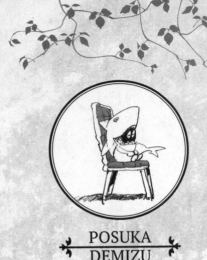

POSUKA DEMIZU

I hope you enjoy volume 19.

The release of this volume was delayed a month in Japan, so I would like to thank everyone who waited patiently.

At the beginning of the story, Isabella was 31 years old, and now she's 33. Unlike Emma and the other kids, her physique hasn't changed much. But her position has gone up and her life has changed, so I tried to draw her with more authority and beauty.

Volume 20 is going to end this series.

Let's meet again then, in the final volume!!

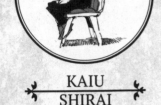

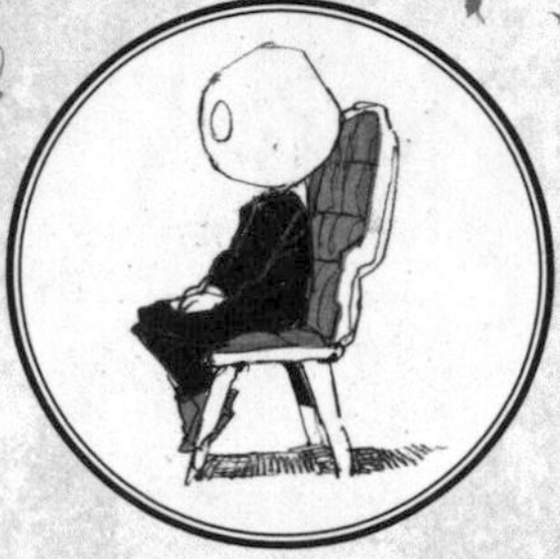

KAIU SHIRAI

Writer Shirai's interesting tidbits for *The Promised Neverland* fanatics, part 7!

In this volume, on page 72, panel 4, her name was revealed for the first time in the series.

But we snuck her name in a while ago in volume 3.

Did you notice?

Hint: the letter!

Please enjoy this volume!

Posuka Demizu debuted as a manga artist with the 2013 *CoroCoro* series *Oreca Monster Bouken Retsuden*. A collection of illustrations, *The Art of Posuka Demizu*, was released in 2016 by PIE International.

Kaiu Shirai debuted in 2015 with *Ashley Gate no Yukue* on the *Shonen Jump+* website. Shirai first worked with Posuka Demizu on the two-shot *Poppy no Negai*, which was released in February 2016.

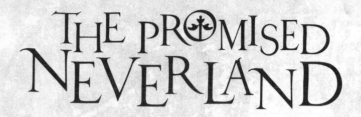

VOLUME 19
SHONEN JUMP Manga Edition

STORY BY KAIU SHIRAI
ART BY POSUKA DEMIZU

Translation/Satsuki Yamashita
Touch-Up Art & Lettering/Mark McMurray
Design/Julian [JR] Robinson
Editor/Alexis Kirsch

YAKUSOKU NO NEVERLAND © 2016 by Kaiu Shirai, Posuka Demizu
All rights reserved.
First published in Japan in 2016 by SHUEISHA Inc., Tokyo.
English translation rights arranged by SHUEISHA Inc.

The stories, characters and incidents mentioned in this publication are entirely fictional.

Printed in the U.S.A.

Published by VIZ Media, LLC
P.O. Box 77010
San Francisco, CA 94107

10 9 8 7 6 5 4 3 2 1
First printing, May 2021

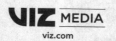
viz.com

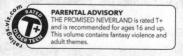
PARENTAL ADVISORY
THE PROMISED NEVERLAND is rated T+ and is recommended for ages 16 and up. This volume contains fantasy violence and adult themes.

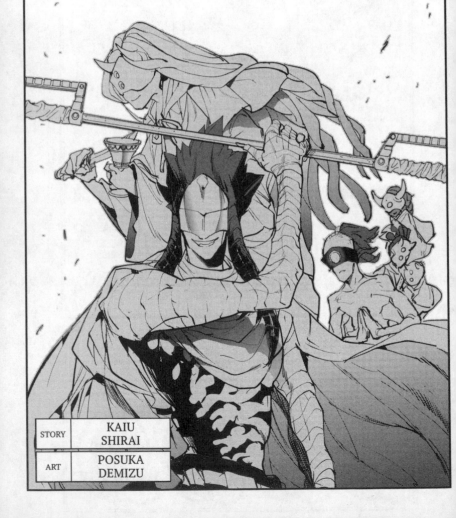

THE PROMISED NEVERLAND

19
Perfect Scores

STORY	KAIU SHIRAI
ART	POSUKA DEMIZU

CHARACTERS

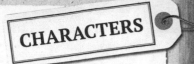

The Children of Grace Field House

They aim to free all of the children who are trapped in Grace Field House within the next two months.

RAY

On the Run

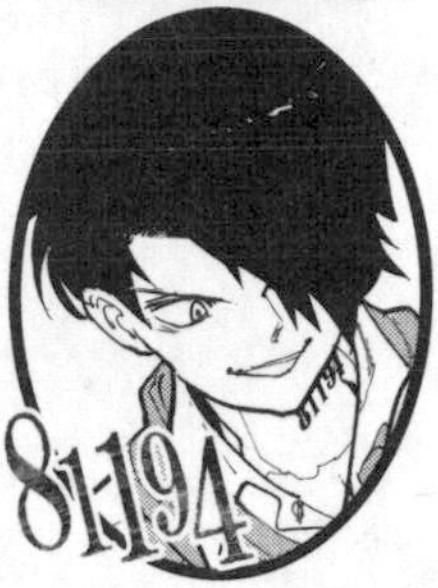
81194

The only one among the Grace Field House children who can match wits with Norman.

EMMA

On the Run

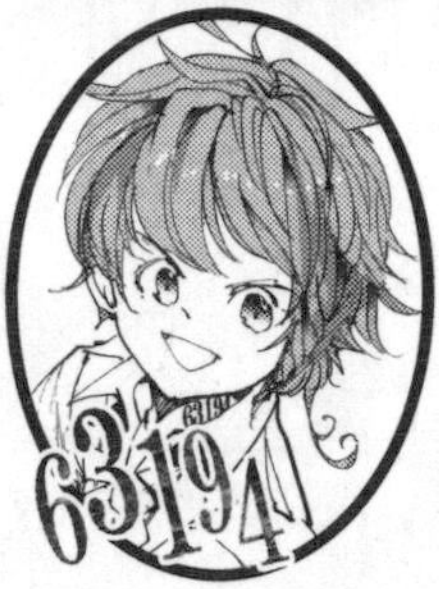
63194

An enthusiastic and optimistic girl with superb athletic and learning abilities.

NORMAN

On the Run

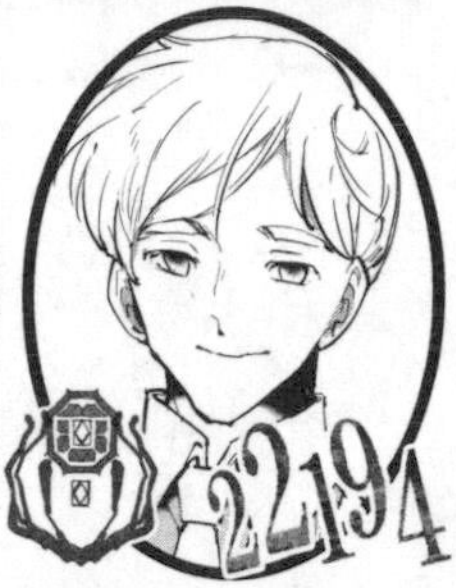
22194

A boy with excellent analytical and decision-making capabilities. He is the smartest of the children from Grace Field House.

CAROL

In Grace Field House

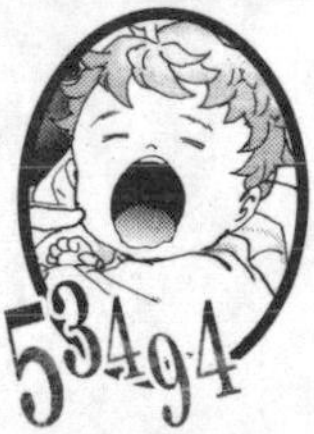
53494

PHIL

In Grace Field House

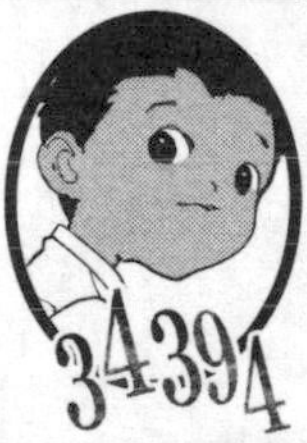
34394

GILDA

On the Run

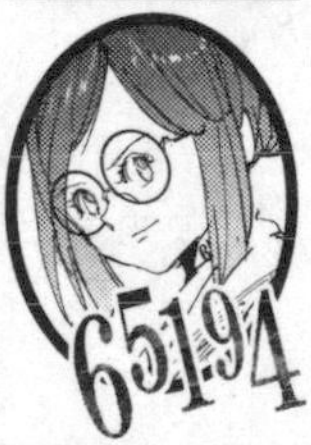
65194

DON

On the Run

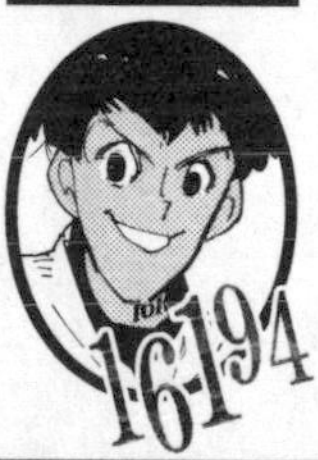
16194

The Escapees of Lambda 7214

They obtained superpowers from being repeatedly experimented on by the demons. They are devoted to Norman and have destroyed many farms with him.

ZAZIE

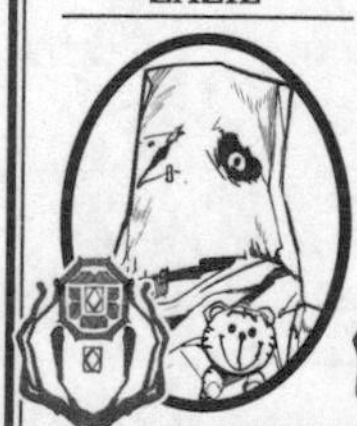

BARBARA

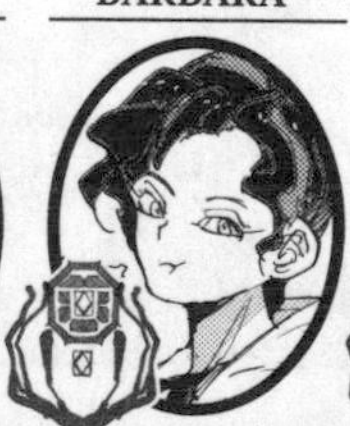

CISLO

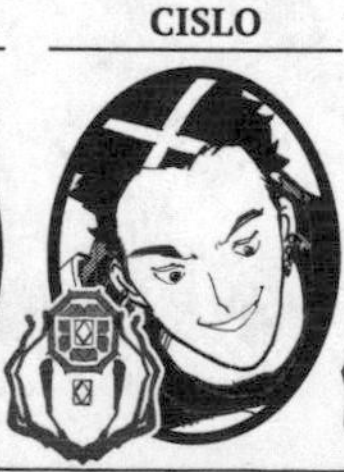

VINCENT

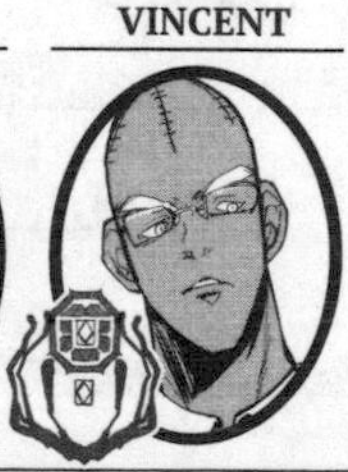

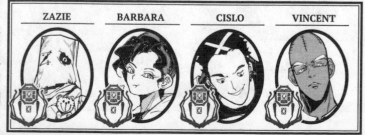

Ratri Clan

Plans to get rid of Emma and her group to keep order in the world.

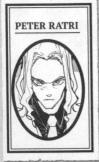

PETER RATRI

Evil-Blooded Girl Group

Thought to have been killed by the royal family for her ability to maintain human form, but Mujika secretly survived.

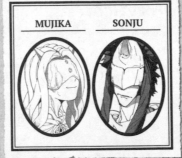

MUJIKA　　**SONJU**

Disposed Child

Stolen from a farm and raised by a demon.

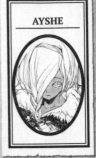

AYSHE

Royal Family

The queen who rules the many subjects of the demon world.

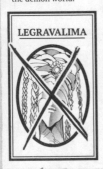

LEGRAVALIMA

The Five Regent Houses

They govern the demon world with the royal family. They also operate the farms that raise humans.

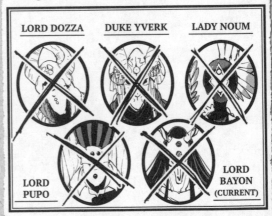

LORD DOZZA　　**DUKE YVERK**　　**LADY NOUM**

LORD PUPO　　**LORD BAYON (CURRENT)**

The Story So Far

Emma is living happily at Grace Field House with her foster siblings. One day, she realizes that they are being bred as food for demons and escapes with a group of other children. After meeting new friends and gaining further information, she decides to free all of the children raised in the farms. To replace the promise made 1,000 years ago that changed the shape of the world, she creates a new promise. The Ratri clan abducts her friends and family, however, forcing Emma to pursue them to Grace Field House. Meanwhile, as a result of Norman subjugating the queen, the demon world has been thrown into confusion. Afraid that the situation will escalate into a major conflict, Sonju and Mujika make their move.

THE PROMISED NEVERLAND

19

Perfect Scores

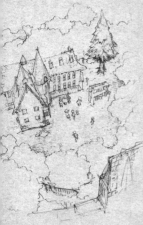

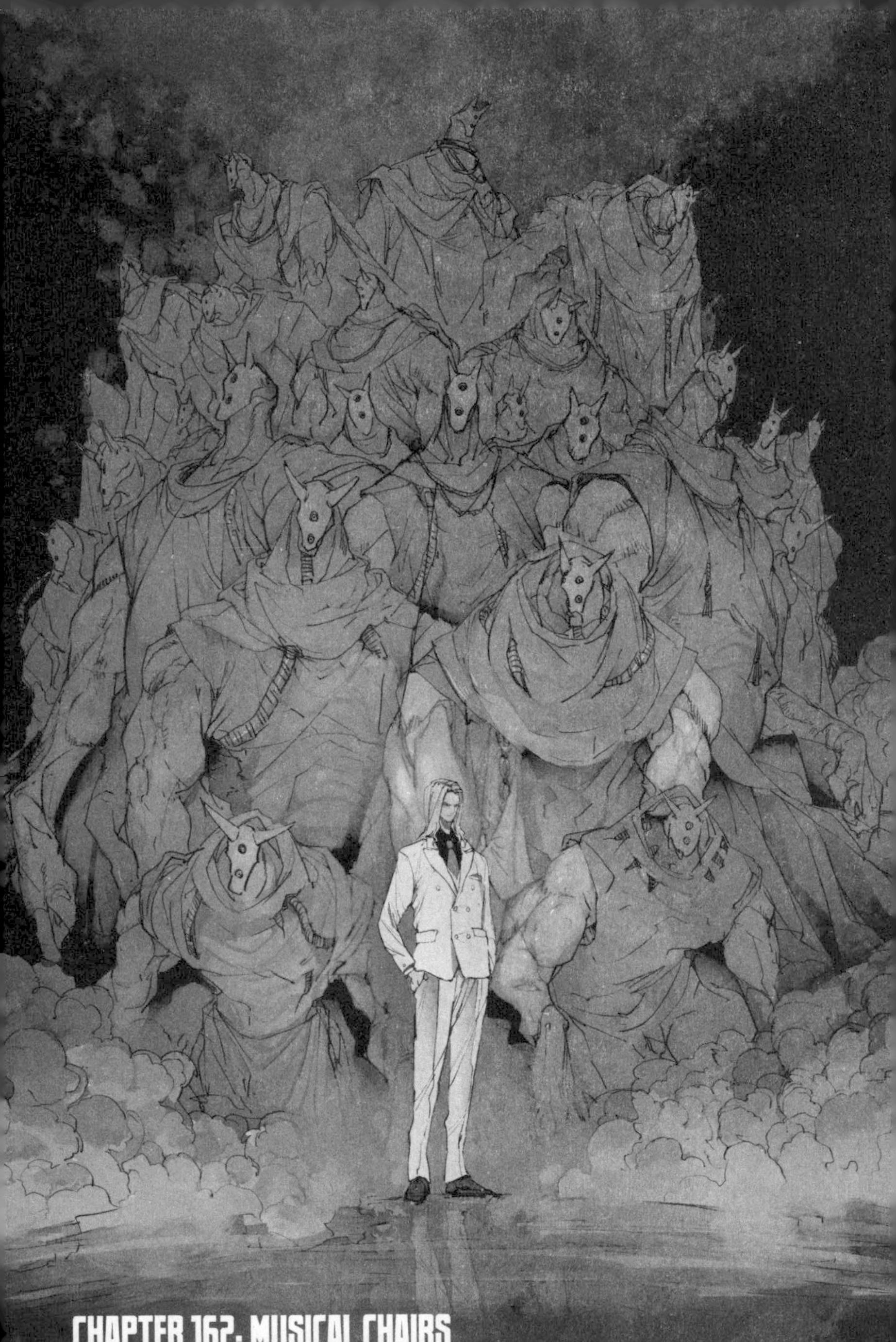

CHAPTER 162: MUSICAL CHAIRS

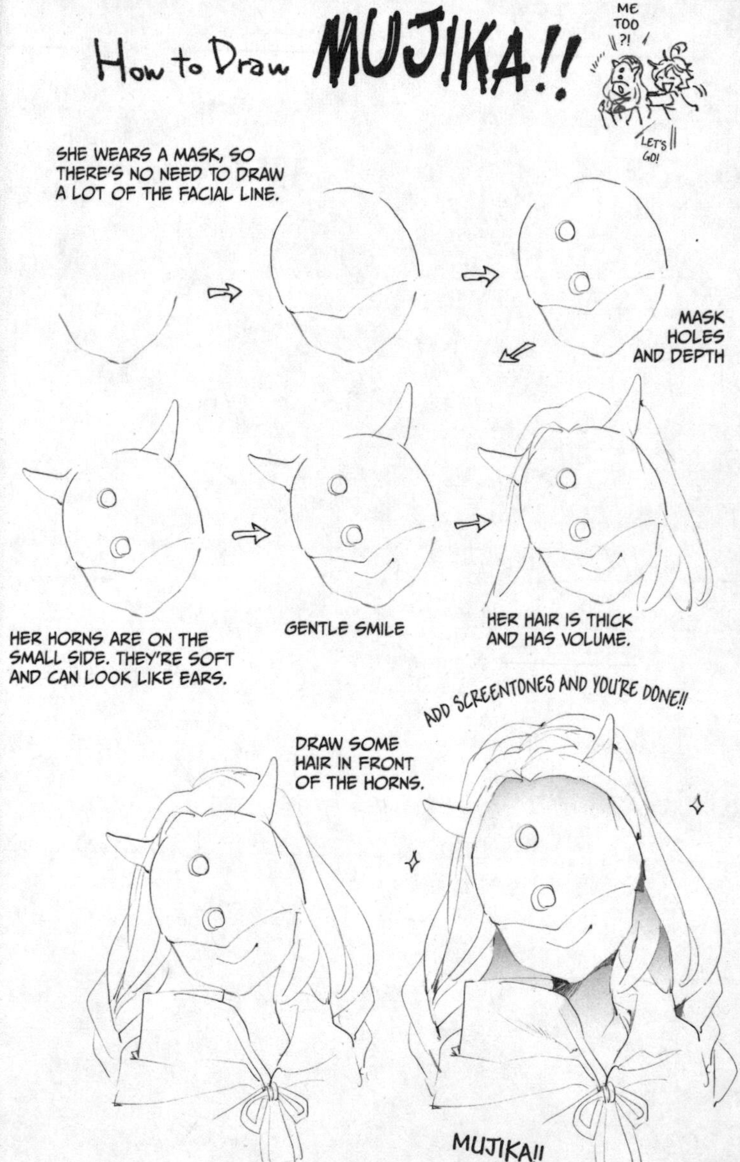

How to Draw MUJIKA!!

ME TOO ?!

LETS GO!

SHE WEARS A MASK, SO THERE'S NO NEED TO DRAW A LOT OF THE FACIAL LINE.

MASK HOLES AND DEPTH

HER HORNS ARE ON THE SMALL SIDE. THEY'RE SOFT AND CAN LOOK LIKE EARS.

GENTLE SMILE

HER HAIR IS THICK AND HAS VOLUME.

ADD SCREENTONES AND YOU'RE DONE!!

DRAW SOME HAIR IN FRONT OF THE HORNS.

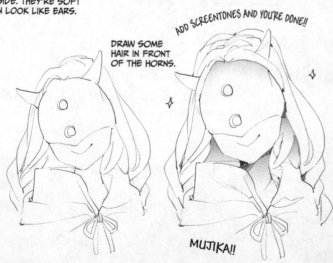

MUJIKA!!

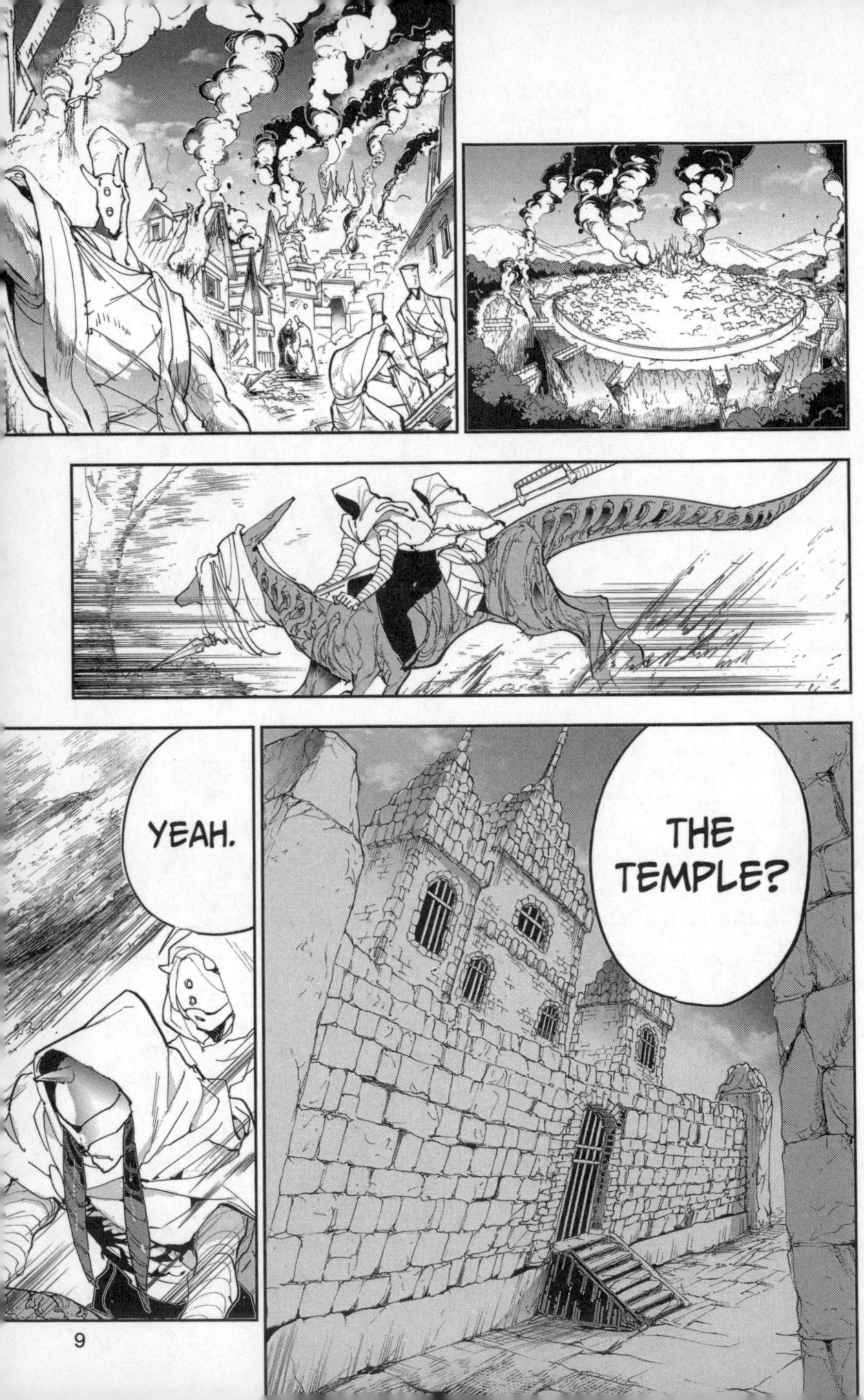
THE TEMPLE?
YEAH.

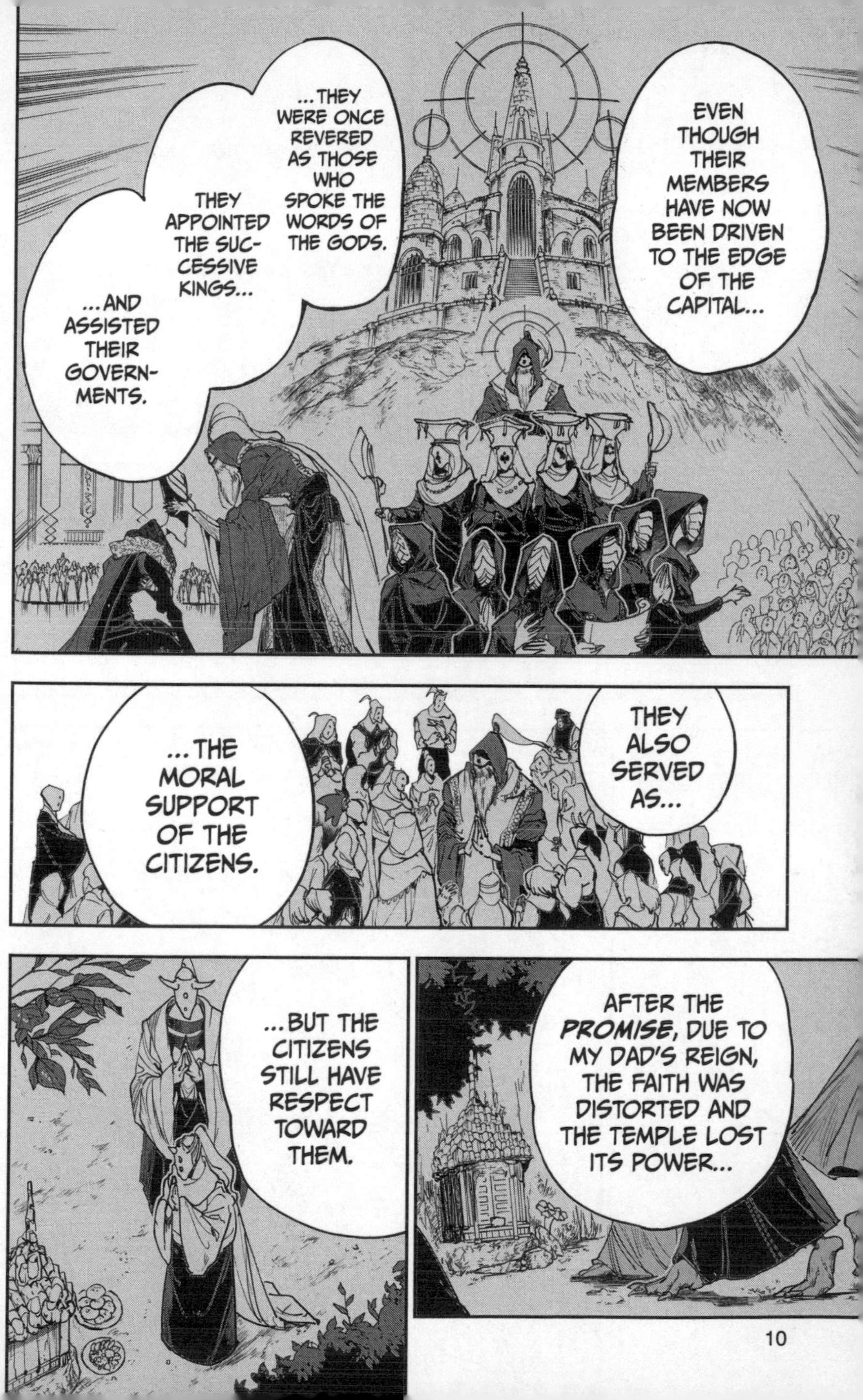
EVEN THOUGH THEIR MEMBERS HAVE NOW BEEN DRIVEN TO THE EDGE OF THE CAPITAL...
...THEY WERE ONCE REVERED AS THOSE WHO SPOKE THE WORDS OF THE GODS.
THEY APPOINTED THE SUC-CESSIVE KINGS...
...AND ASSISTED THEIR GOVERN-MENTS.
THEY ALSO SERVED AS...
...THE MORAL SUPPORT OF THE CITIZENS.
AFTER THE *PROMISE*, DUE TO MY DAD'S REIGN, THE FAITH WAS DISTORTED AND THE TEMPLE LOST ITS POWER...
...BUT THE CITIZENS STILL HAVE RESPECT TOWARD THEM.

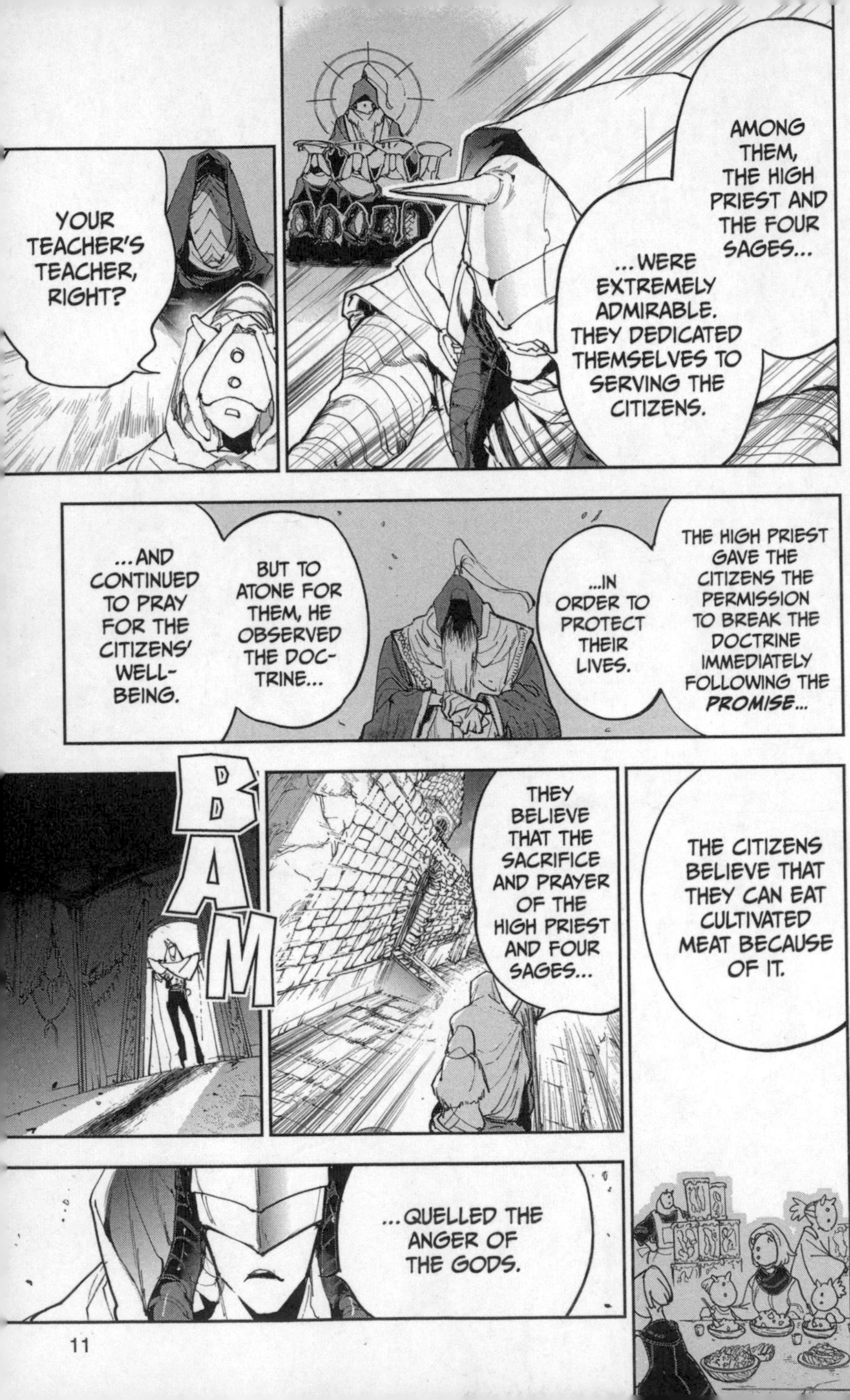
AMONG THEM, THE HIGH PRIEST AND THE FOUR SAGES...
...WERE EXTREMELY ADMIRABLE. THEY DEDICATED THEMSELVES TO SERVING THE CITIZENS.
YOUR TEACHER'S TEACHER, RIGHT?
THE HIGH PRIEST GAVE THE CITIZENS THE PERMISSION TO BREAK THE DOCTRINE IMMEDIATELY FOLLOWING THE *PROMISE*...
...IN ORDER TO PROTECT THEIR LIVES.
BUT TO ATONE FOR THEM, HE OBSERVED THE DOC-TRINE...
...AND CONTINUED TO PRAY FOR THE CITIZENS' WELL-BEING.
THE CITIZENS BELIEVE THAT THEY CAN EAT CULTIVATED MEAT BECAUSE OF IT.
THEY BELIEVE THAT THE SACRIFICE AND PRAYER OF THE HIGH PRIEST AND FOUR SAGES...
BAM
...QUELLED THE ANGER OF THE GODS.

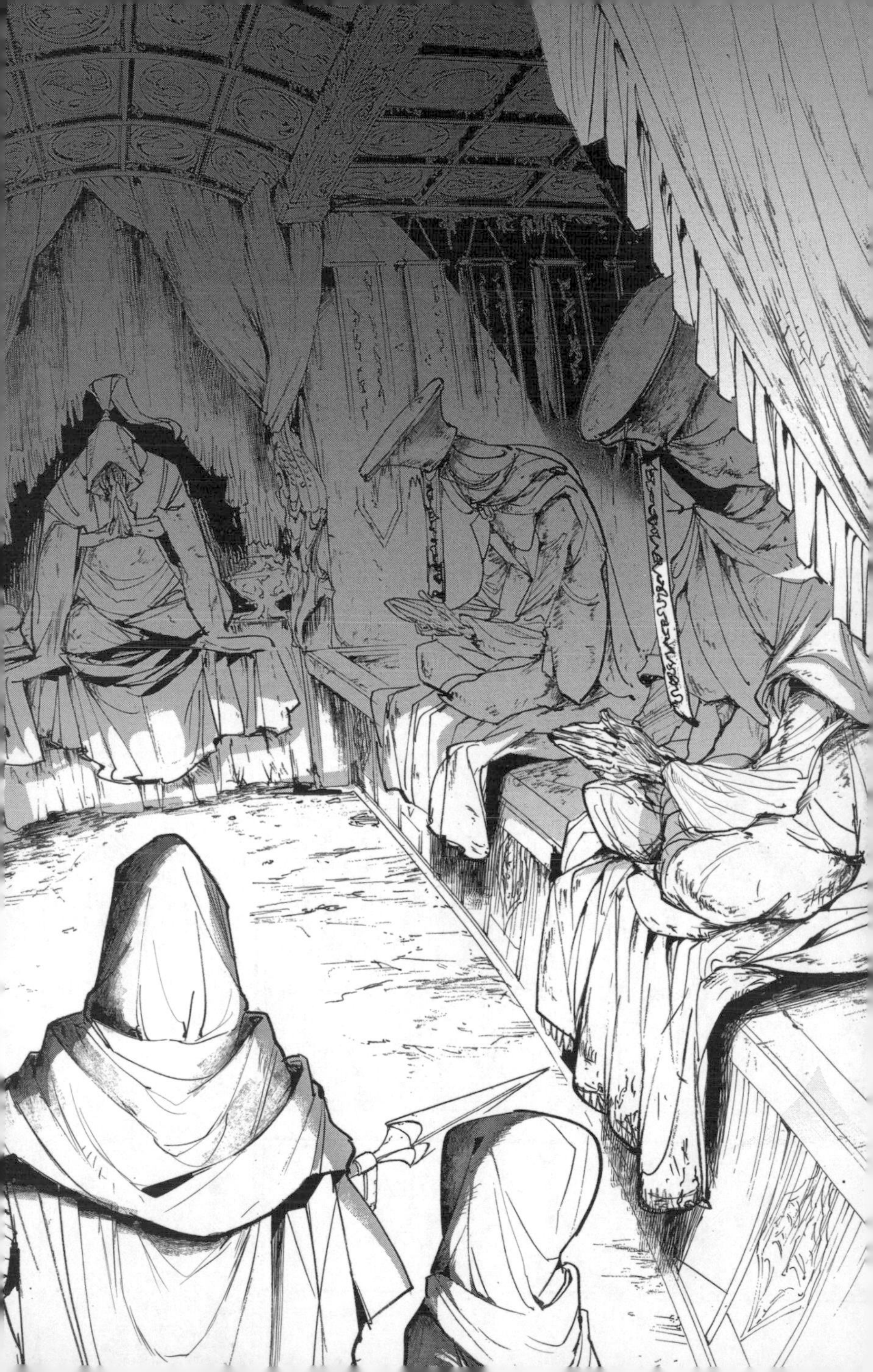

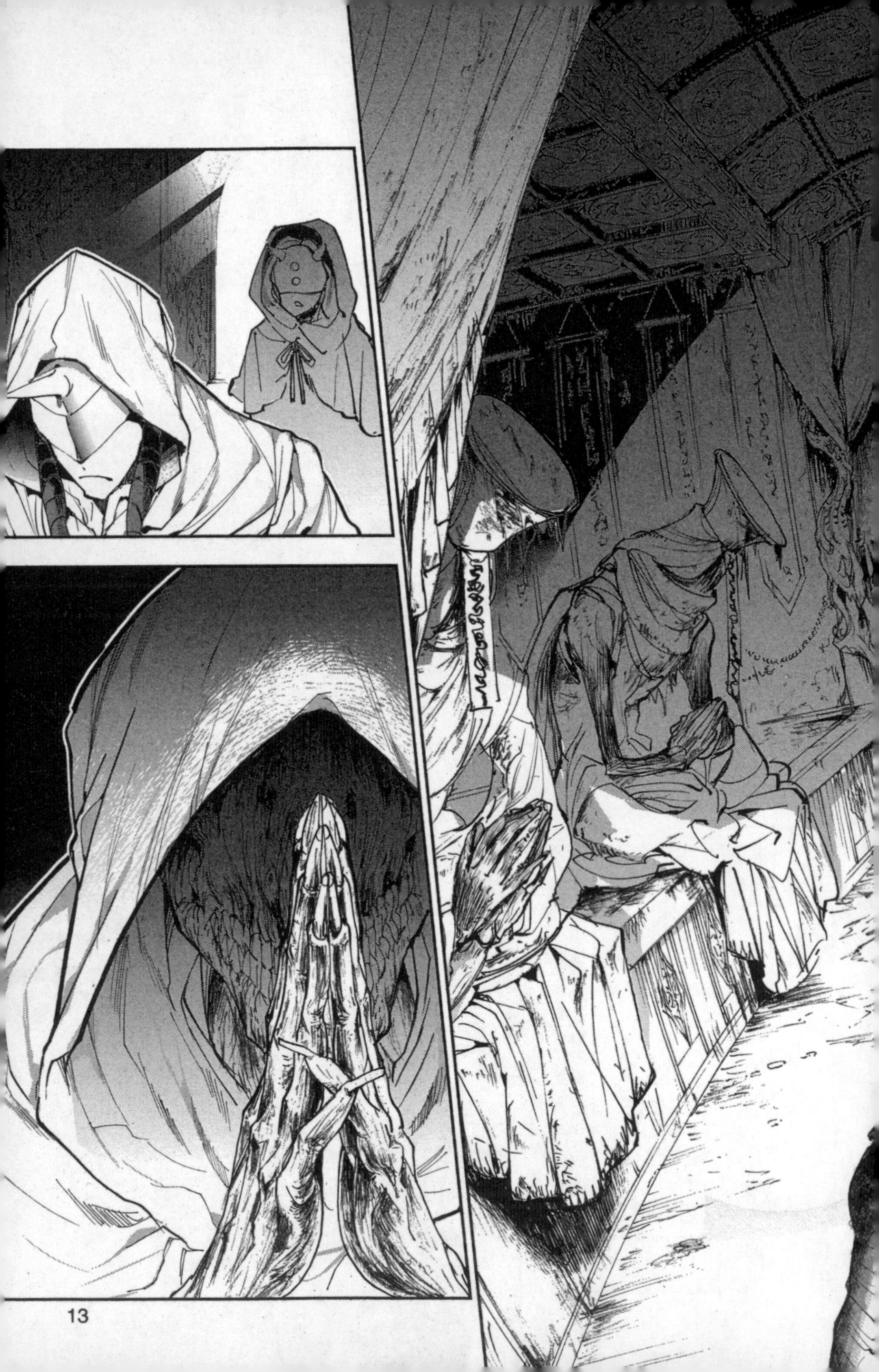

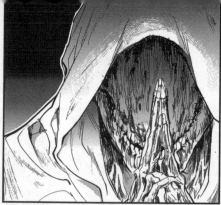

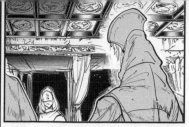

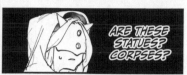
ARE THESE STATUES? CORPSES?

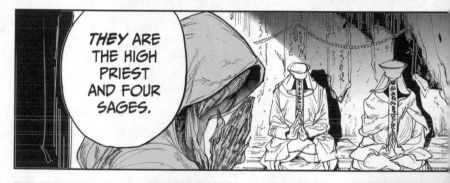
THEY ARE THE HIGH PRIEST AND FOUR SAGES.

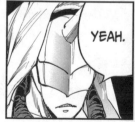
YEAH.

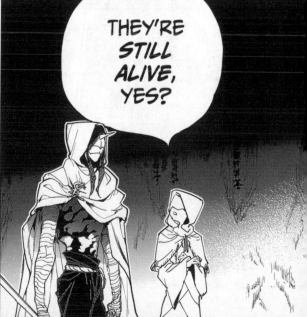
THEY'RE STILL ALIVE, YES?

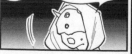
...HOW DID THEY...

NO WAY. FOR 1,000 YEARS, WITHOUT EATING HUMANS...

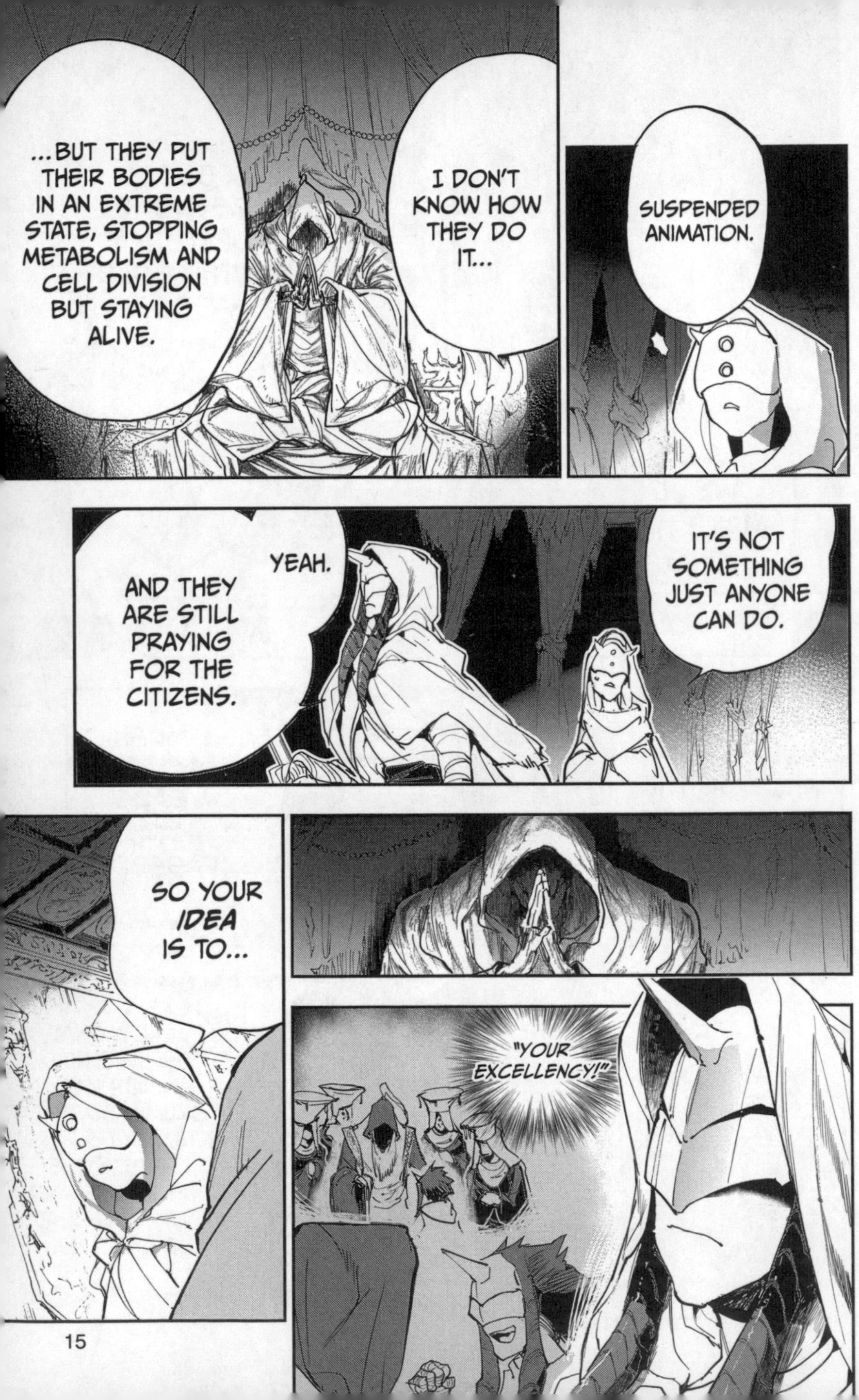
SUSPENDED ANIMATION.
I DON'T KNOW HOW THEY DO IT...
...BUT THEY PUT THEIR BODIES IN AN EXTREME STATE, STOPPING METABOLISM AND CELL DIVISION BUT STAYING ALIVE.
IT'S NOT SOMETHING JUST ANYONE CAN DO.
YEAH.
AND THEY ARE STILL PRAYING FOR THE CITIZENS.
"YOUR EXCELLENCY!"
SO YOUR *IDEA* IS TO...

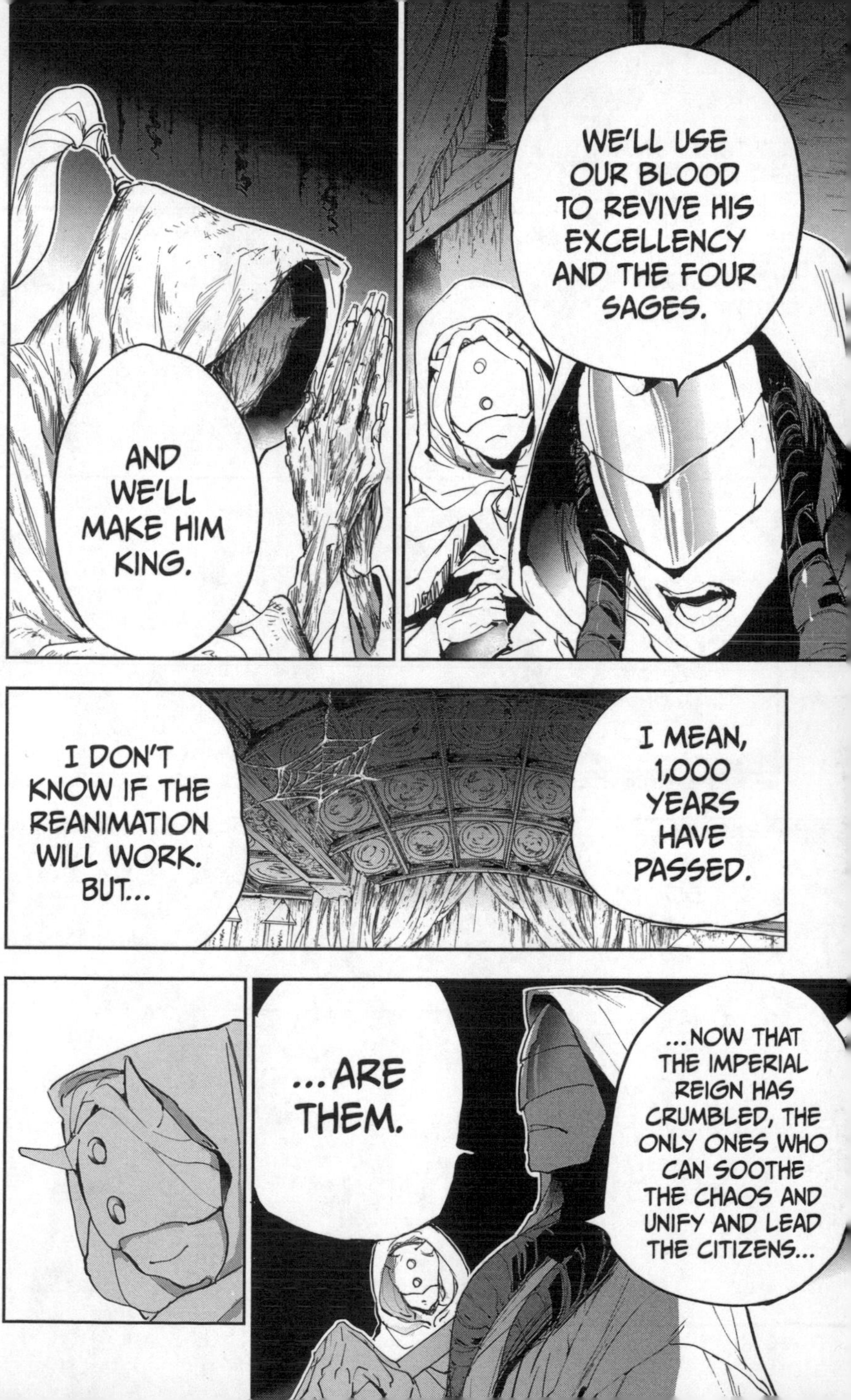
WE'LL USE OUR BLOOD TO REVIVE HIS EXCELLENCY AND THE FOUR SAGES.
AND WE'LL MAKE HIM KING.
I MEAN, 1,000 YEARS HAVE PASSED.
I DON'T KNOW IF THE REANIMATION WILL WORK. BUT...
...NOW THAT THE IMPERIAL REIGN HAS CRUMBLED, THE ONLY ONES WHO CAN SOOTHE THE CHAOS AND UNIFY AND LEAD THE CITIZENS...
...ARE THEM.

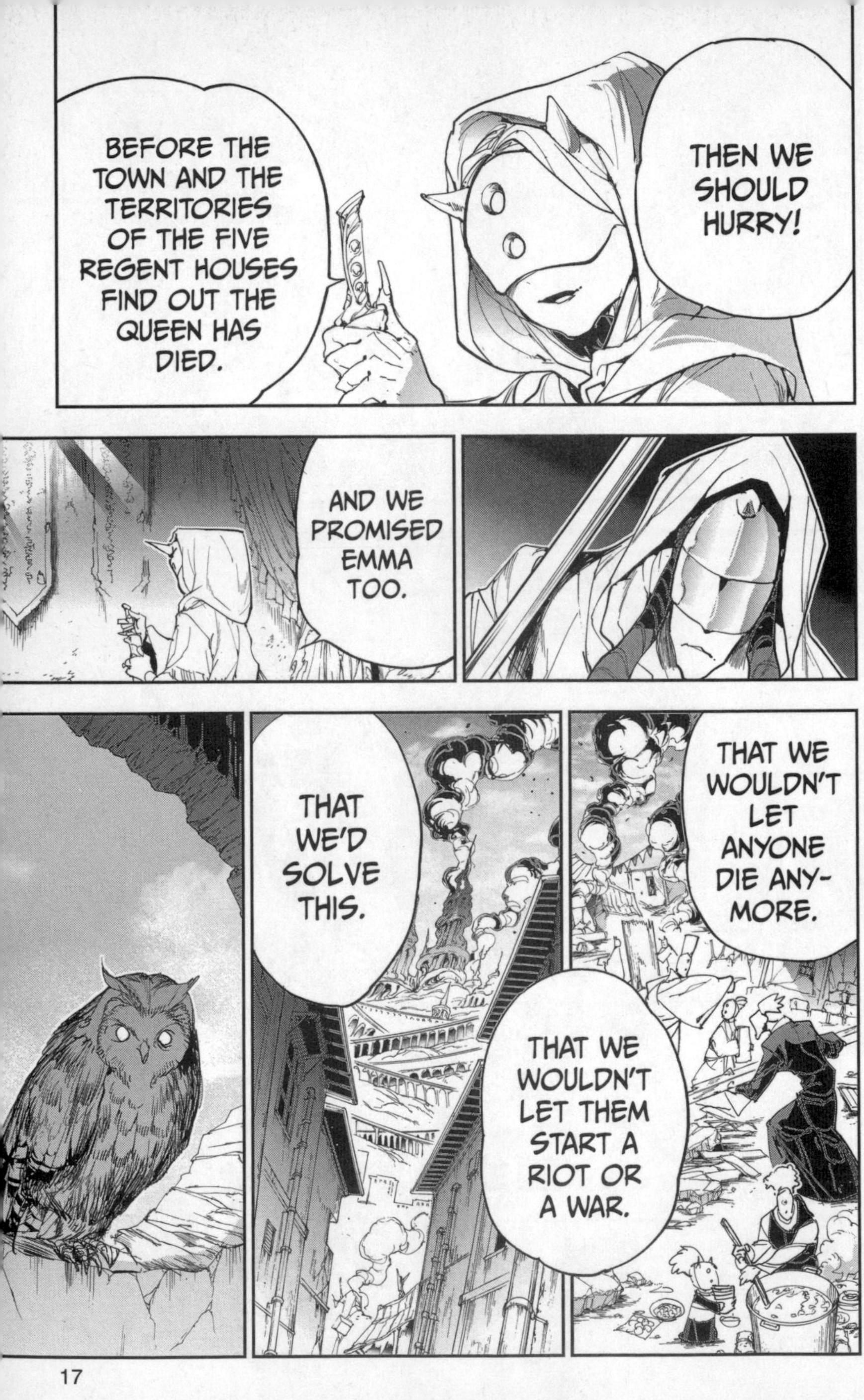
THEN WE SHOULD HURRY!
BEFORE THE TOWN AND THE TERRITORIES OF THE FIVE REGENT HOUSES FIND OUT THE QUEEN HAS DIED.
AND WE PROMISED EMMA TOO.
THAT WE WOULDN'T LET ANYONE DIE ANY-MORE.
THAT WE'D SOLVE THIS.
THAT WE WOULDN'T LET THEM START A RIOT OR A WAR.

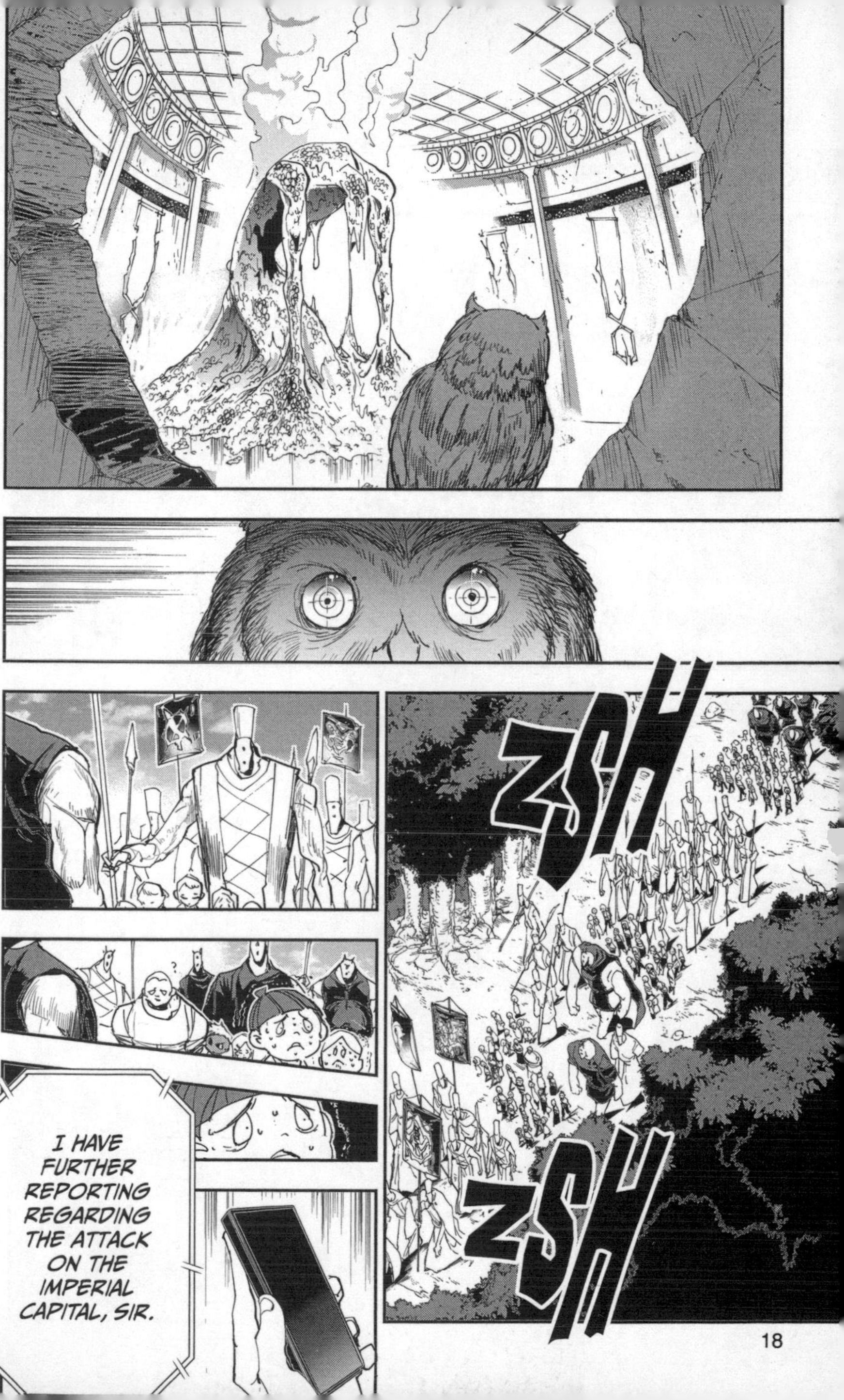
ZSH
ZSH
I HAVE FURTHER REPORTING REGARDING THE ATTACK ON THE IMPERIAL CAPITAL, SIR.

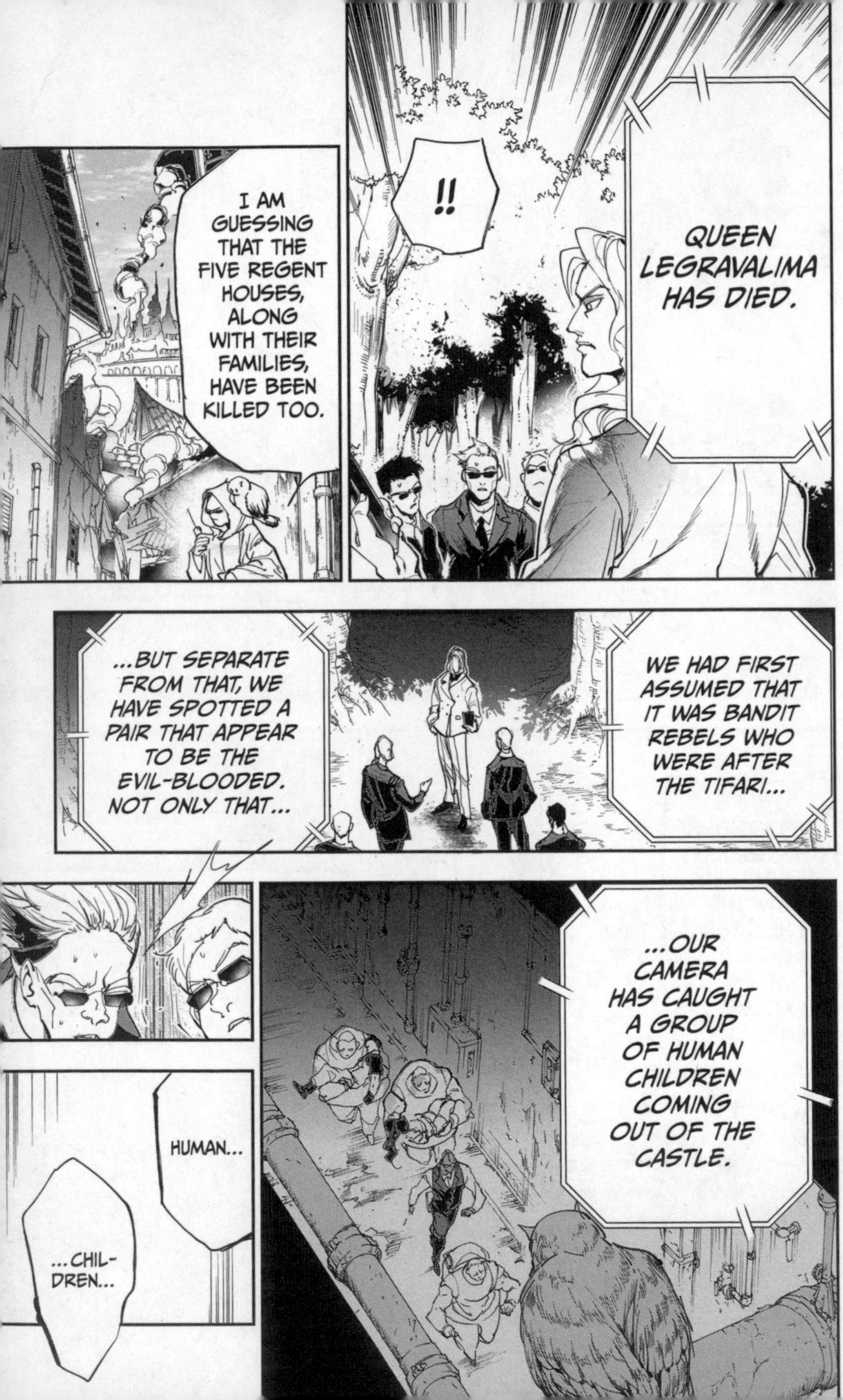
QUEEN LEGRAVALIMA HAS DIED.
!!
I AM GUESSING THAT THE FIVE REGENT HOUSES, ALONG WITH THEIR FAMILIES, HAVE BEEN KILLED TOO.
WE HAD FIRST ASSUMED THAT IT WAS BANDIT REBELS WHO WERE AFTER THE TIFARI...
...BUT SEPARATE FROM THAT, WE HAVE SPOTTED A PAIR THAT APPEAR TO BE THE EVIL-BLOODED. NOT ONLY THAT...
...OUR CAMERA HAS CAUGHT A GROUP OF HUMAN CHILDREN COMING OUT OF THE CASTLE.
HUMAN...
...CHIL-DREN...

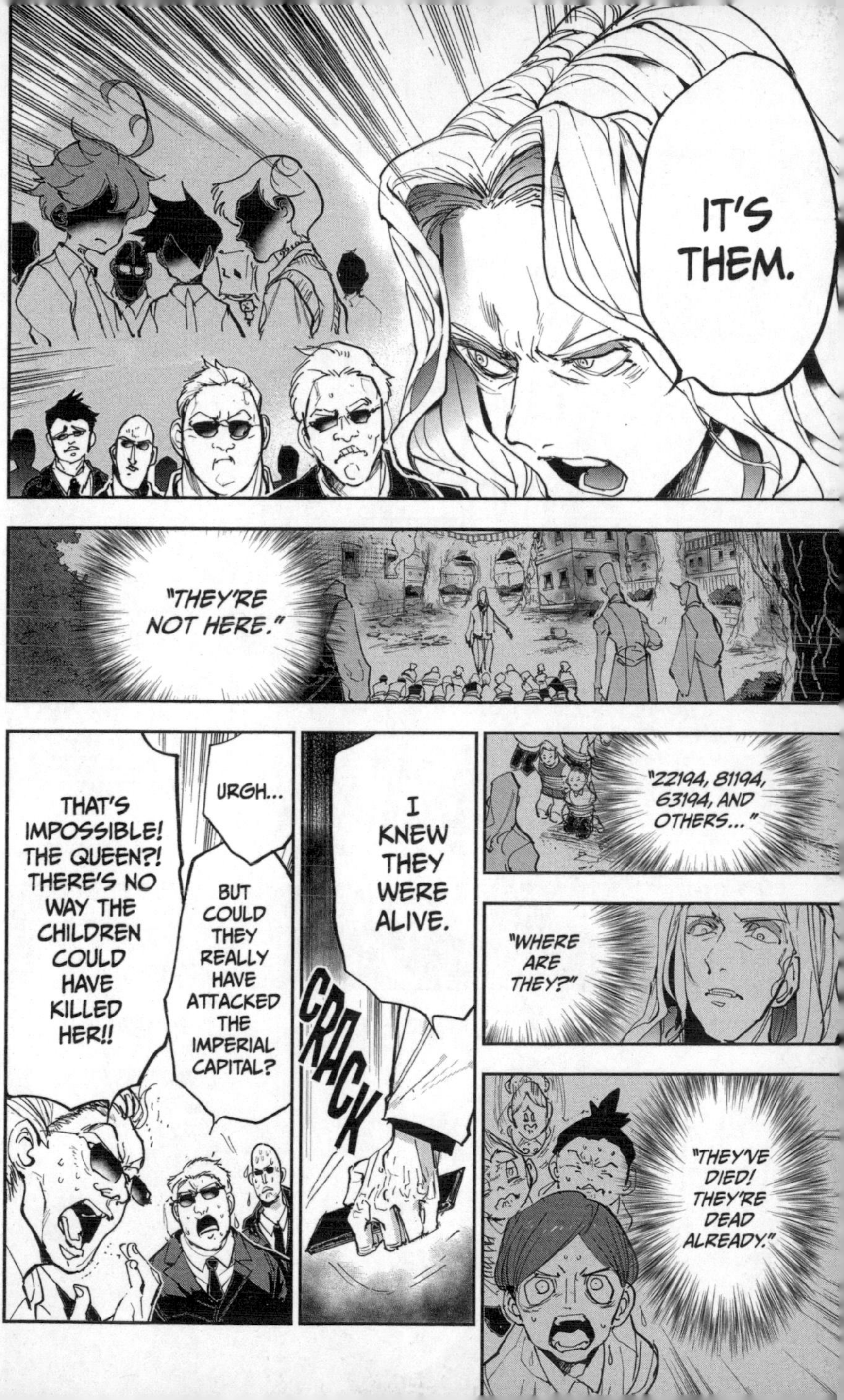
IT'S THEM.
"THEY'RE NOT HERE."
"22194, 81194, 63194, AND OTHERS..."
"WHERE ARE THEY?"
"THEY'VE DIED! THEY'RE DEAD ALREADY."
I KNEW THEY WERE ALIVE.
CRACK
URGH...
BUT COULD THEY REALLY HAVE ATTACKED THE IMPERIAL CAPITAL?
THAT'S IMPOSSIBLE! THE QUEEN?! THERE'S NO WAY THE CHILDREN COULD HAVE KILLED HER!!

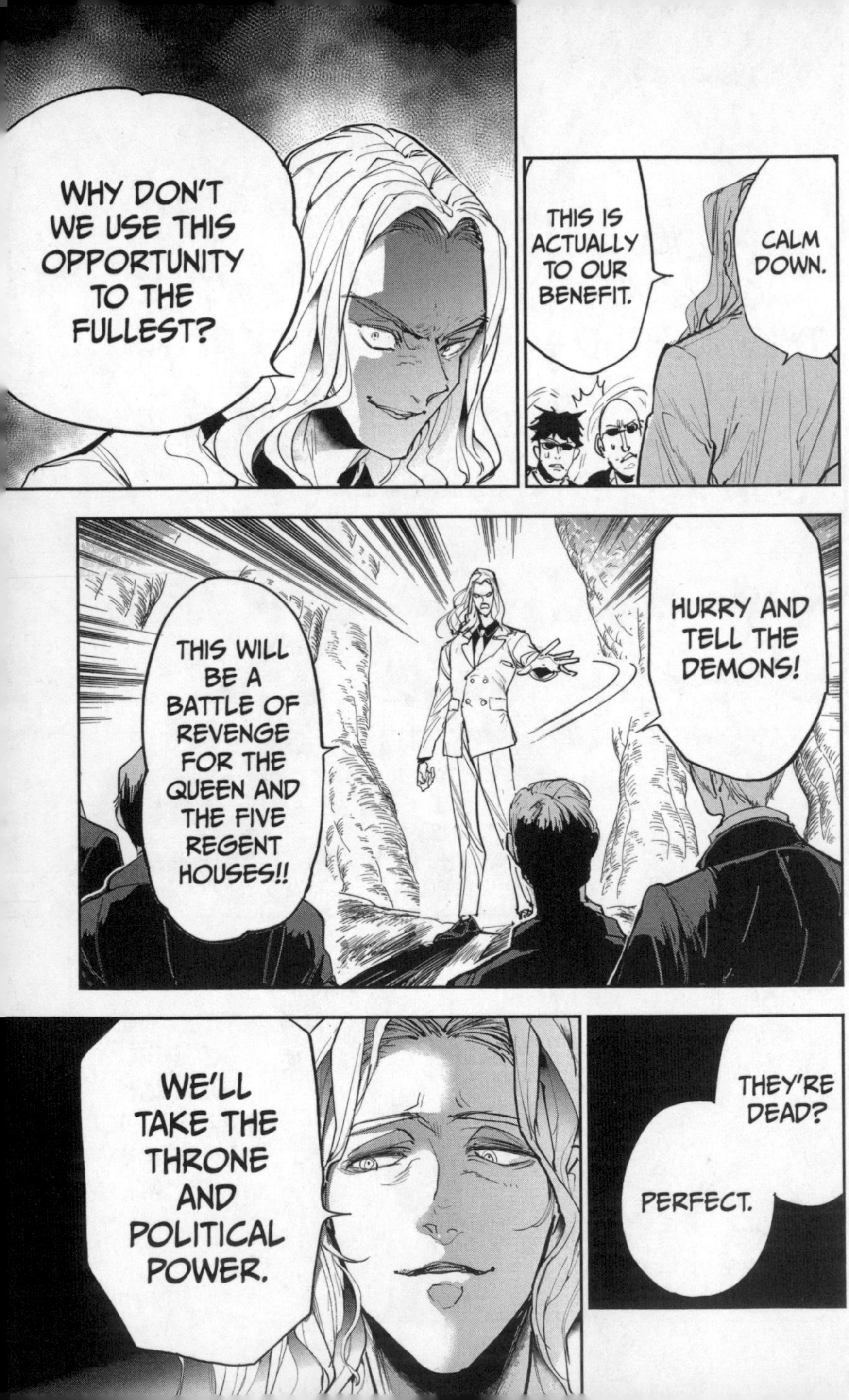
CALM DOWN.
THIS IS ACTUALLY TO OUR BENEFIT.
WHY DON'T WE USE THIS OPPORTUNITY TO THE FULLEST?
HURRY AND TELL THE DEMONS!
THIS WILL BE A BATTLE OF REVENGE FOR THE QUEEN AND THE FIVE REGENT HOUSES!!
THEY'RE DEAD?
PERFECT.
WE'LL TAKE THE THRONE AND POLITICAL POWER.

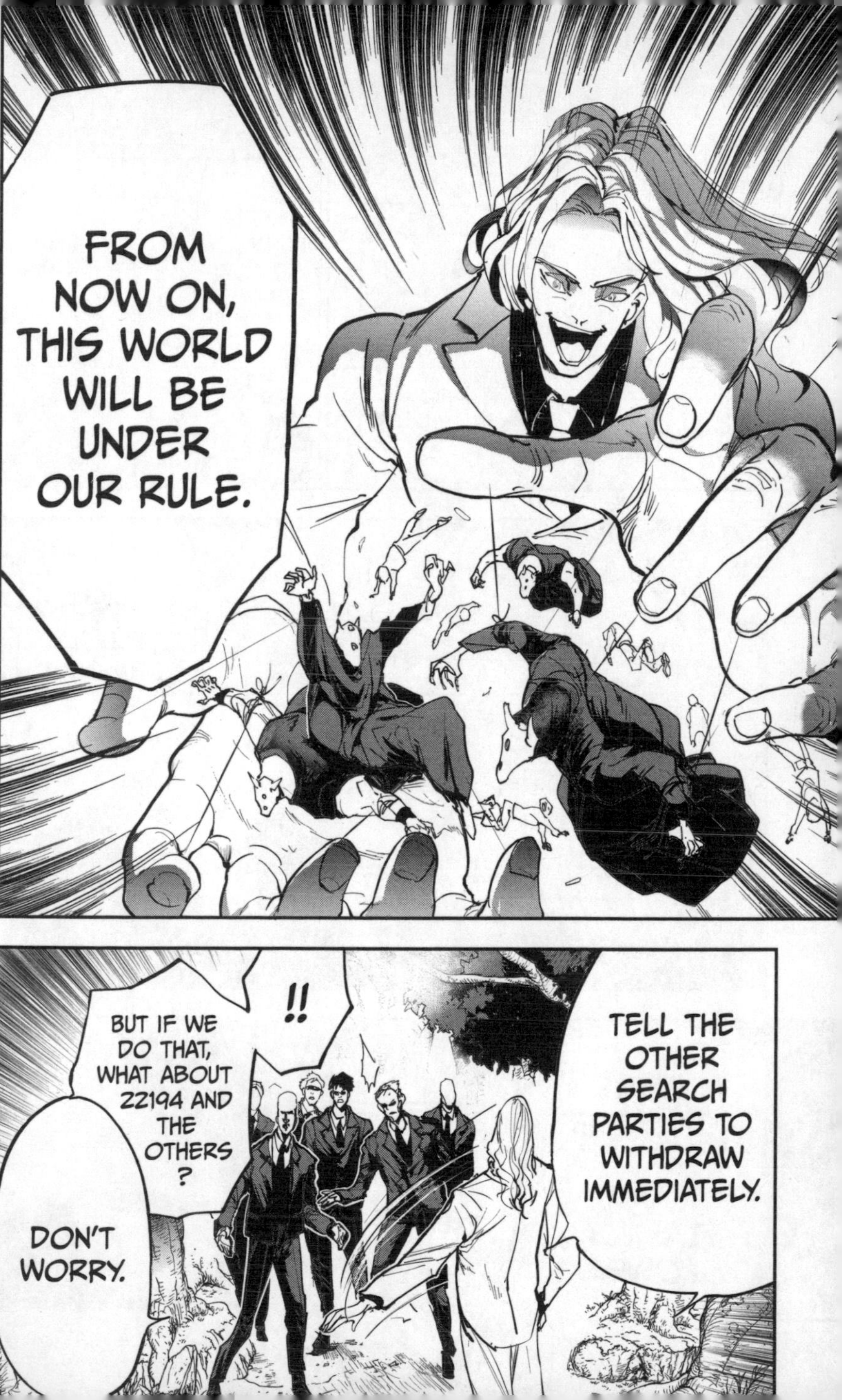
FROM NOW ON, THIS WORLD WILL BE UNDER OUR RULE.
TELL THE OTHER SEARCH PARTIES TO WITHDRAW IMMEDIATELY.
!!
BUT IF WE DO THAT, WHAT ABOUT 22194 AND THE OTHERS?
DON'T WORRY.

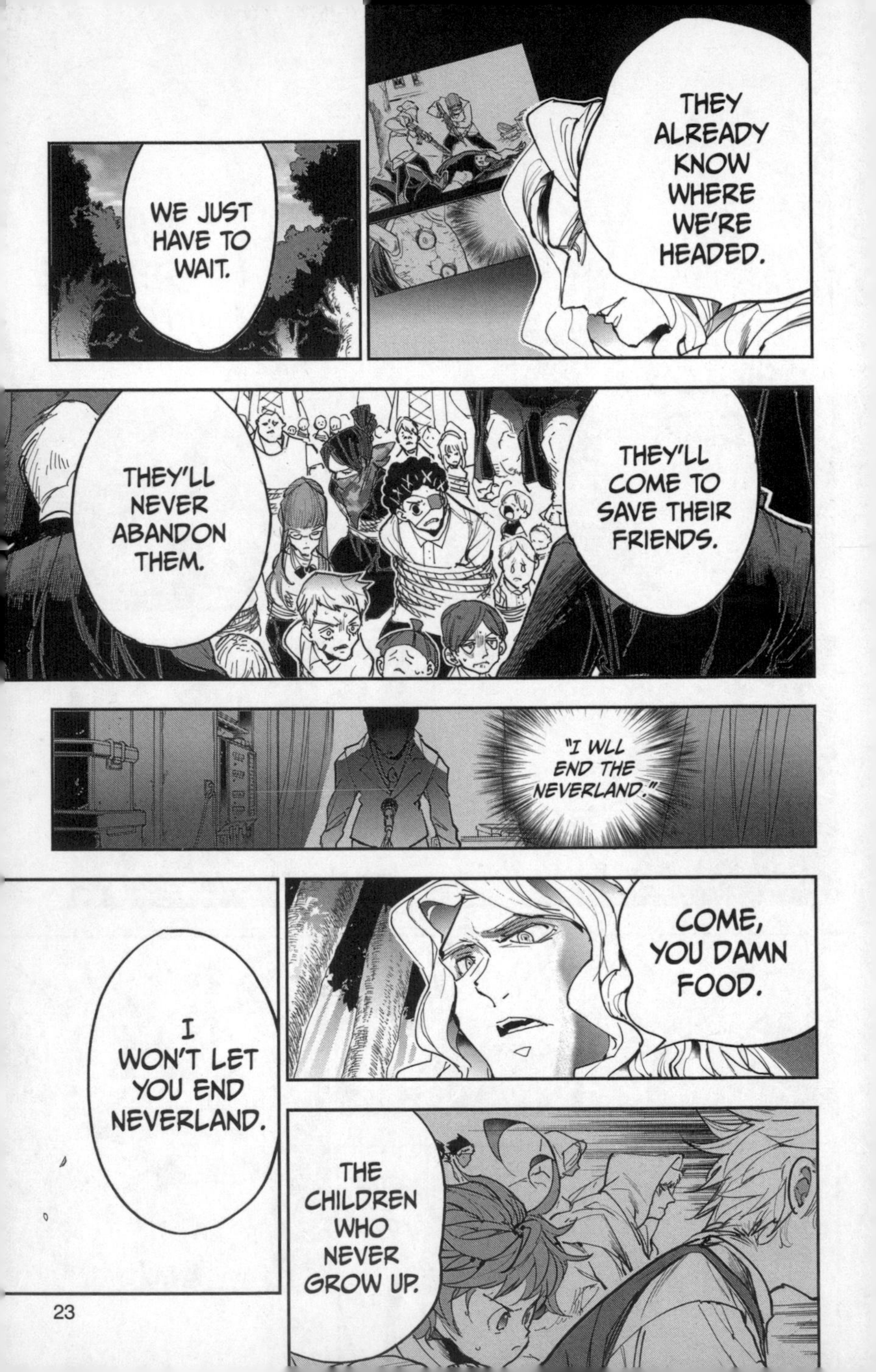
THEY ALREADY KNOW WHERE WE'RE HEADED.
WE JUST HAVE TO WAIT.
THEY'LL COME TO SAVE THEIR FRIENDS.
THEY'LL NEVER ABANDON THEM.
"I WLL END THE NEVERLAND."
COME, YOU DAMN FOOD.
THE CHILDREN WHO NEVER GROW UP.
I WON'T LET YOU END NEVERLAND.

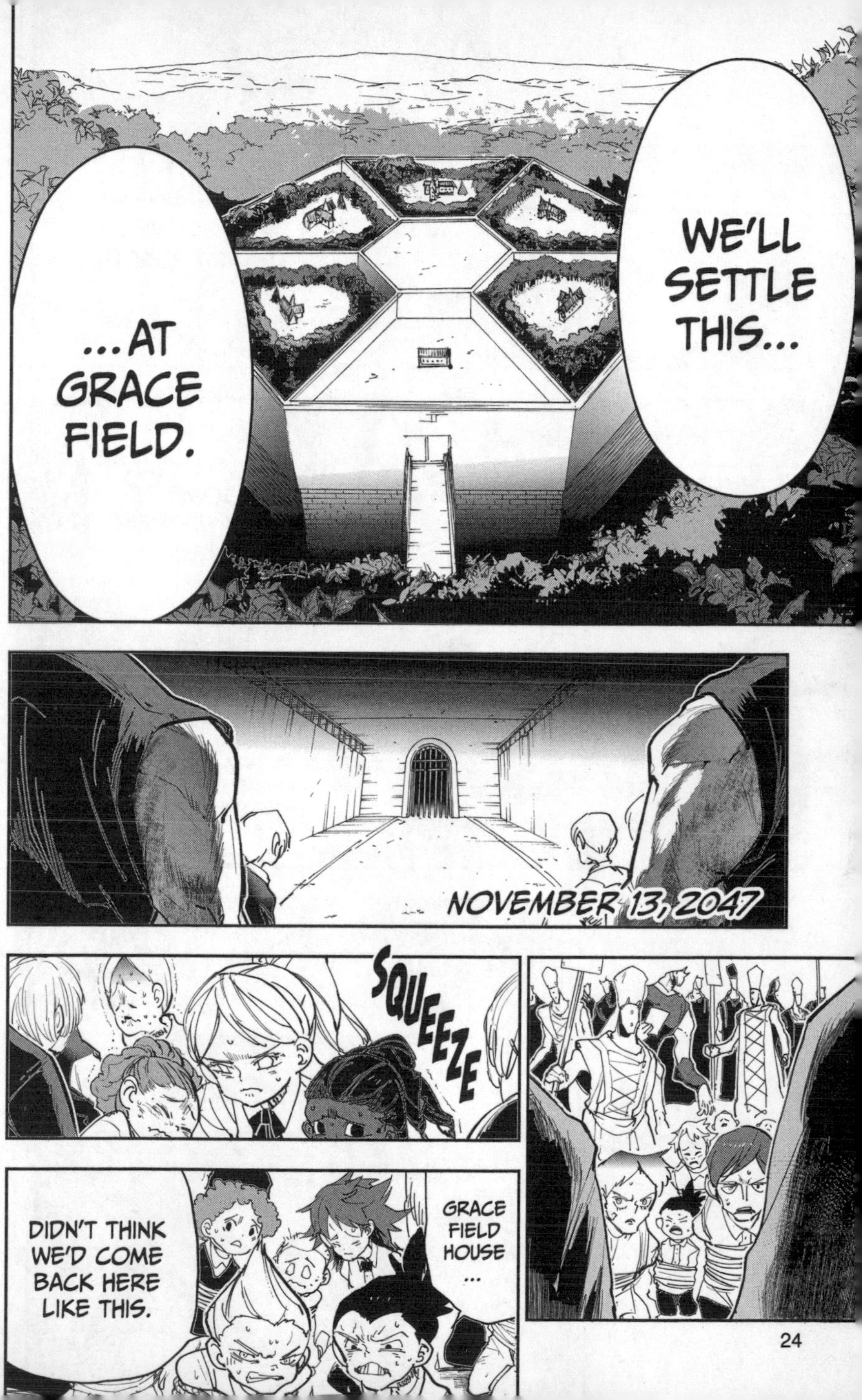
WE'LL SETTLE THIS...
...AT GRACE FIELD.
NOVEMBER 13, 2047
SQUEEZE
GRACE FIELD HOUSE ...
DIDN'T THINK WE'D COME BACK HERE LIKE THIS.

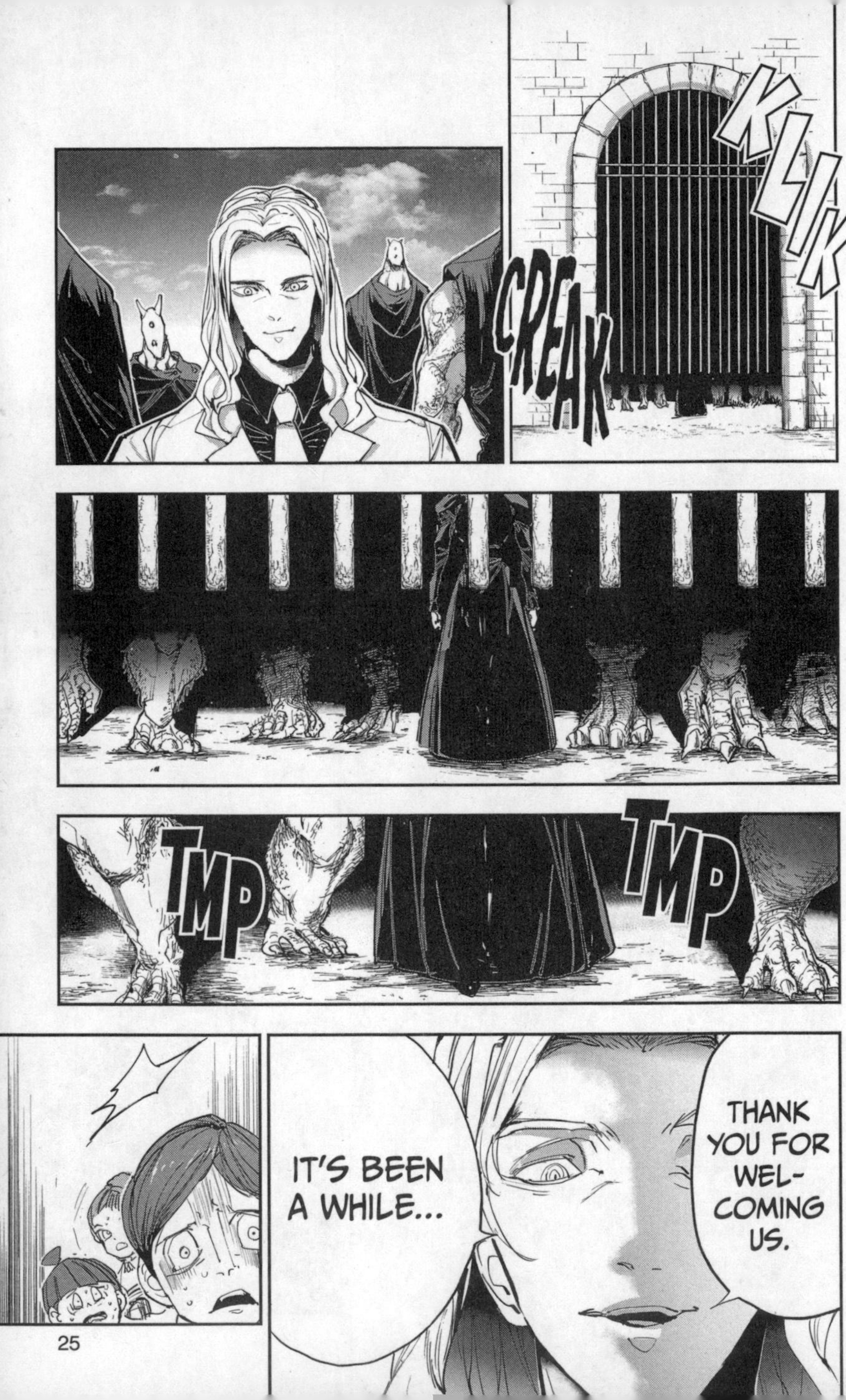
KLIK
CREAK
TMP
TMP
THANK YOU FOR WEL-COMING US.
IT'S BEEN A WHILE...

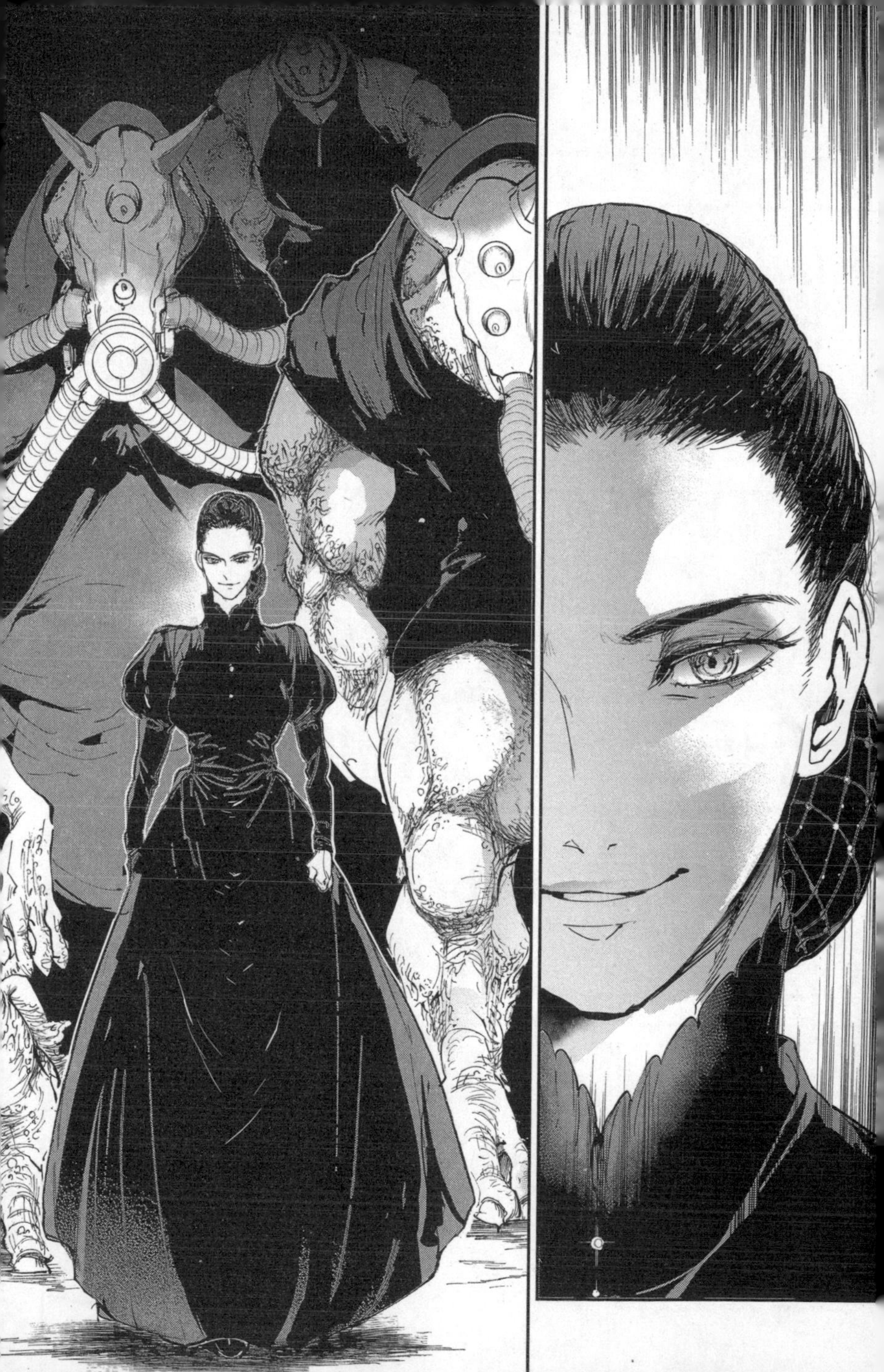

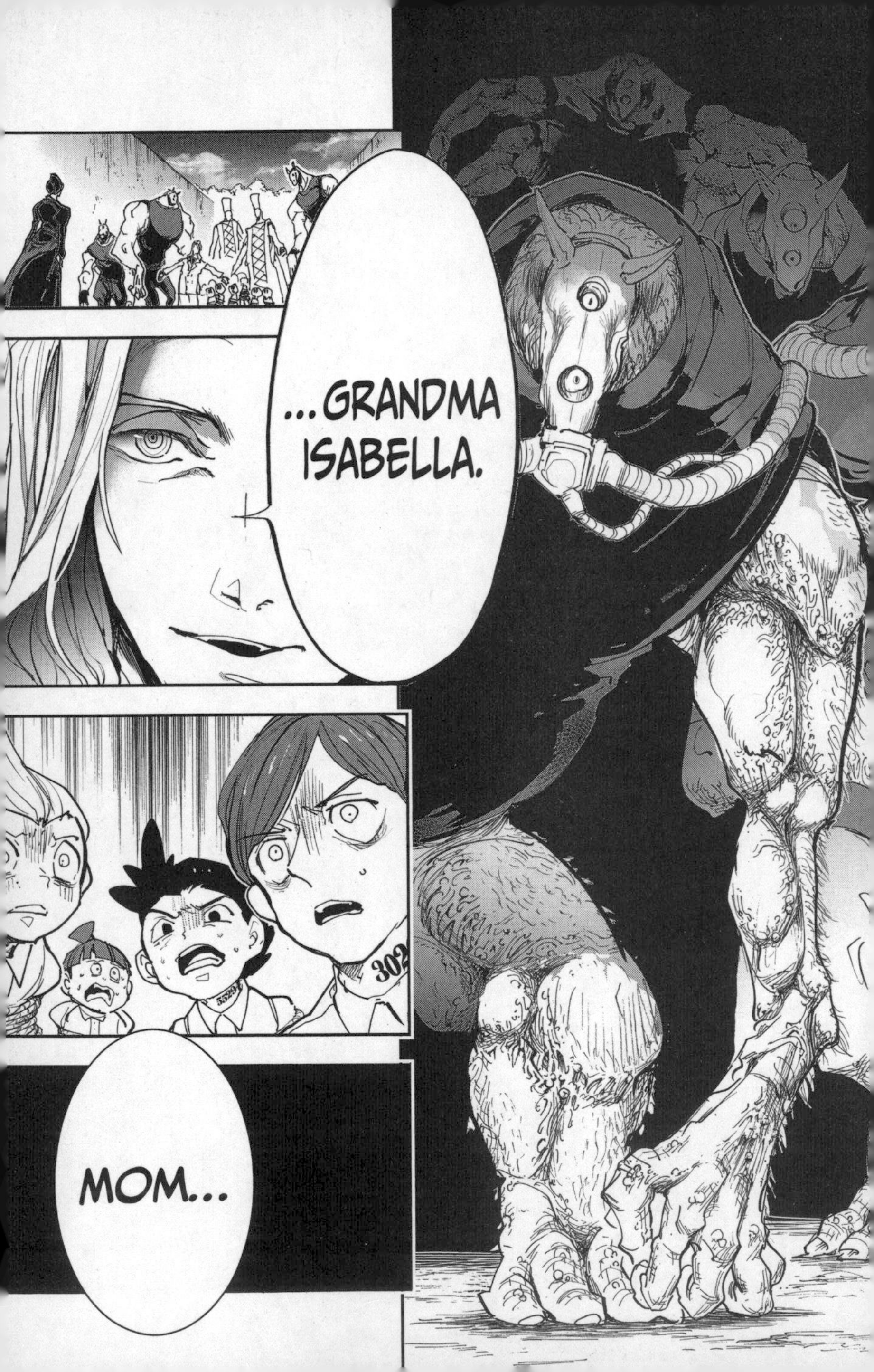
...GRANDMA ISABELLA.
MOM...

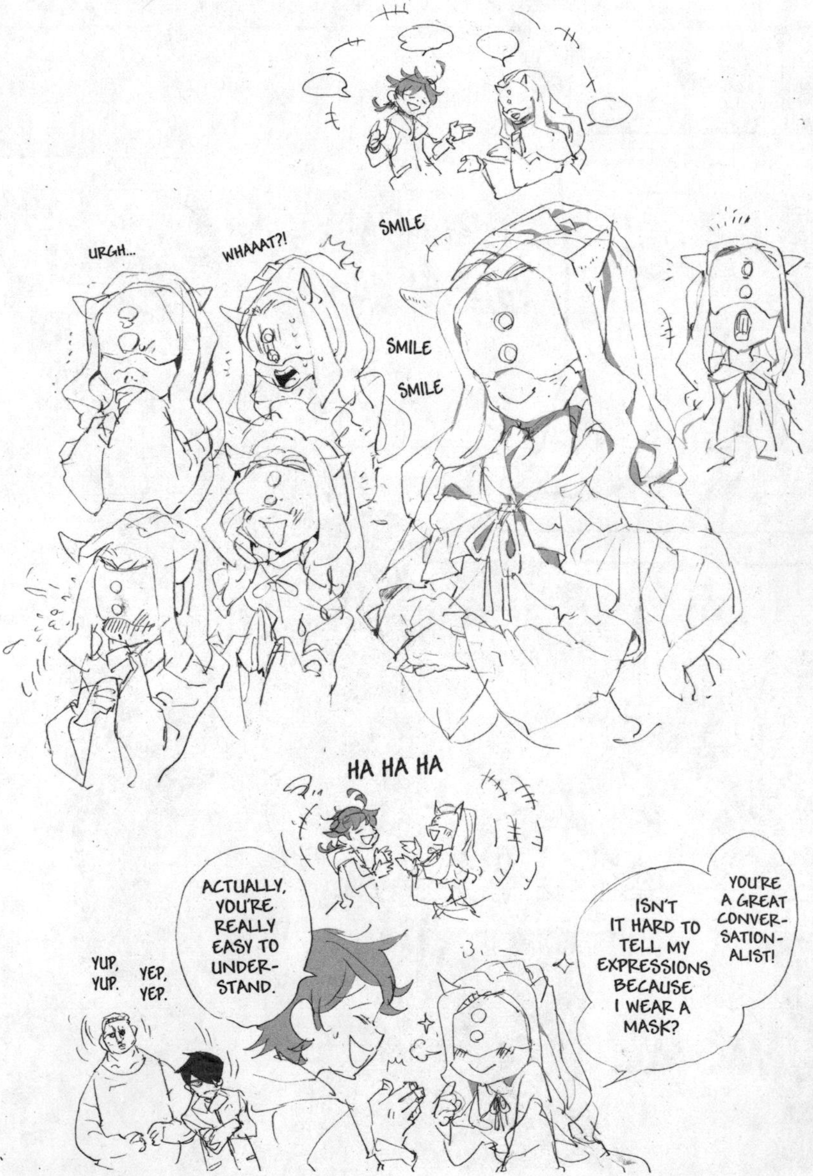
SMILE
SMILE
SMILE
WHAAAT?!
URGH...
HA HA HA
YOU'RE A GREAT CONVERSATIONALIST!
ISN'T IT HARD TO TELL MY EXPRESSIONS BECAUSE I WEAR A MASK?
ACTUALLY, YOU'RE REALLY EASY TO UNDERSTAND.
YEP, YEP.
YUP, YUP.

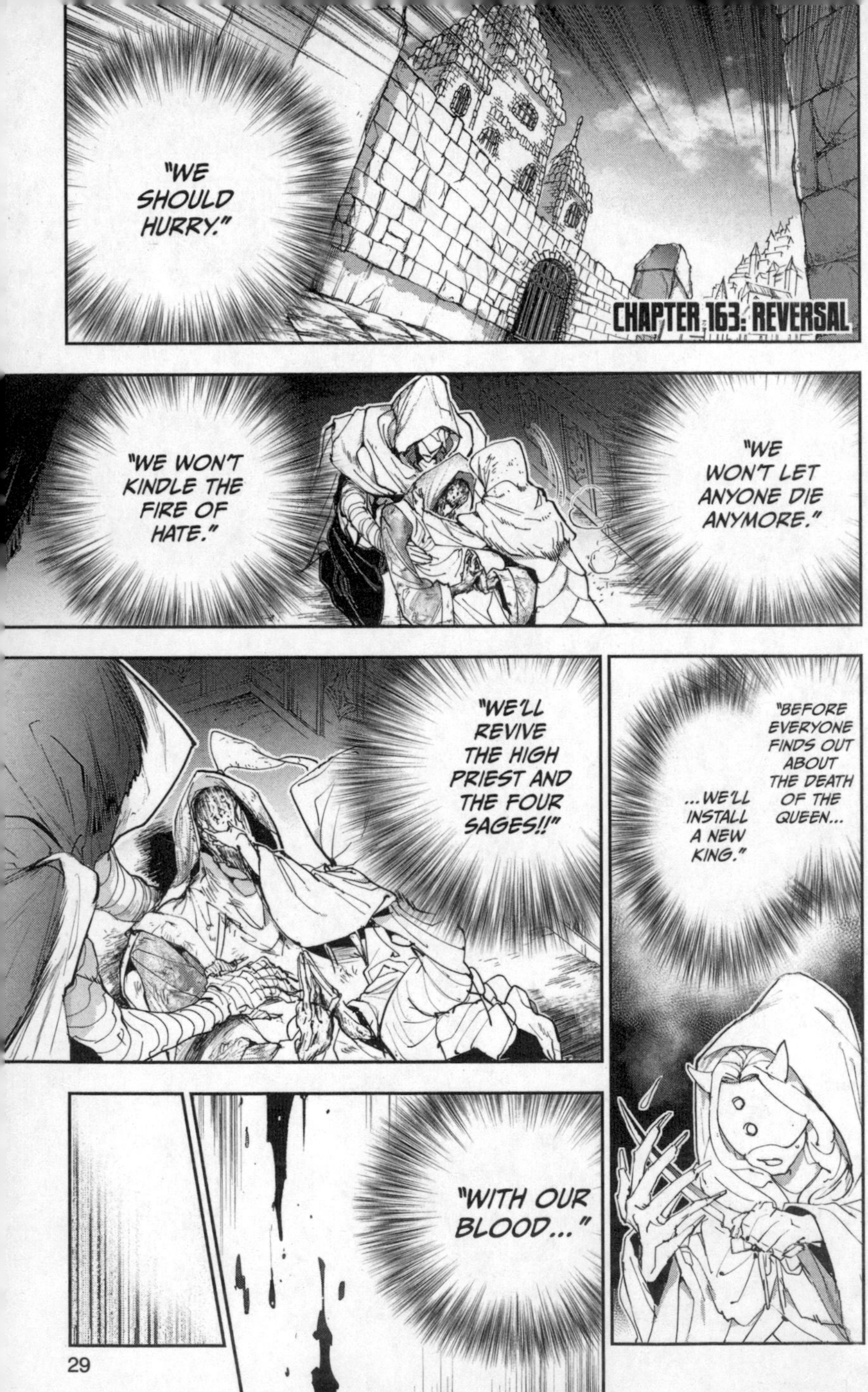
"WE SHOULD HURRY."
CHAPTER 163: REVERSAL
"WE WON'T LET ANYONE DIE ANYMORE."
"WE WON'T KINDLE THE FIRE OF HATE."
"BEFORE EVERYONE FINDS OUT ABOUT THE DEATH OF THE QUEEN...
...WE'LL INSTALL A NEW KING."
"WE'LL REVIVE THE HIGH PRIEST AND THE FOUR SAGES!!"
"WITH OUR BLOOD..."

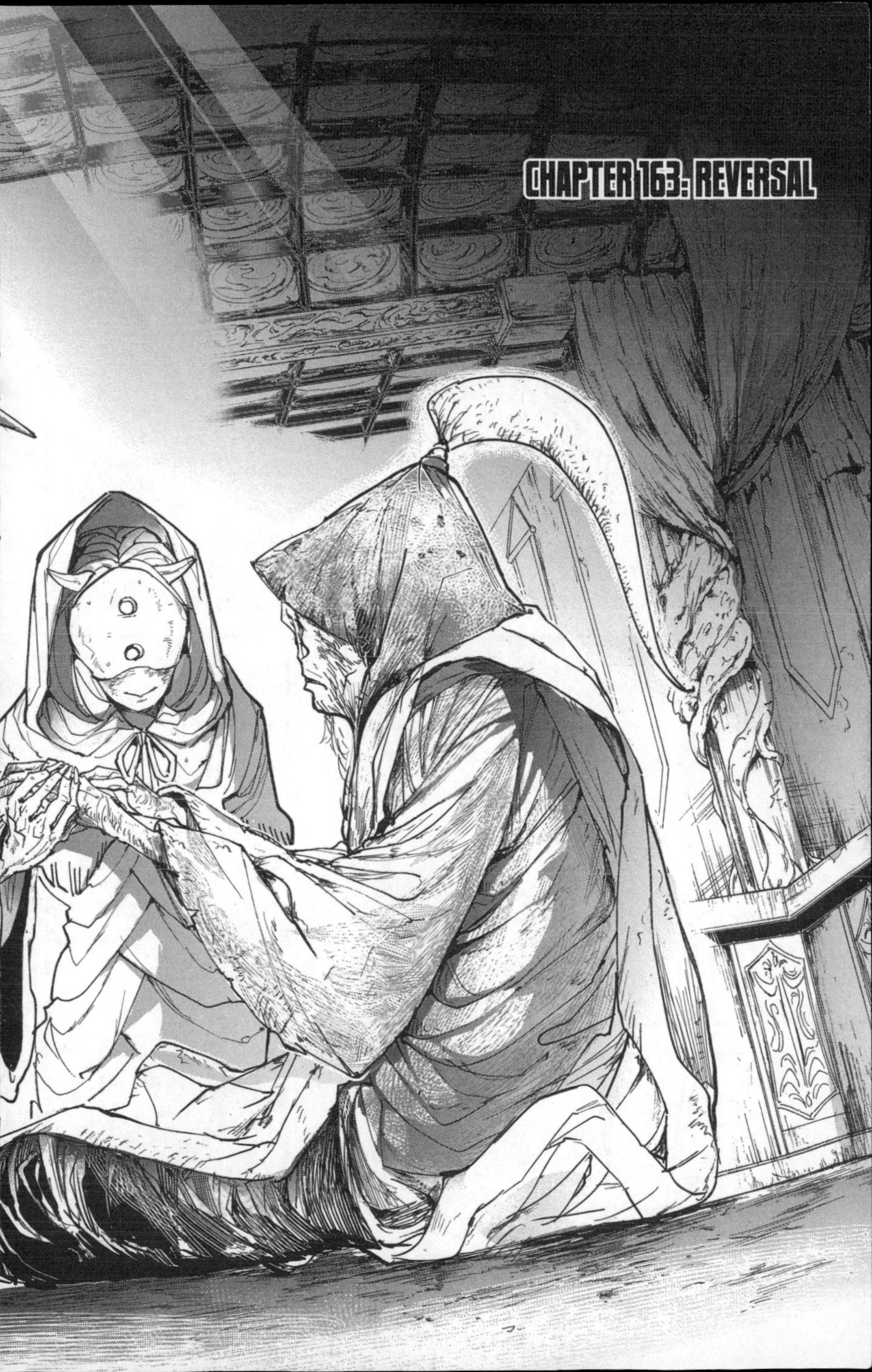
CHAPTER 163: REVERSAL

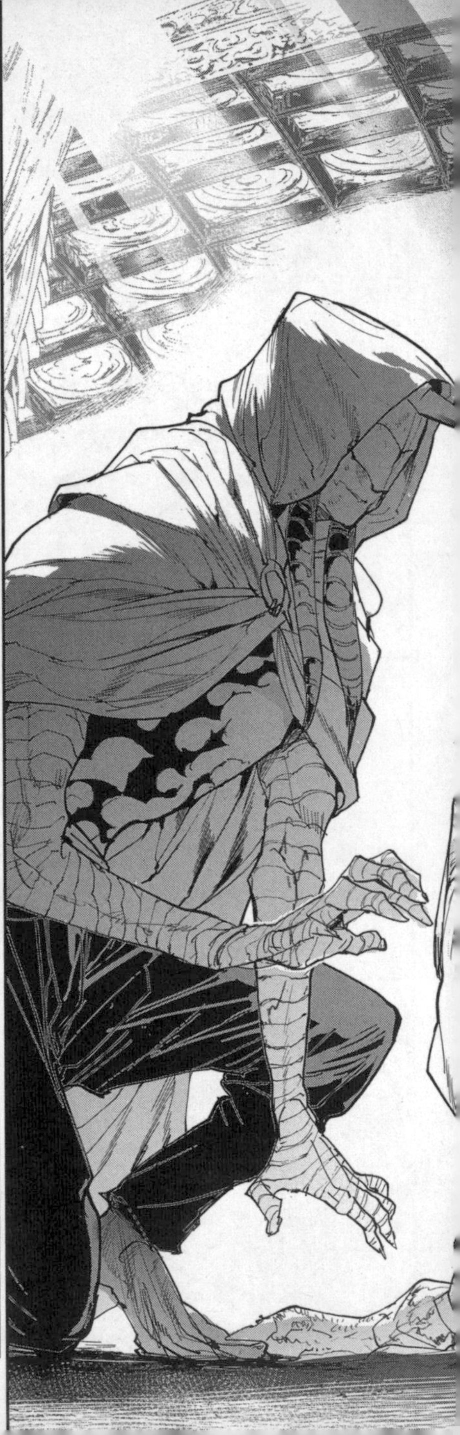

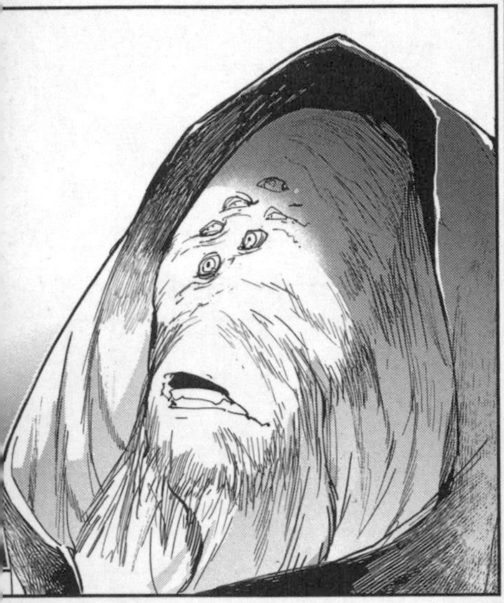

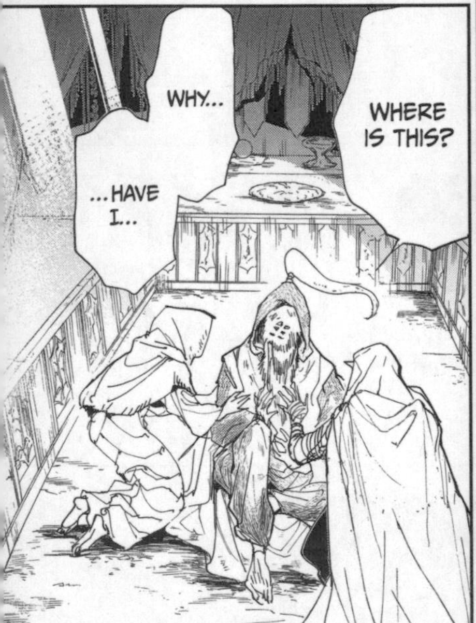
WHERE IS THIS?
WHY...
...HAVE I...

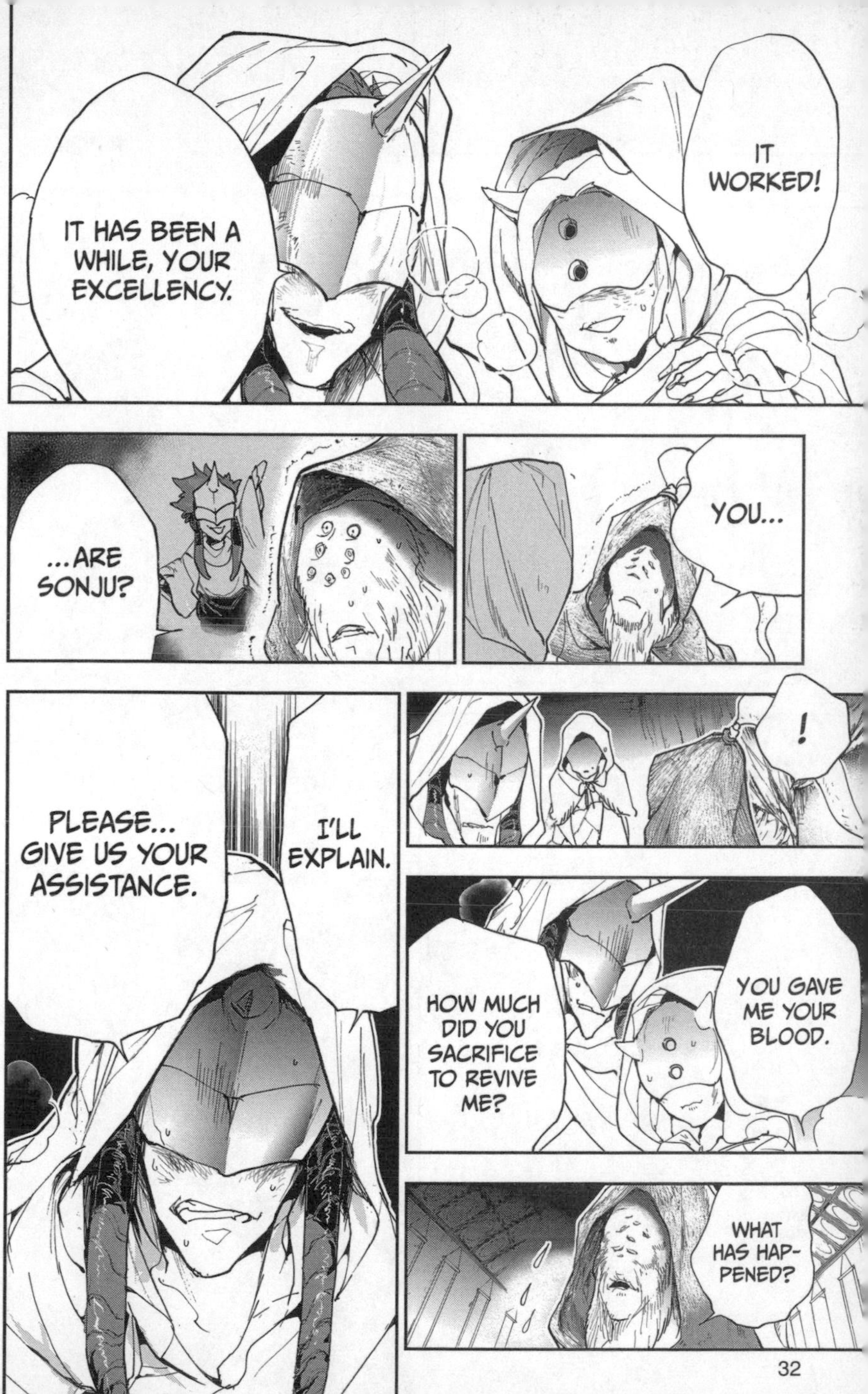
IT WORKED!
IT HAS BEEN A WHILE, YOUR EXCELLENCY.
YOU...
...ARE SONJU?
!
YOU GAVE ME YOUR BLOOD.
HOW MUCH DID YOU SACRIFICE TO REVIVE ME?
WHAT HAS HAP-PENED?
I'LL EXPLAIN.
PLEASE... GIVE US YOUR ASSISTANCE.

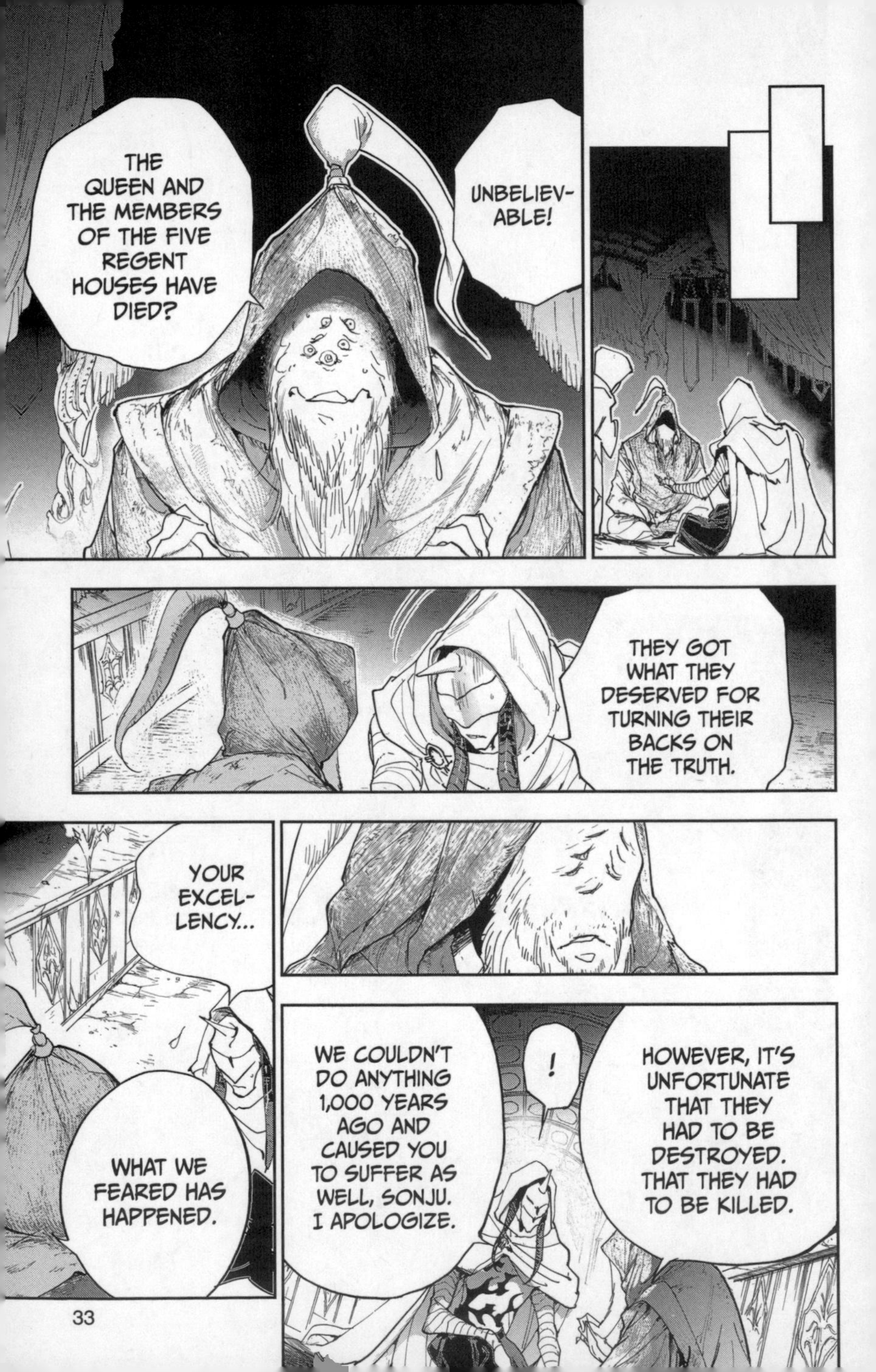
UNBELIEV-ABLE!
THE QUEEN AND THE MEMBERS OF THE FIVE REGENT HOUSES HAVE DIED?
THEY GOT WHAT THEY DESERVED FOR TURNING THEIR BACKS ON THE TRUTH.
HOWEVER, IT'S UNFORTUNATE THAT THEY HAD TO BE DESTROYED. THAT THEY HAD TO BE KILLED.
!
WE COULDN'T DO ANYTHING 1,000 YEARS AGO AND CAUSED YOU TO SUFFER AS WELL, SONJU. I APOLOGIZE.
YOUR EXCEL-LENCY...
WHAT WE FEARED HAS HAPPENED.

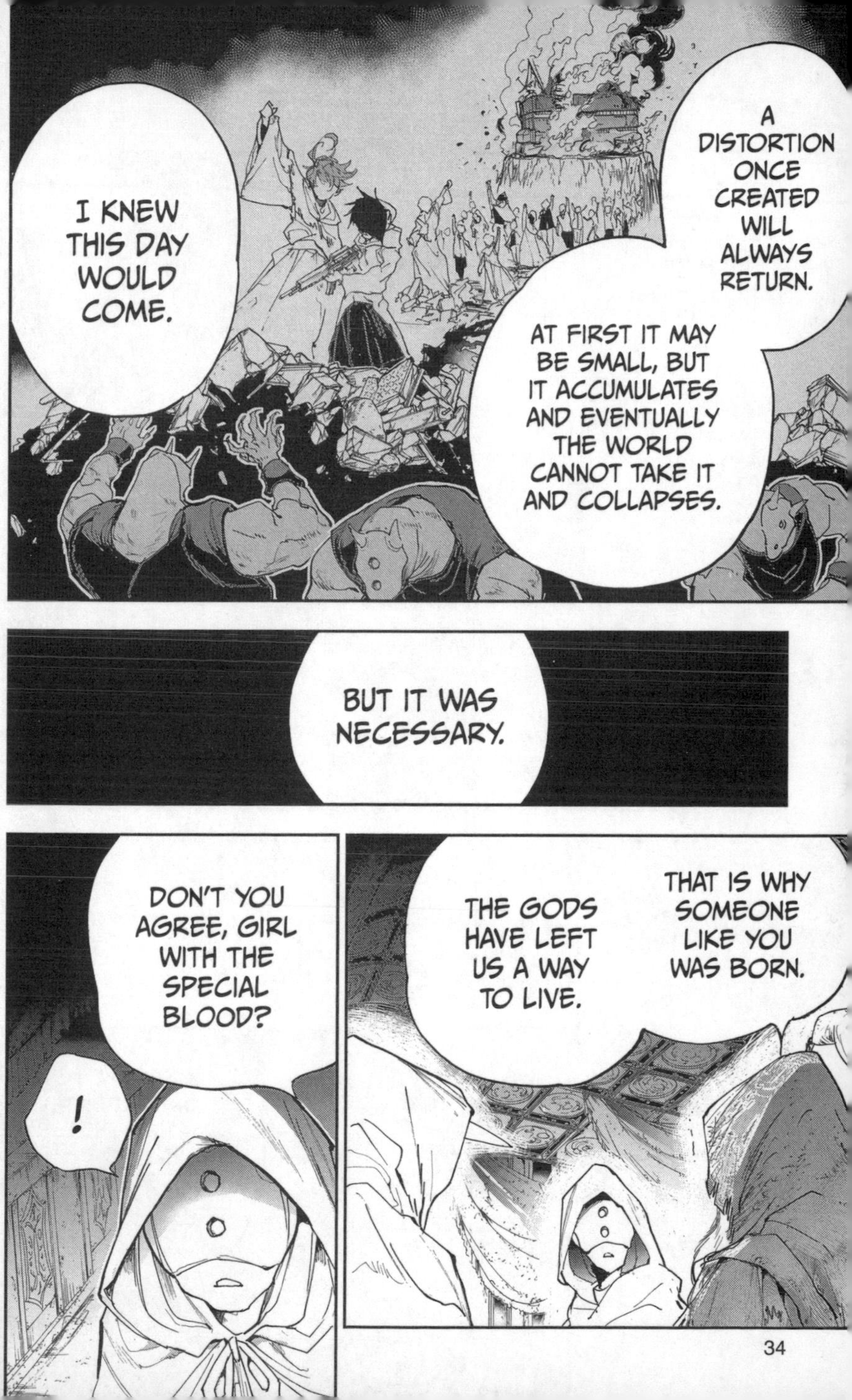
A DISTORTION ONCE CREATED WILL ALWAYS RETURN.
AT FIRST IT MAY BE SMALL, BUT IT ACCUMULATES AND EVENTUALLY THE WORLD CANNOT TAKE IT AND COLLAPSES.
I KNEW THIS DAY WOULD COME.
BUT IT WAS NECESSARY.
THAT IS WHY SOMEONE LIKE YOU WAS BORN.
THE GODS HAVE LEFT US A WAY TO LIVE.
DON'T YOU AGREE, GIRL WITH THE SPECIAL BLOOD?
!

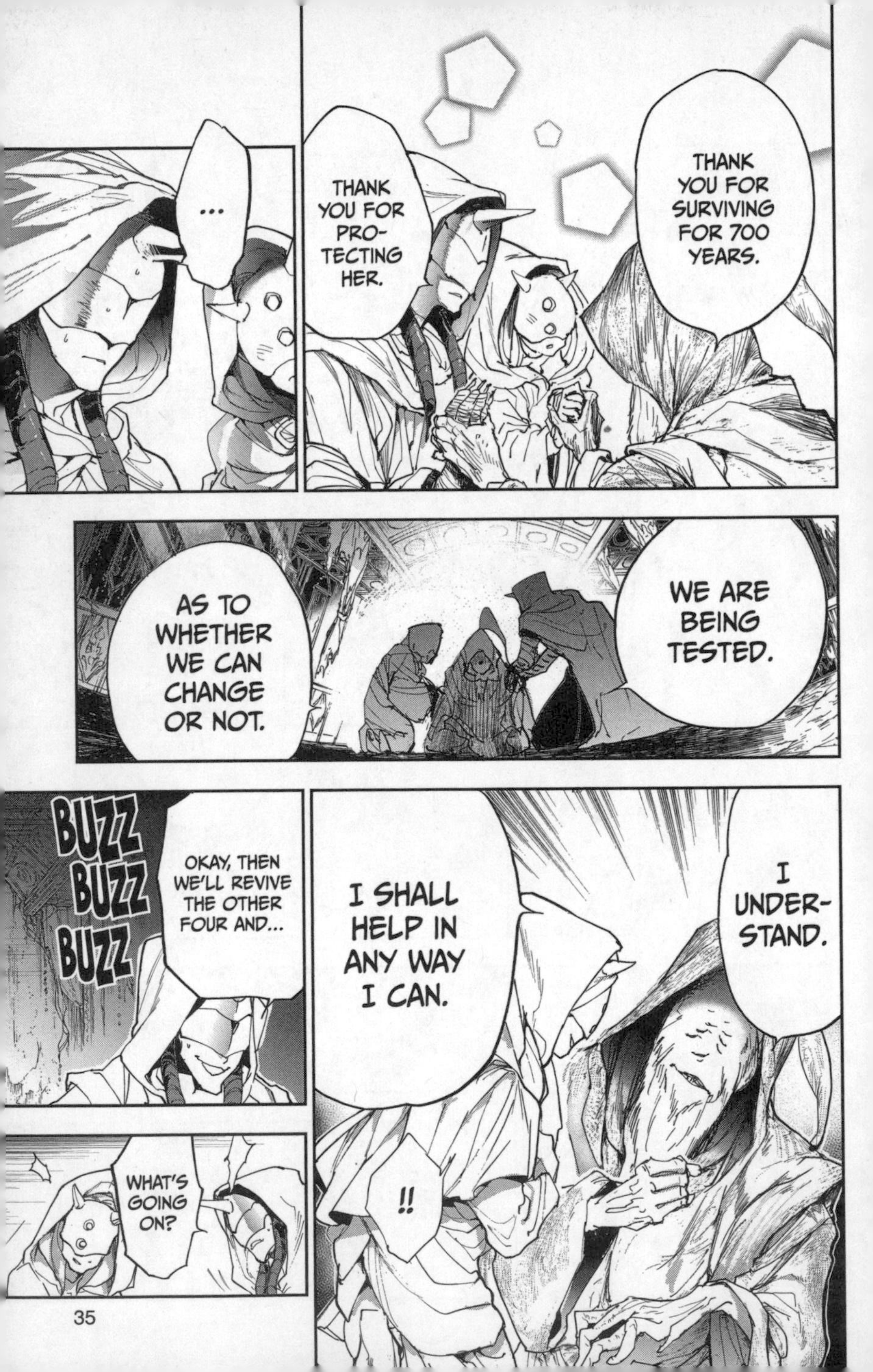
THANK YOU FOR SURVIVING FOR 700 YEARS.
THANK YOU FOR PRO-TECTING HER.
...
WE ARE BEING TESTED.
AS TO WHETHER WE CAN CHANGE OR NOT.
I UNDER-STAND.
I SHALL HELP IN ANY WAY I CAN.
!!
OKAY, THEN WE'LL REVIVE THE OTHER FOUR AND...
BUZZ BUZZ BUZZ
WHAT'S GOING ON?

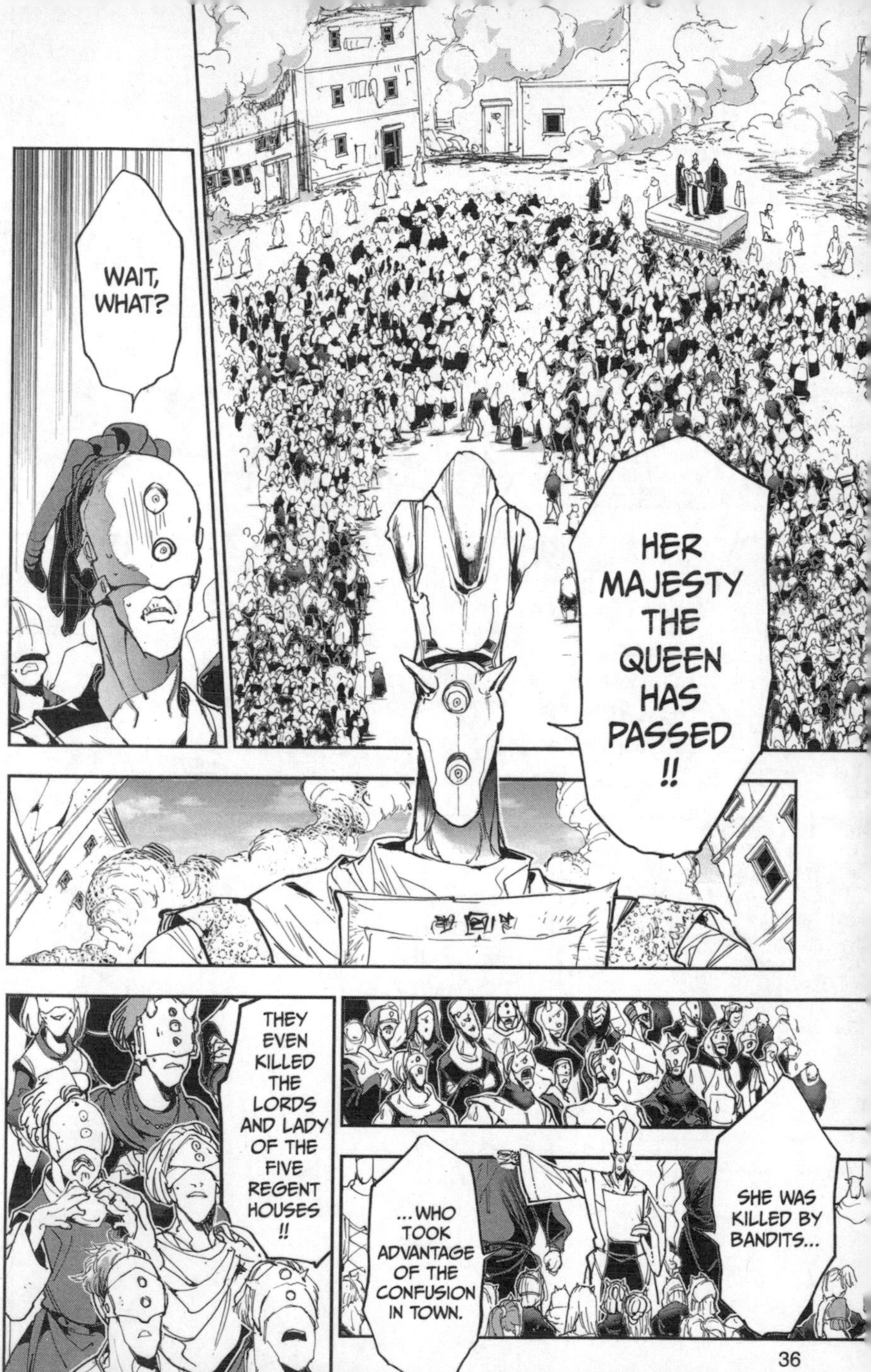
HER MAJESTY THE QUEEN HAS PASSED!!
WAIT, WHAT?
SHE WAS KILLED BY BANDITS...
...WHO TOOK ADVANTAGE OF THE CONFUSION IN TOWN.
THEY EVEN KILLED THE LORDS AND LADY OF THE FIVE REGENT HOUSES!!

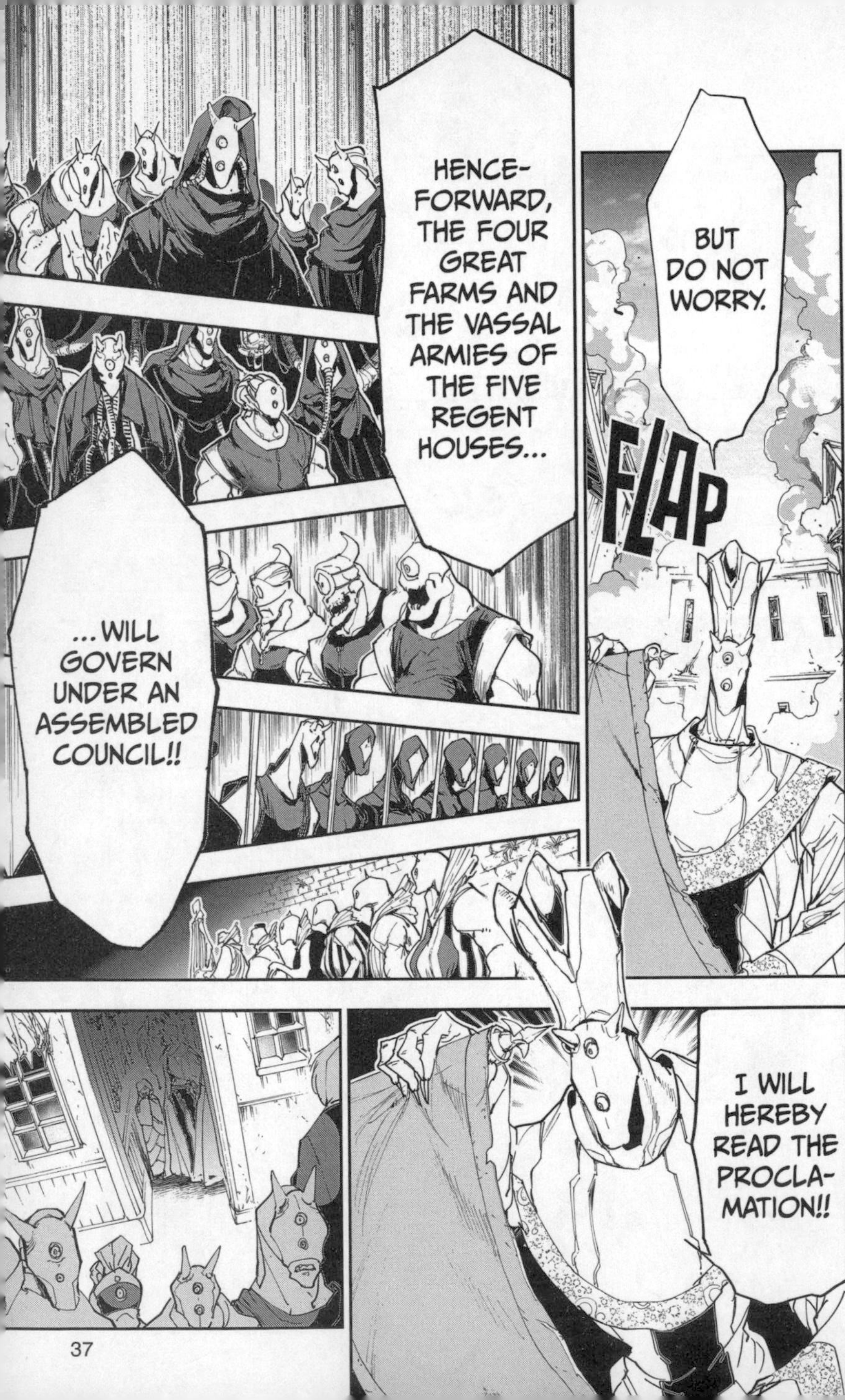
BUT DO NOT WORRY.
FLAP
HENCE-FORWARD, THE FOUR GREAT FARMS AND THE VASSAL ARMIES OF THE FIVE REGENT HOUSES...
...WILL GOVERN UNDER AN ASSEMBLED COUNCIL!!
I WILL HEREBY READ THE PROCLA-MATION!!

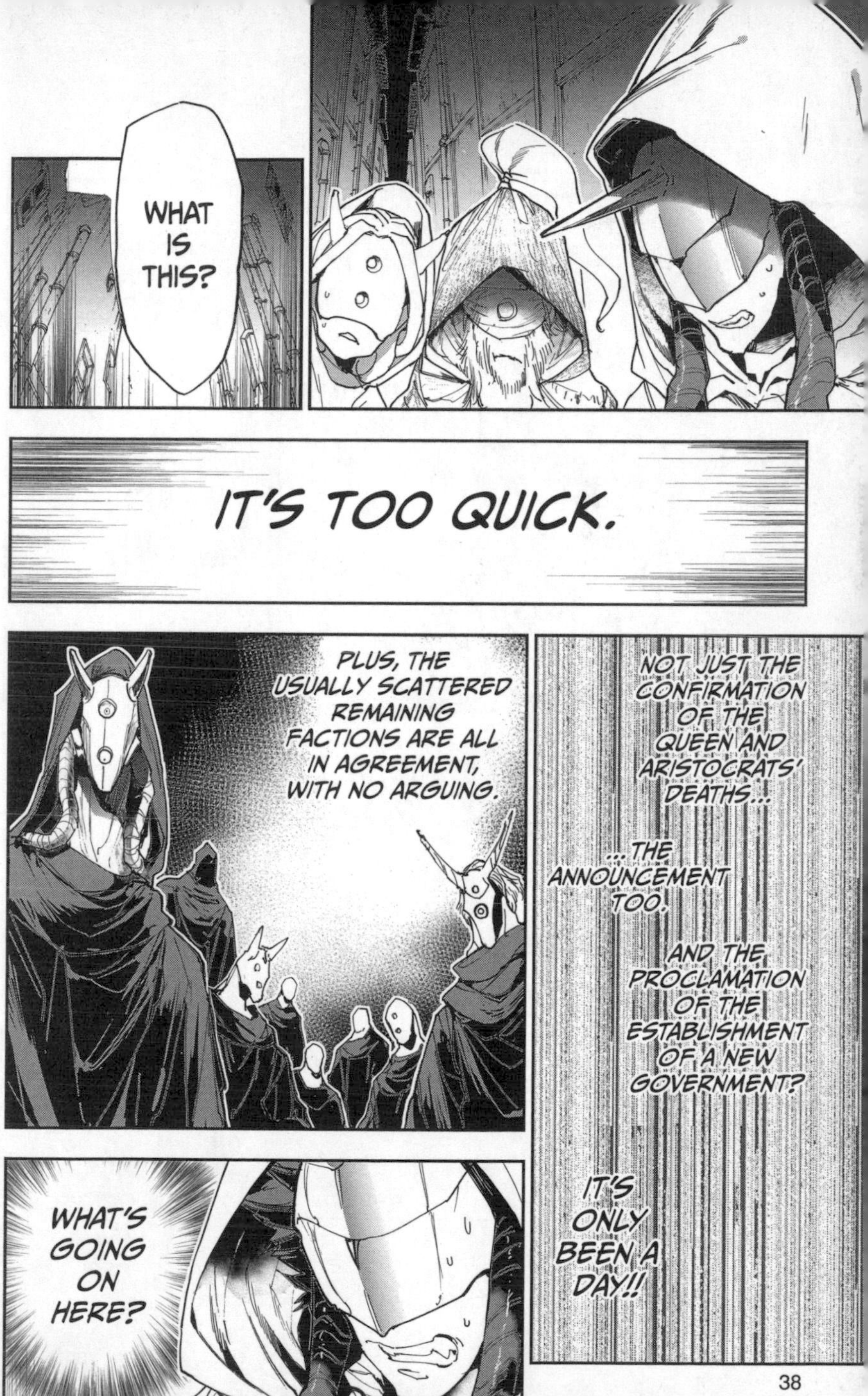
WHAT IS THIS?
IT'S TOO QUICK.
NOT JUST THE CONFIRMATION OF THE QUEEN AND ARISTOCRATS' DEATHS...
...THE ANNOUNCEMENT TOO.
AND THE PROCLAMATION OF THE ESTABLISHMENT OF A NEW GOVERNMENT?
IT'S ONLY BEEN A DAY!!
PLUS, THE USUALLY SCATTERED REMAINING FACTIONS ARE ALL IN AGREEMENT, WITH NO ARGUING.
WHAT'S GOING ON HERE?

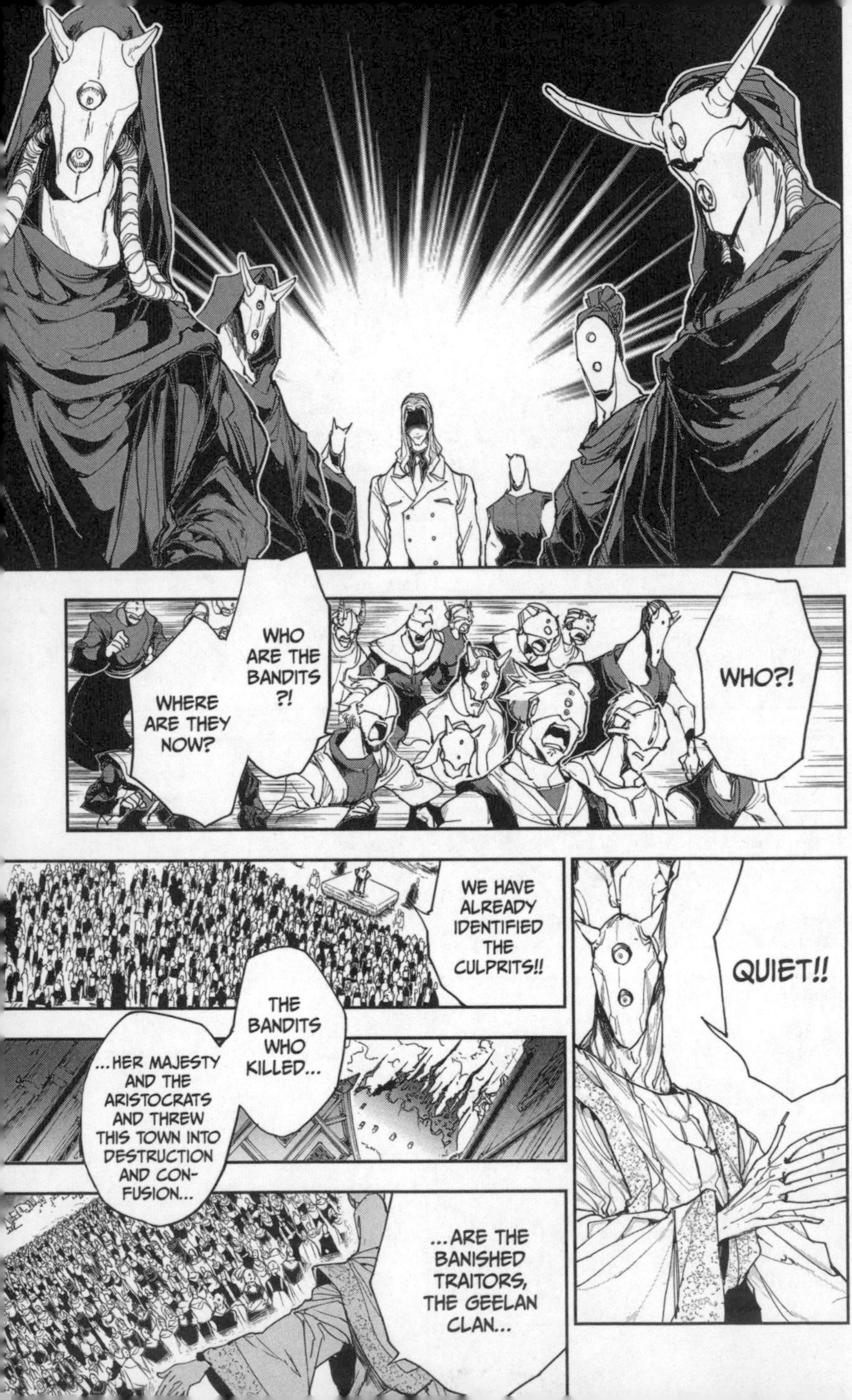
WHO?!
WHO ARE THE BANDITS?!
WHERE ARE THEY NOW?
QUIET!!
WE HAVE ALREADY IDENTIFIED THE CULPRITS!!
THE BANDITS WHO KILLED...
...HER MAJESTY AND THE ARISTOCRATS AND THREW THIS TOWN INTO DESTRUCTION AND CONFUSION...
...ARE THE BANISHED TRAITORS, THE GEELAN CLAN...

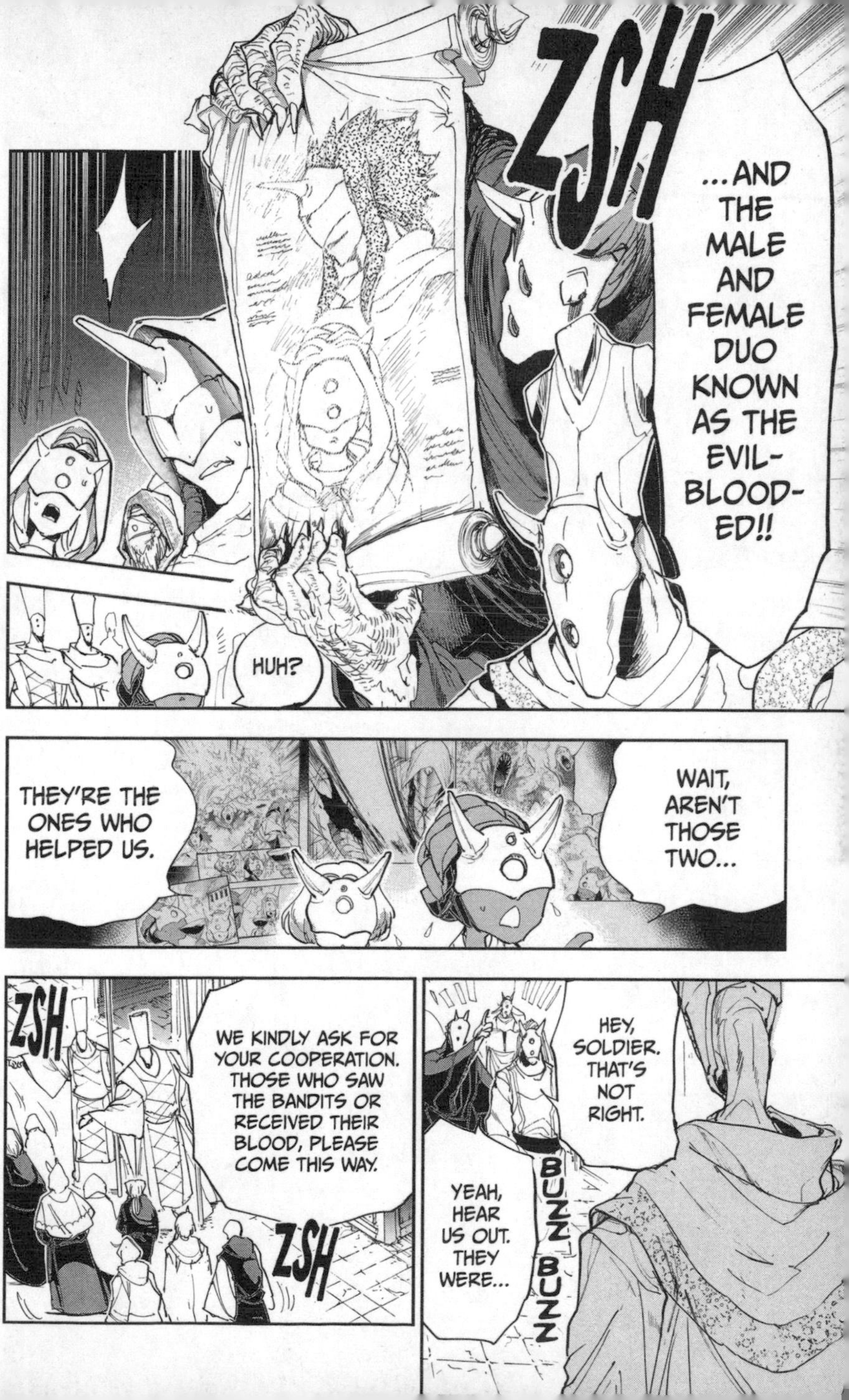
ZSH
...AND THE MALE AND FEMALE DUO KNOWN AS THE EVIL-BLOODED!!
HUH?
WAIT, AREN'T THOSE TWO...
THEY'RE THE ONES WHO HELPED US.
HEY, SOLDIER. THAT'S NOT RIGHT.
BUZZ BUZZ
YEAH, HEAR US OUT. THEY WERE...
ZSH
WE KINDLY ASK FOR YOUR COOPERATION. THOSE WHO SAW THE BANDITS OR RECEIVED THEIR BLOOD, PLEASE COME THIS WAY.
ZSH

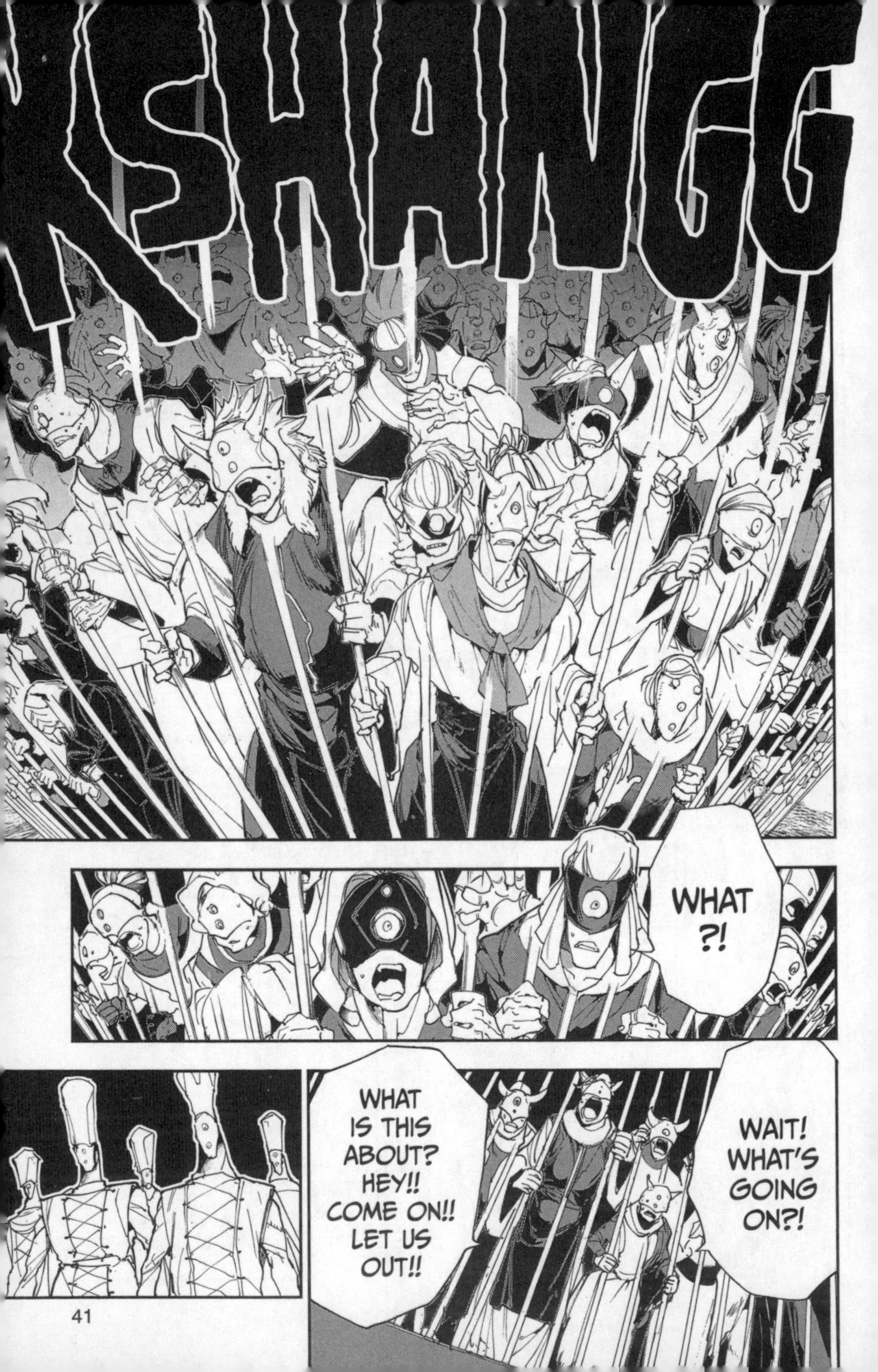
KSHANGG
WHAT ?!
WAIT! WHAT'S GOING ON?!
WHAT IS THIS ABOUT? HEY!! COME ON!! LET US OUT!!

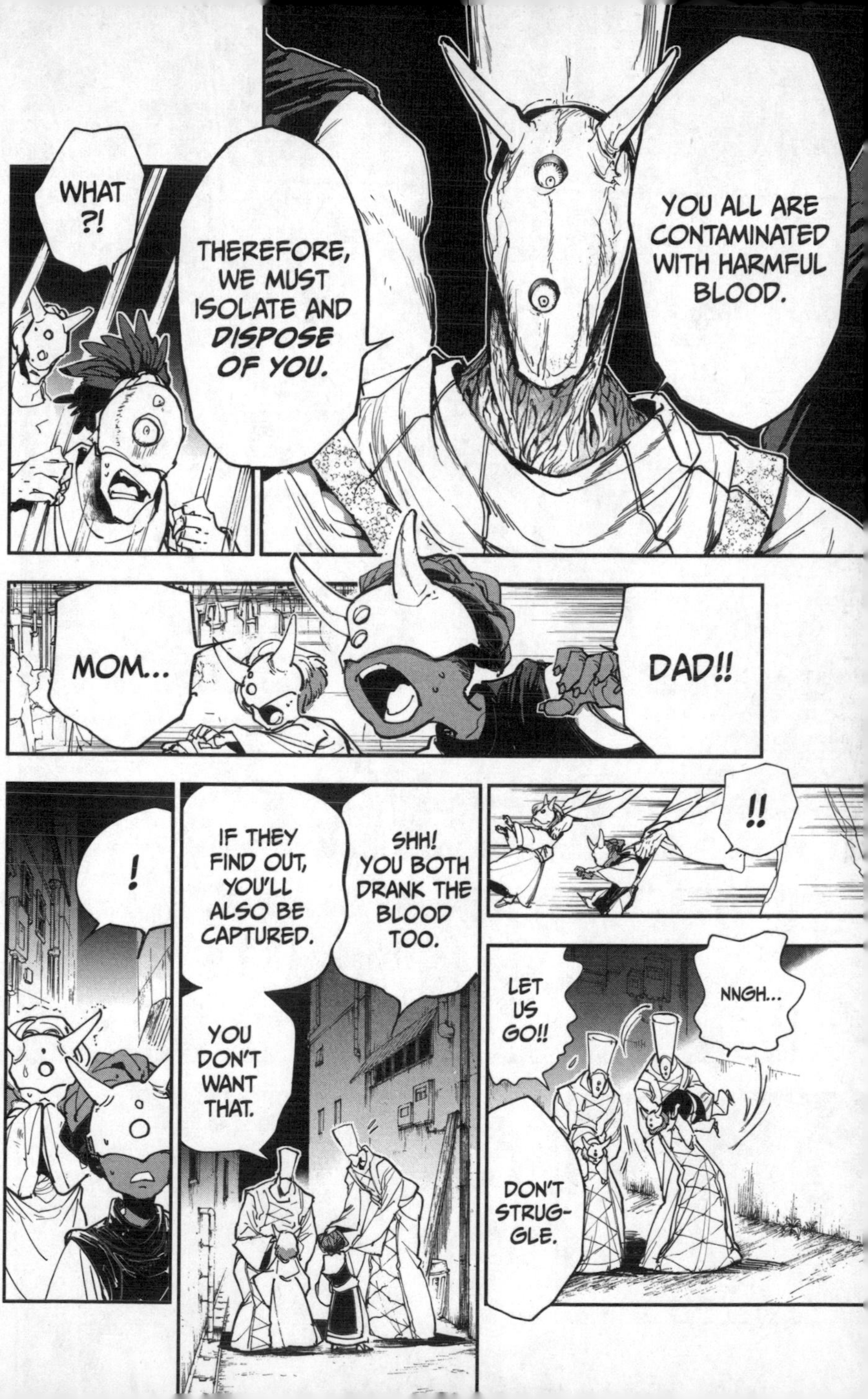
YOU ALL ARE CONTAMINATED WITH HARMFUL BLOOD.
THEREFORE, WE MUST ISOLATE AND DISPOSE OF YOU.
WHAT ?!
DAD!!
MOM...
!!
NNGH...
LET US GO!!
DON'T STRUG-GLE.
SHH! YOU BOTH DRANK THE BLOOD TOO.
IF THEY FIND OUT, YOU'LL ALSO BE CAPTURED.
YOU DON'T WANT THAT.
!

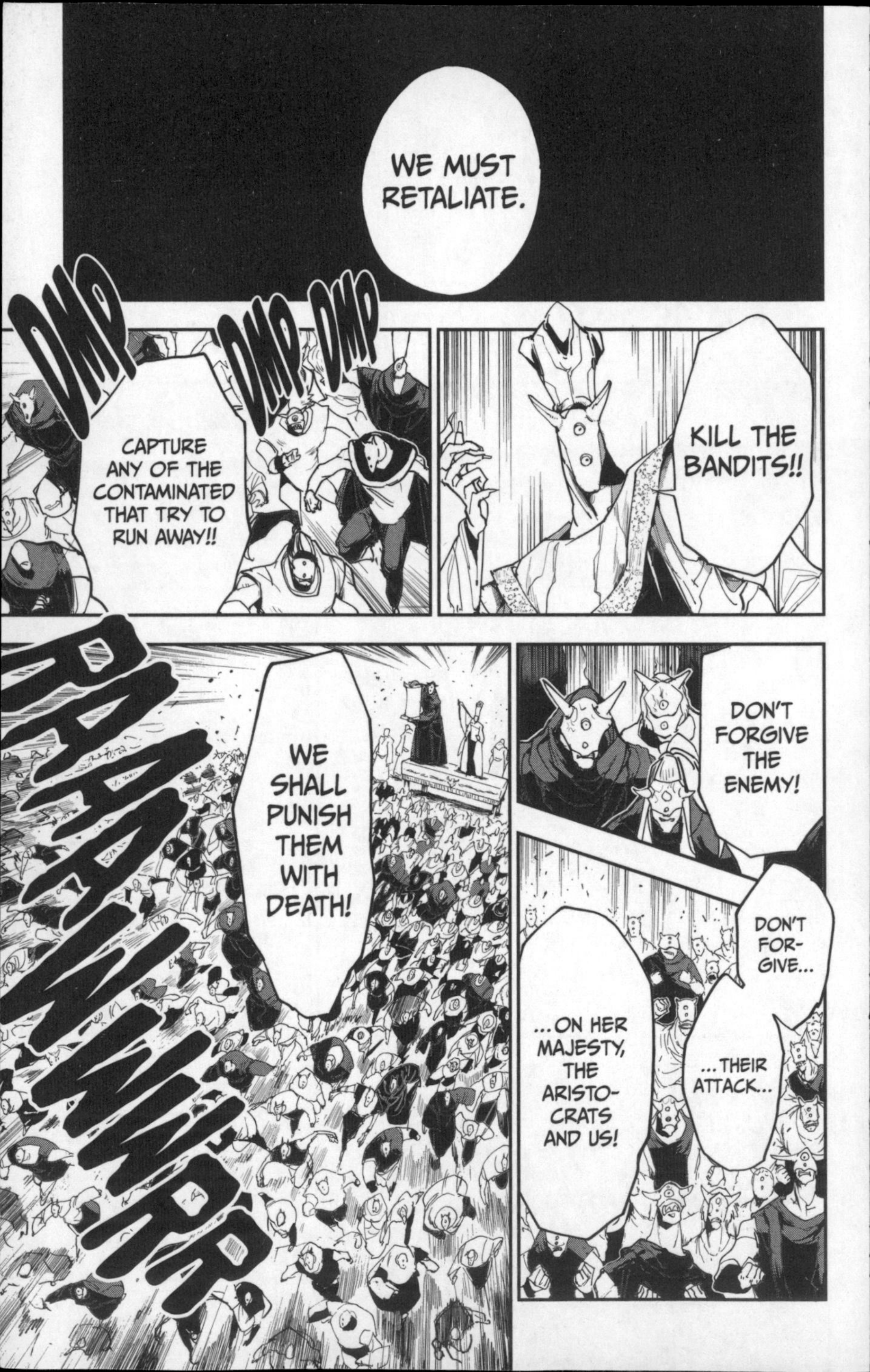

WE MUST RETALIATE.
KILL THE BANDITS!!
DMP
DMP DMP
CAPTURE ANY OF THE CONTAMINATED THAT TRY TO RUN AWAY!!
DON'T FORGIVE THE ENEMY!
DON'T FOR-GIVE...
...THEIR ATTACK...
...ON HER MAJESTY, THE ARISTO-CRATS AND US!
WE SHALL PUNISH THEM WITH DEATH!
RAAWWWRR

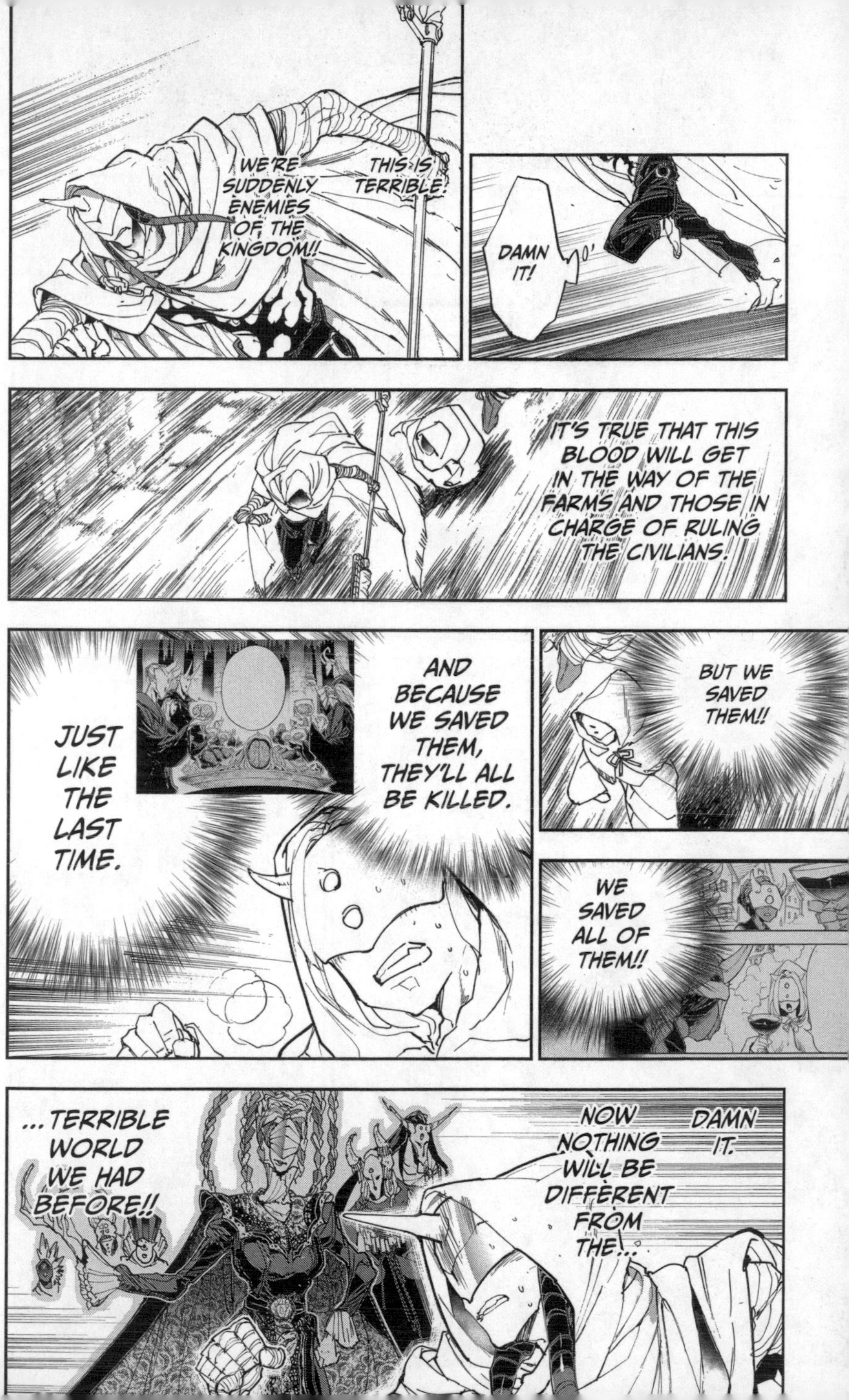
DAMN IT!
THIS IS TERRIBLE!
WE'RE SUDDENLY ENEMIES OF THE KINGDOM!!
IT'S TRUE THAT THIS BLOOD WILL GET IN THE WAY OF THE FARMS AND THOSE IN CHARGE OF RULING THE CIVILIANS.
BUT WE SAVED THEM!!
WE SAVED ALL OF THEM!!
AND BECAUSE WE SAVED THEM, THEY'LL ALL BE KILLED.
JUST LIKE THE LAST TIME.
DAMN IT.
NOW NOTHING WILL BE DIFFERENT FROM THE...
...TERRIBLE WORLD WE HAD BEFORE!!

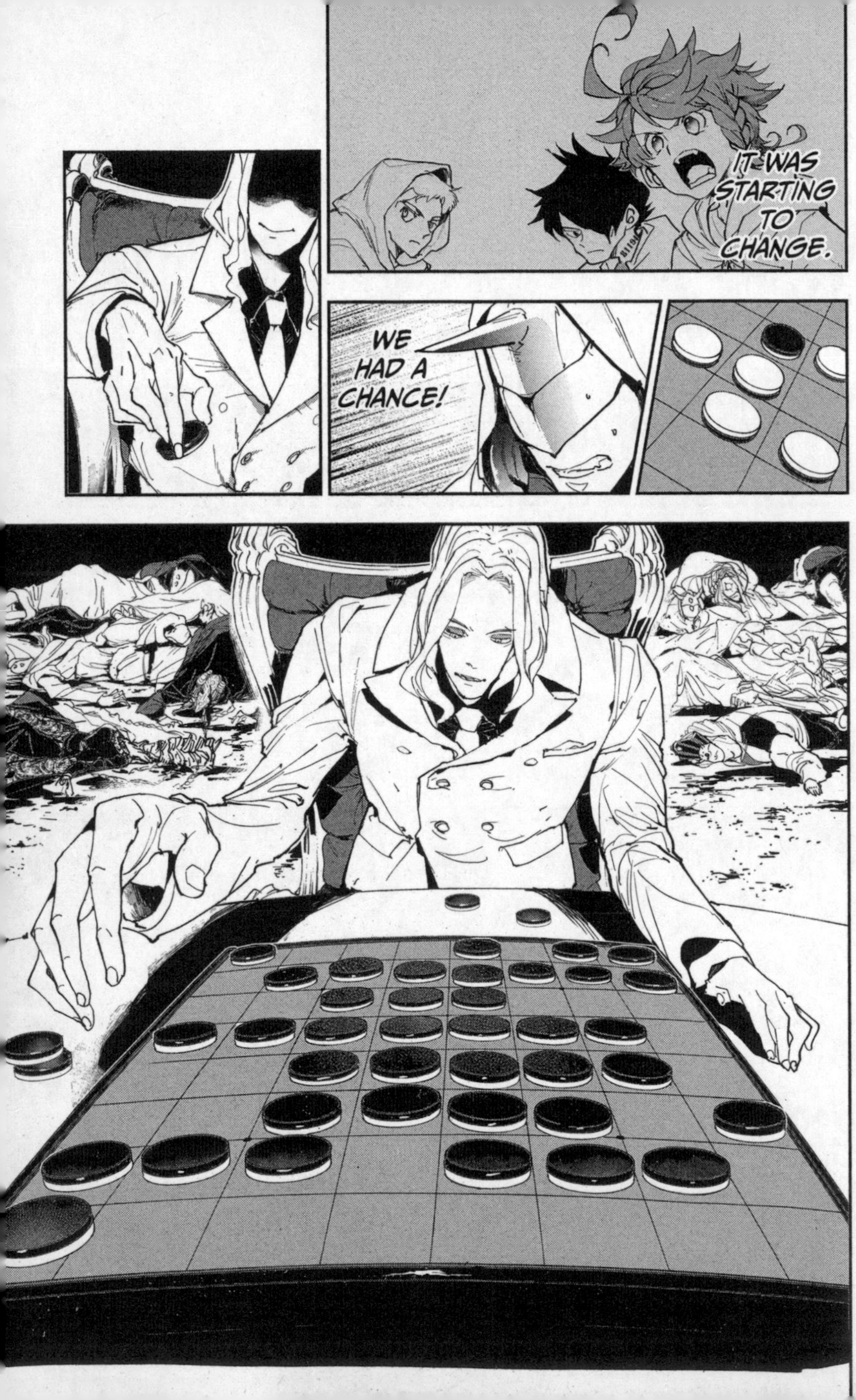
IT WAS STARTING TO CHANGE.
WE HAD A CHANCE!

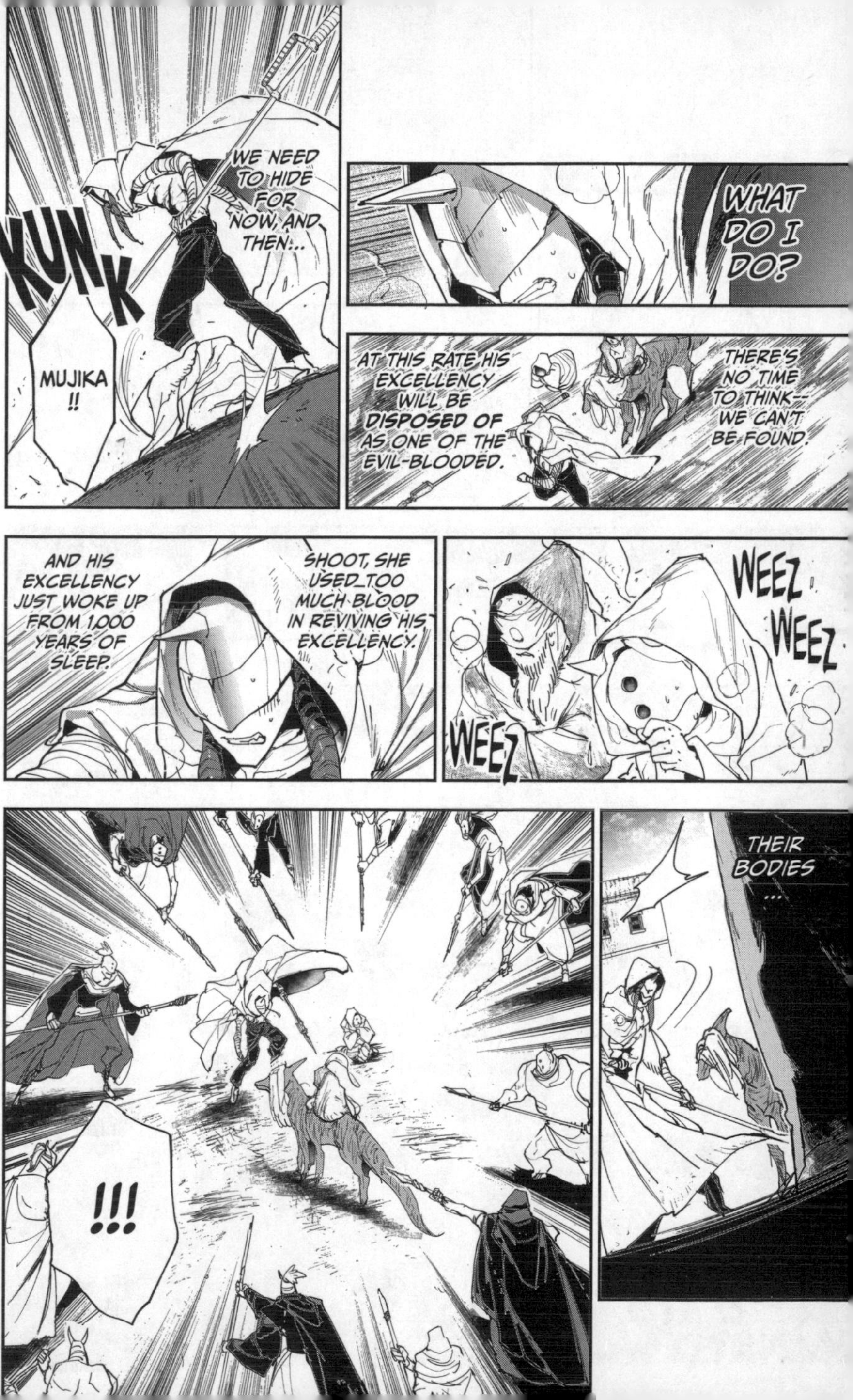
WHAT DO I DO?
THERE'S NO TIME TO THINK-- WE CAN'T BE FOUND.
AT THIS RATE HIS EXCELLENCY WILL BE DISPOSED OF AS ONE OF THE EVIL-BLOODED.
WE NEED TO HIDE FOR NOW, AND THEN...
KUNK
MUJIKA !!
WEEZ
WEEZ
WEEZ
SHOOT, SHE USED TOO MUCH BLOOD IN REVIVING HIS EXCELLENCY.
AND HIS EXCELLENCY JUST WOKE UP FROM 1,000 YEARS OF SLEEP.
THEIR BODIES ...
!!!

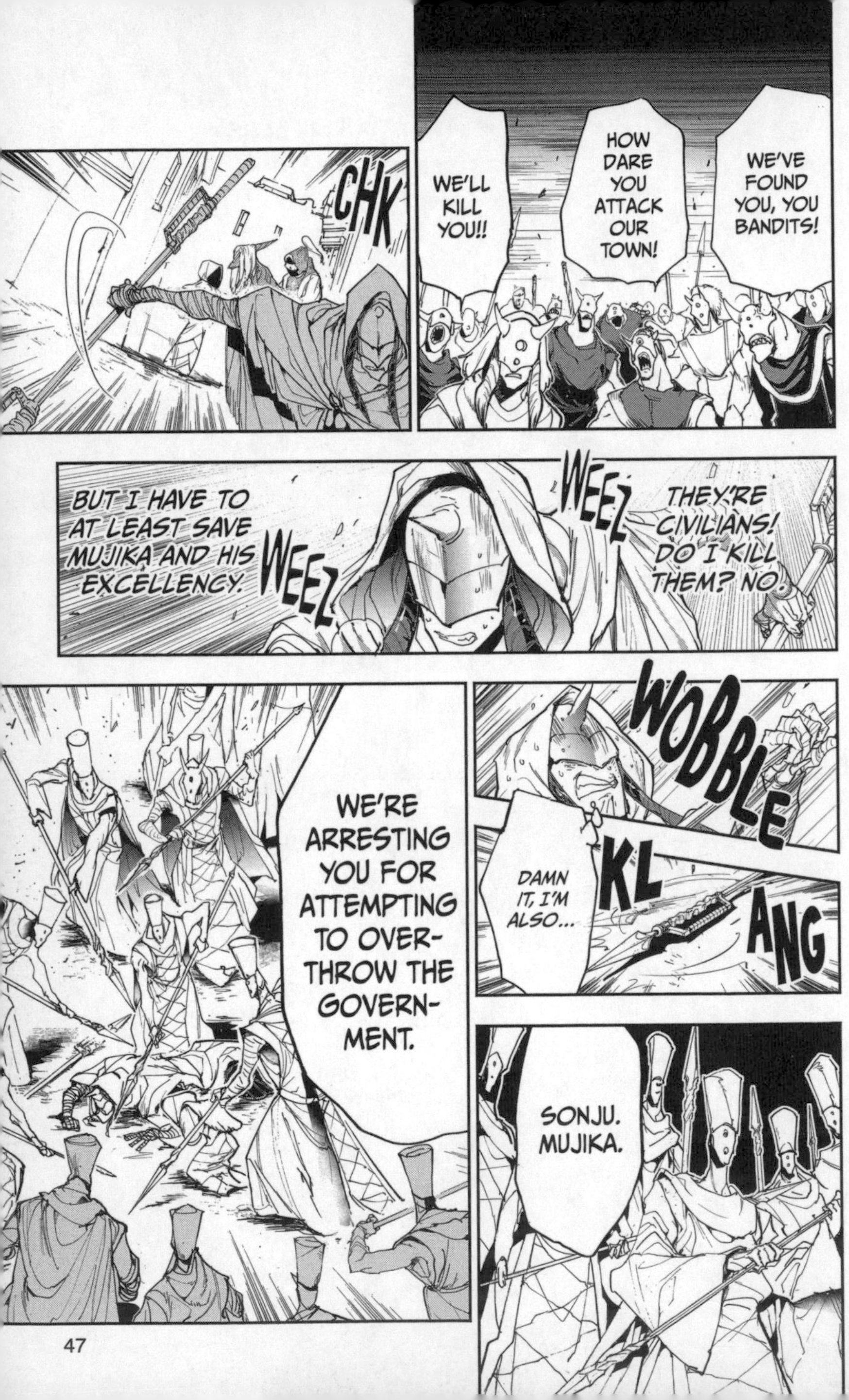
WE'VE FOUND YOU, YOU BANDITS!
HOW DARE YOU ATTACK OUR TOWN!
WE'LL KILL YOU!!
CHK
WEEZ
THEY'RE CIVILIANS! DO I KILL THEM? NO.
WEEZ
BUT I HAVE TO AT LEAST SAVE MUJIKA AND HIS EXCELLENCY.
WOBBLE
KLANG
DAMN IT, I'M ALSO...
SONJU. MUJIKA.
WE'RE ARRESTING YOU FOR ATTEMPTING TO OVERTHROW THE GOVERNMENT.

SUPER BLUE

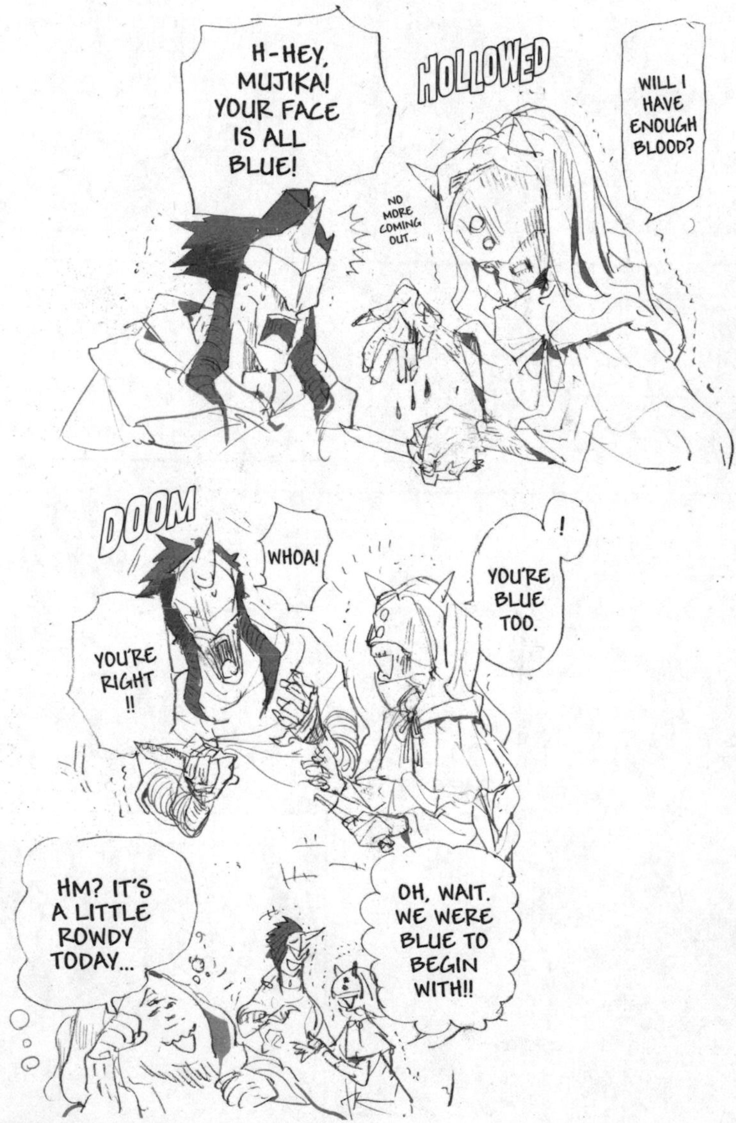
WILL I HAVE ENOUGH BLOOD?
HOLLOWED
H-HEY, MUJIKA! YOUR FACE IS ALL BLUE!
NO MORE COMING OUT...
!
YOU'RE BLUE TOO.
WHOA!
DOOM
YOU'RE RIGHT !!
OH, WAIT. WE WERE BLUE TO BEGIN WITH!!
HM? IT'S A LITTLE ROWDY TODAY...

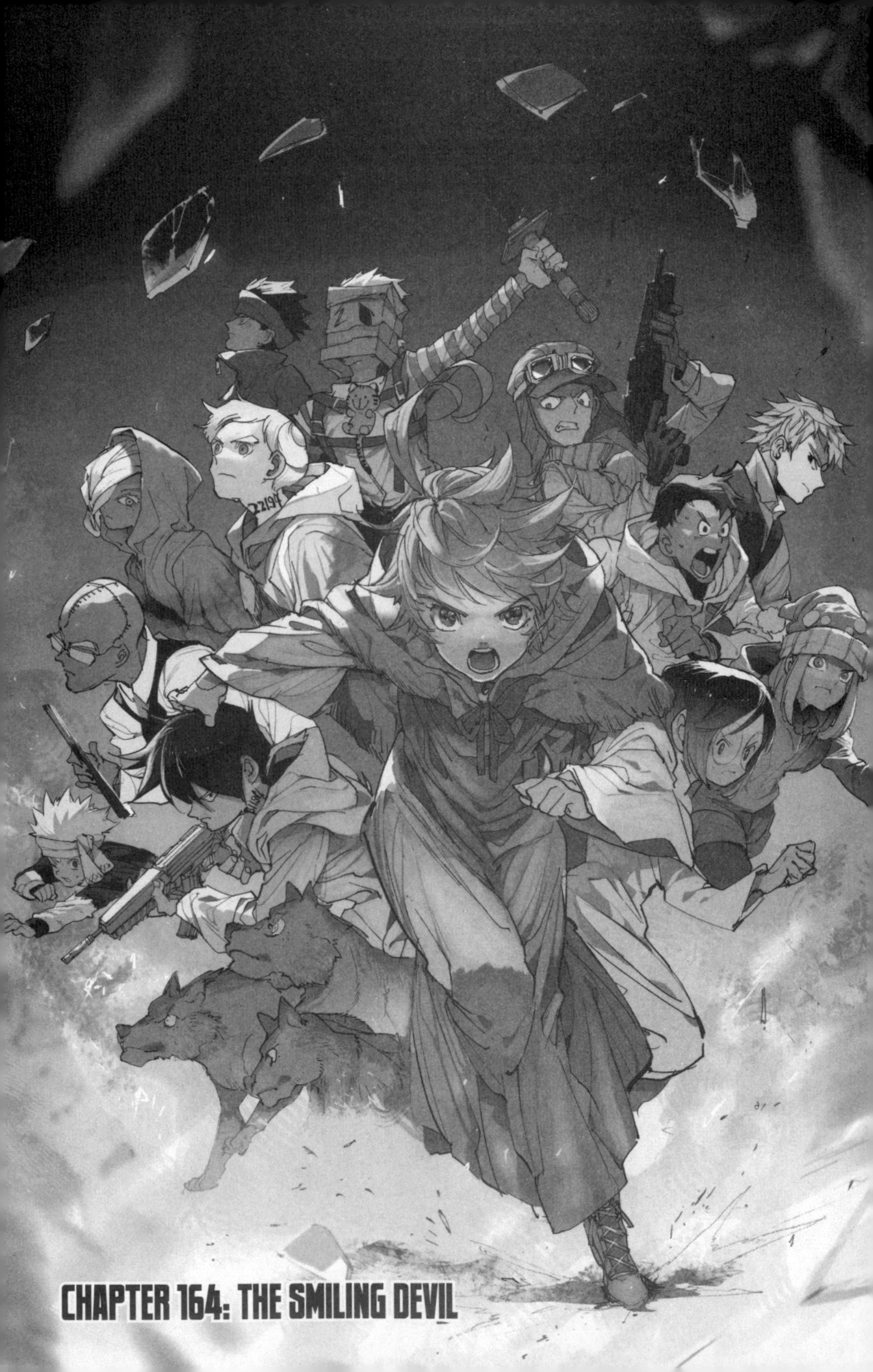

CHAPTER 164: THE SMILING DEVIL

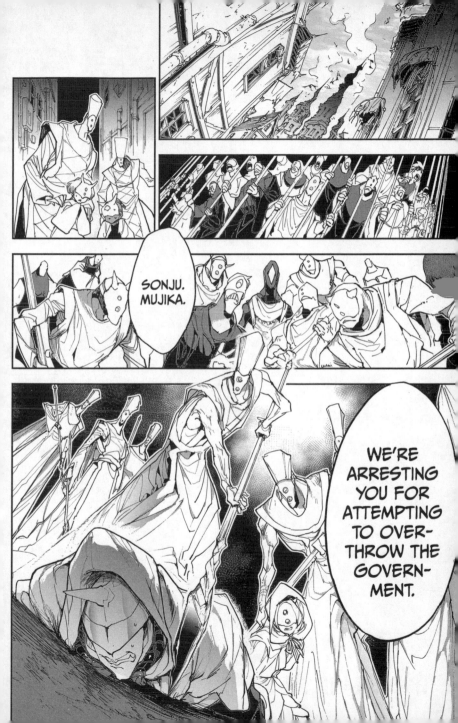

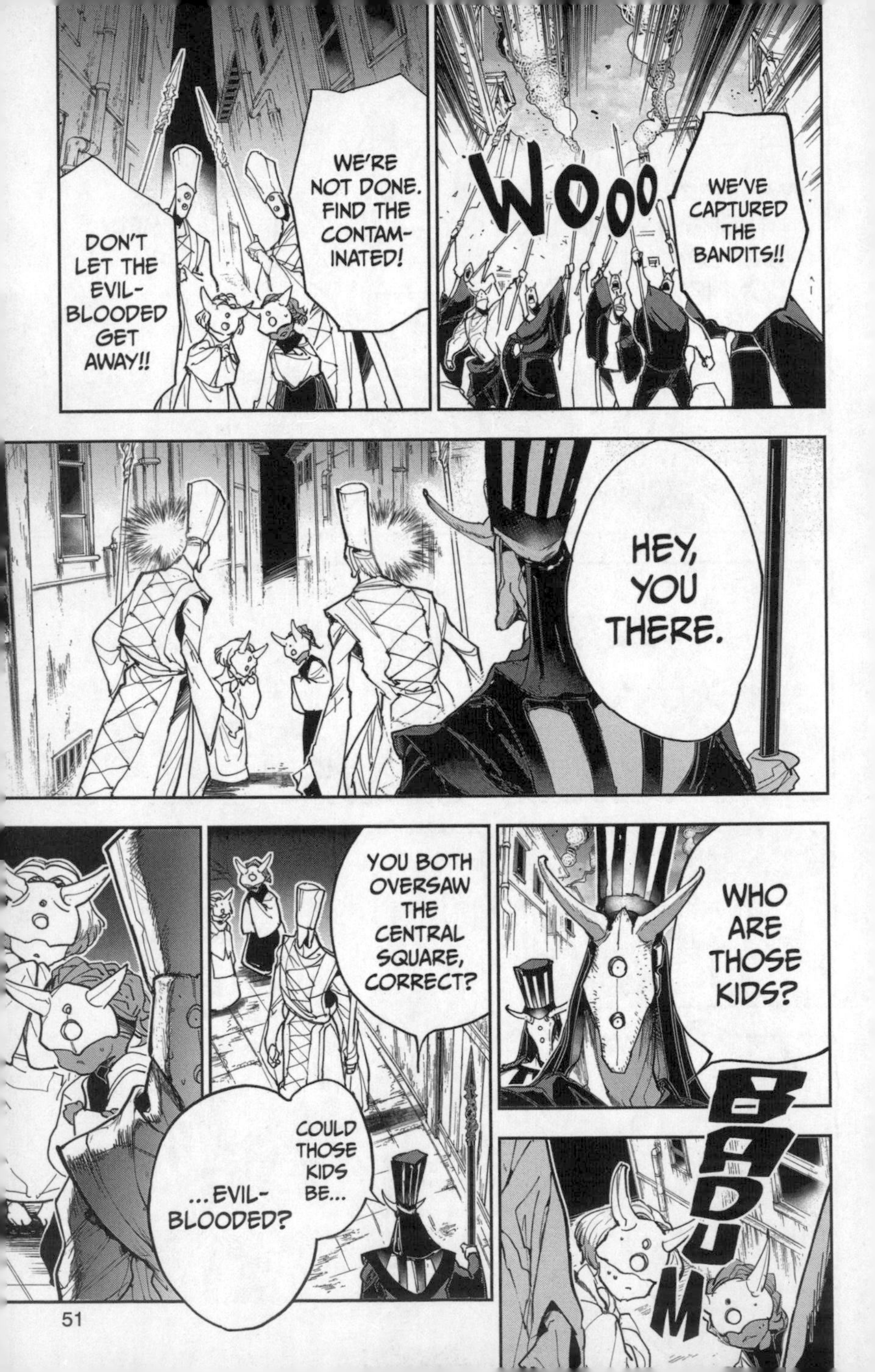
WOOO
WE'VE CAPTURED THE BANDITS!!
WE'RE NOT DONE. FIND THE CONTAM-INATED!
DON'T LET THE EVIL-BLOODED GET AWAY!!
HEY, YOU THERE.
WHO ARE THOSE KIDS?
B-BADUM
YOU BOTH OVERSAW THE CENTRAL SQUARE, CORRECT?
COULD THOSE KIDS BE...
...EVIL-BLOODED?

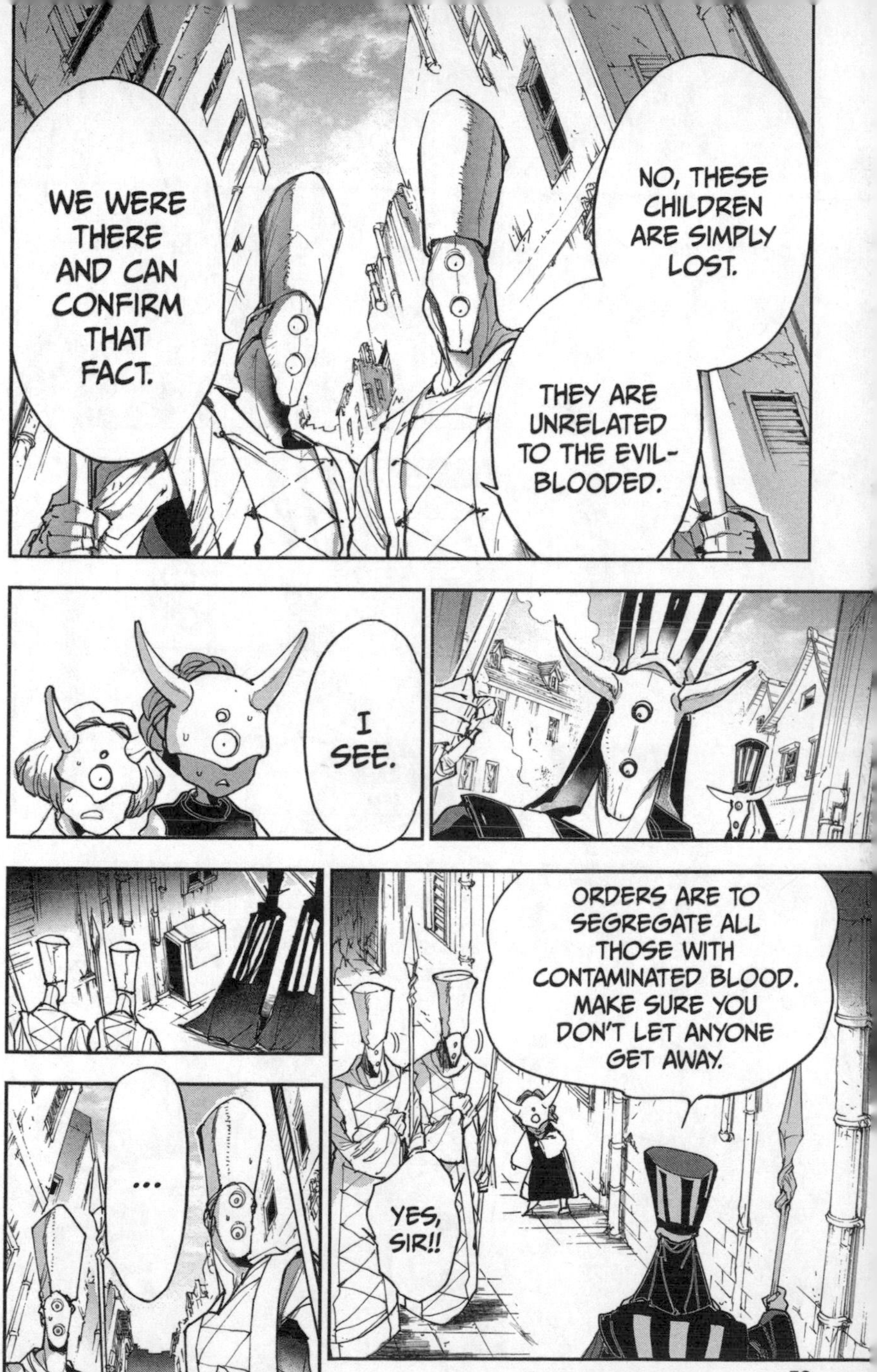
NO, THESE CHILDREN ARE SIMPLY LOST.
THEY ARE UNRELATED TO THE EVIL-BLOODED.
WE WERE THERE AND CAN CONFIRM THAT FACT.
I SEE.
ORDERS ARE TO SEGREGATE ALL THOSE WITH CONTAMINATED BLOOD. MAKE SURE YOU DON'T LET ANYONE GET AWAY.
YES, SIR!!
...

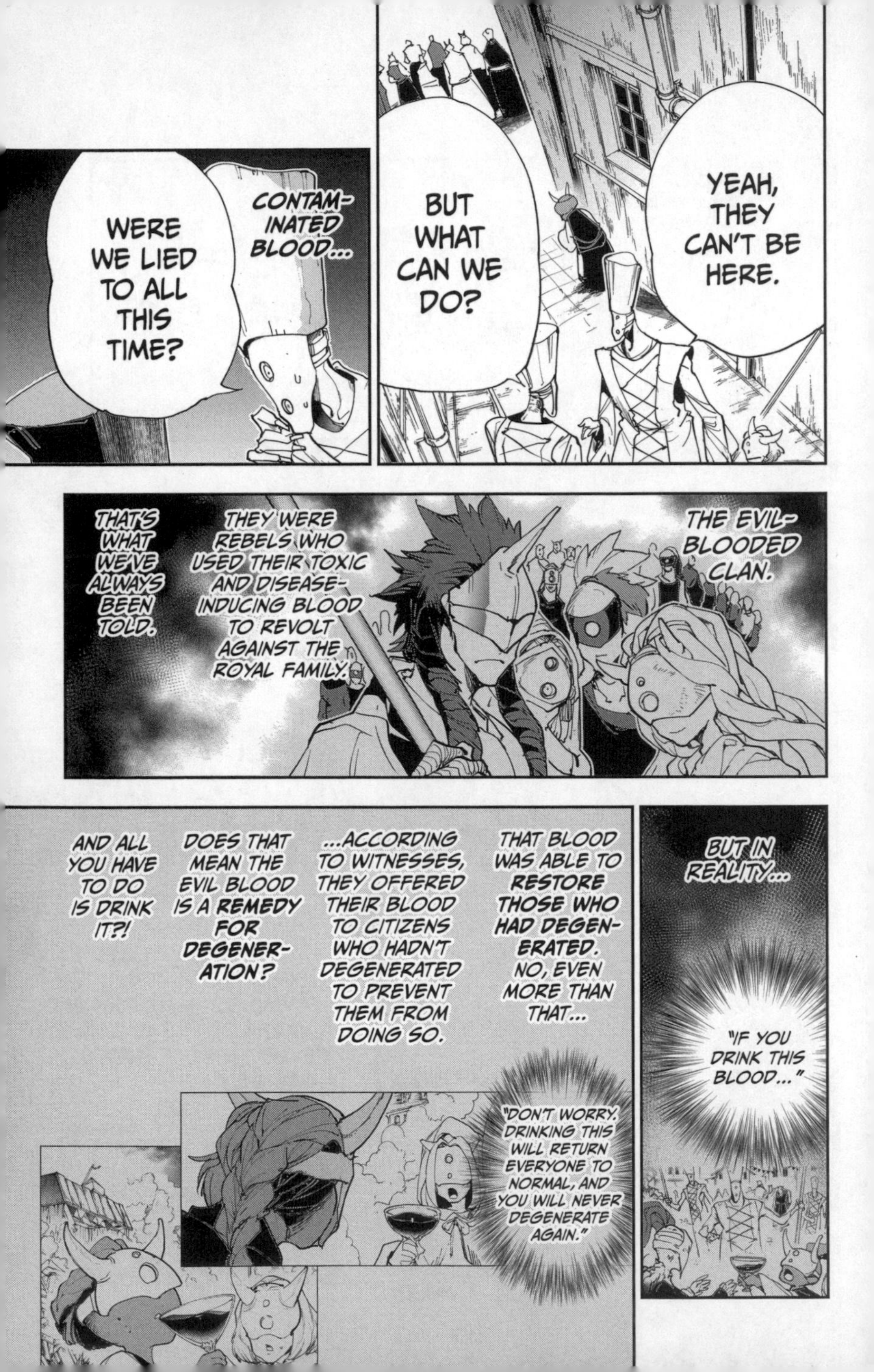
YEAH, THEY CAN'T BE HERE.
BUT WHAT CAN WE DO?
CONTAMINATED BLOOD...
WERE WE LIED TO ALL THIS TIME?
THE EVIL-BLOODED CLAN.
THEY WERE REBELS WHO USED THEIR TOXIC AND DISEASE-INDUCING BLOOD TO REVOLT AGAINST THE ROYAL FAMILY.
THAT'S WHAT WE'VE ALWAYS BEEN TOLD.
BUT IN REALITY...
"IF YOU DRINK THIS BLOOD..."
THAT BLOOD WAS ABLE TO **RESTORE THOSE WHO HAD DEGENERATED.** NO, EVEN MORE THAN THAT...
...ACCORDING TO WITNESSES, THEY OFFERED THEIR BLOOD TO CITIZENS WHO HADN'T DEGENERATED TO PREVENT THEM FROM DOING SO.
DOES THAT MEAN THE EVIL BLOOD IS A **REMEDY FOR DEGENERATION?**
AND ALL YOU HAVE TO DO IS DRINK IT?!
"DON'T WORRY. DRINKING THIS WILL RETURN EVERYONE TO NORMAL, AND YOU WILL NEVER DEGENERATE AGAIN."

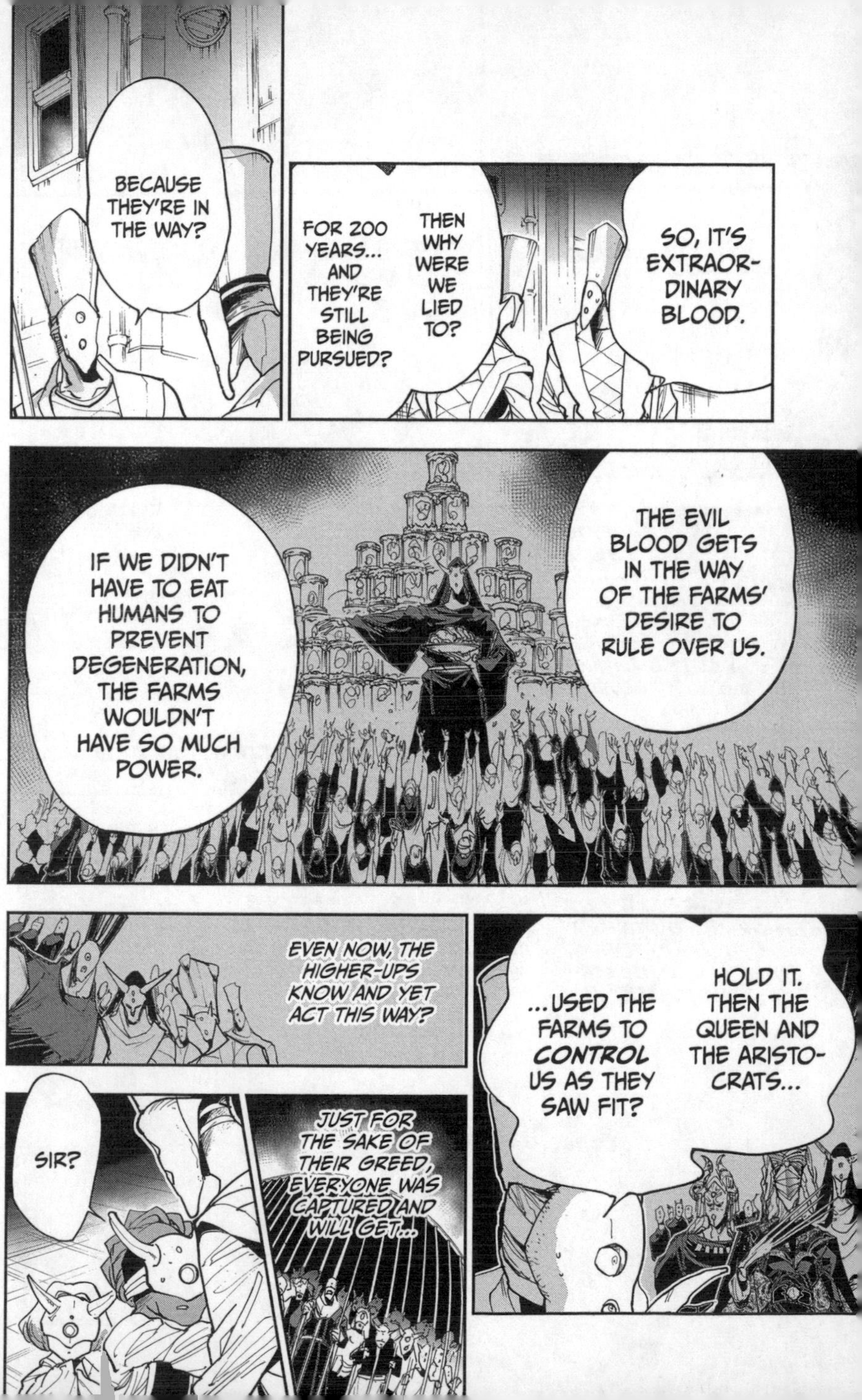
SO, IT'S EXTRAOR-DINARY BLOOD.
THEN WHY WERE WE LIED TO?
FOR 200 YEARS... AND THEY'RE STILL BEING PURSUED?
BECAUSE THEY'RE IN THE WAY?
THE EVIL BLOOD GETS IN THE WAY OF THE FARMS' DESIRE TO RULE OVER US.
IF WE DIDN'T HAVE TO EAT HUMANS TO PREVENT DEGENERATION, THE FARMS WOULDN'T HAVE SO MUCH POWER.
HOLD IT. THEN THE QUEEN AND THE ARISTO-CRATS...
...USED THE FARMS TO CONTROL US AS THEY SAW FIT?
EVEN NOW, THE HIGHER-UPS KNOW AND YET ACT THIS WAY?
JUST FOR THE SAKE OF THEIR GREED, EVERYONE WAS CAPTURED AND WILL GET...
SIR?

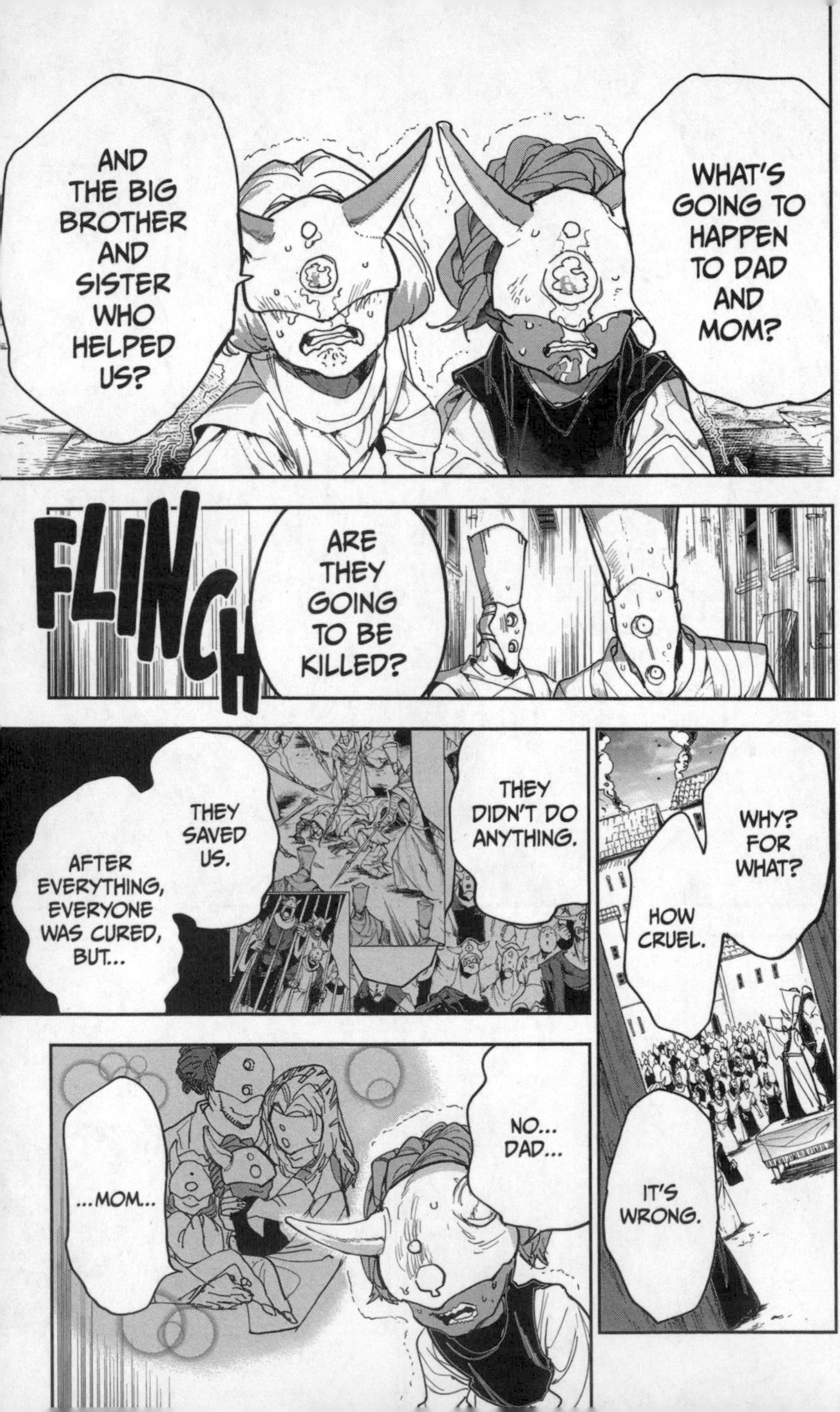
WHAT'S GOING TO HAPPEN TO DAD AND MOM?
AND THE BIG BROTHER AND SISTER WHO HELPED US?
ARE THEY GOING TO BE KILLED?
FLINCH
WHY? FOR WHAT?
HOW CRUEL.
IT'S WRONG.
THEY DIDN'T DO ANYTHING.
THEY SAVED US.
AFTER EVERYTHING, EVERYONE WAS CURED, BUT...
NO... DAD...
...MOM...

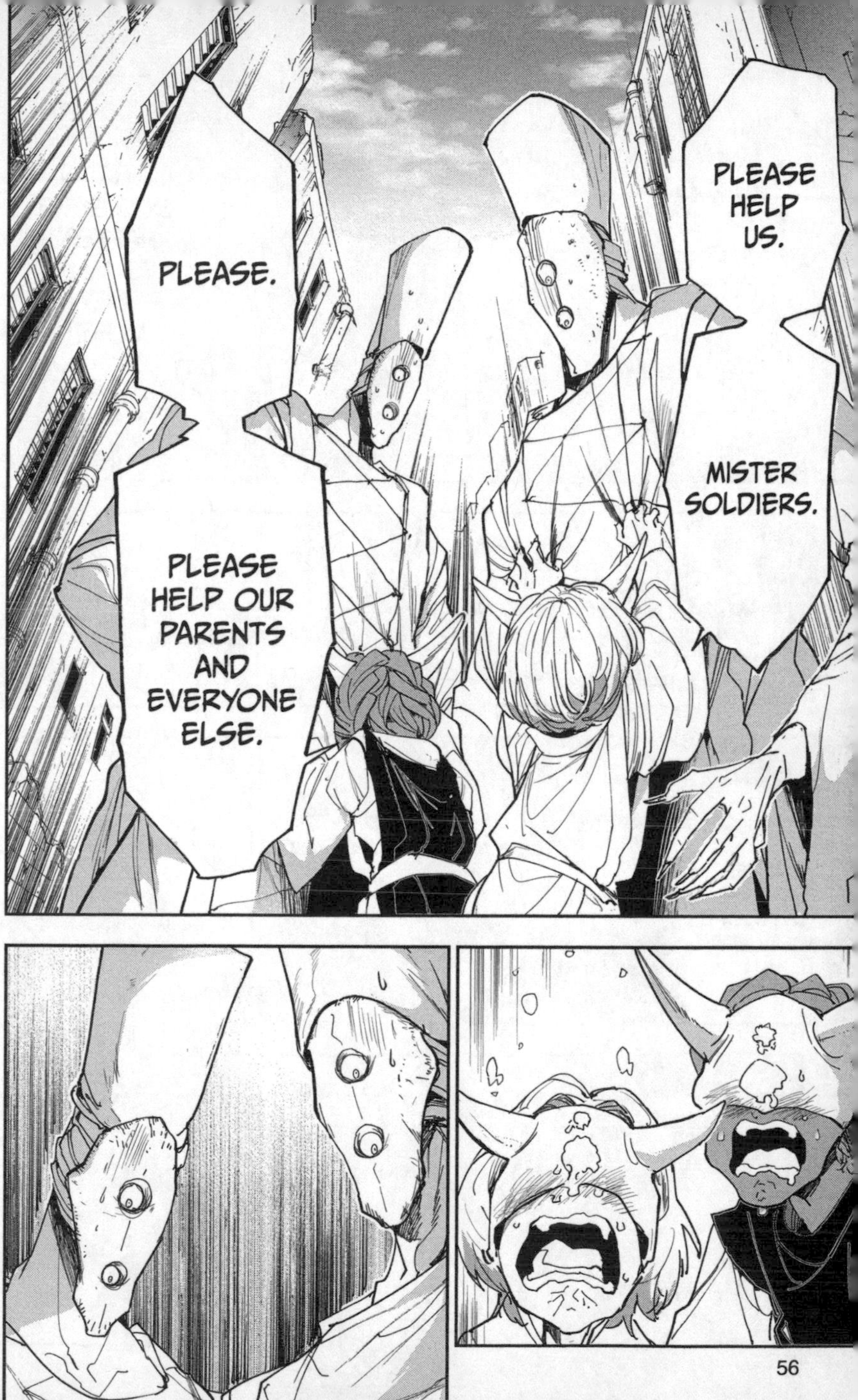
PLEASE HELP US.
MISTER SOLDIERS.
PLEASE.
PLEASE HELP OUR PARENTS AND EVERYONE ELSE.

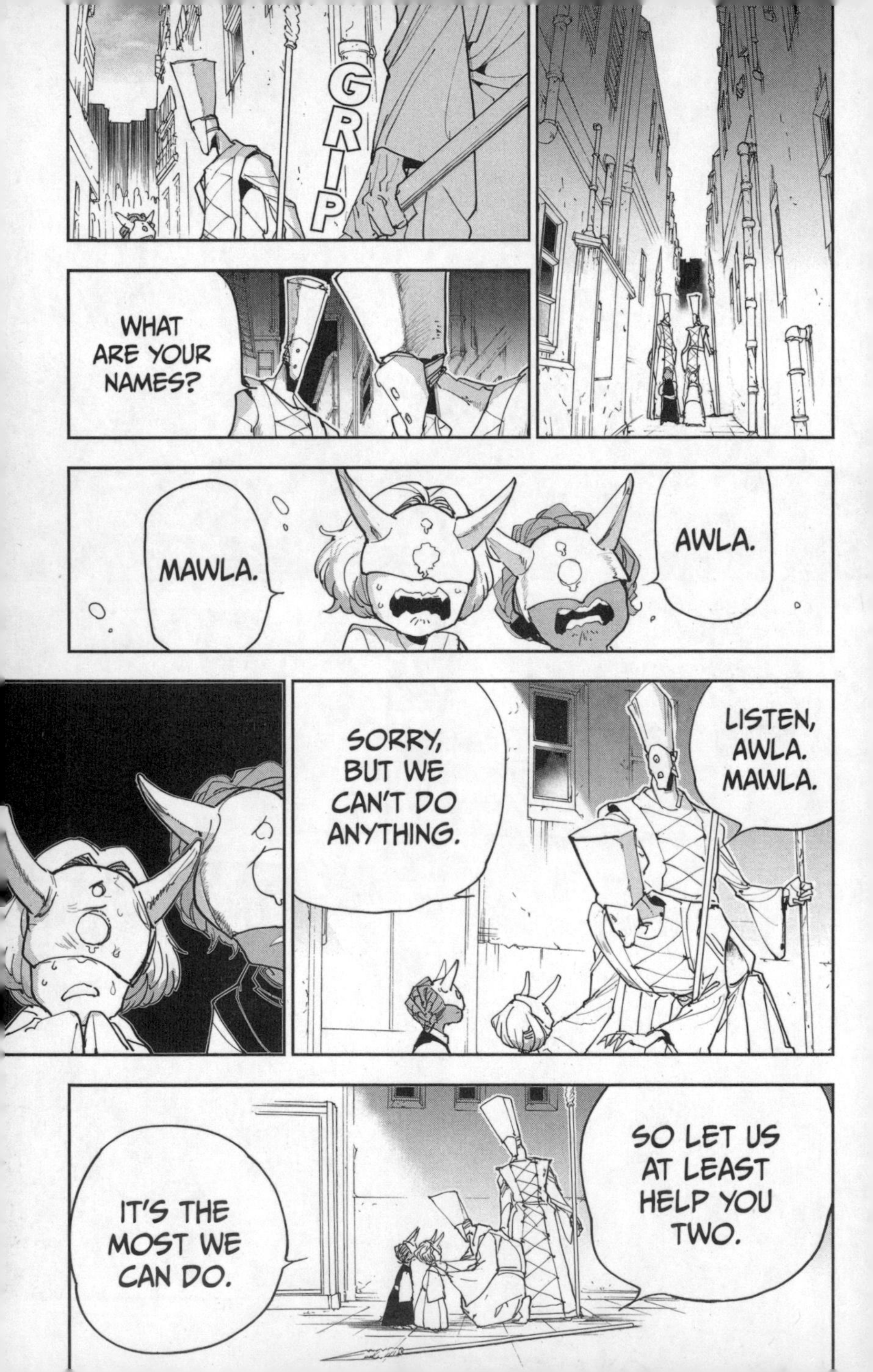
GRIP
WHAT ARE YOUR NAMES?
AWLA.
MAWLA.
LISTEN, AWLA. MAWLA.
SORRY, BUT WE CAN'T DO ANYTHING.
SO LET US AT LEAST HELP YOU TWO.
IT'S THE MOST WE CAN DO.

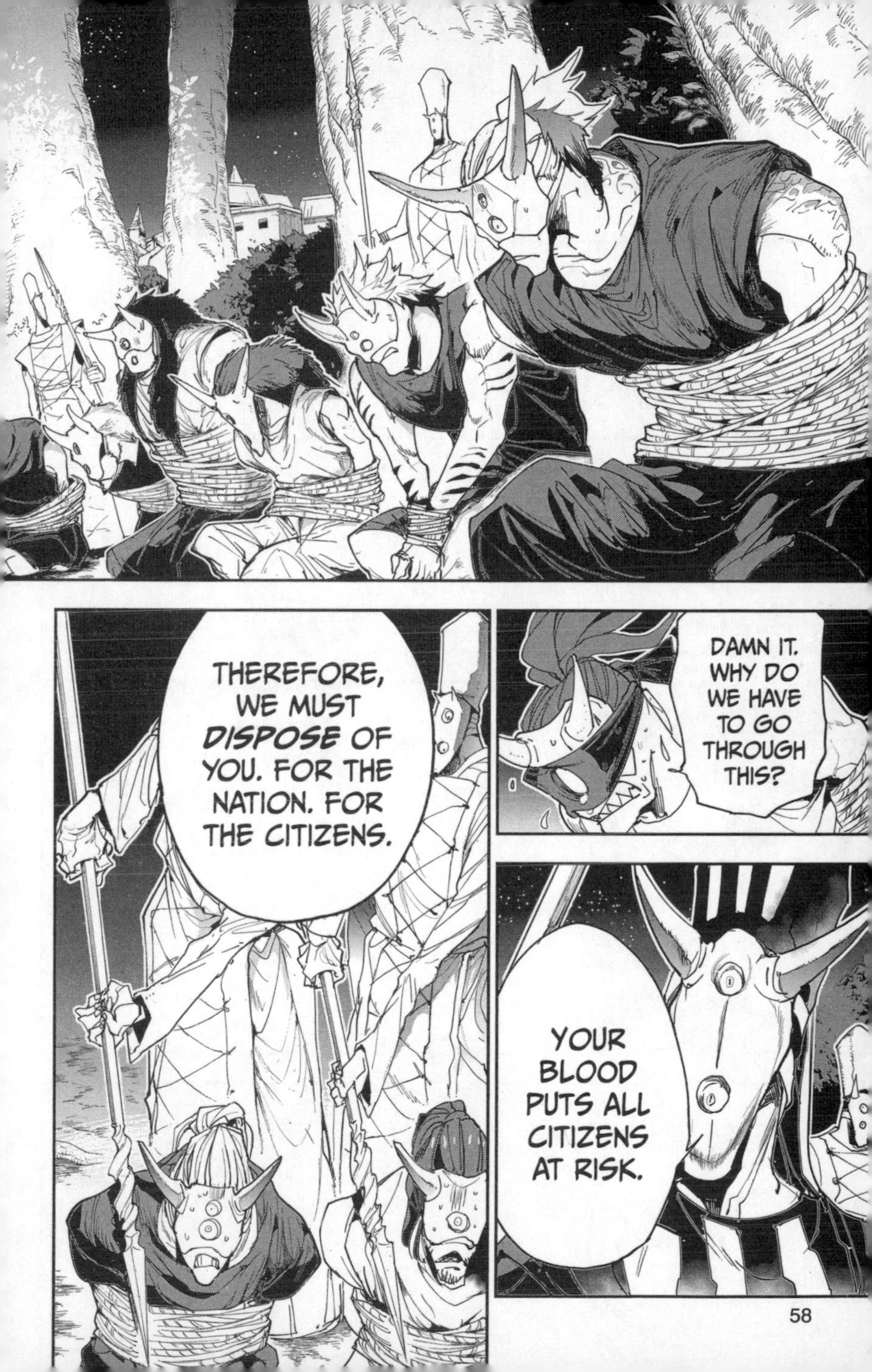
DAMN IT. WHY DO WE HAVE TO GO THROUGH THIS?
YOUR BLOOD PUTS ALL CITIZENS AT RISK.
THEREFORE, WE MUST *DISPOSE* OF YOU. FOR THE NATION. FOR THE CITIZENS.

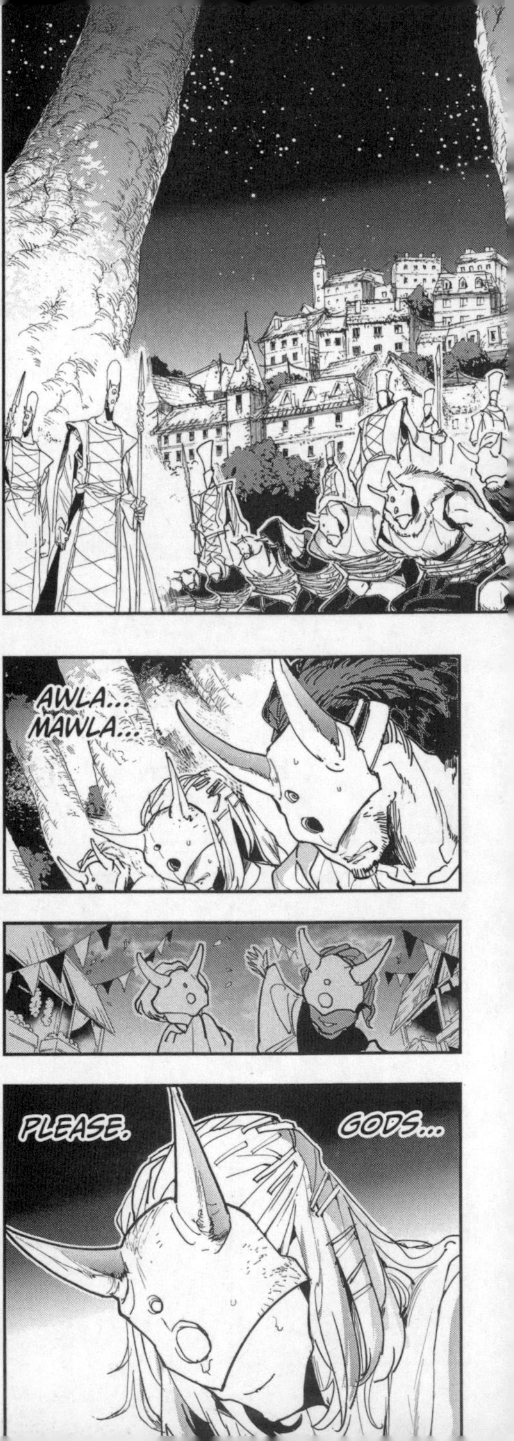
AWLA... MAWLA...
GODS...
PLEASE.
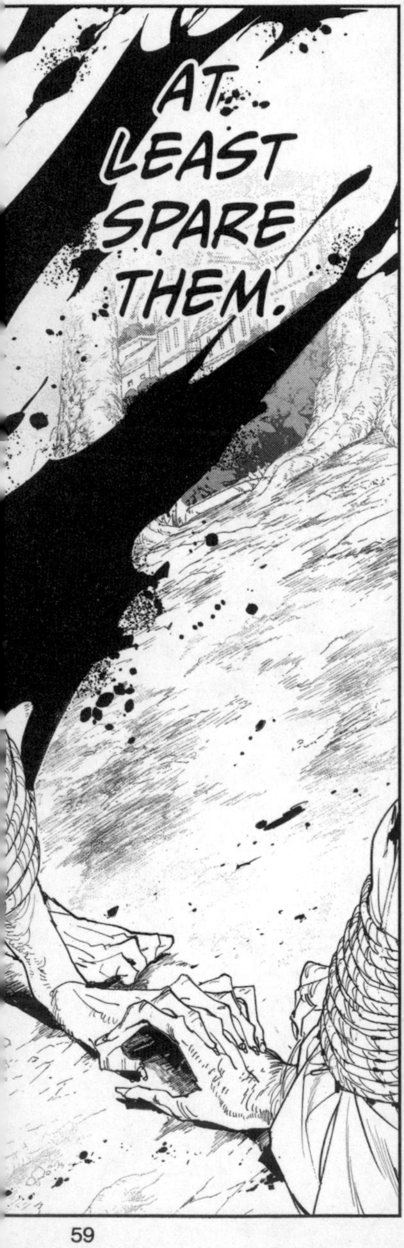
AT LEAST SPARE THEM.

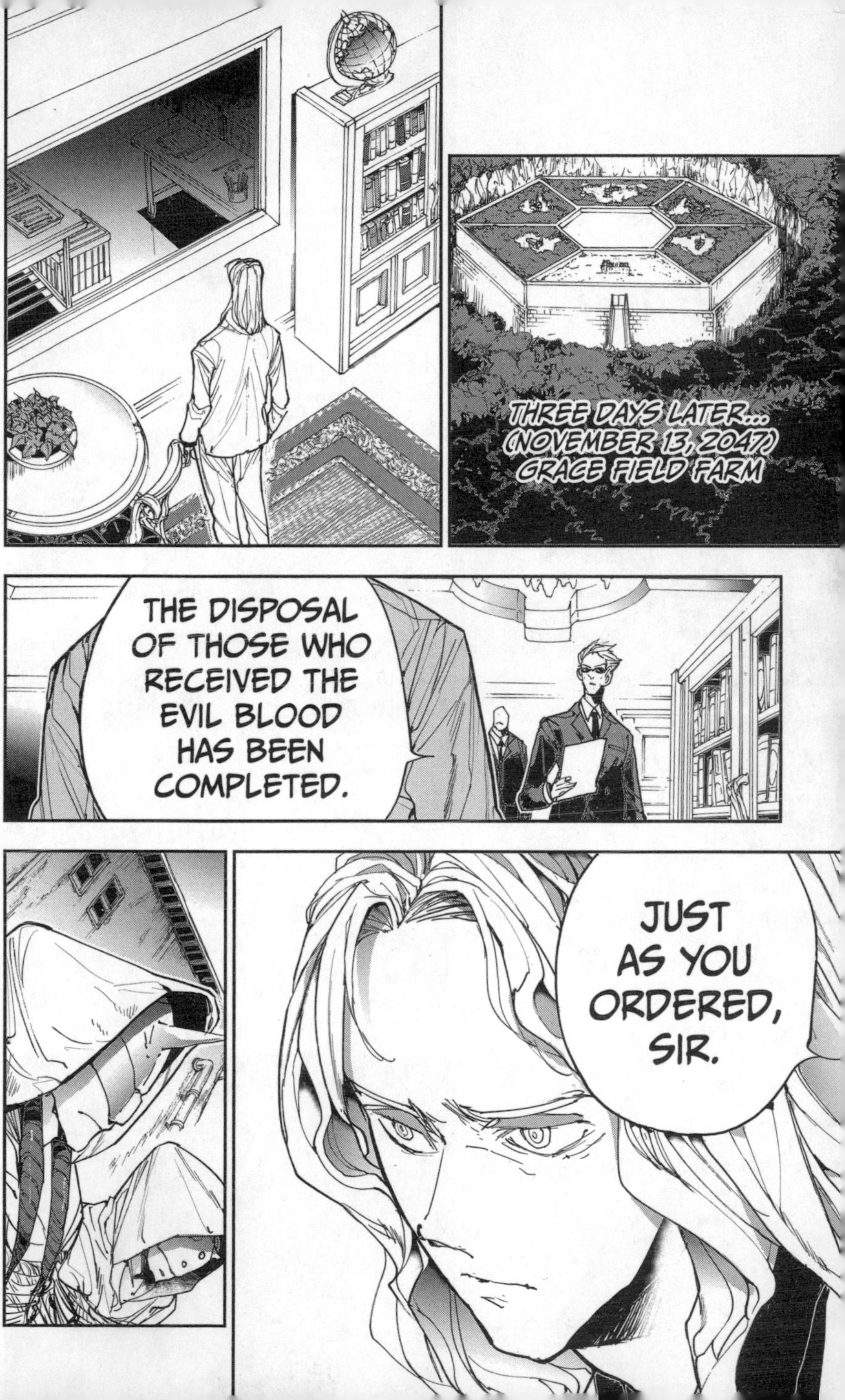
THREE DAYS LATER...
(NOVEMBER 13, 2047)
GRACE FIELD FARM
THE DISPOSAL OF THOSE WHO RECEIVED THE EVIL BLOOD HAS BEEN COMPLETED.
JUST AS YOU ORDERED, SIR.

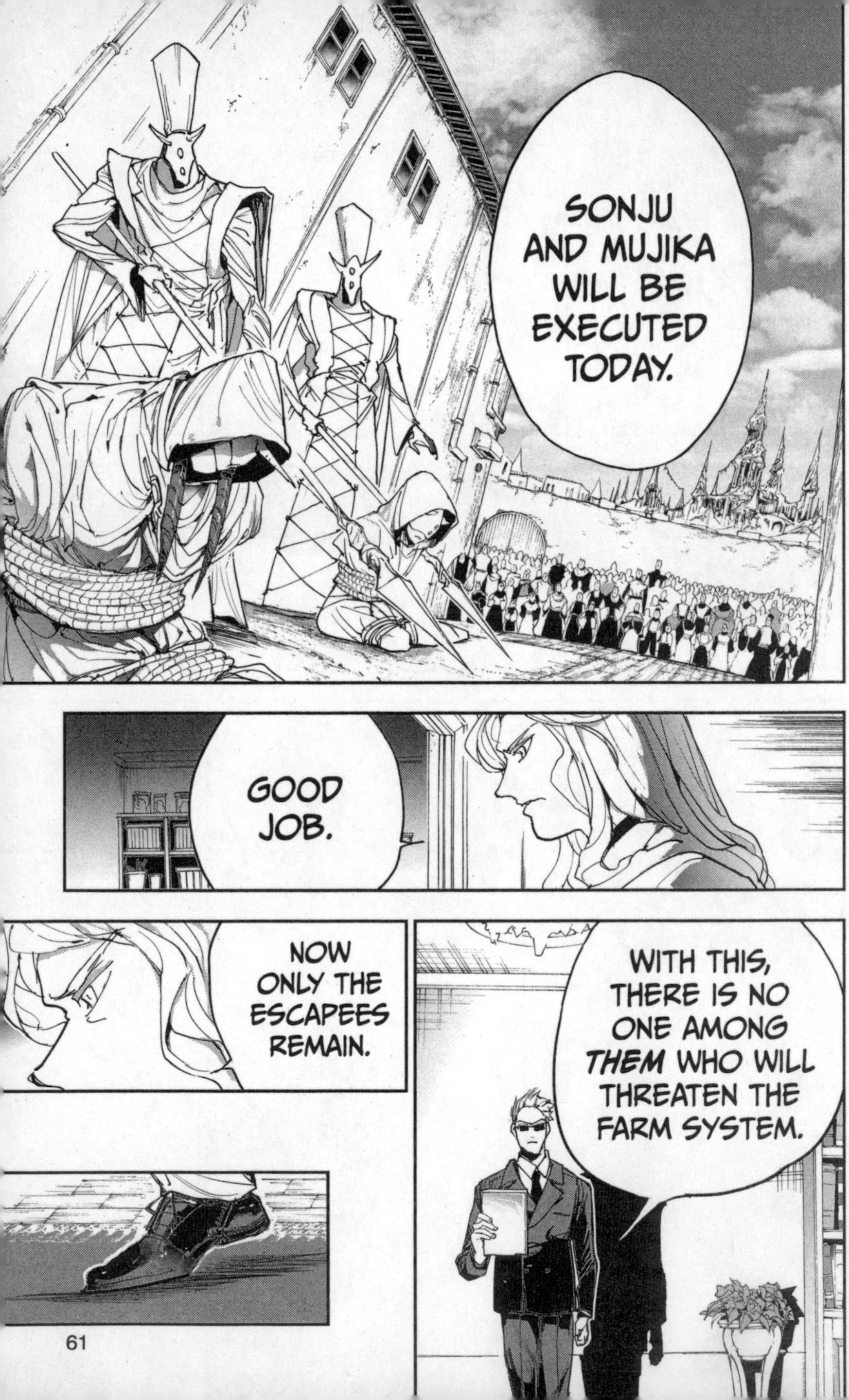
SONJU AND MUJIKA WILL BE EXECUTED TODAY.
GOOD JOB.
WITH THIS, THERE IS NO ONE AMONG *THEM* WHO WILL THREATEN THE FARM SYSTEM.
NOW ONLY THE ESCAPEES REMAIN.

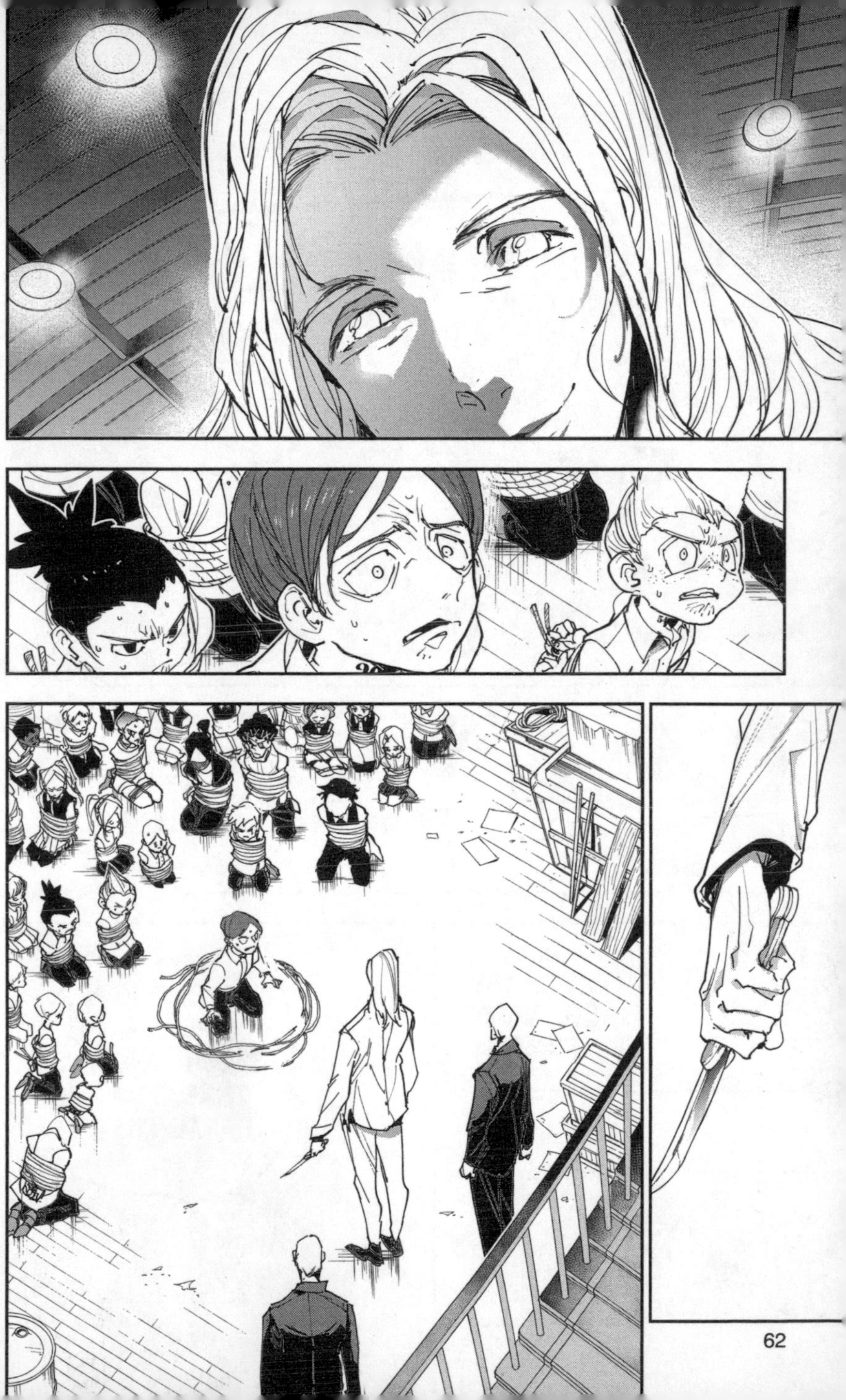

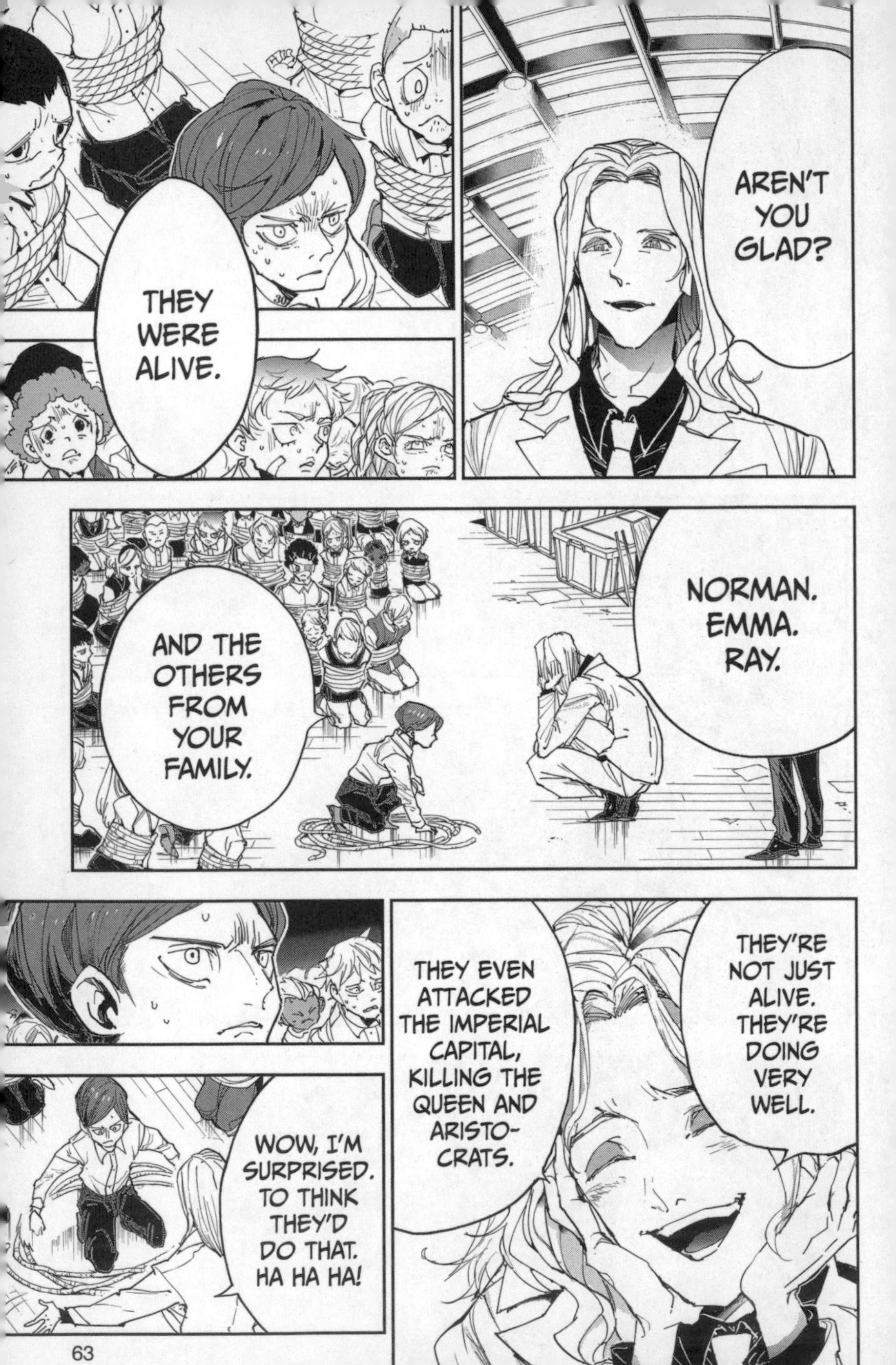
AREN'T YOU GLAD?
THEY WERE ALIVE.
NORMAN. EMMA. RAY.
AND THE OTHERS FROM YOUR FAMILY.
THEY'RE NOT JUST ALIVE. THEY'RE DOING VERY WELL.
THEY EVEN ATTACKED THE IMPERIAL CAPITAL, KILLING THE QUEEN AND ARISTO-CRATS.
WOW, I'M SURPRISED. TO THINK THEY'D DO THAT. HA HA HA!

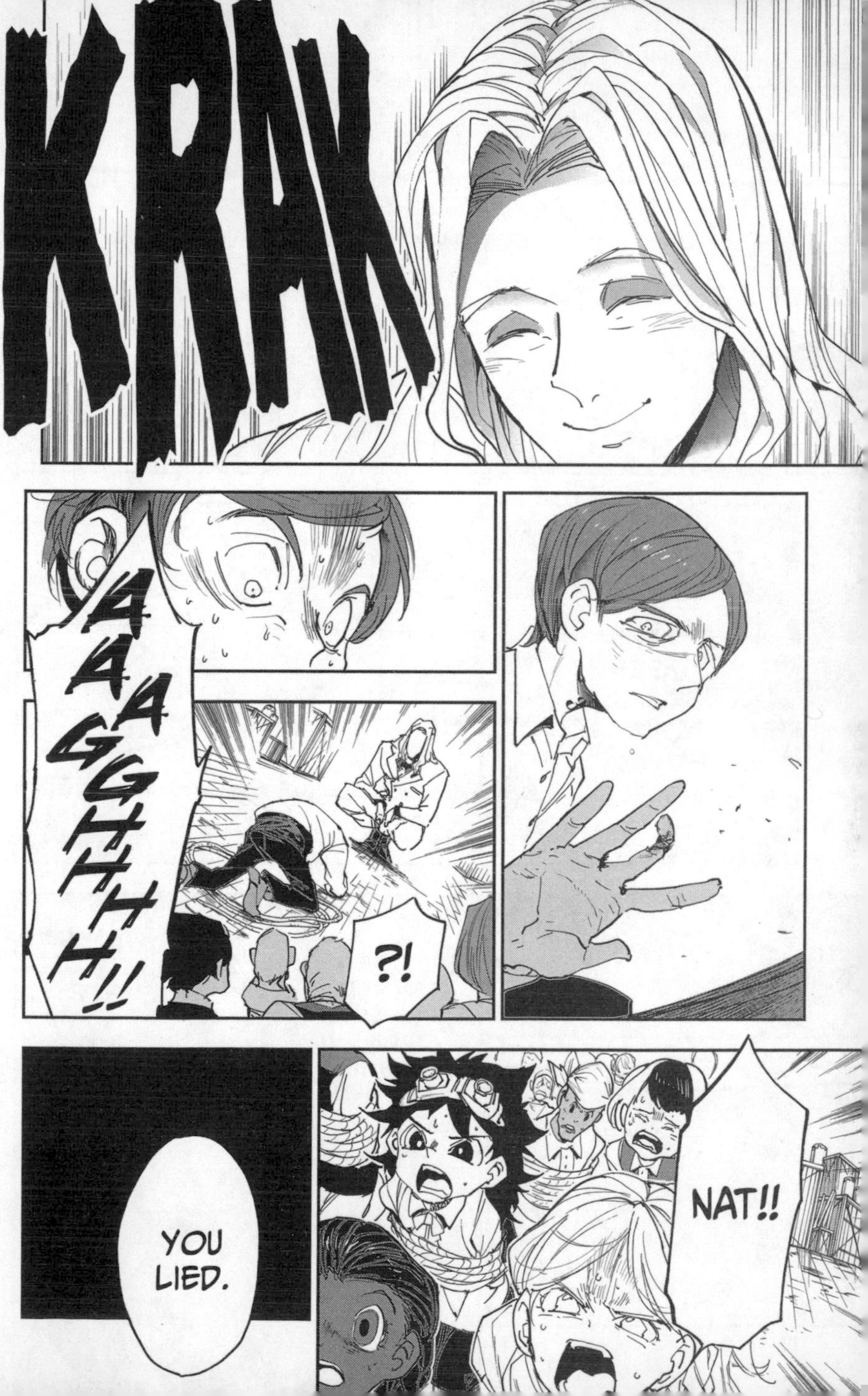
KRAK
YAAAGGHHHHH!!
?!
NAT!!
YOU LIED.

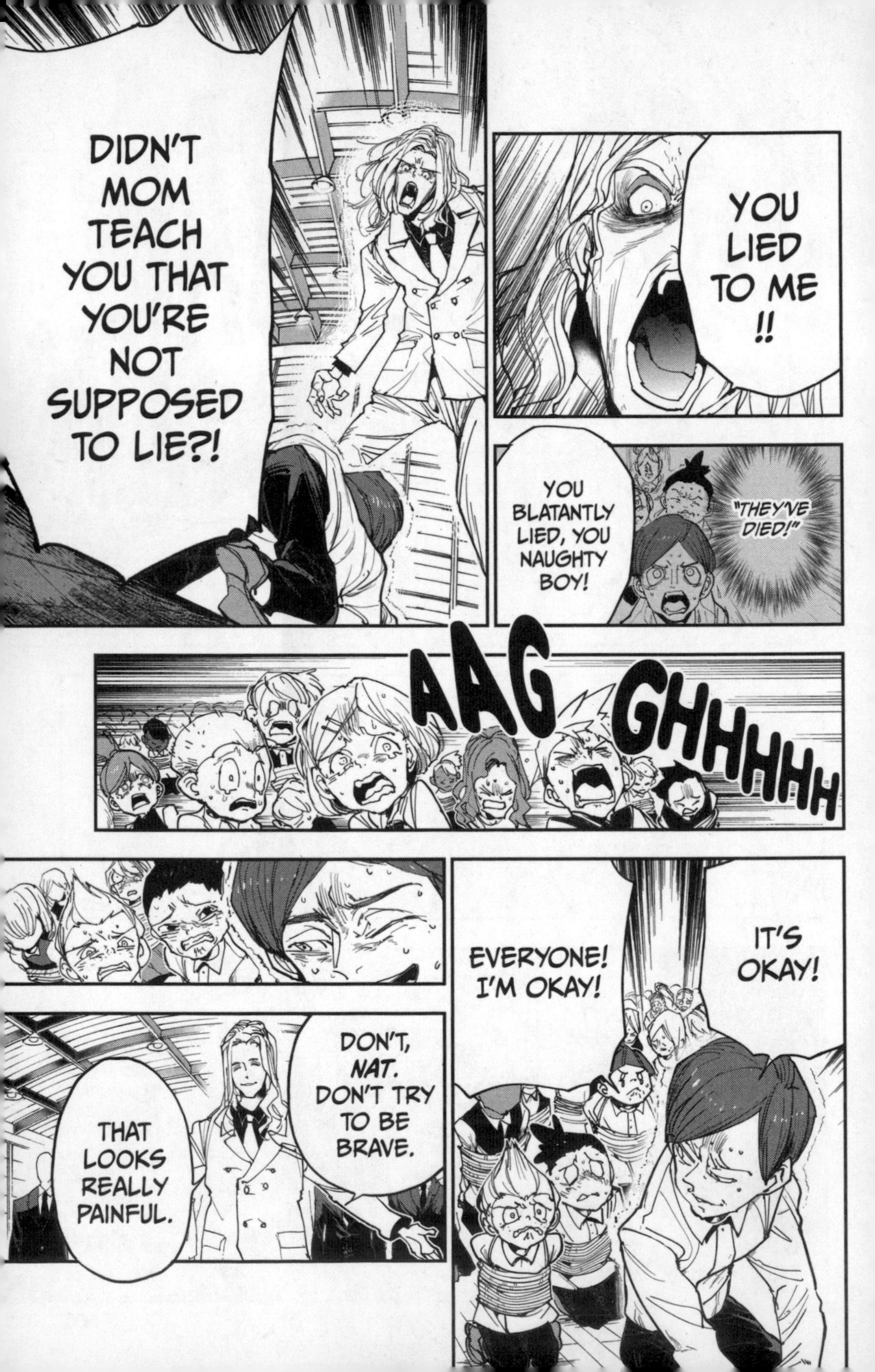
YOU LIED TO ME !!
YOU BLATANTLY LIED, YOU NAUGHTY BOY!
"THEY'VE DIED!"
DIDN'T MOM TEACH YOU THAT YOU'RE NOT SUPPOSED TO LIE?!
AAGGHHHHHH
IT'S OKAY!
EVERYONE! I'M OKAY!
DON'T, *NAT*. DON'T TRY TO BE BRAVE.
THAT LOOKS REALLY PAINFUL.

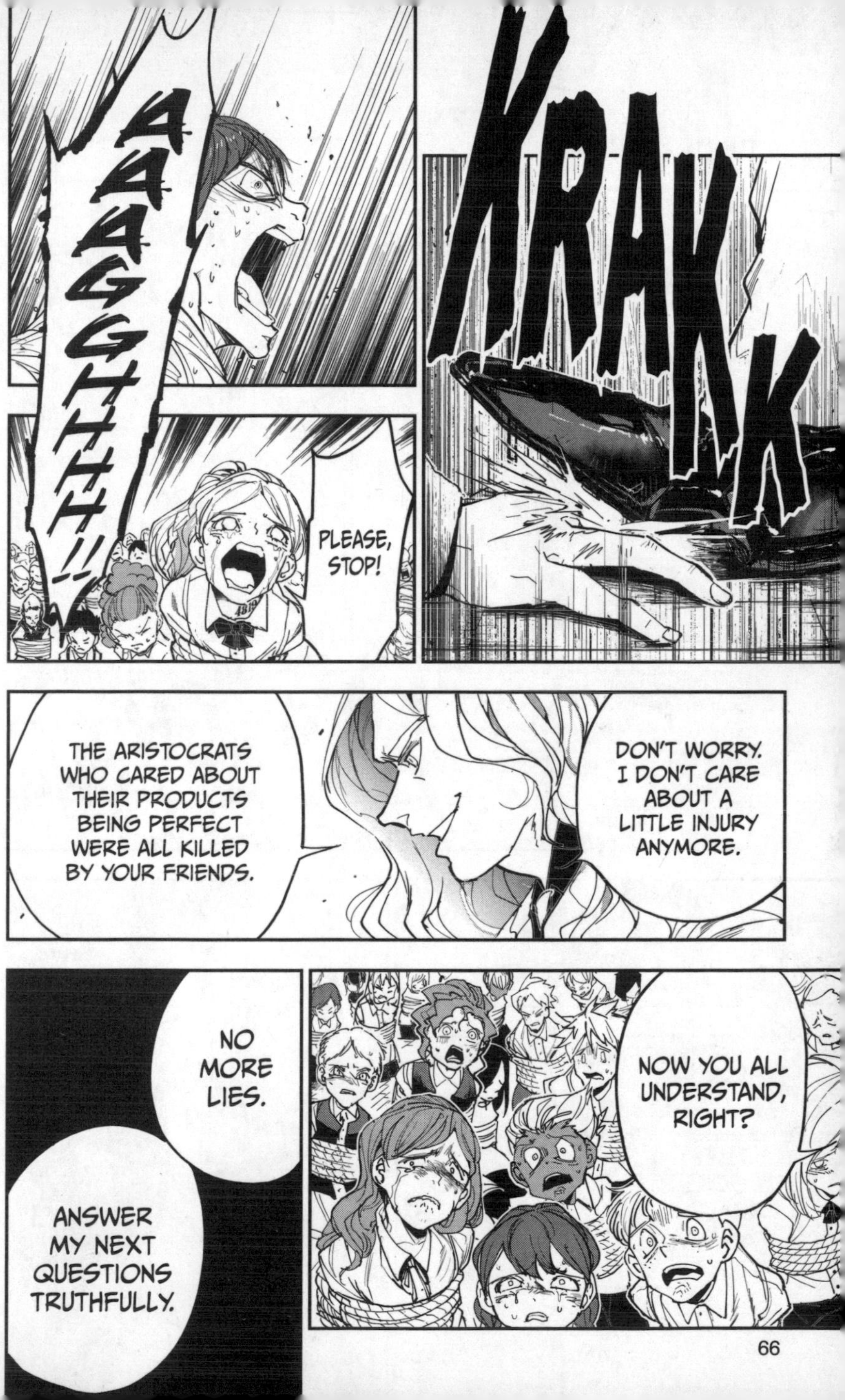
KRAKK
AAAGGHHHHH!!
PLEASE, STOP!
DON'T WORRY. I DON'T CARE ABOUT A LITTLE INJURY ANYMORE.
THE ARISTOCRATS WHO CARED ABOUT THEIR PRODUCTS BEING PERFECT WERE ALL KILLED BY YOUR FRIENDS.
NOW YOU ALL UNDERSTAND, RIGHT?
NO MORE LIES.
ANSWER MY NEXT QUESTIONS TRUTHFULLY.

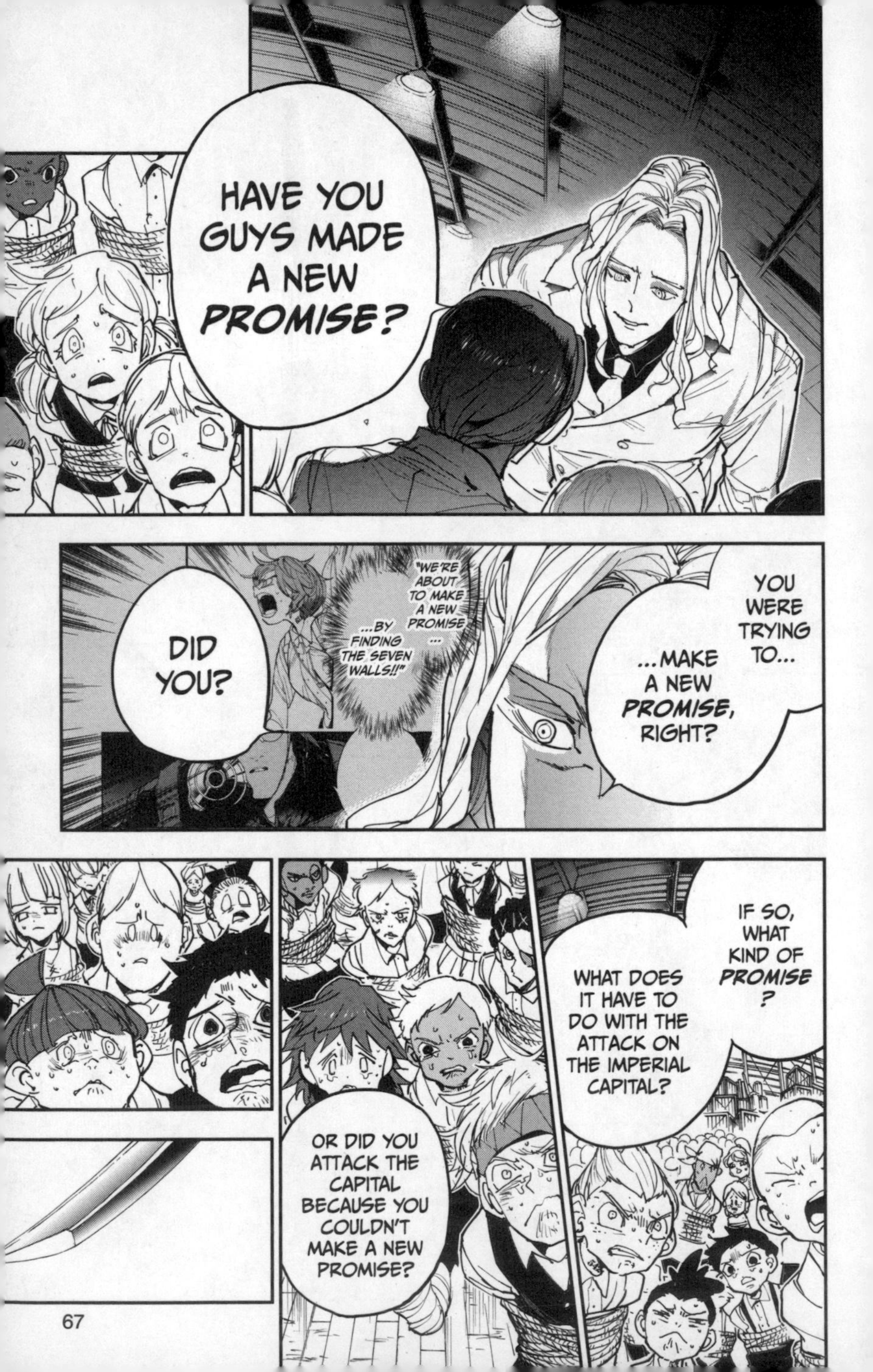
HAVE YOU GUYS MADE A NEW PROMISE?
YOU WERE TRYING TO...
...MAKE A NEW PROMISE, RIGHT?
"WE'RE ABOUT TO MAKE A NEW PROMISE...
...BY FINDING THE SEVEN WALLS!!"
DID YOU?
IF SO, WHAT KIND OF PROMISE?
WHAT DOES IT HAVE TO DO WITH THE ATTACK ON THE IMPERIAL CAPITAL?
OR DID YOU ATTACK THE CAPITAL BECAUSE YOU COULDN'T MAKE A NEW PROMISE?

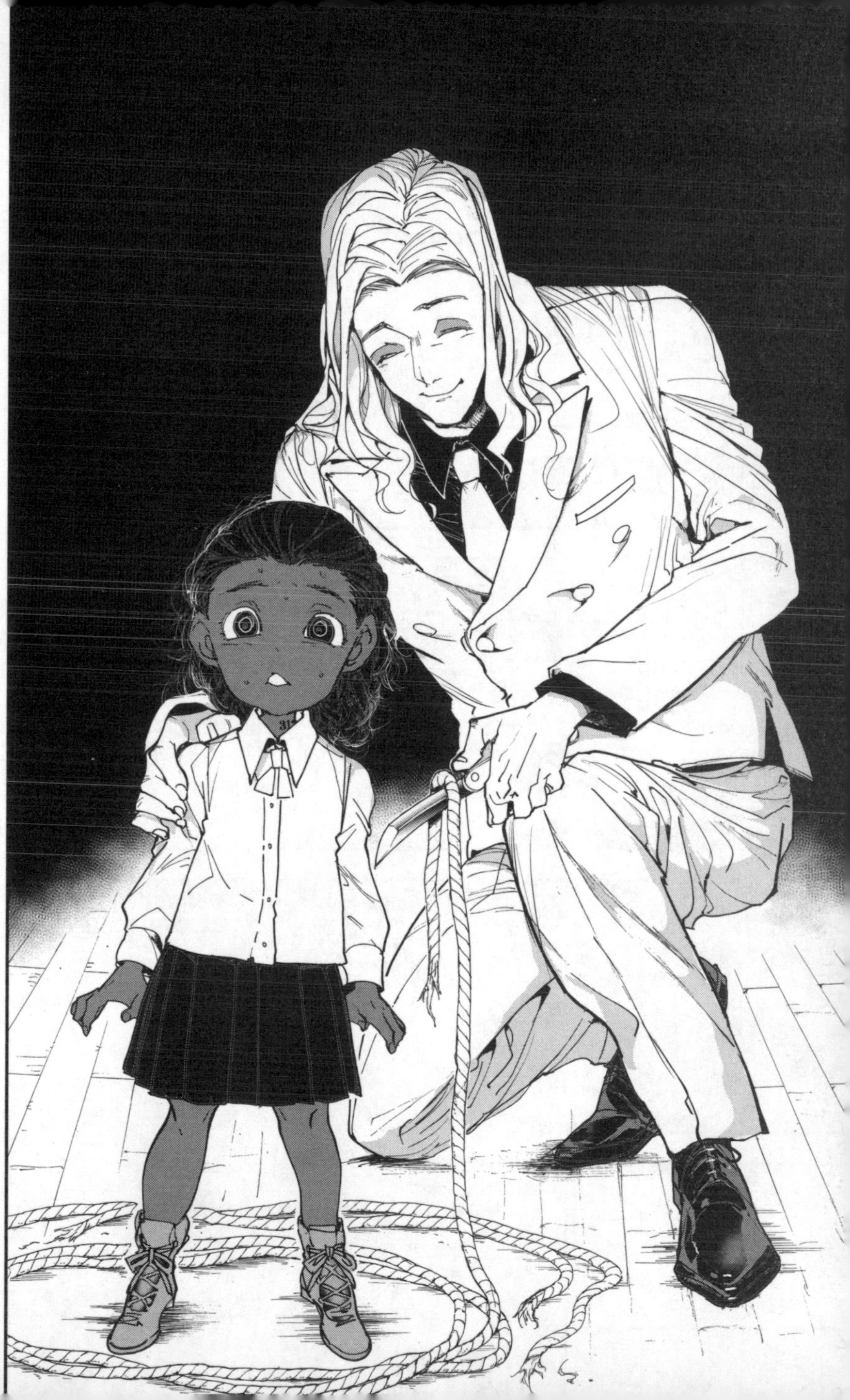

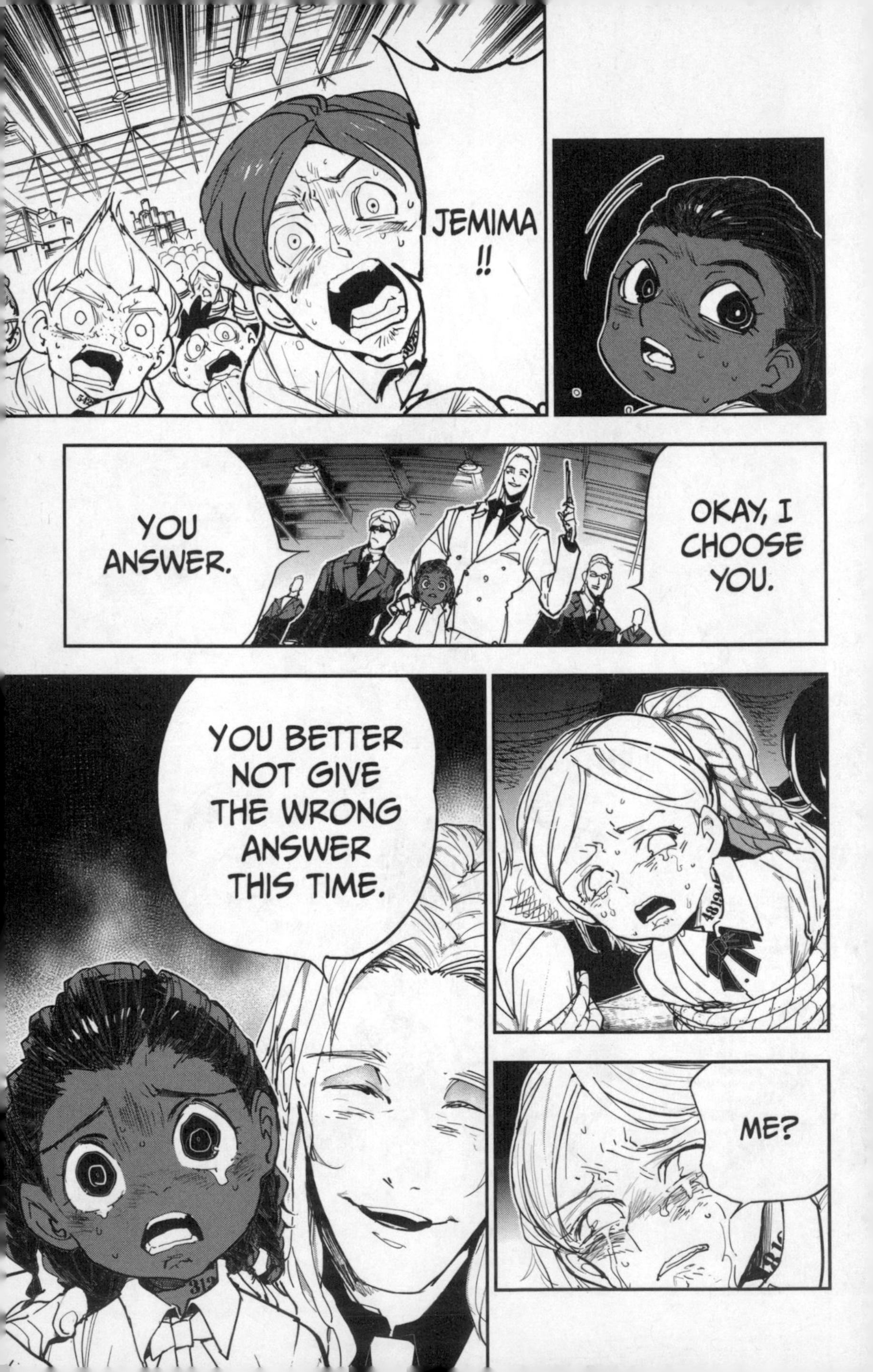
JEMIMA!!
OKAY, I CHOOSE YOU.
YOU ANSWER.
ME?
YOU BETTER NOT GIVE THE WRONG ANSWER THIS TIME.

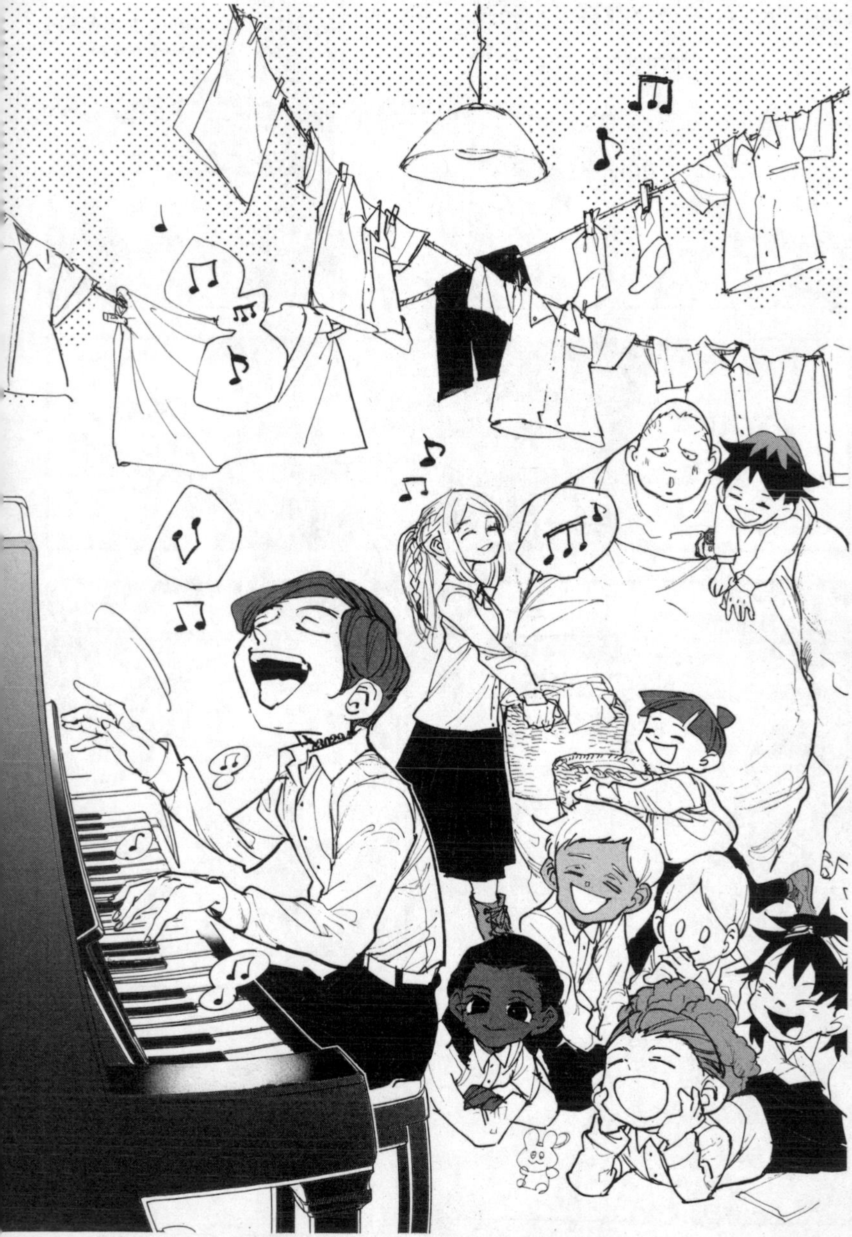

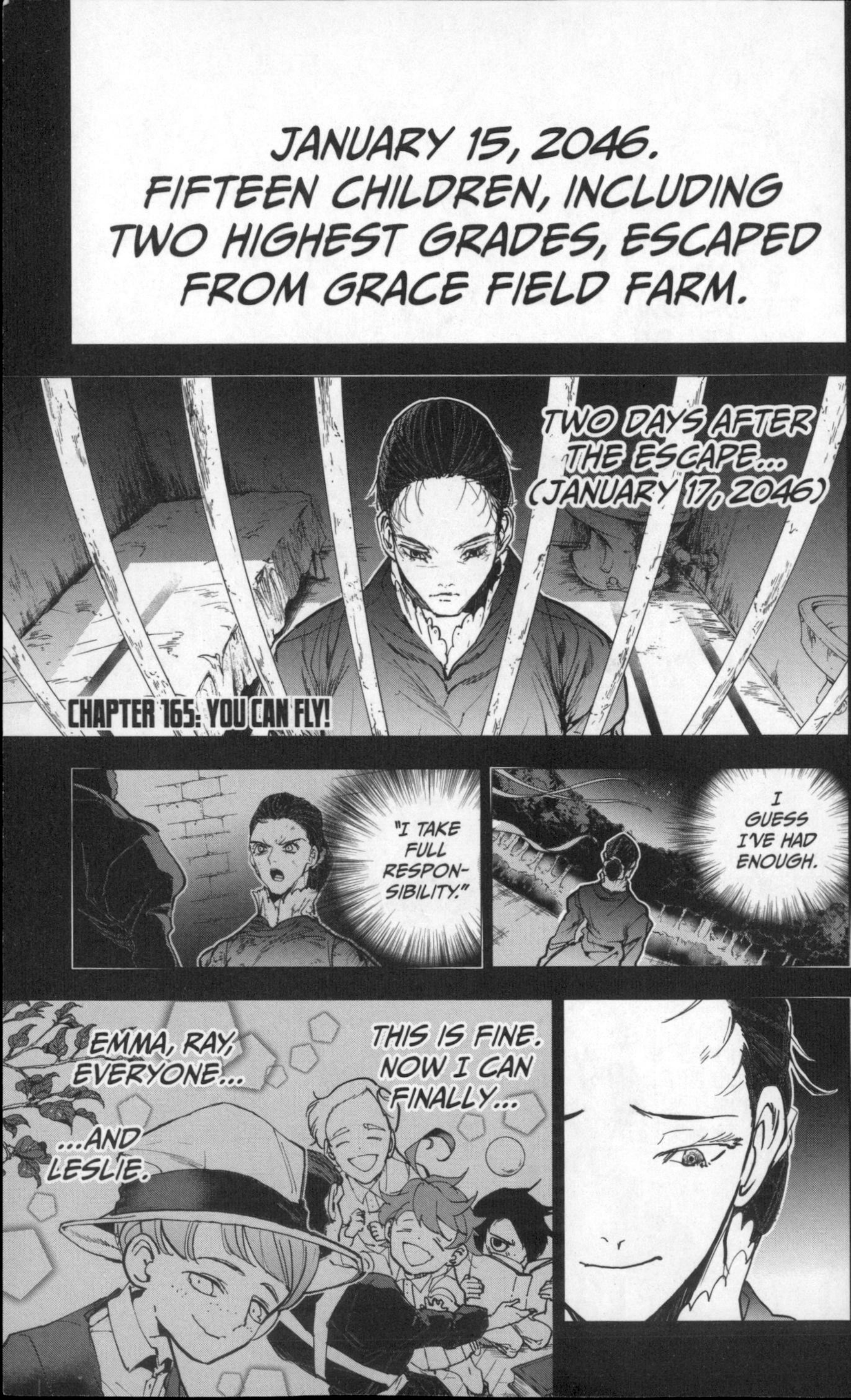
JANUARY 15, 2046. FIFTEEN CHILDREN, INCLUDING TWO HIGHEST GRADES, ESCAPED FROM GRACE FIELD FARM.
TWO DAYS AFTER THE ESCAPE... (JANUARY 17, 2046)
CHAPTER 165: YOU CAN FLY!
I GUESS I'VE HAD ENOUGH.
"I TAKE FULL RESPON-SIBILITY."
THIS IS FINE. NOW I CAN FINALLY...
EMMA, RAY, EVERYONE...
...AND LESLIE.

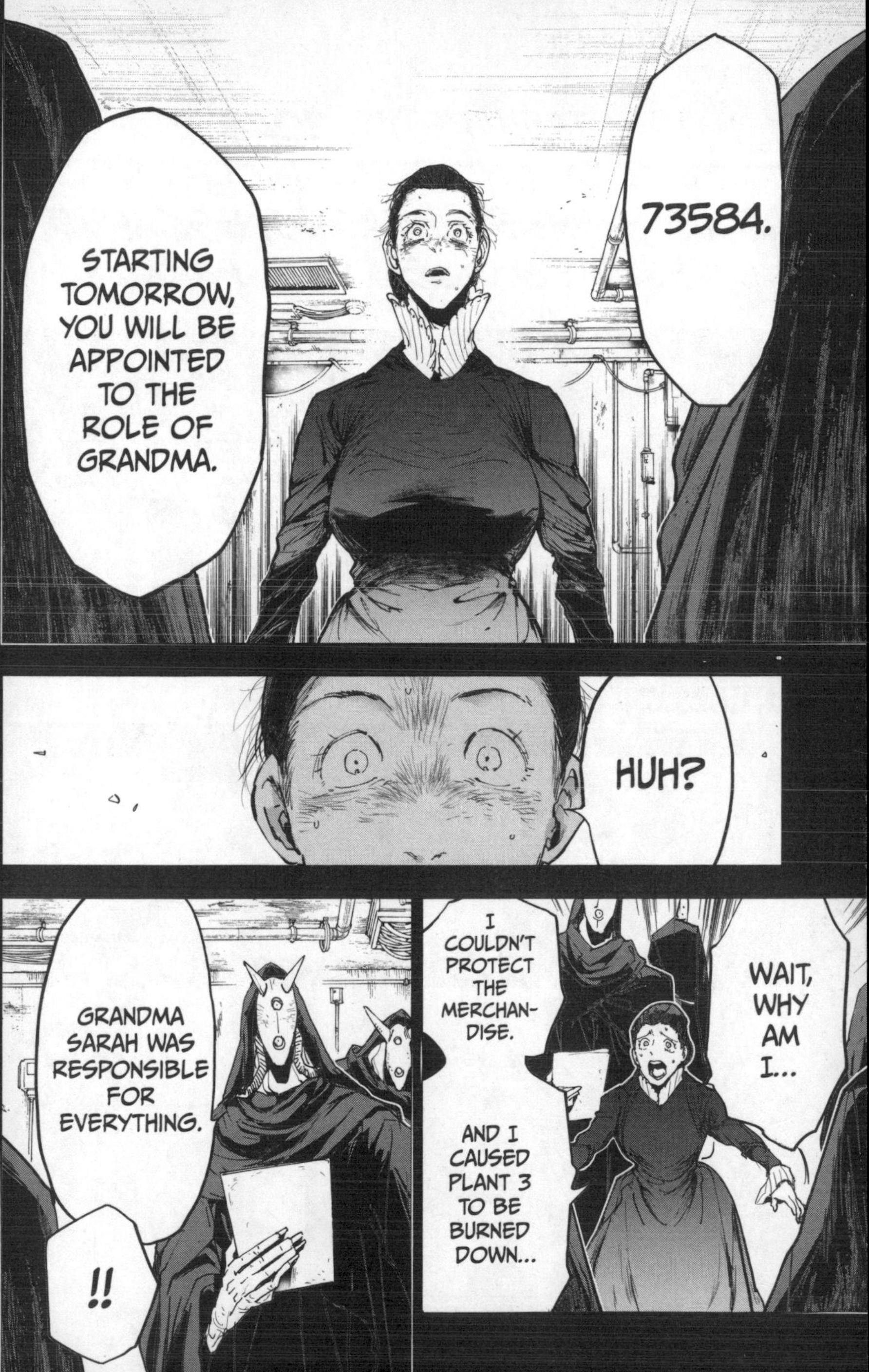
73584.
STARTING TOMORROW, YOU WILL BE APPOINTED TO THE ROLE OF GRANDMA.
HUH?
WAIT, WHY AM I...
I COULDN'T PROTECT THE MERCHAN-DISE.
AND I CAUSED PLANT 3 TO BE BURNED DOWN...
GRANDMA SARAH WAS RESPONSIBLE FOR EVERYTHING.
!!

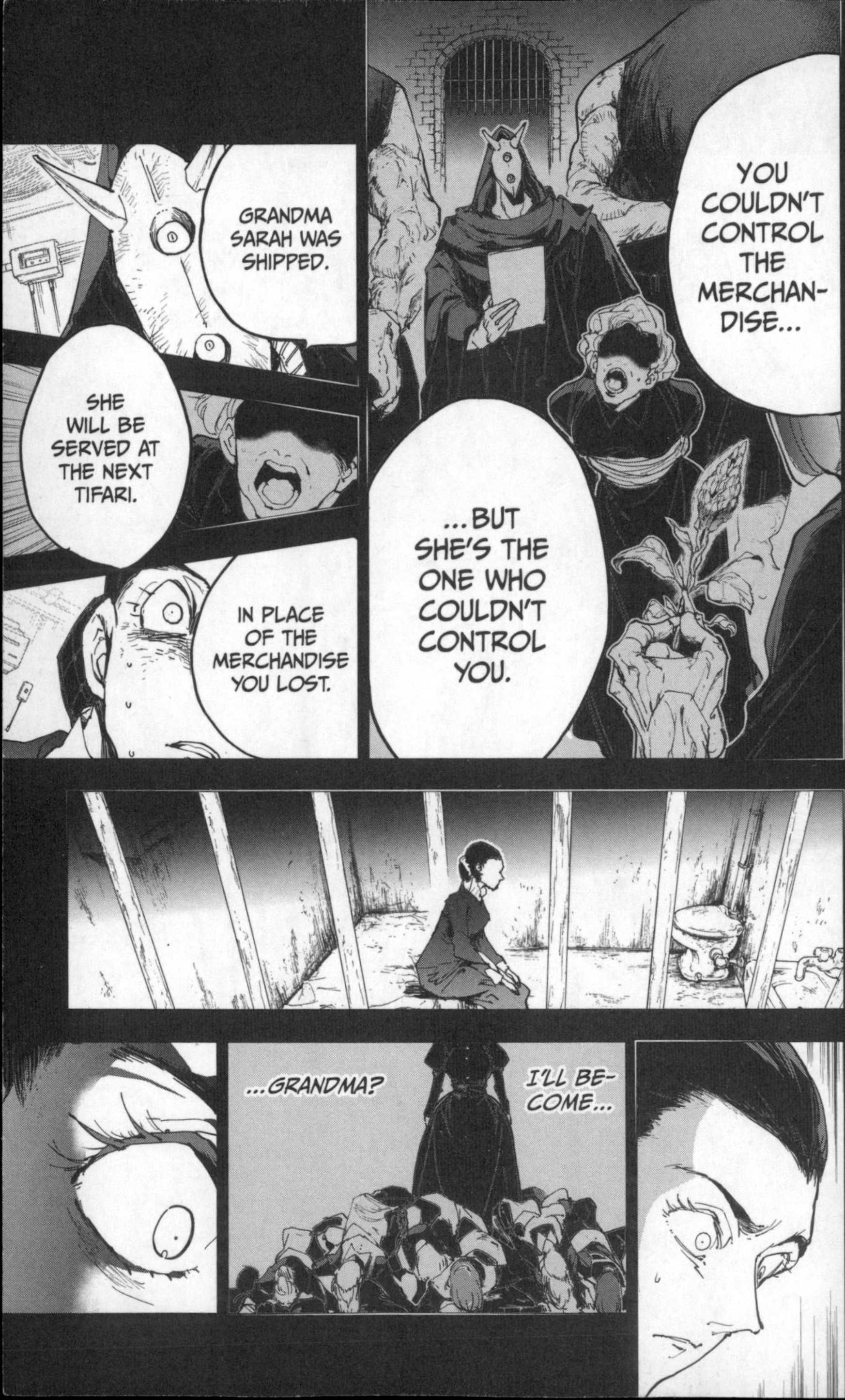
YOU COULDN'T CONTROL THE MERCHAN-DISE...
...BUT SHE'S THE ONE WHO COULDN'T CONTROL YOU.
GRANDMA SARAH WAS SHIPPED.
SHE WILL BE SERVED AT THE NEXT TIFARI.
IN PLACE OF THE MERCHANDISE YOU LOST.
I'LL BE-COME...
...GRANDMA?

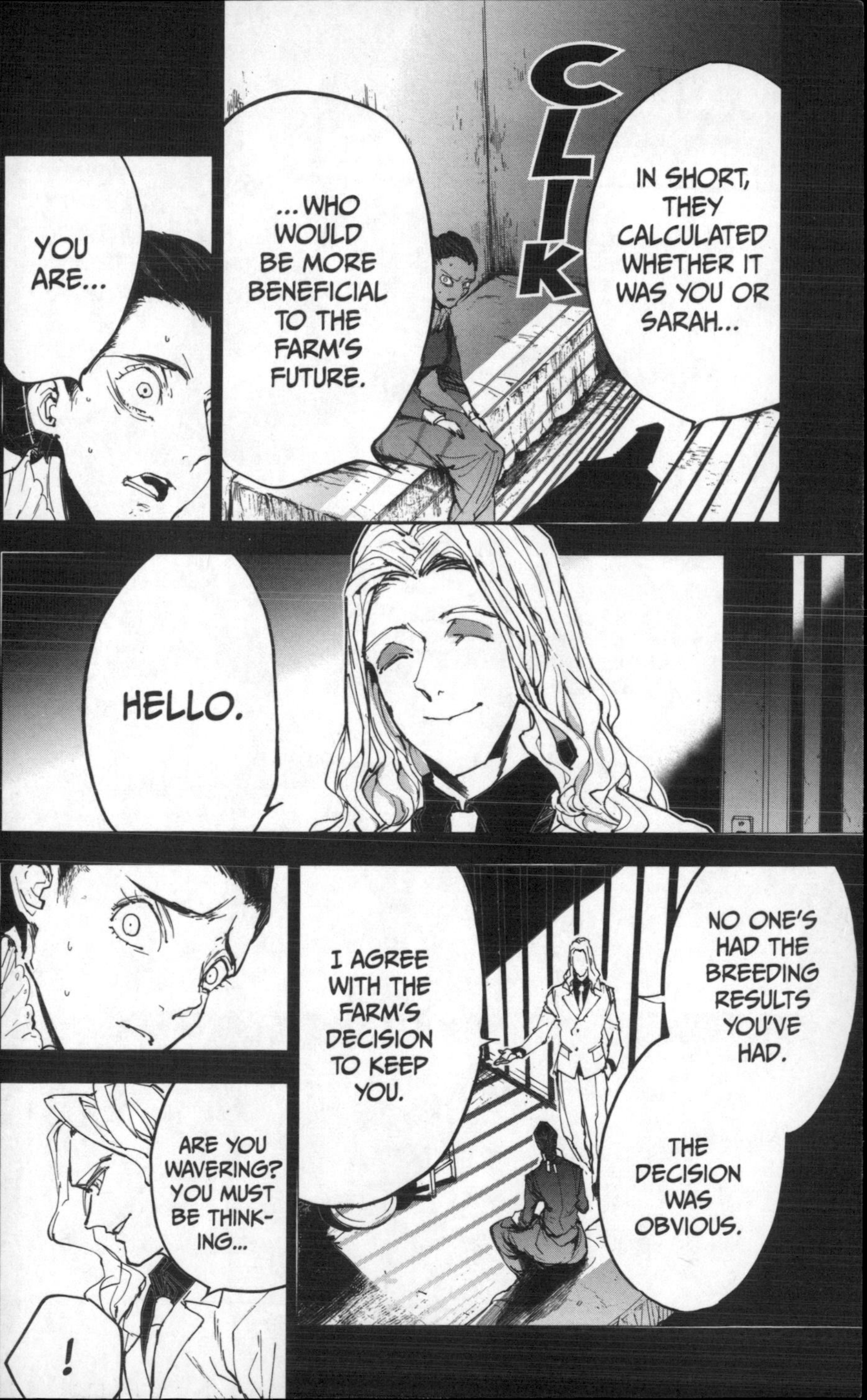

CLIK
IN SHORT, THEY CALCULATED WHETHER IT WAS YOU OR SARAH...
...WHO WOULD BE MORE BENEFICIAL TO THE FARM'S FUTURE.
YOU ARE...
HELLO.
NO ONE'S HAD THE BREEDING RESULTS YOU'VE HAD.
I AGREE WITH THE FARM'S DECISION TO KEEP YOU.
THE DECISION WAS OBVIOUS.
ARE YOU WAVERING? YOU MUST BE THINK-ING...
!

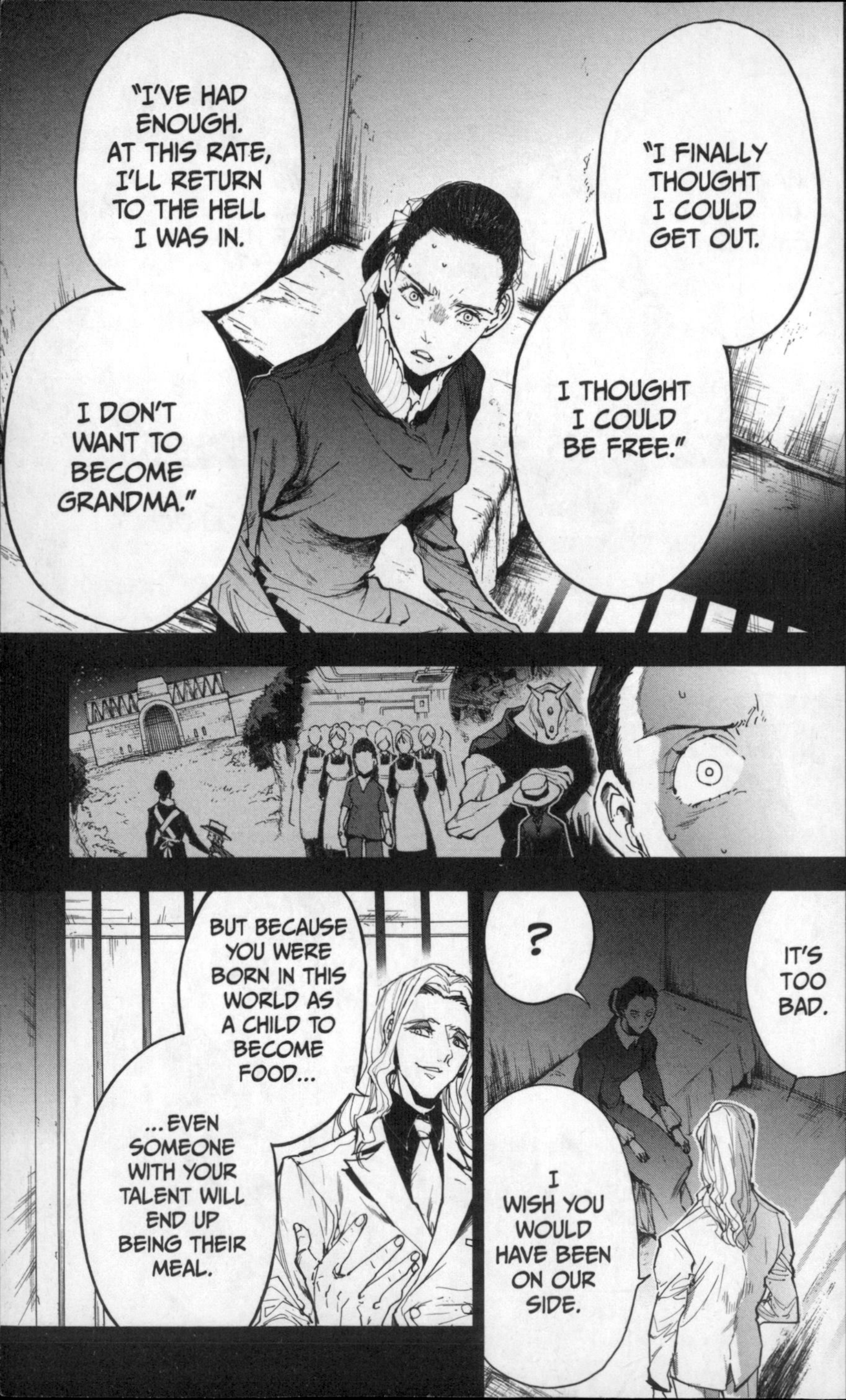
"I FINALLY THOUGHT I COULD GET OUT.
I THOUGHT I COULD BE FREE."
"I'VE HAD ENOUGH. AT THIS RATE, I'LL RETURN TO THE HELL I WAS IN.
I DON'T WANT TO BECOME GRANDMA."
IT'S TOO BAD.
?
I WISH YOU WOULD HAVE BEEN ON OUR SIDE.
BUT BECAUSE YOU WERE BORN IN THIS WORLD AS A CHILD TO BECOME FOOD...
...EVEN SOMEONE WITH YOUR TALENT WILL END UP BEING THEIR MEAL.

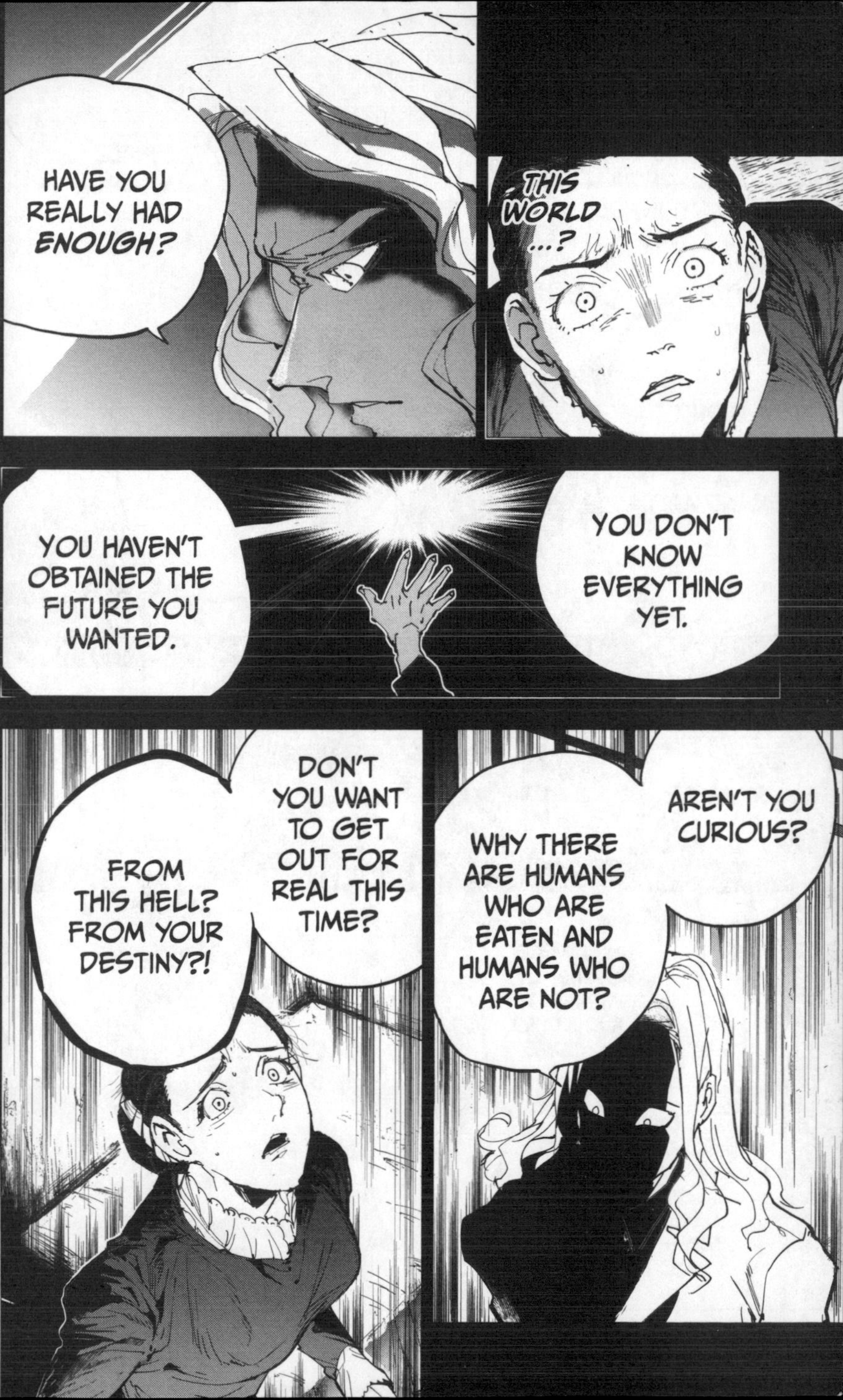
...THIS WORLD ...?
HAVE YOU REALLY HAD *ENOUGH?*
YOU DON'T KNOW EVERYTHING YET.
YOU HAVEN'T OBTAINED THE FUTURE YOU WANTED.
AREN'T YOU CURIOUS?
WHY THERE ARE HUMANS WHO ARE EATEN AND HUMANS WHO ARE NOT?
DON'T YOU WANT TO GET OUT FOR REAL THIS TIME?
FROM THIS HELL? FROM YOUR DESTINY?!

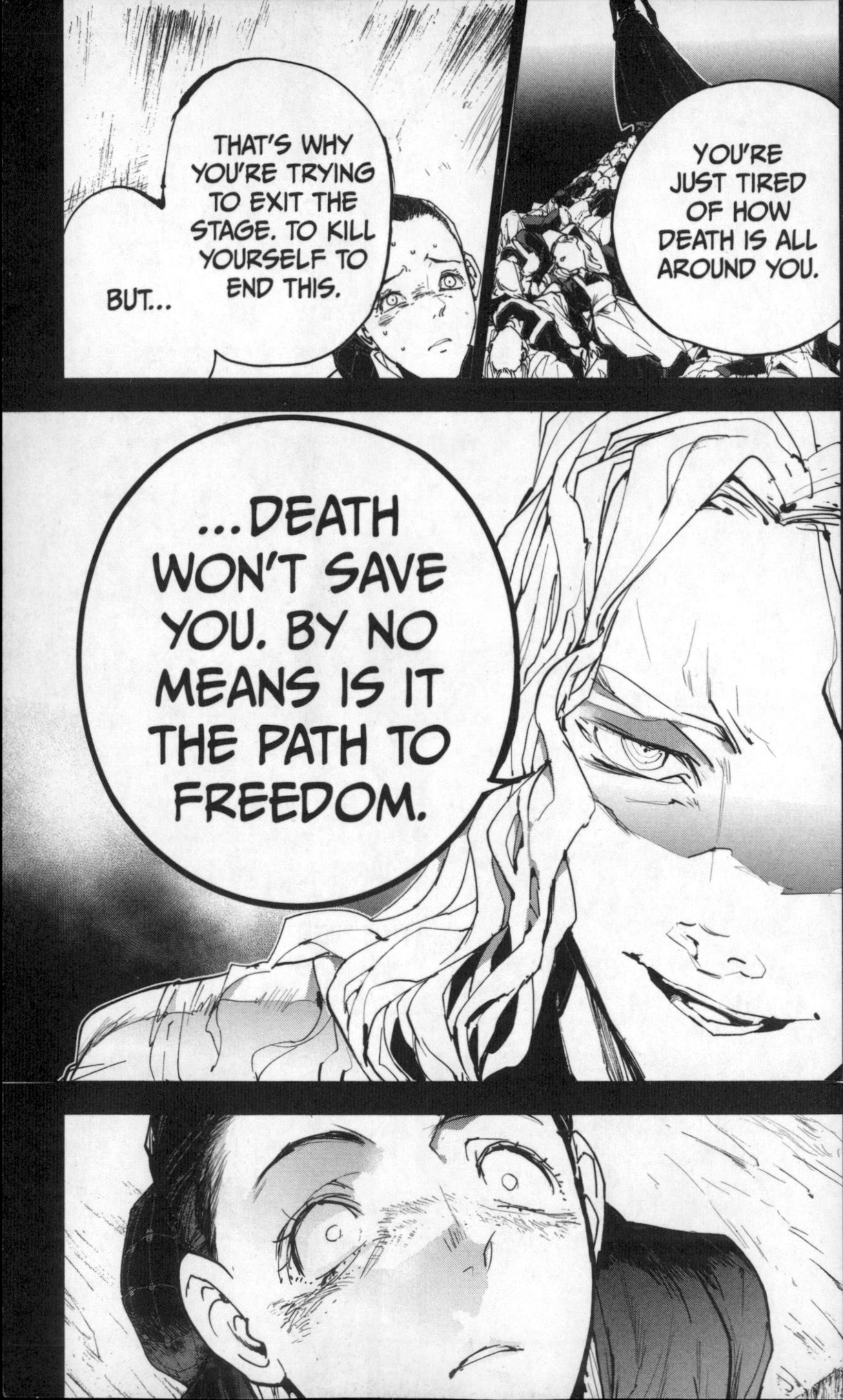
YOU'RE JUST TIRED OF HOW DEATH IS ALL AROUND YOU.
THAT'S WHY YOU'RE TRYING TO EXIT THE STAGE. TO KILL YOURSELF TO END THIS.
BUT...
...DEATH WON'T SAVE YOU. BY NO MEANS IS IT THE PATH TO FREEDOM.

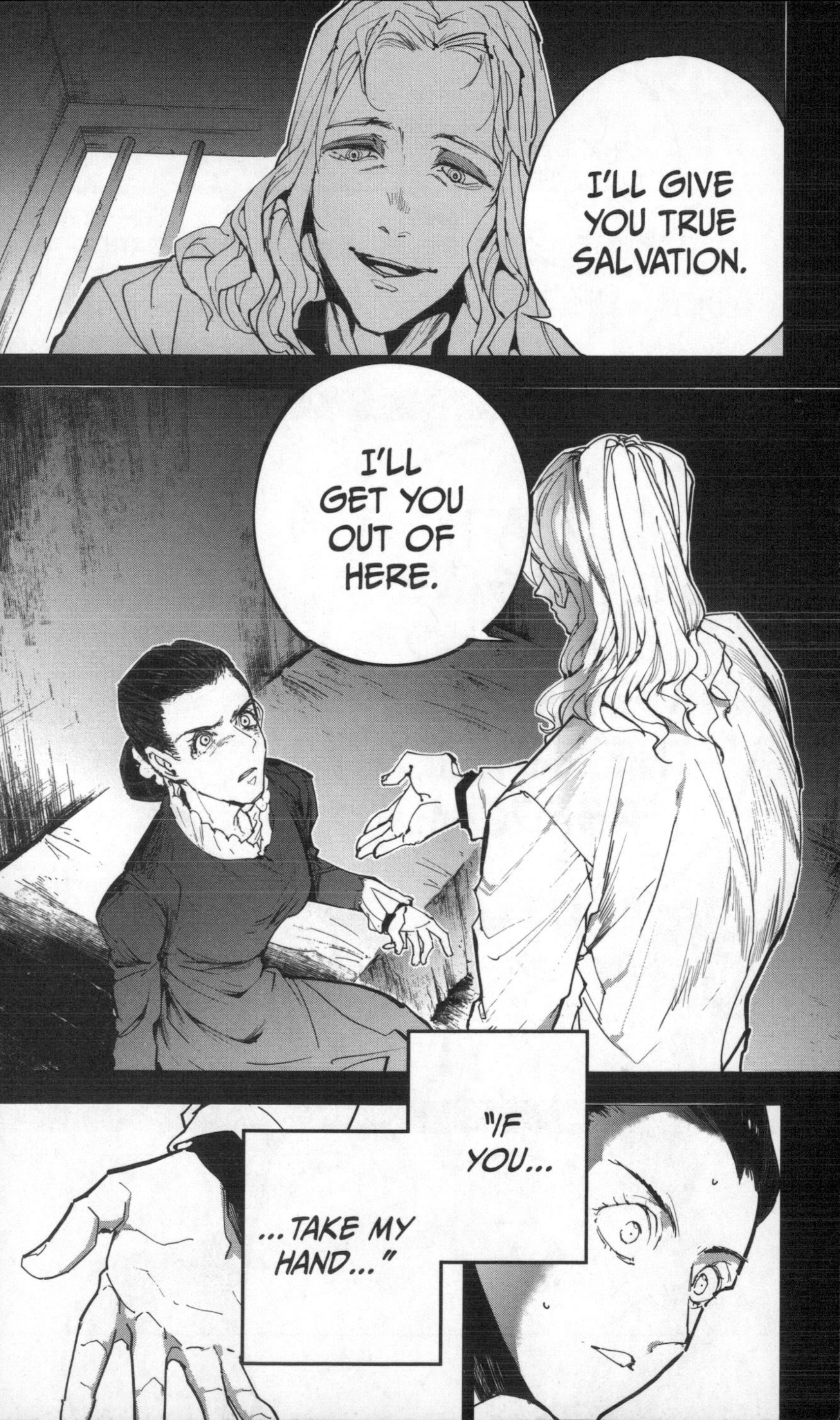
I'LL GIVE YOU TRUE SALVATION.
I'LL GET YOU OUT OF HERE.
"IF YOU...
...TAKE MY HAND..."

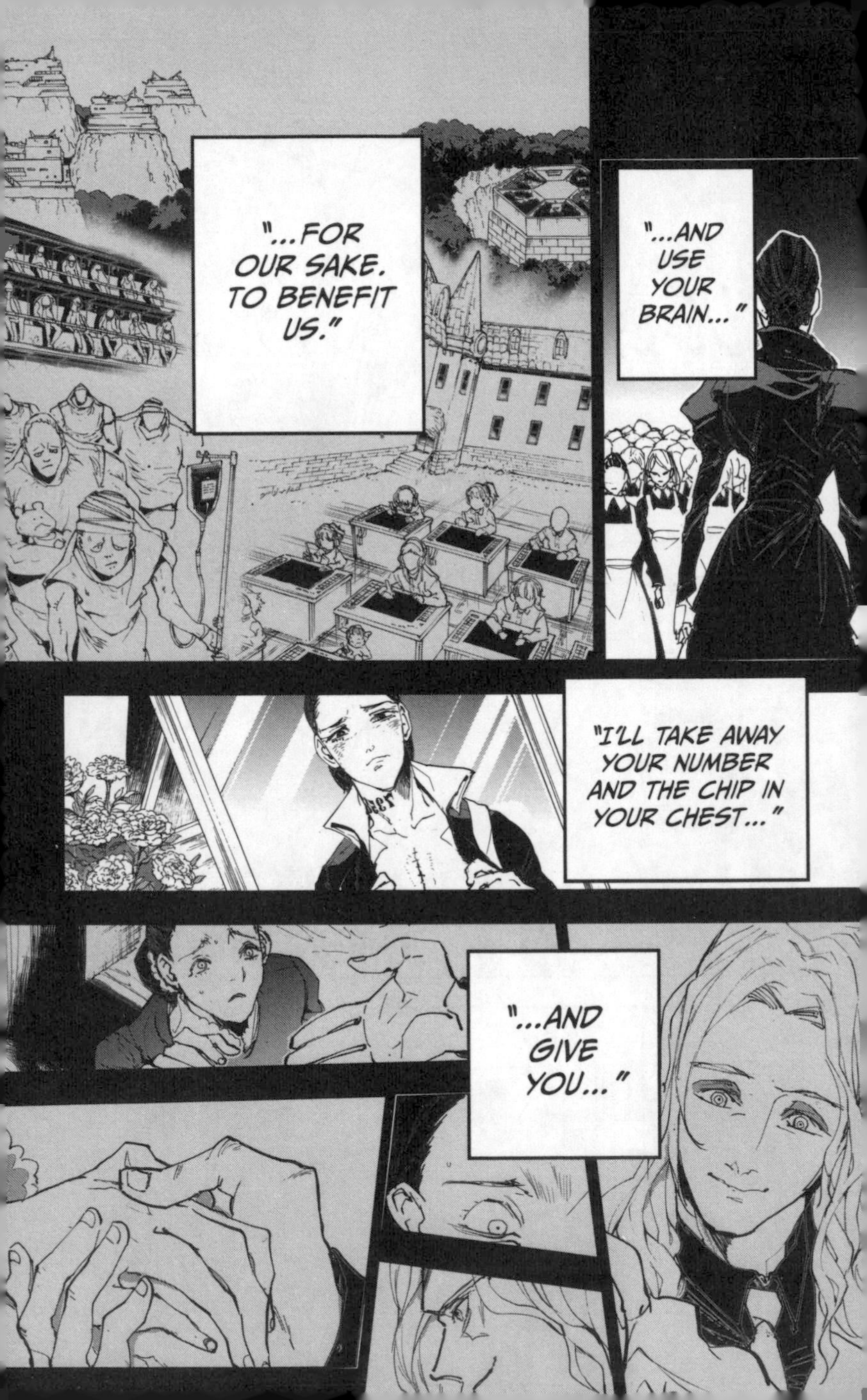
"...AND USE YOUR BRAIN..."
"...FOR OUR SAKE. TO BENEFIT US."
"I'LL TAKE AWAY YOUR NUMBER AND THE CHIP IN YOUR CHEST..."
"...AND GIVE YOU..."

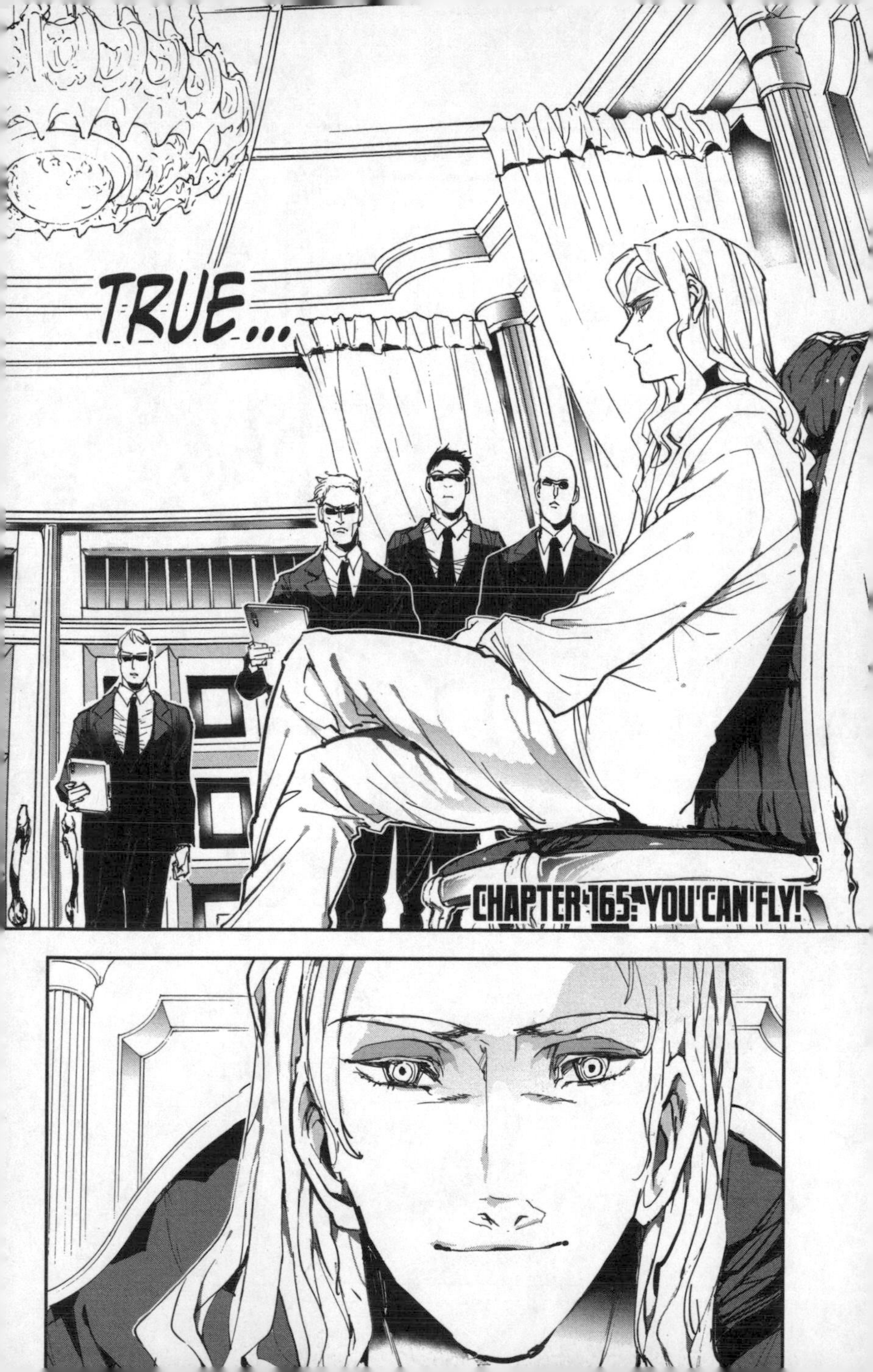
TRUE...
CHAPTER 165: YOU CAN FLY!

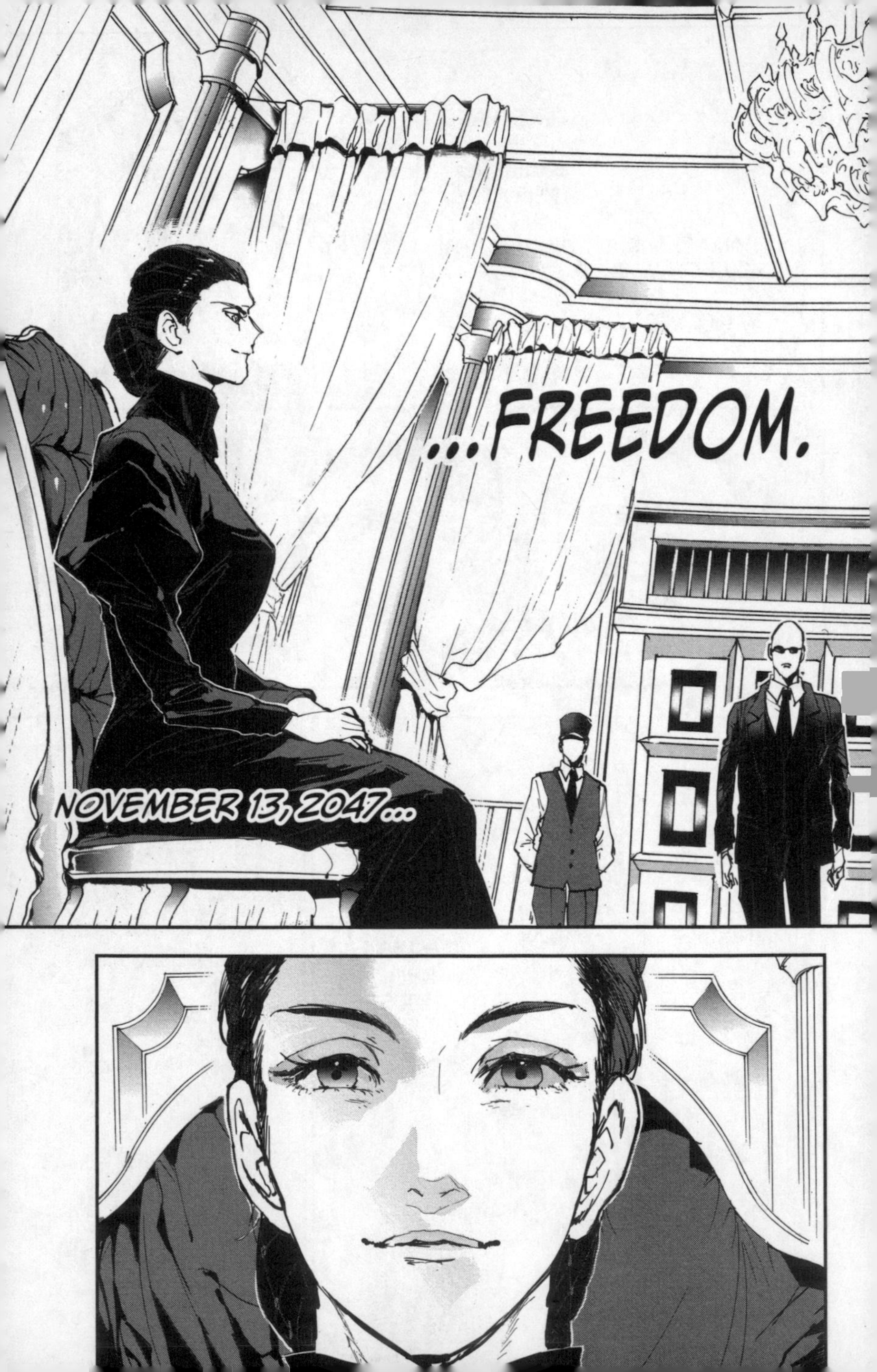
...FREEDOM.
NOVEMBER 13, 2047...

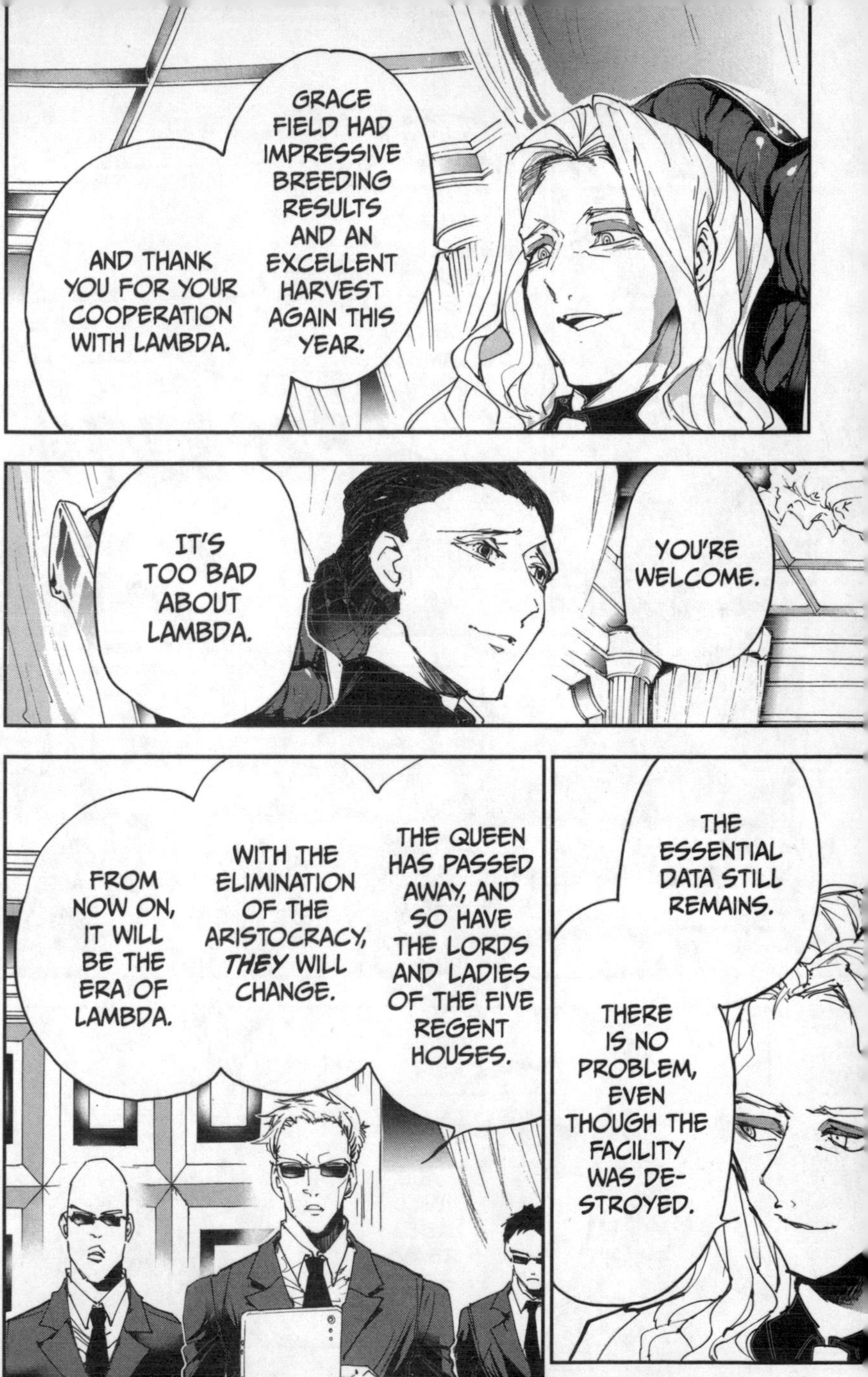
GRACE FIELD HAD IMPRESSIVE BREEDING RESULTS AND AN EXCELLENT HARVEST AGAIN THIS YEAR.
AND THANK YOU FOR YOUR COOPERATION WITH LAMBDA.
YOU'RE WELCOME.
IT'S TOO BAD ABOUT LAMBDA.
THE ESSENTIAL DATA STILL REMAINS.
THERE IS NO PROBLEM, EVEN THOUGH THE FACILITY WAS DE-STROYED.
THE QUEEN HAS PASSED AWAY, AND SO HAVE THE LORDS AND LADIES OF THE FIVE REGENT HOUSES.
WITH THE ELIMINATION OF THE ARISTOCRACY, *THEY* WILL CHANGE.
FROM NOW ON, IT WILL BE THE ERA OF LAMBDA.

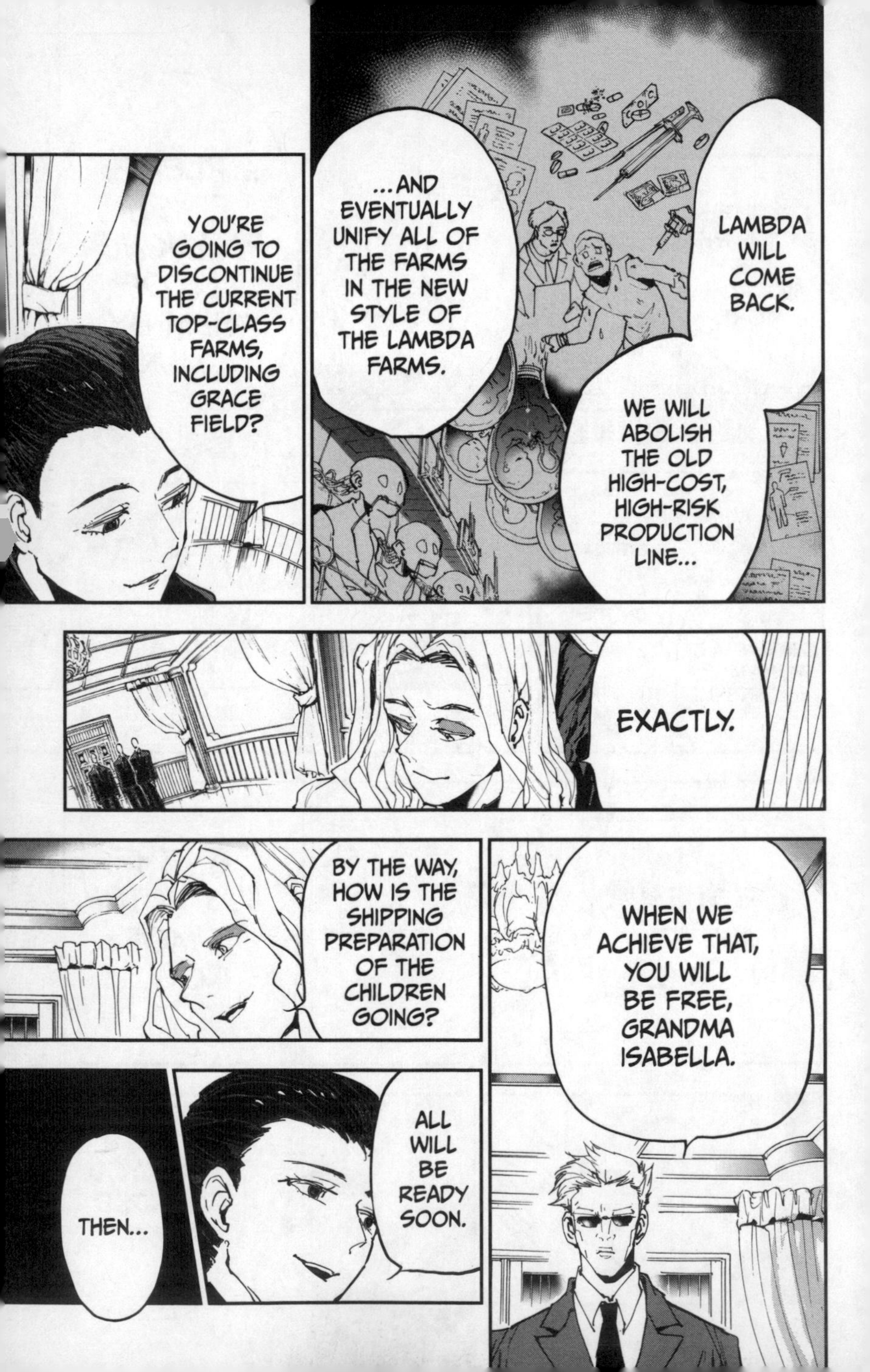
LAMBDA WILL COME BACK.
WE WILL ABOLISH THE OLD HIGH-COST, HIGH-RISK PRODUCTION LINE...
...AND EVENTUALLY UNIFY ALL OF THE FARMS IN THE NEW STYLE OF THE LAMBDA FARMS.
YOU'RE GOING TO DISCONTINUE THE CURRENT TOP-CLASS FARMS, INCLUDING GRACE FIELD?
EXACTLY.
WHEN WE ACHIEVE THAT, YOU WILL BE FREE, GRANDMA ISABELLA.
BY THE WAY, HOW IS THE SHIPPING PREPARATION OF THE CHILDREN GOING?
ALL WILL BE READY SOON.
THEN...

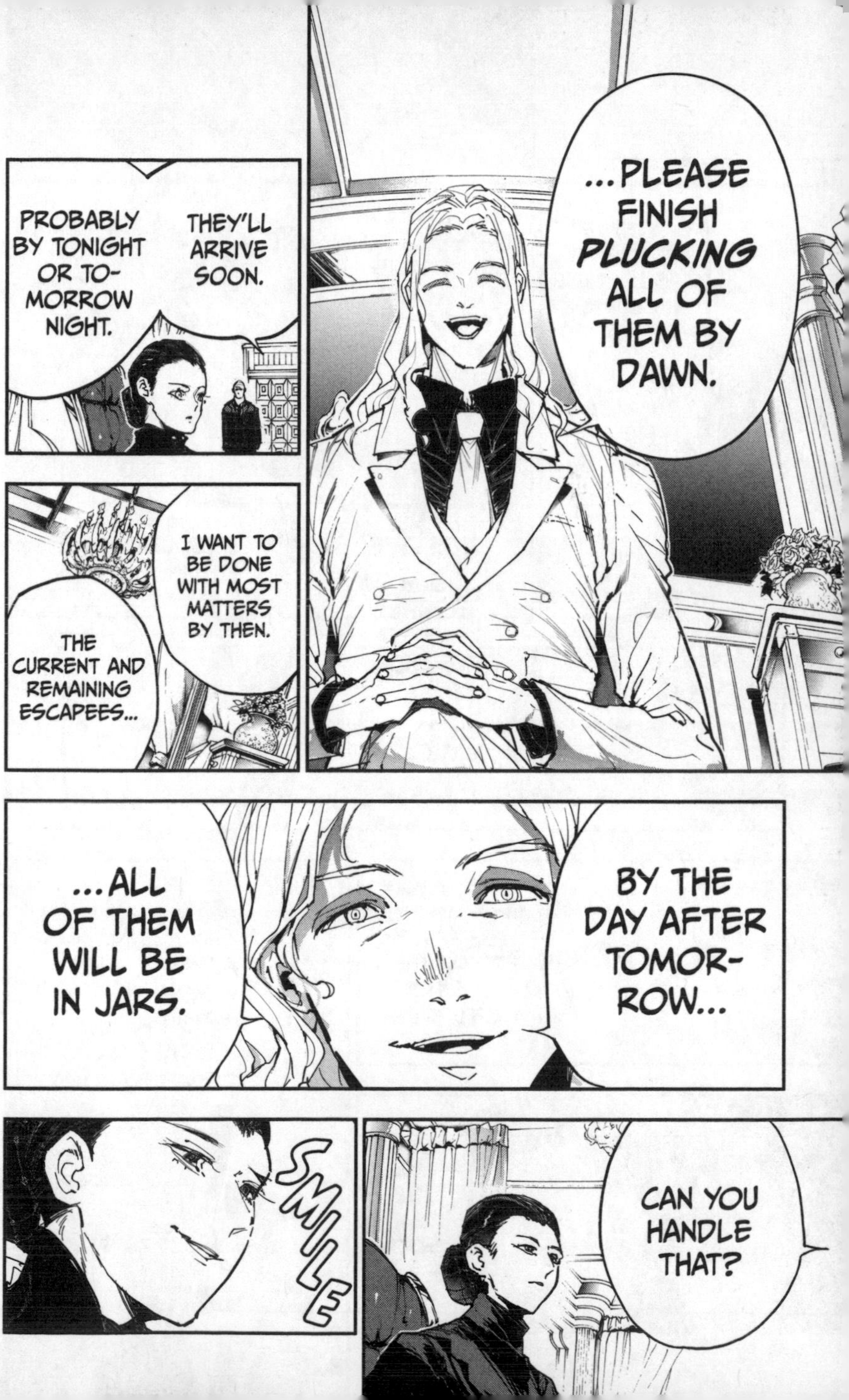
...PLEASE FINISH PLUCKING ALL OF THEM BY DAWN.
THEY'LL ARRIVE SOON.
PROBABLY BY TONIGHT OR TO-MORROW NIGHT.
I WANT TO BE DONE WITH MOST MATTERS BY THEN.
THE CURRENT AND REMAINING ESCAPEES...
BY THE DAY AFTER TOMOR-ROW...
...ALL OF THEM WILL BE IN JARS.
CAN YOU HANDLE THAT?
SMILE

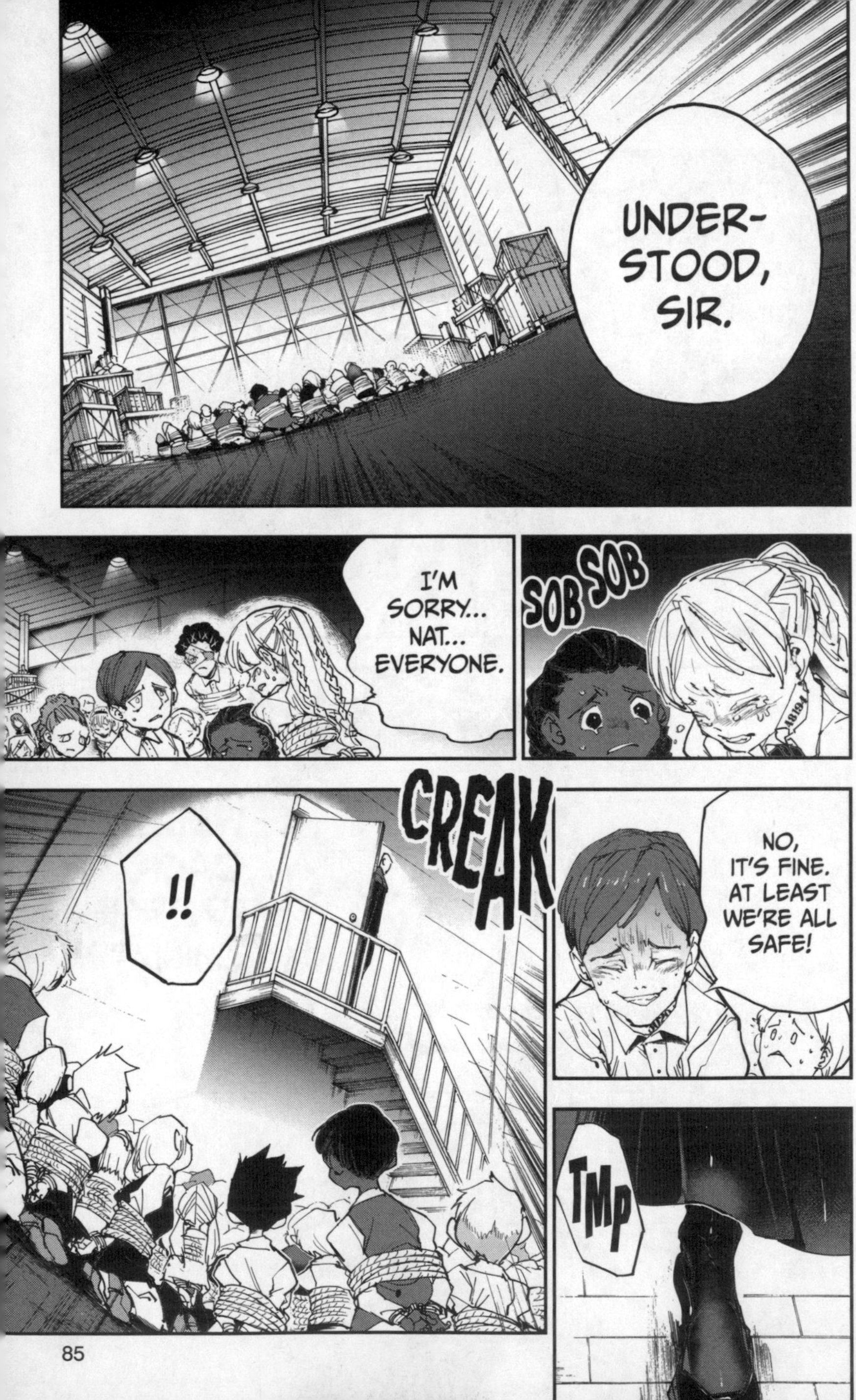
UNDER-STOOD, SIR.
SOB SOB
I'M SORRY... NAT... EVERYONE.
NO, IT'S FINE. AT LEAST WE'RE ALL SAFE!
TMP
CREAK
!!

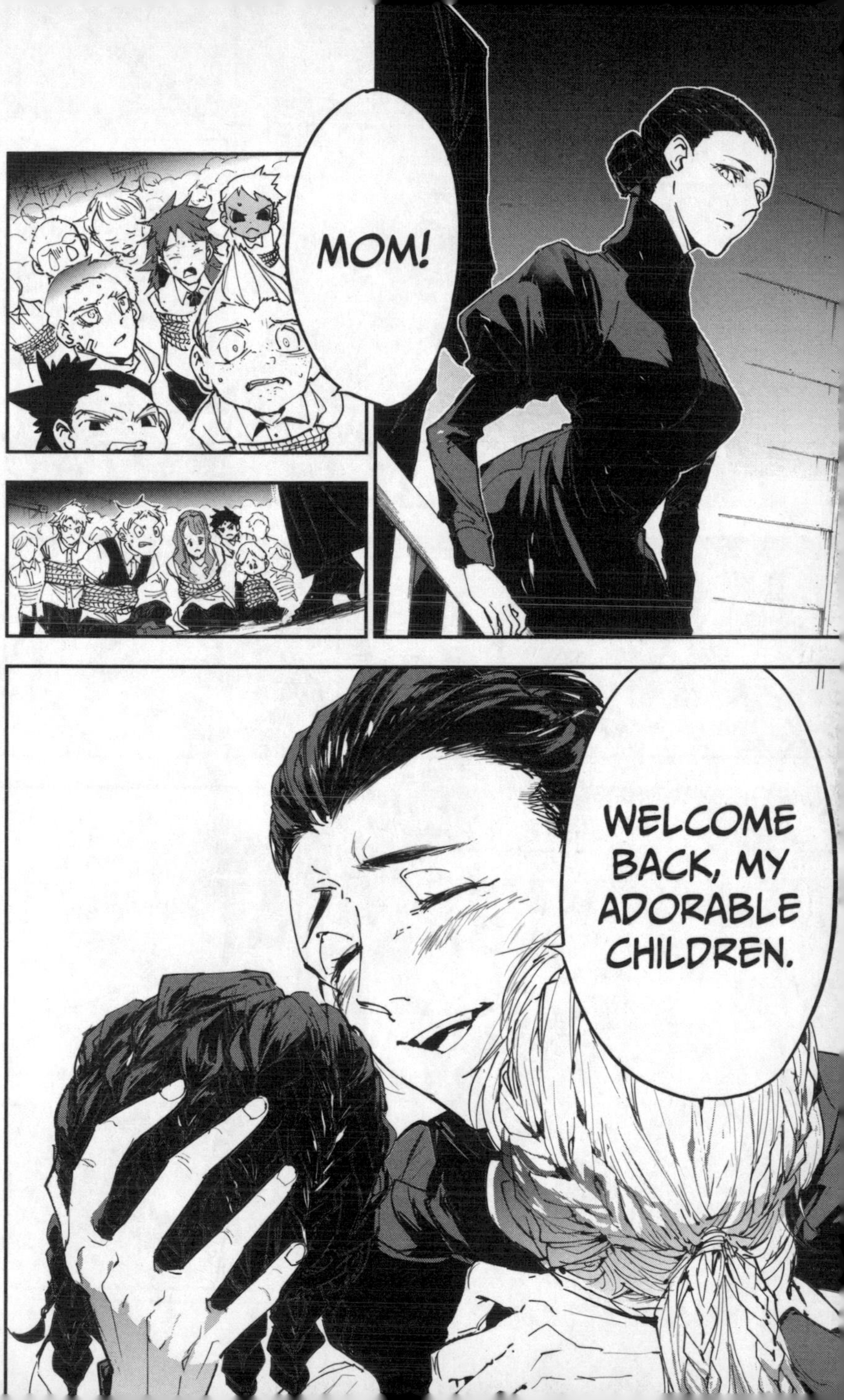
MOM!
WELCOME BACK, MY ADORABLE CHILDREN.

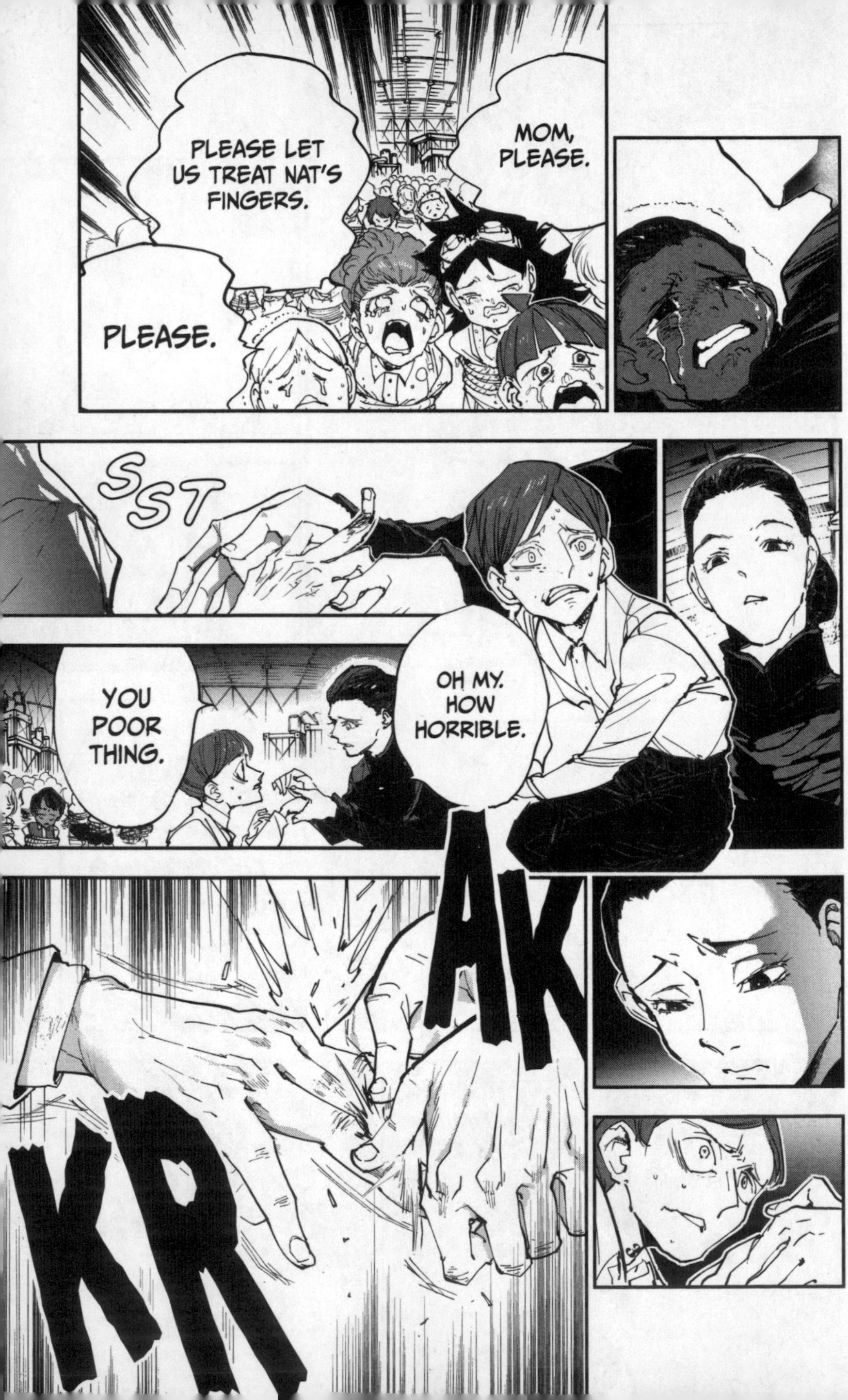
MOM, PLEASE.
PLEASE LET US TREAT NAT'S FINGERS.
PLEASE.
SST
OH MY. HOW HORRIBLE.
YOU POOR THING.
KRAK

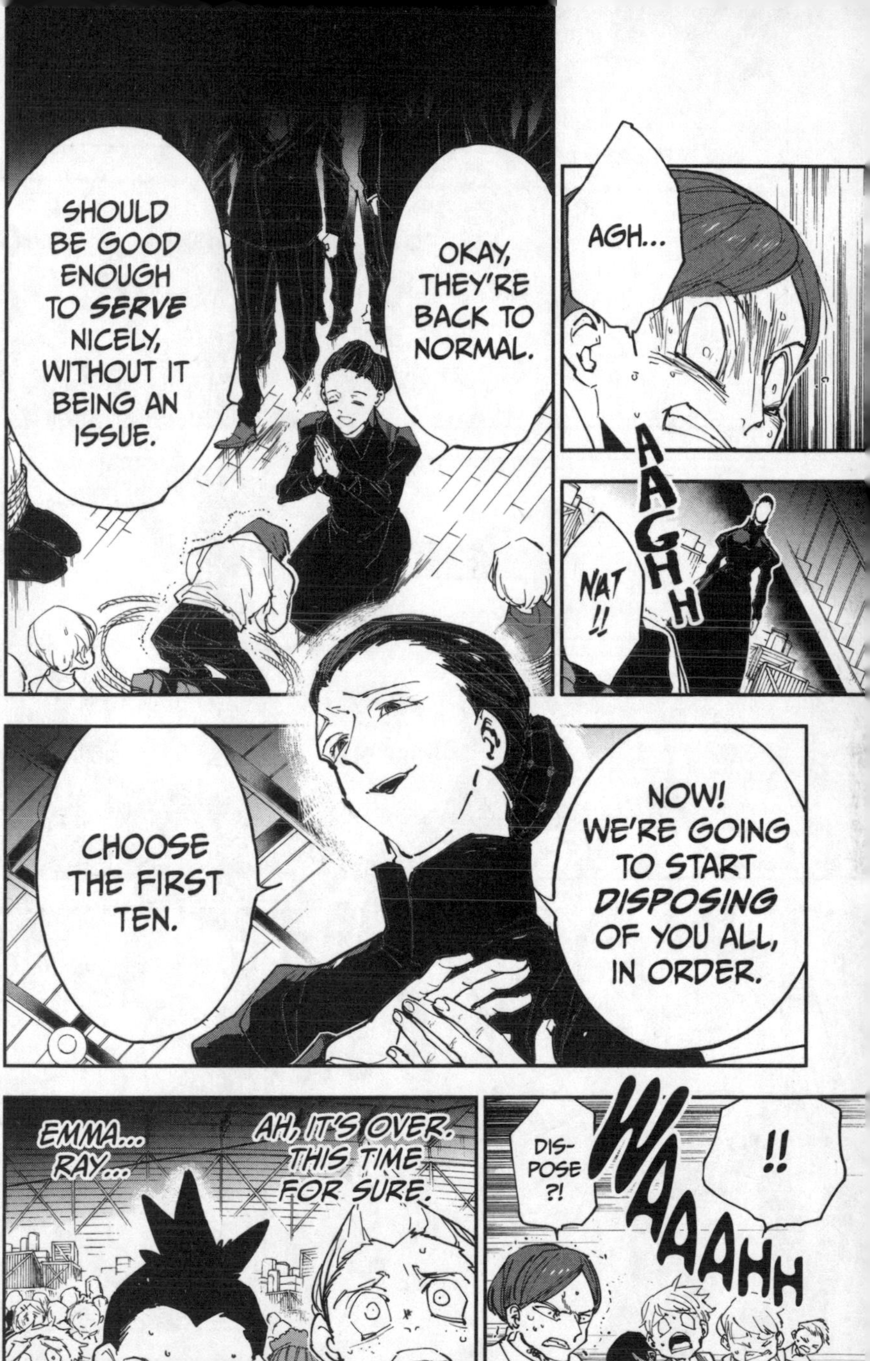
AGH...
AAGHH
NAT!!
OKAY, THEY'RE BACK TO NORMAL.
SHOULD BE GOOD ENOUGH TO *SERVE* NICELY, WITHOUT IT BEING AN ISSUE.
NOW! WE'RE GOING TO START *DISPOSING* OF YOU ALL, IN ORDER.
CHOOSE THE FIRST TEN.
!!
WAAAAHH
DIS-POSE?!
AH, IT'S OVER. THIS TIME FOR SURE.
EMMA... RAY...

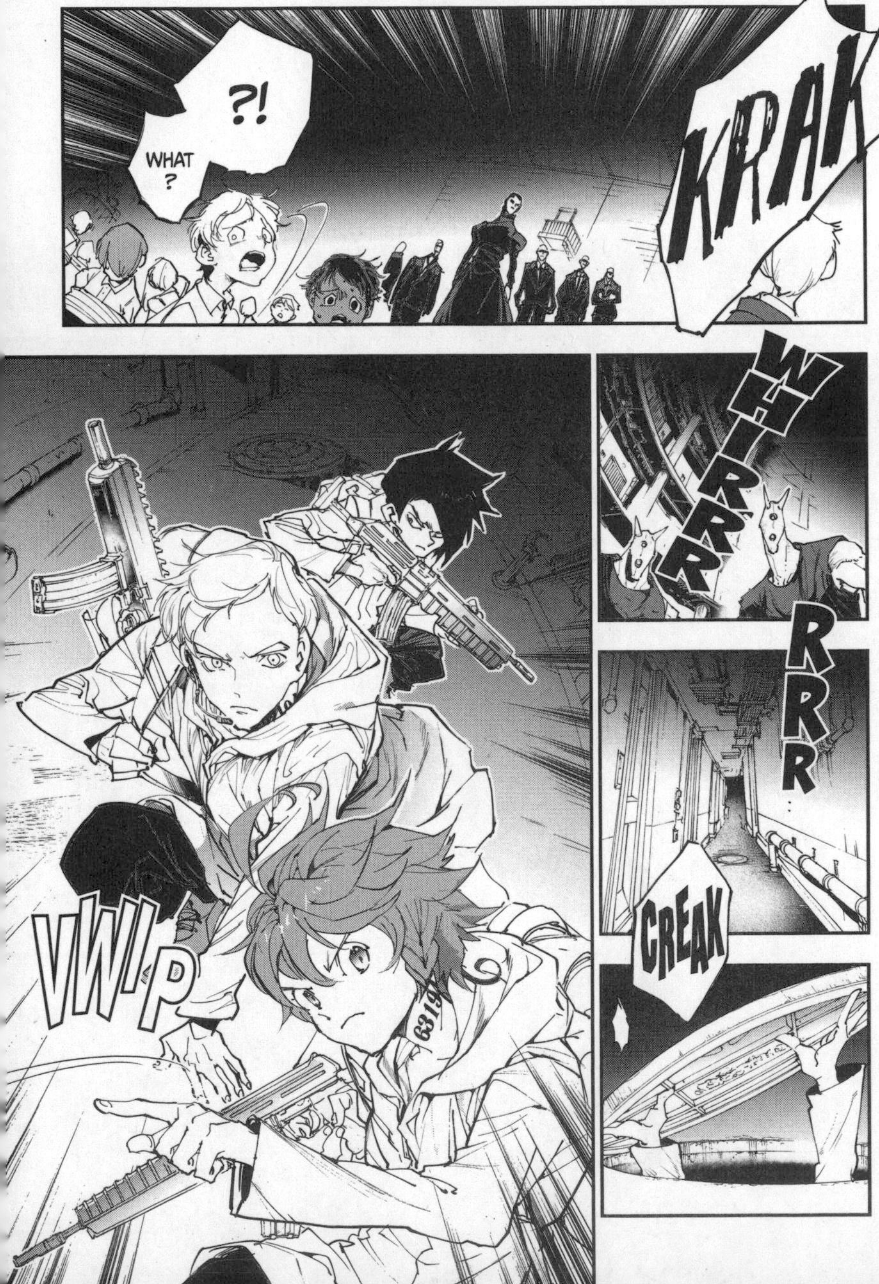
KRAK
?!
WHAT ?
WHIRRRRR
RRR...
CREAK
VWIP

EVEN MORE THAN BEFORE

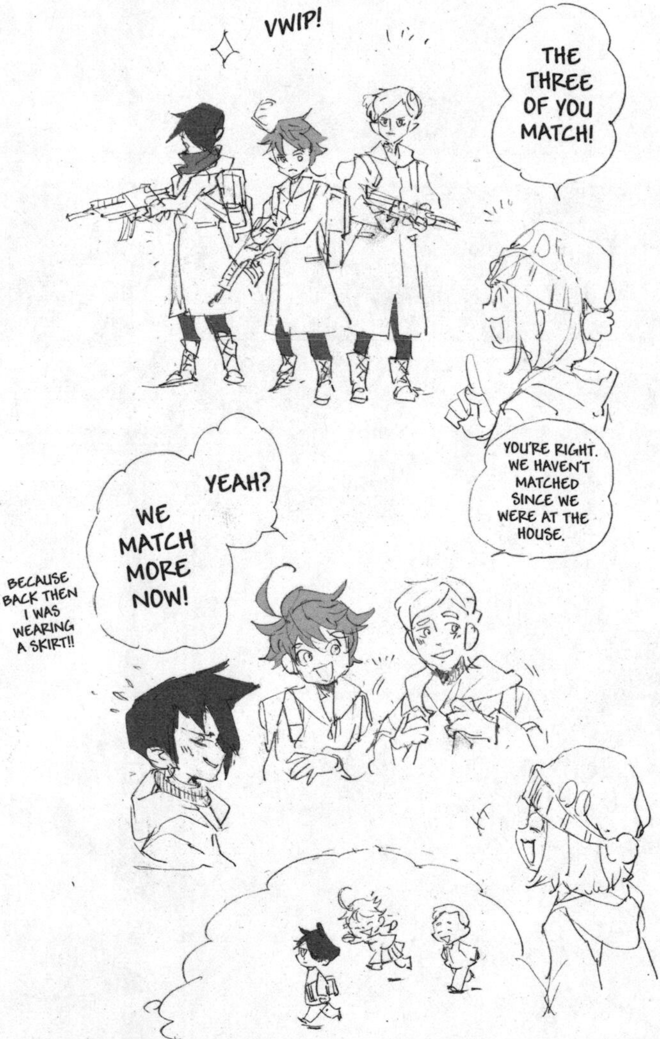
VWIP!
THE THREE OF YOU MATCH!
YOU'RE RIGHT. WE HAVEN'T MATCHED SINCE WE WERE AT THE HOUSE.
YEAH?
WE MATCH MORE NOW!
BECAUSE BACK THEN I WAS WEARING A SKIRT!!

CHAPTER 166: GOING BACK HOME

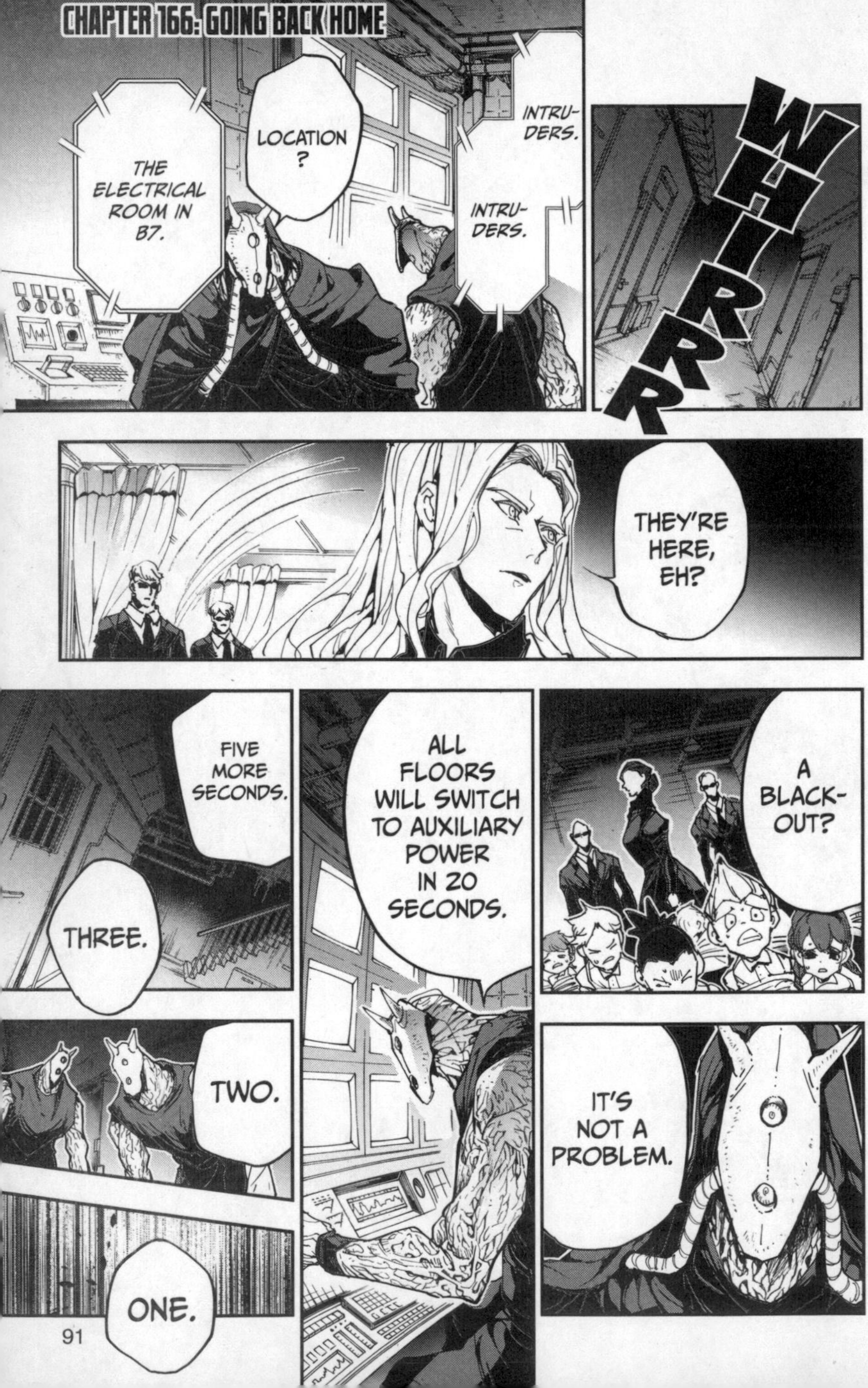
WHIRRR
INTRU-DERS.
INTRU-DERS.
LOCATION?
THE ELECTRICAL ROOM IN B7.
THEY'RE HERE, EH?
A BLACK-OUT?
IT'S NOT A PROBLEM.
ALL FLOORS WILL SWITCH TO AUXILIARY POWER IN 20 SECONDS.
FIVE MORE SECONDS.
THREE.
TWO.
ONE.

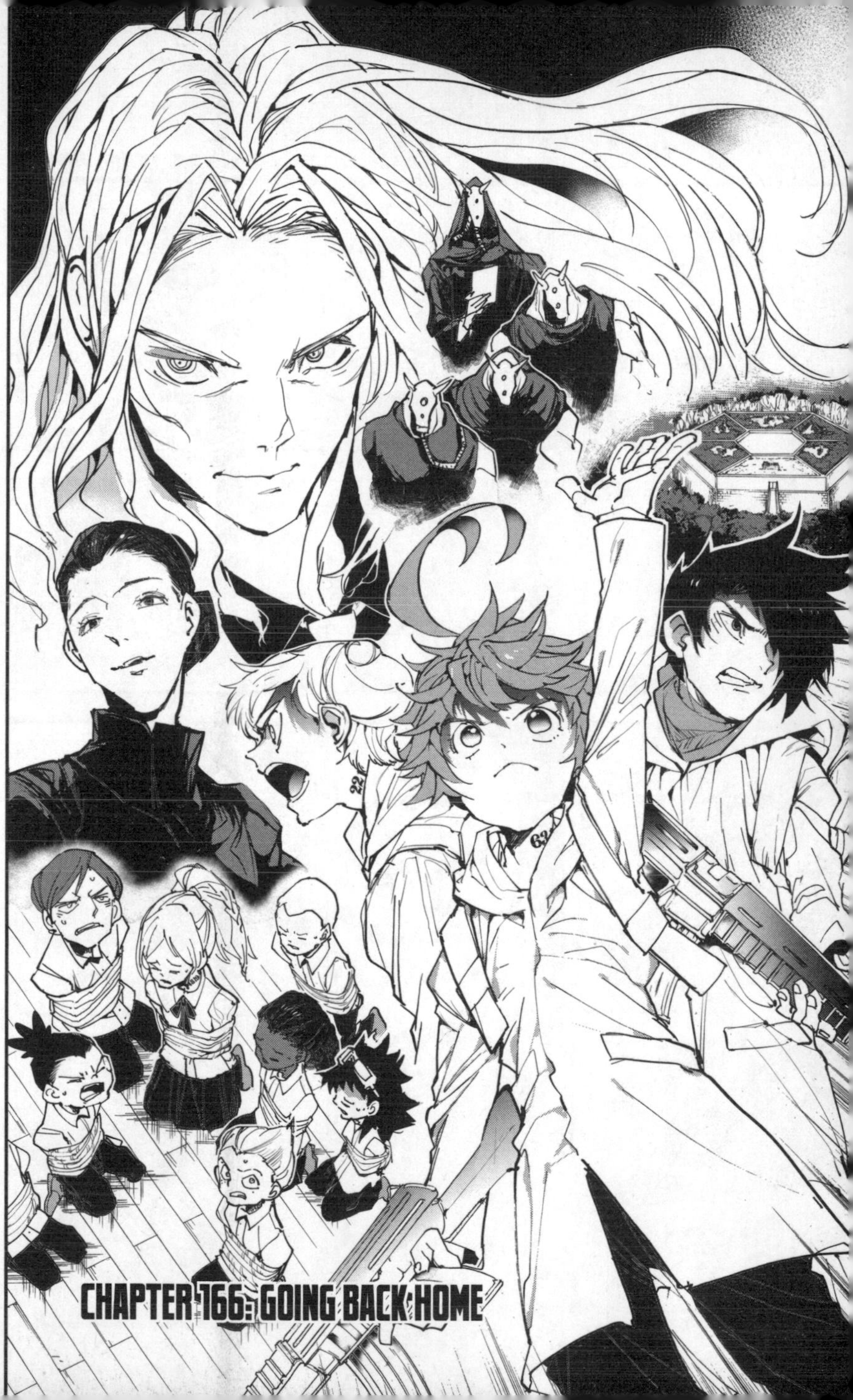
CHAPTER 166: GOING BACK HOME

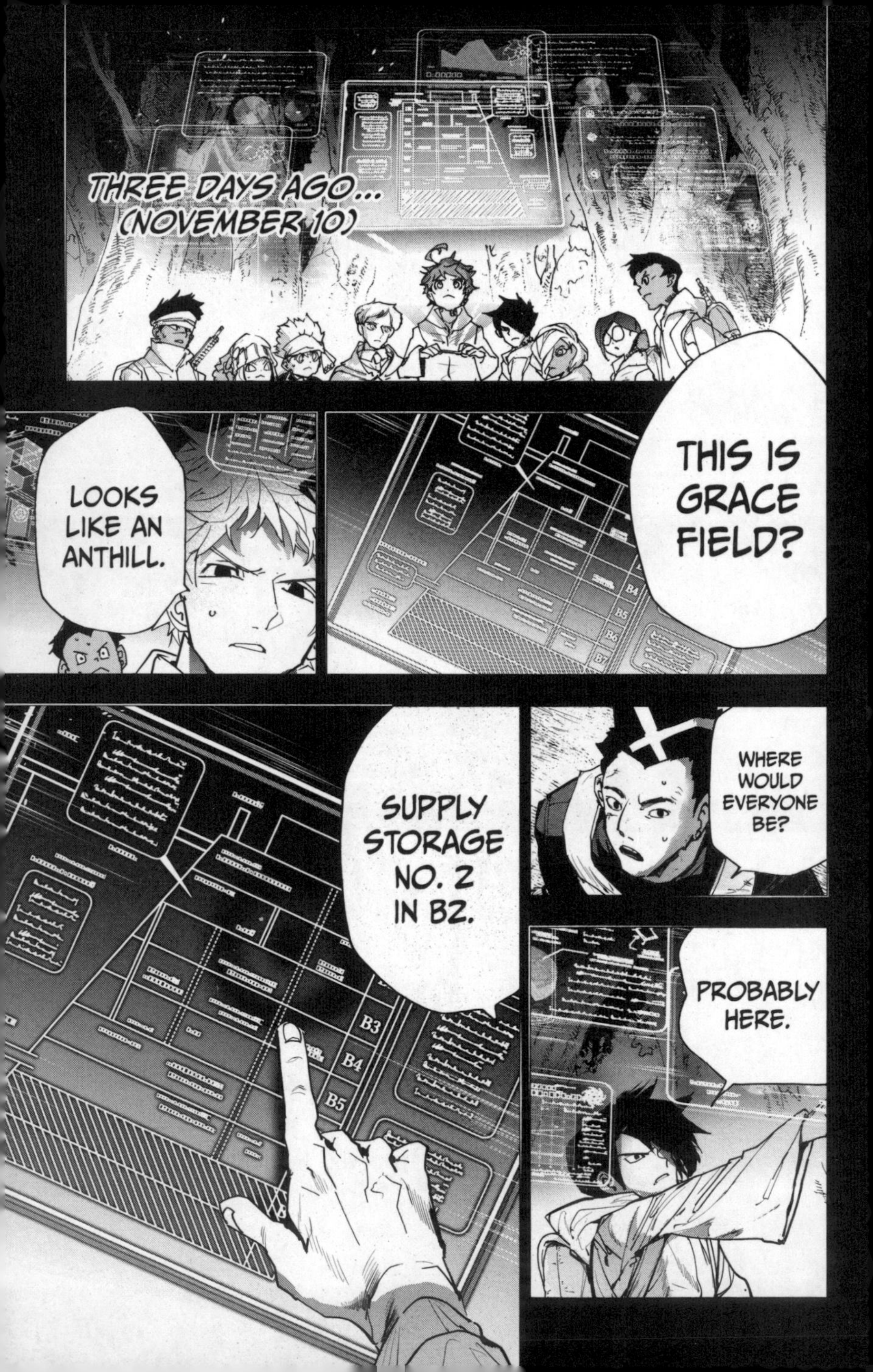
THREE DAYS AGO... (NOVEMBER 10)
THIS IS GRACE FIELD?
LOOKS LIKE AN ANTHILL.
WHERE WOULD EVERYONE BE?
PROBABLY HERE.
SUPPLY STORAGE NO. 2 IN B2.

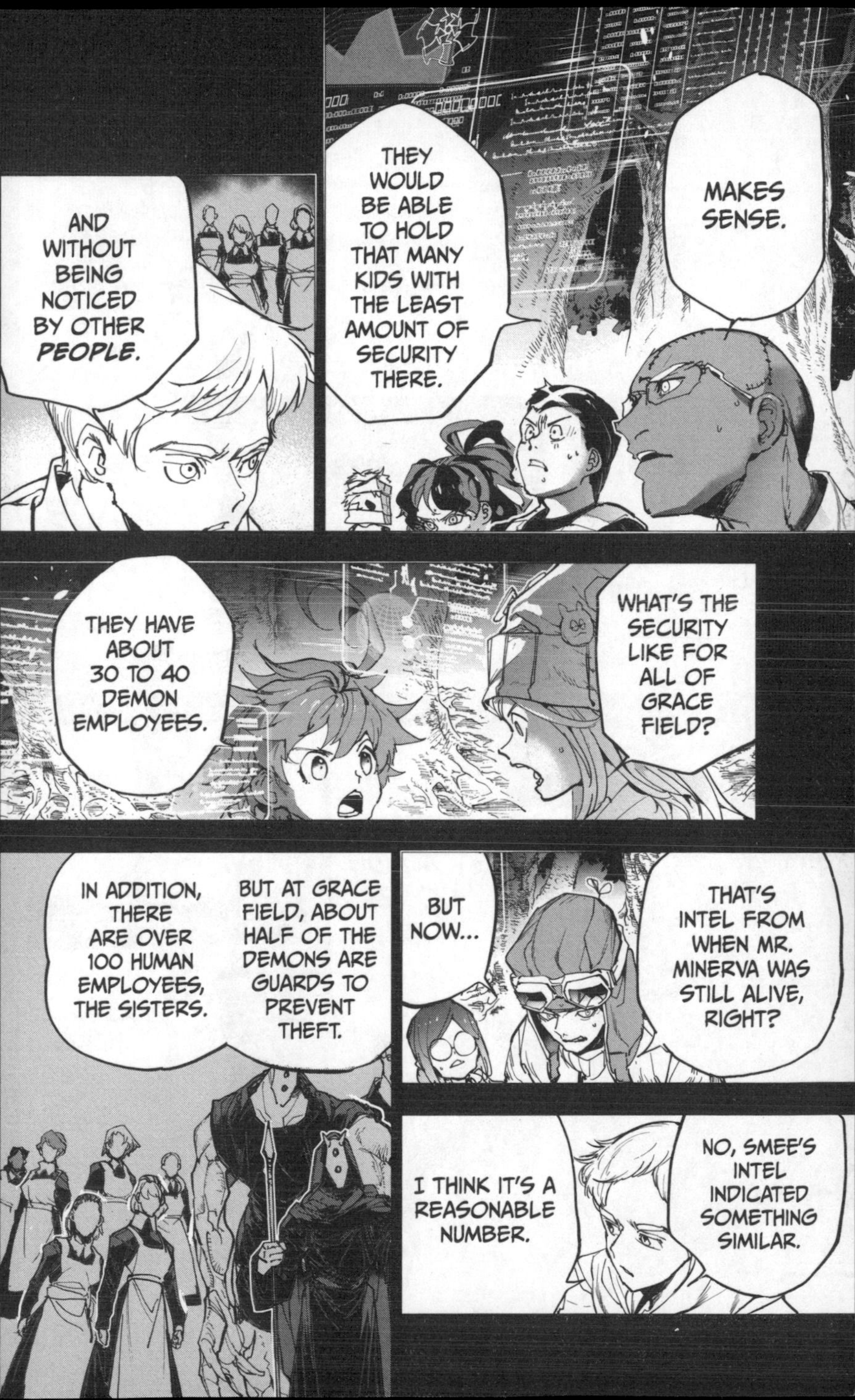
MAKES SENSE.
THEY WOULD BE ABLE TO HOLD THAT MANY KIDS WITH THE LEAST AMOUNT OF SECURITY THERE.
AND WITHOUT BEING NOTICED BY OTHER *PEOPLE*.
WHAT'S THE SECURITY LIKE FOR ALL OF GRACE FIELD?
THEY HAVE ABOUT 30 TO 40 DEMON EMPLOYEES.
THAT'S INTEL FROM WHEN MR. MINERVA WAS STILL ALIVE, RIGHT?
BUT NOW...
NO, SMEE'S INTEL INDICATED SOMETHING SIMILAR.
I THINK IT'S A REASONABLE NUMBER.
BUT AT GRACE FIELD, ABOUT HALF OF THE DEMONS ARE GUARDS TO PREVENT THEFT.
IN ADDITION, THERE ARE OVER 100 HUMAN EMPLOYEES, THE SISTERS.

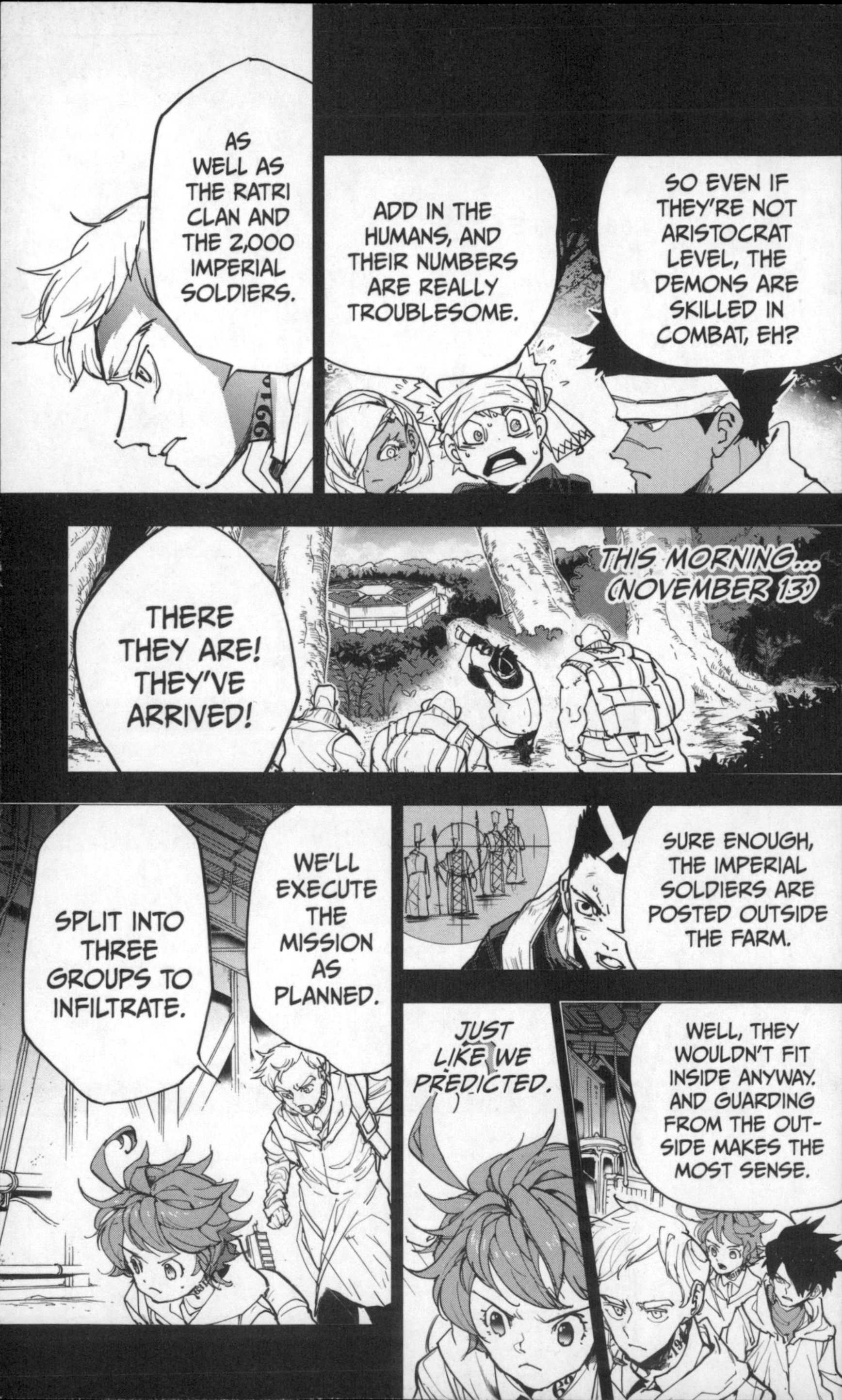
SO EVEN IF THEY'RE NOT ARISTOCRAT LEVEL, THE DEMONS ARE SKILLED IN COMBAT, EH?
ADD IN THE HUMANS, AND THEIR NUMBERS ARE REALLY TROUBLESOME.
AS WELL AS THE RATRI CLAN AND THE 2,000 IMPERIAL SOLDIERS.
THIS MORNING... (NOVEMBER 13)
THERE THEY ARE! THEY'VE ARRIVED!
SURE ENOUGH, THE IMPERIAL SOLDIERS ARE POSTED OUTSIDE THE FARM.
WELL, THEY WOULDN'T FIT INSIDE ANYWAY. AND GUARDING FROM THE OUT-SIDE MAKES THE MOST SENSE.
JUST LIKE WE PREDICTED.
WE'LL EXECUTE THE MISSION AS PLANNED.
SPLIT INTO THREE GROUPS TO INFILTRATE.

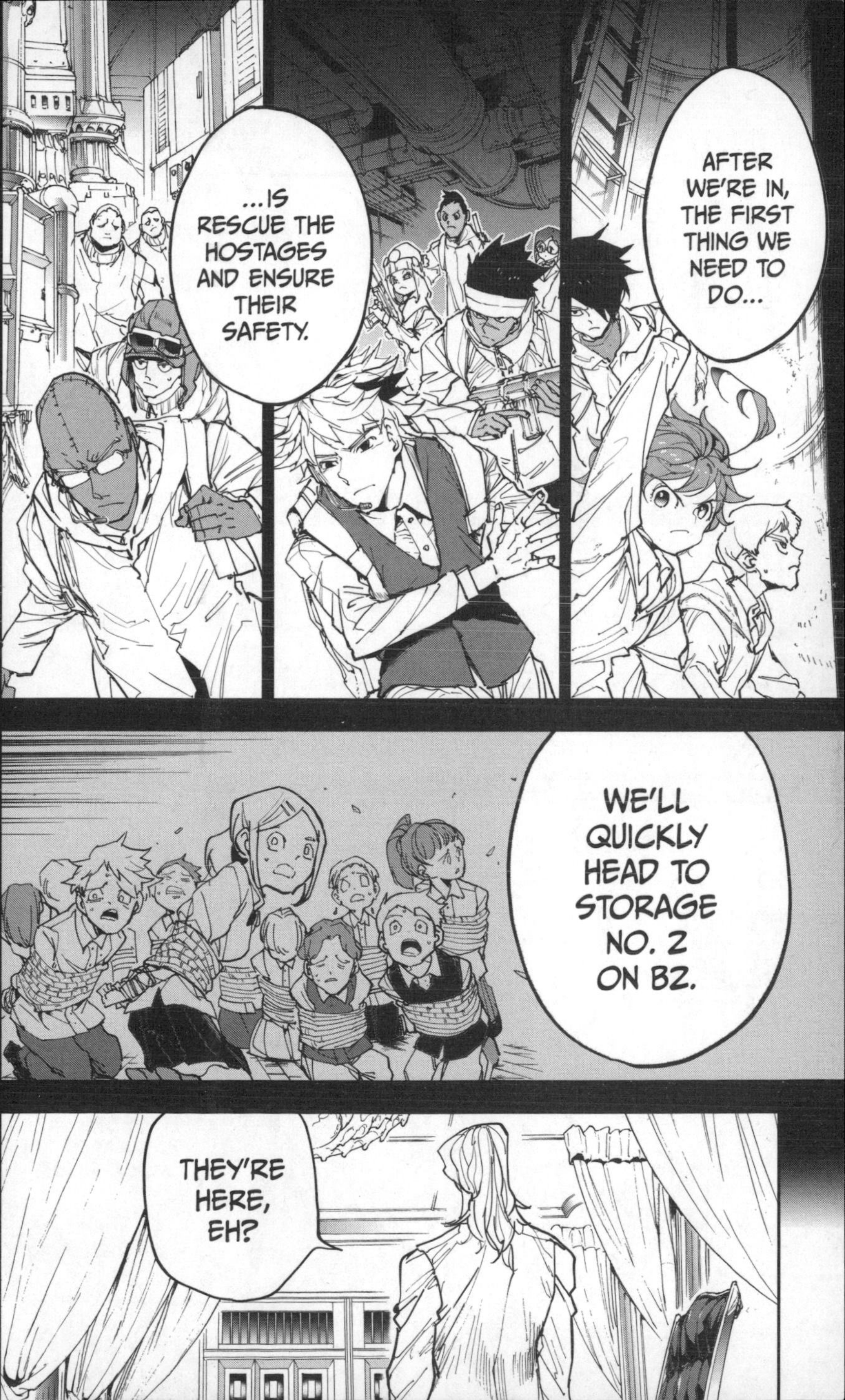
AFTER WE'RE IN, THE FIRST THING WE NEED TO DO...
...IS RESCUE THE HOSTAGES AND ENSURE THEIR SAFETY.
WE'LL QUICKLY HEAD TO STORAGE NO. 2 ON B2.
THEY'RE HERE, EH?

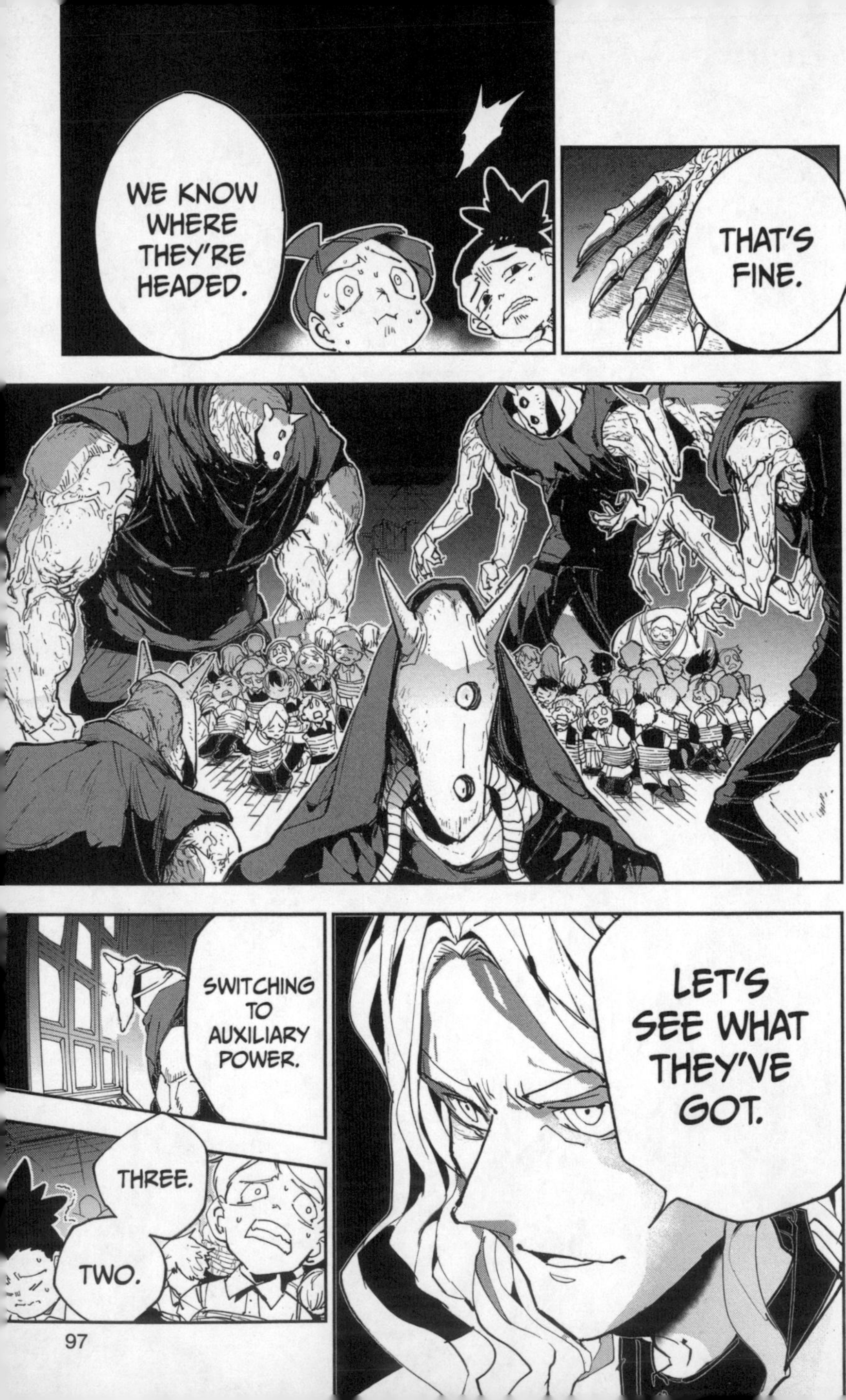
THAT'S FINE.
WE KNOW WHERE THEY'RE HEADED.
LET'S SEE WHAT THEY'VE GOT.
SWITCHING TO AUXILIARY POWER.
THREE.
TWO.

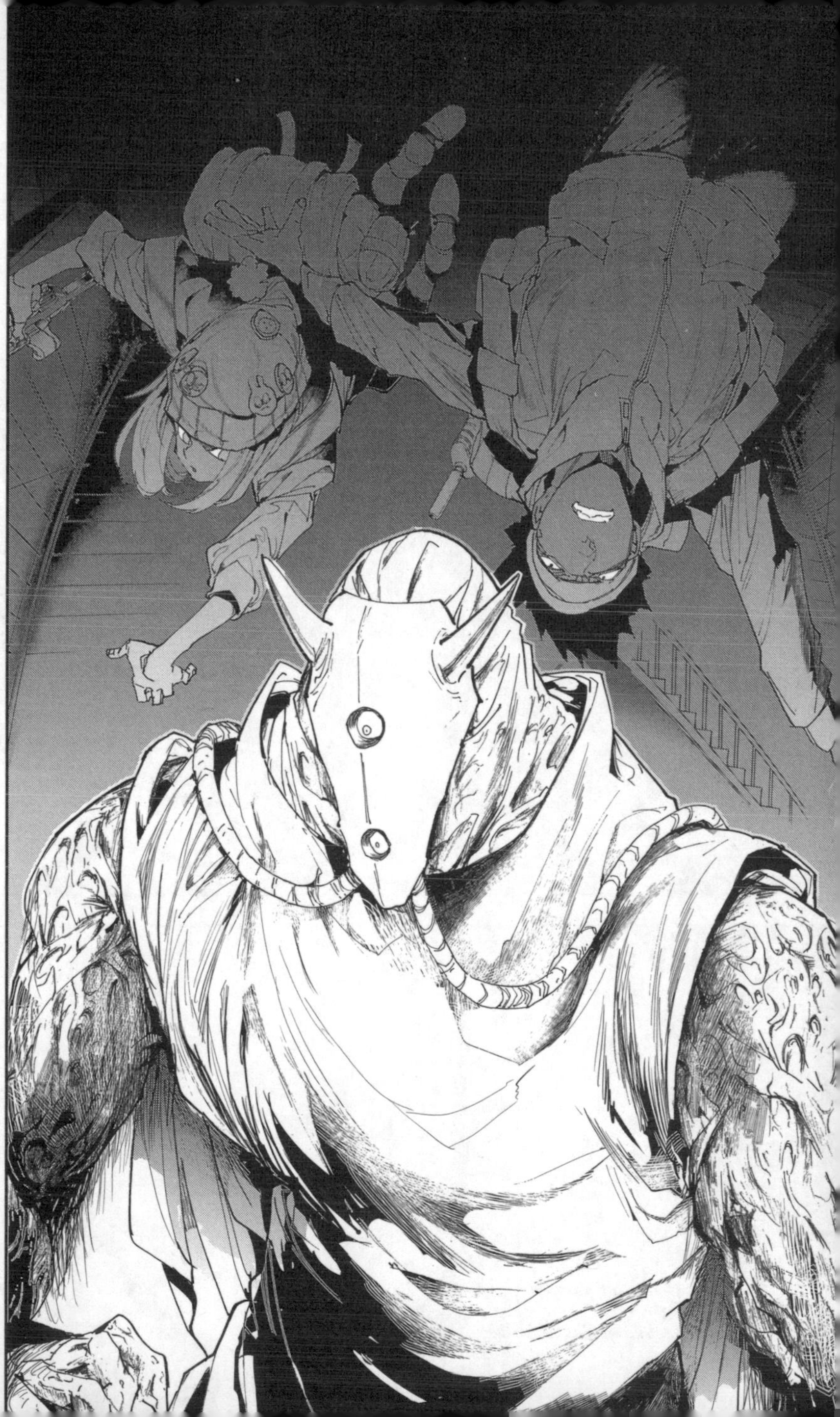

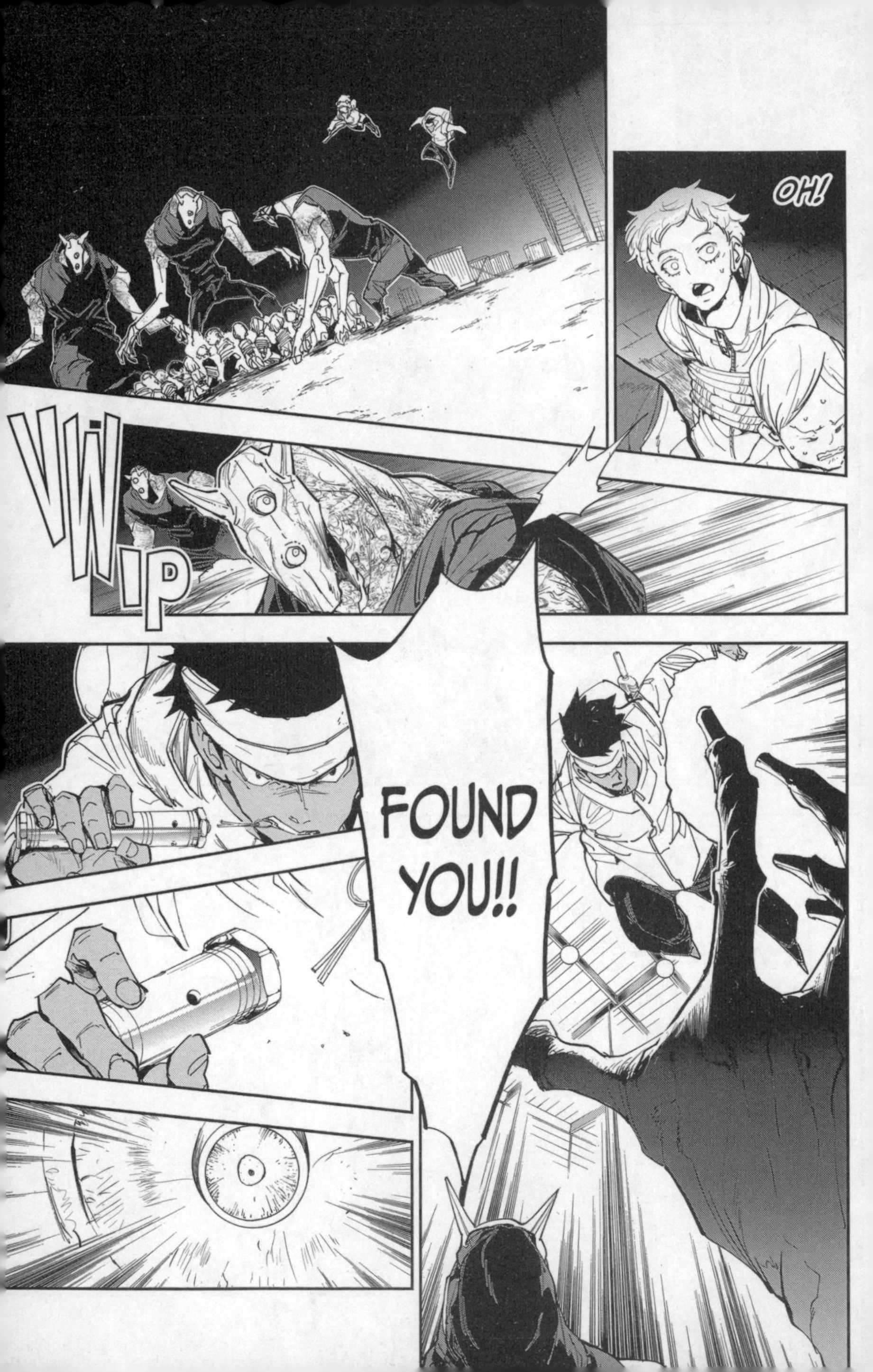
OH!
VWIP
FOUND YOU!!

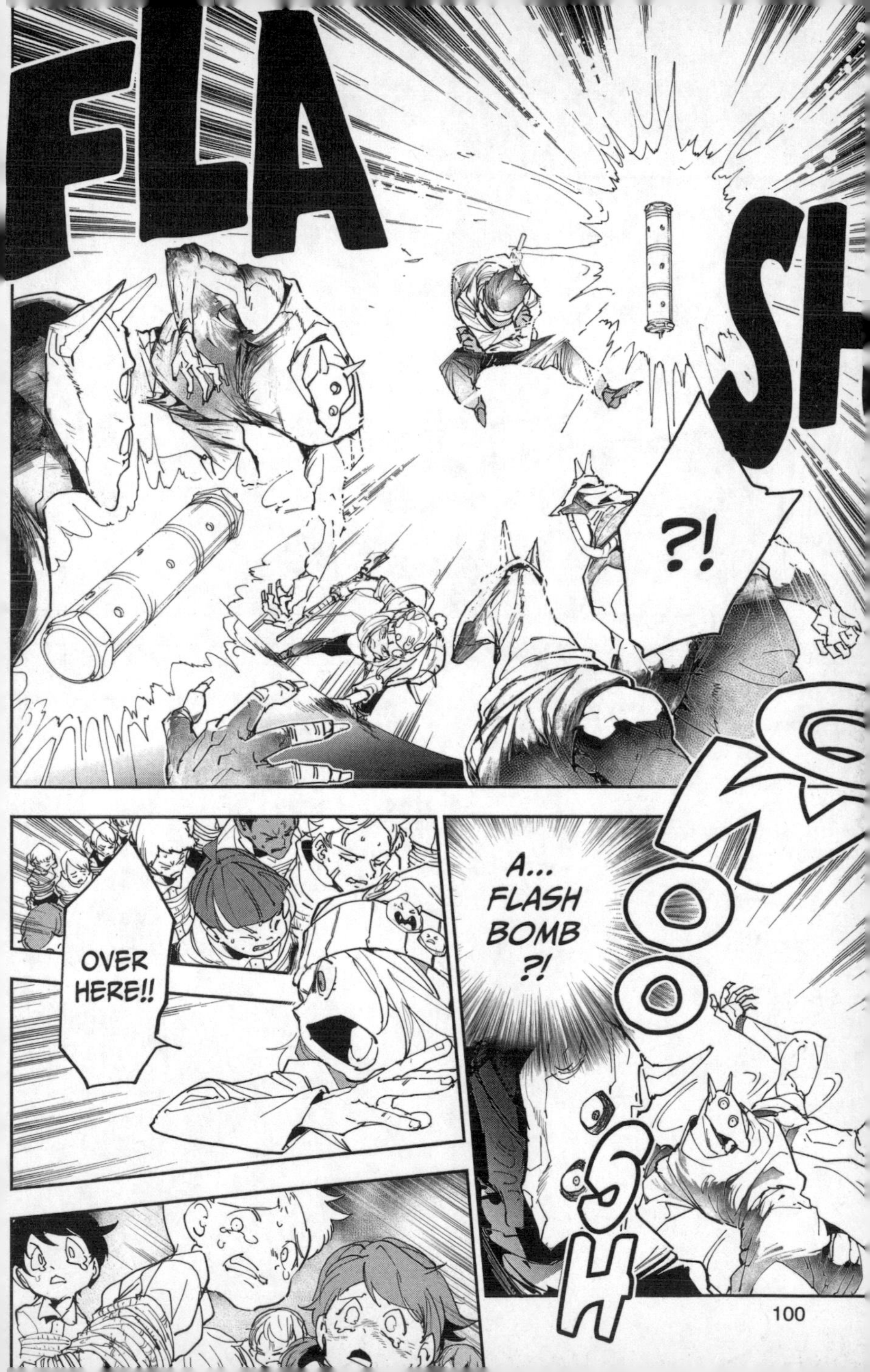
FLA
SH
?!
A... FLASH BOMB ?!
OVER HERE!!

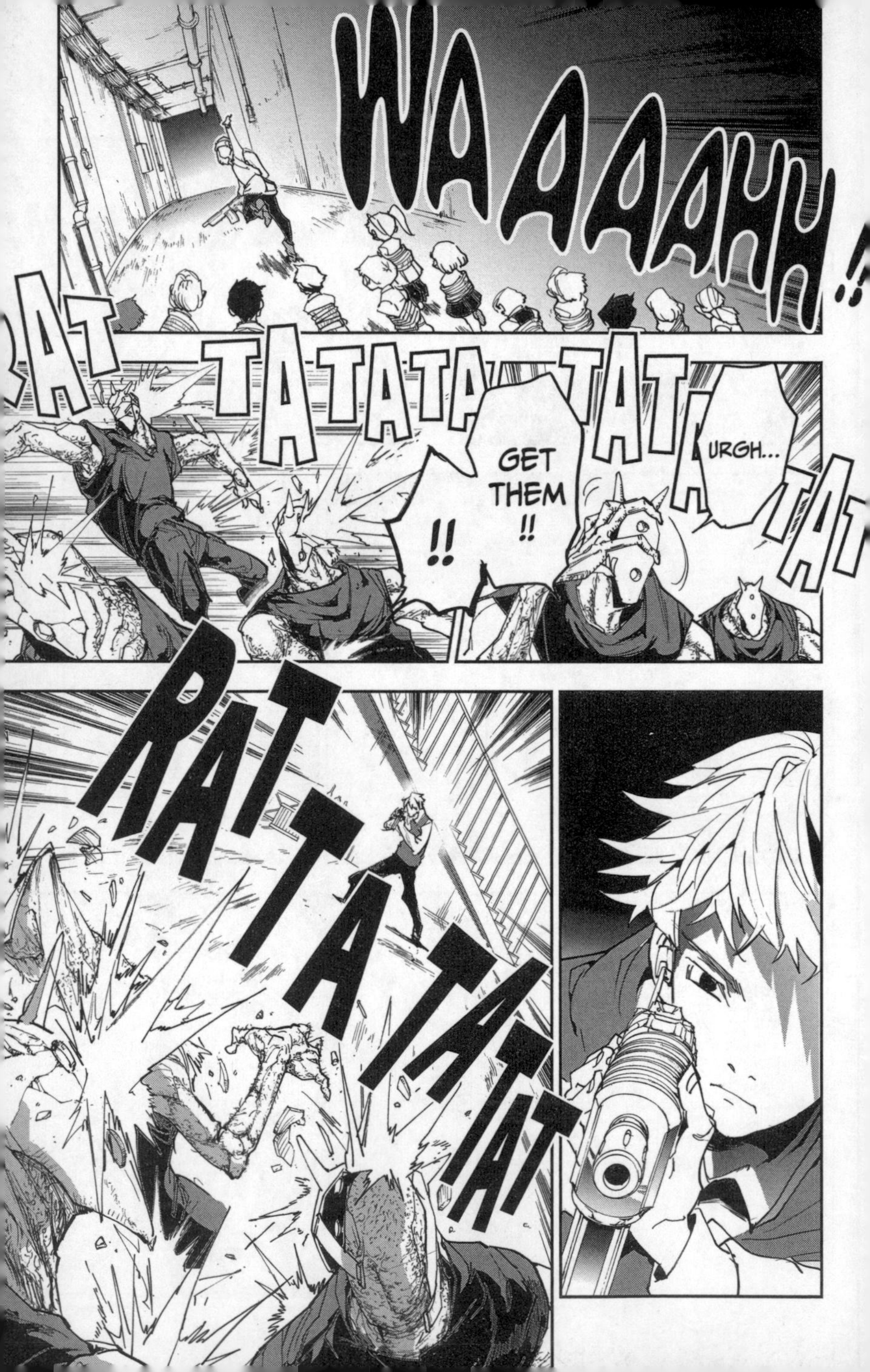
WAAAAAH!!
RATATATATATATAT
URGH...
GET THEM!!
!!
RATATATATAT

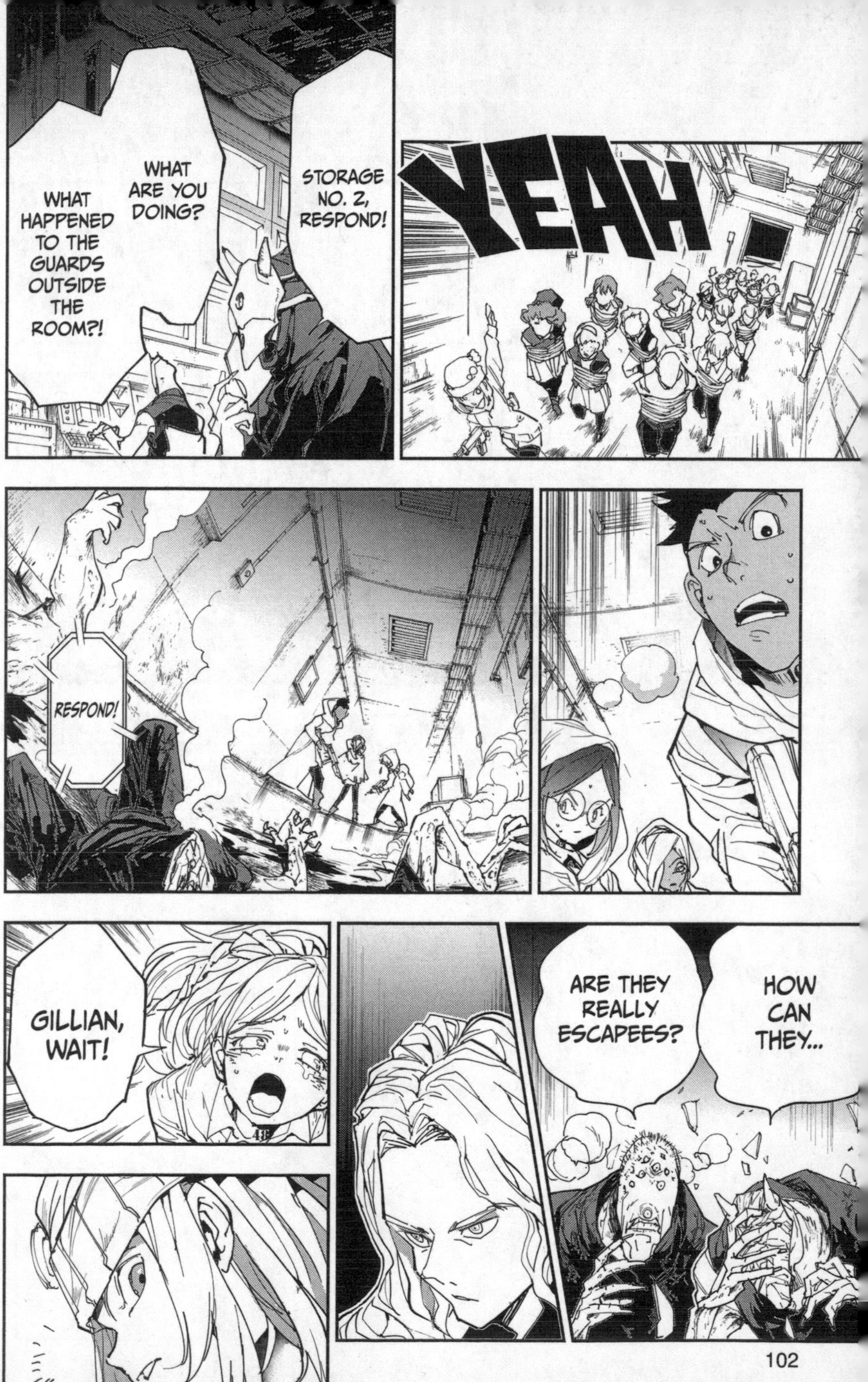
YEAH
STORAGE NO. 2, RESPOND!
WHAT ARE YOU DOING?
WHAT HAPPENED TO THE GUARDS OUTSIDE THE ROOM?!
RESPOND!
HOW CAN THEY...
ARE THEY REALLY ESCAPEES?
GILLIAN, WAIT!

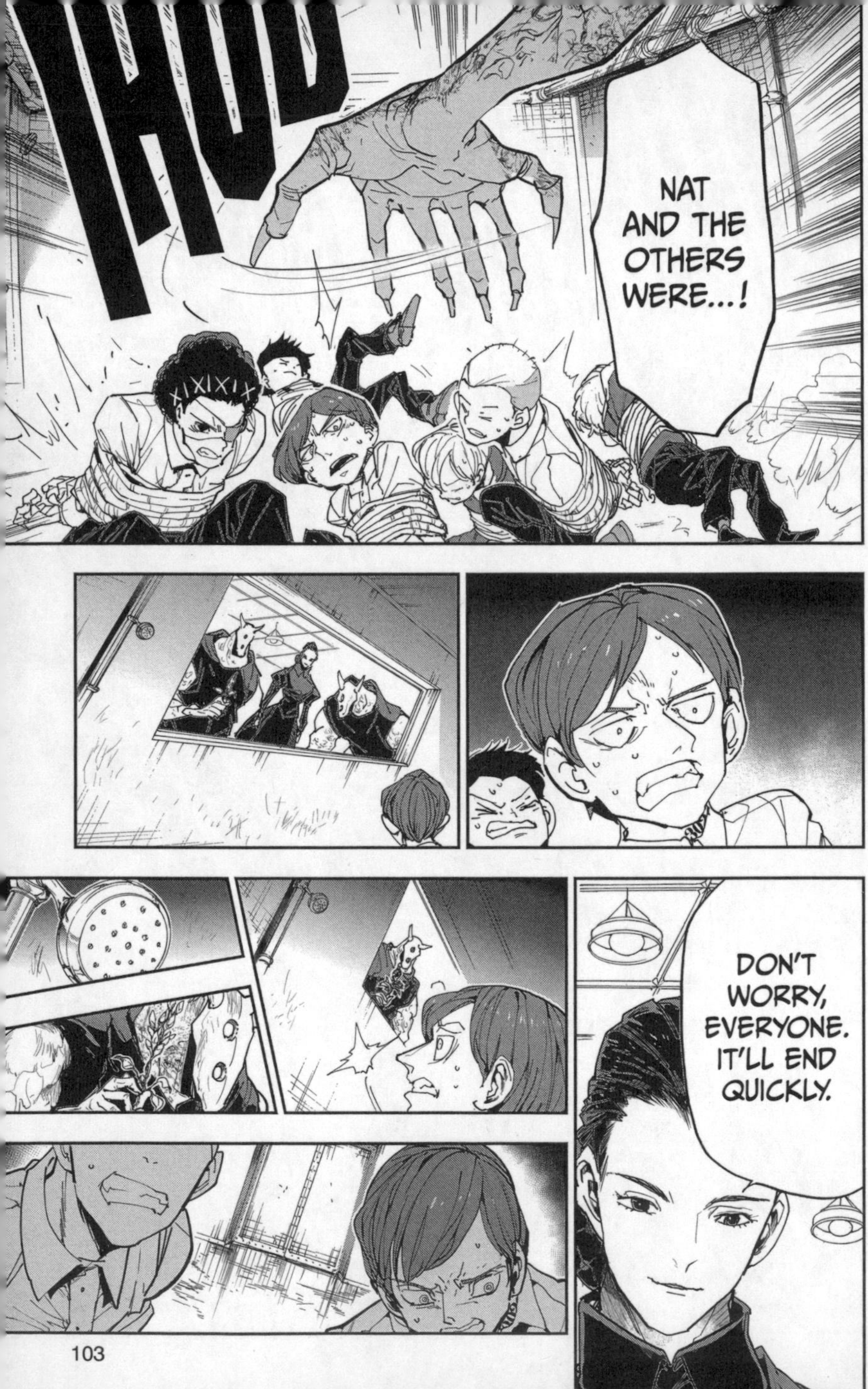
THUD
NAT AND THE OTHERS WERE...!
DON'T WORRY, EVERYONE. IT'LL END QUICKLY.

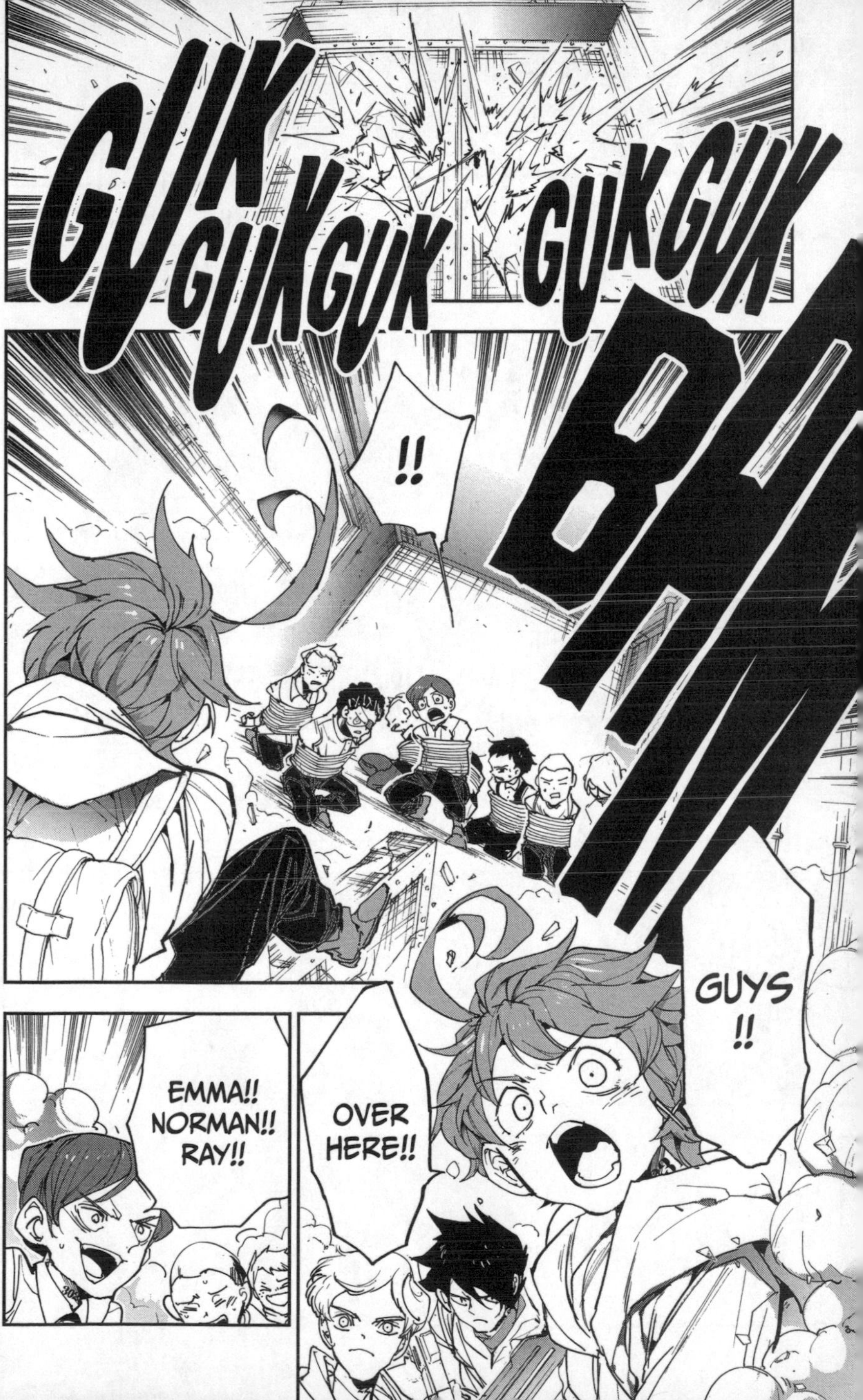
GUKGUK
GUK GUKGUK
!!
GUYS !!
OVER HERE!!
EMMA!! NORMAN!! RAY!!

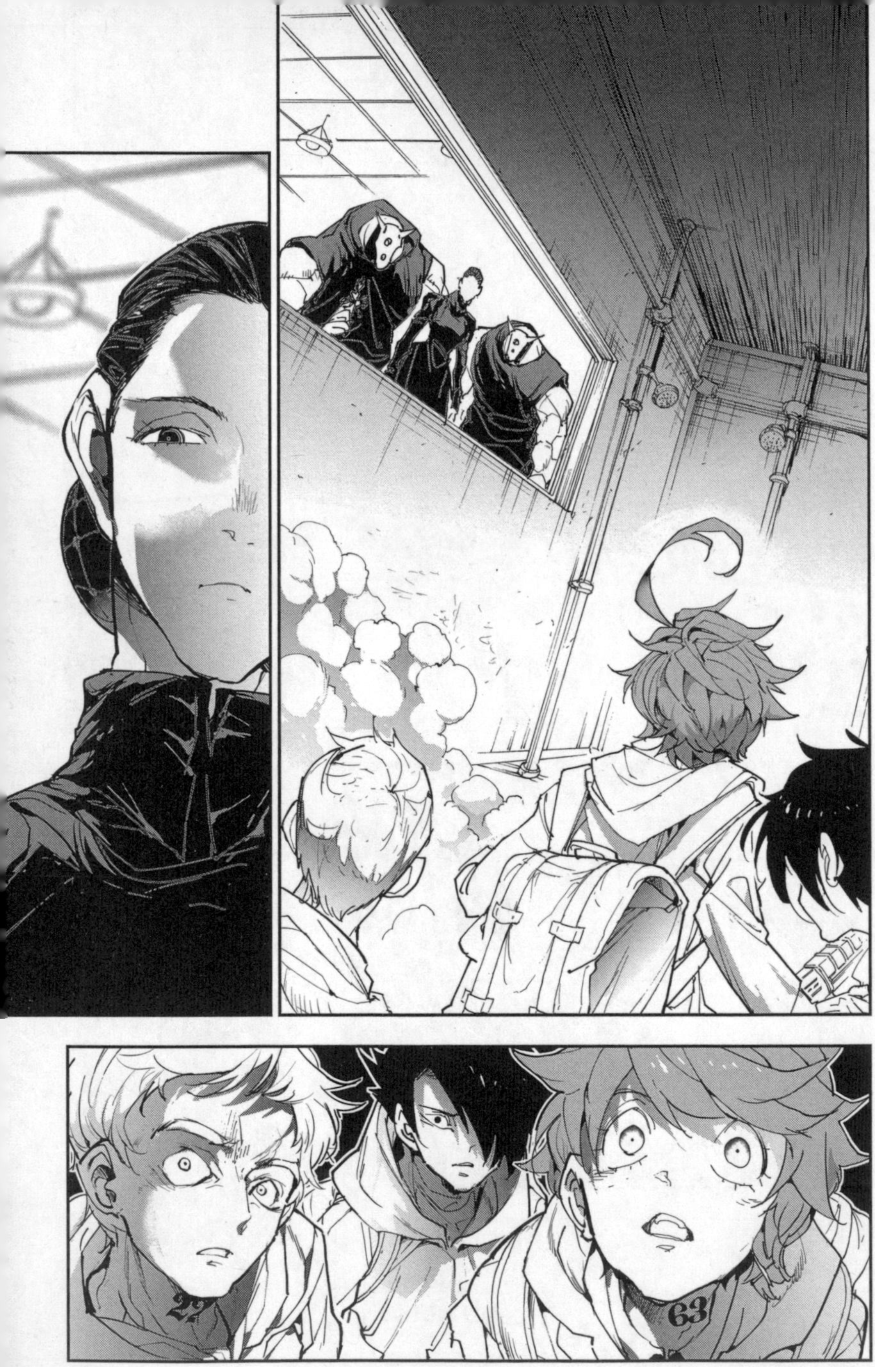
63

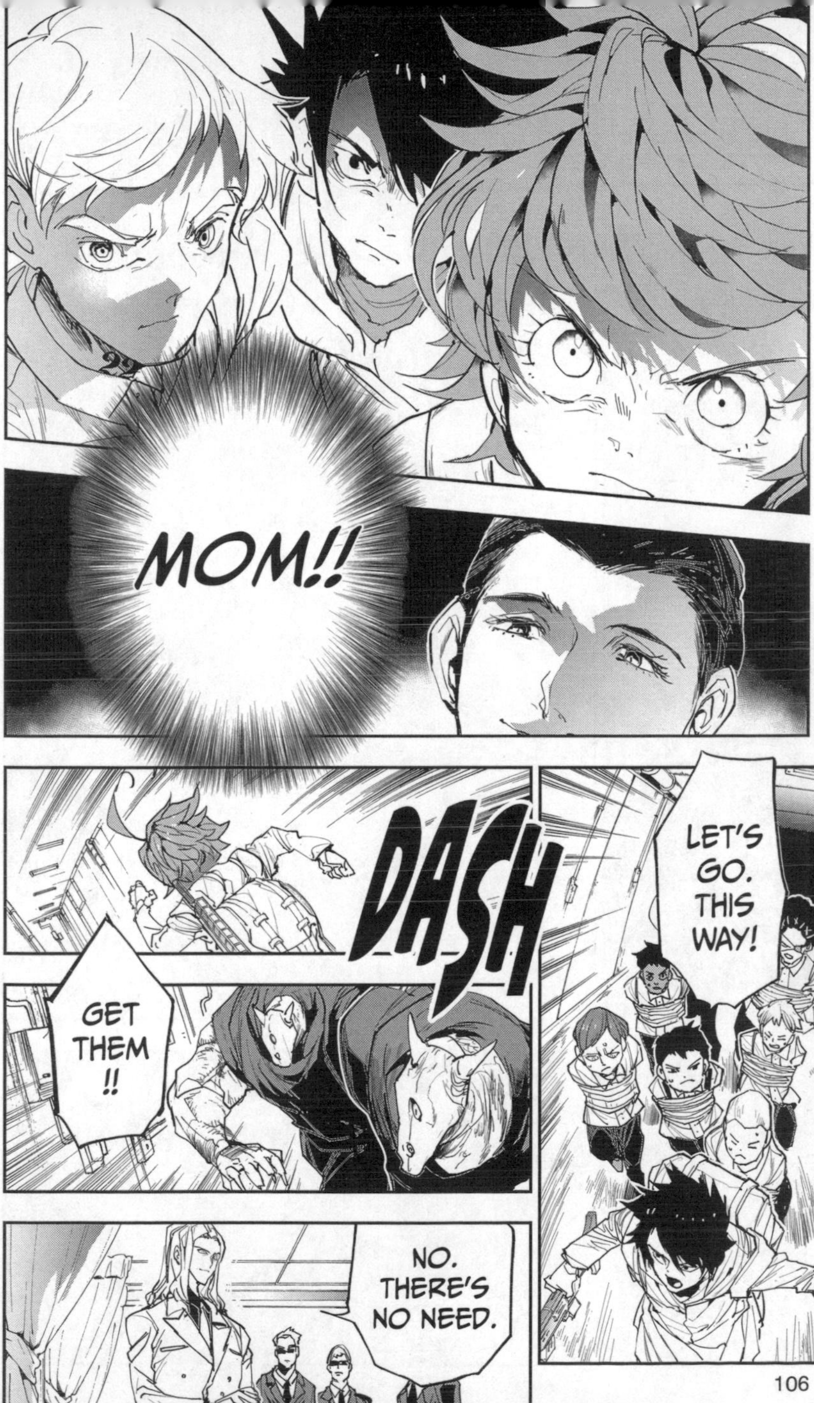
MOM!!
LET'S GO. THIS WAY!
DASH
GET THEM!!
NO. THERE'S NO NEED.

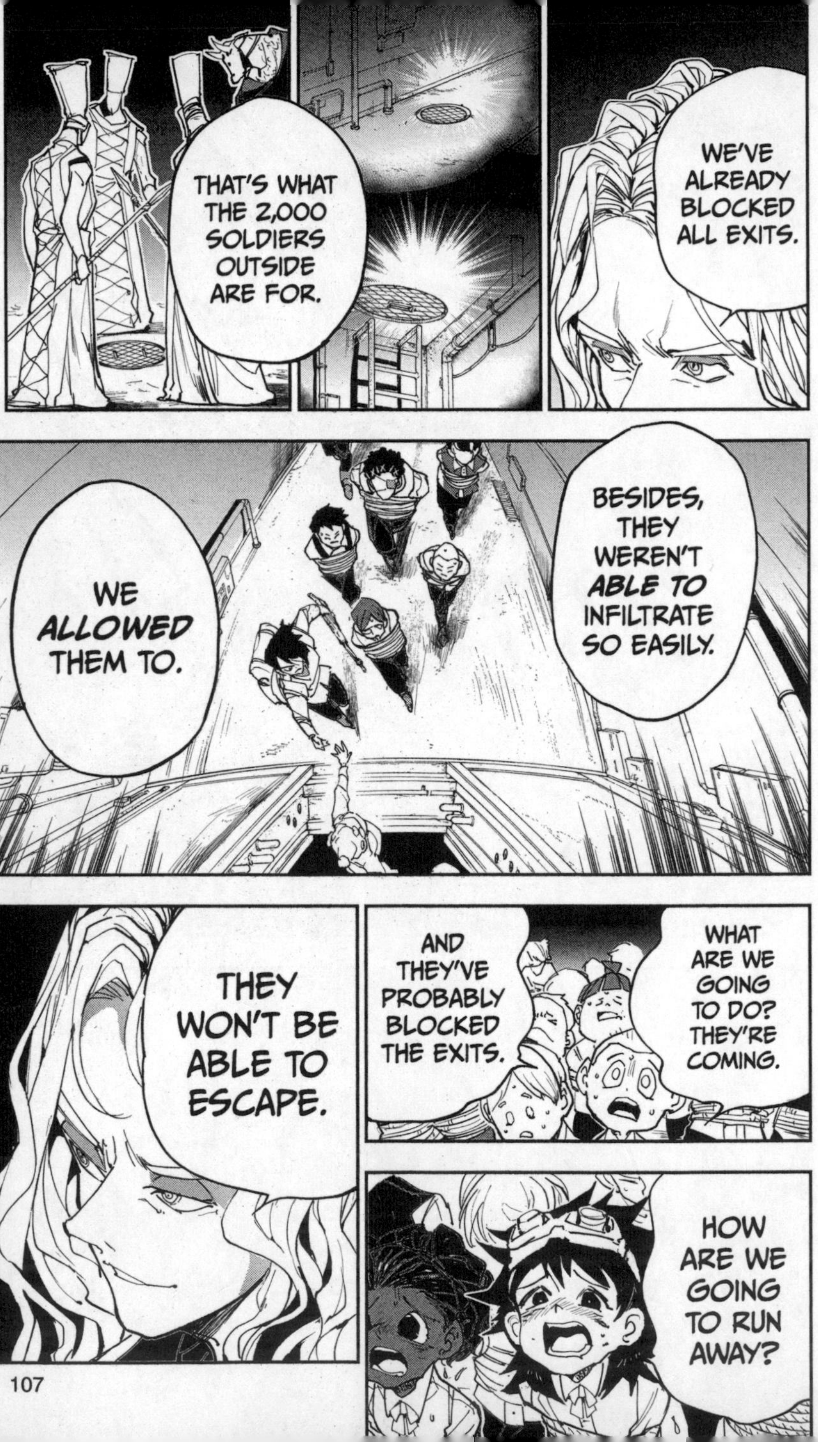
WE'VE ALREADY BLOCKED ALL EXITS.
THAT'S WHAT THE 2,000 SOLDIERS OUTSIDE ARE FOR.
BESIDES, THEY WEREN'T *ABLE TO* INFILTRATE SO EASILY.
WE *ALLOWED* THEM TO.
WHAT ARE WE GOING TO DO? THEY'RE COMING.
AND THEY'VE PROBABLY BLOCKED THE EXITS.
HOW ARE WE GOING TO RUN AWAY?
THEY WON'T BE ABLE TO ESCAPE.

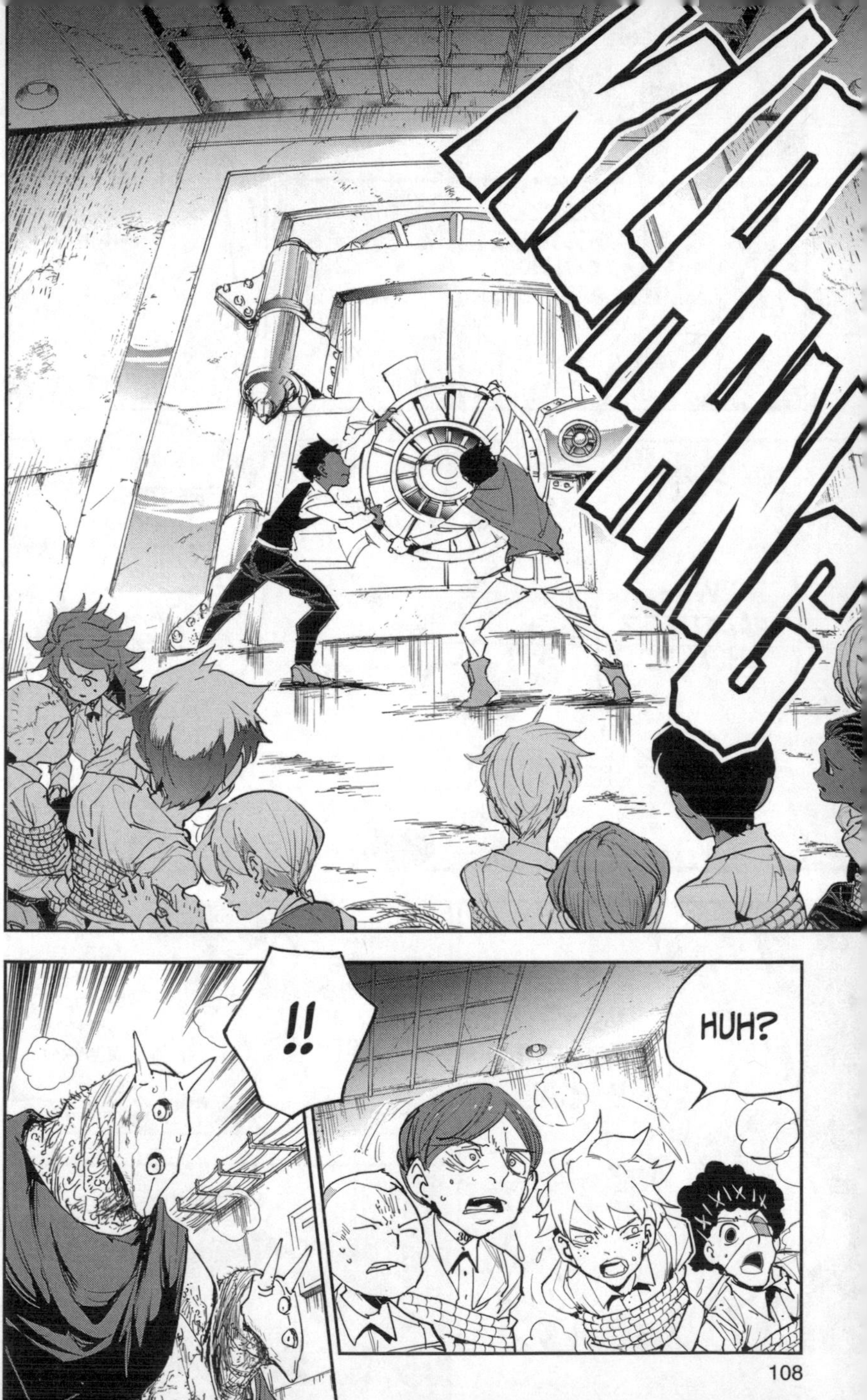
HUH?
!!

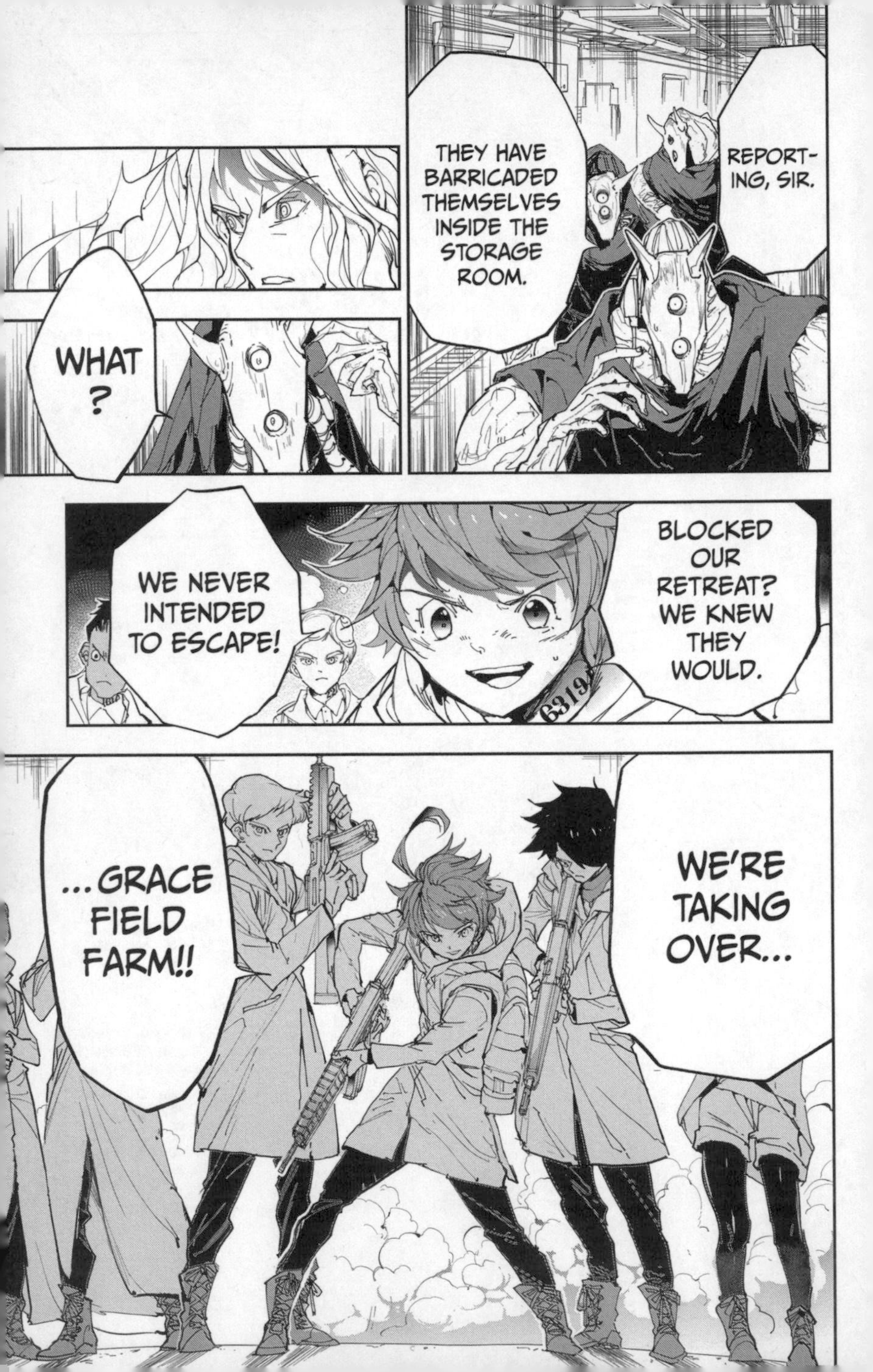
REPORTING, SIR.
THEY HAVE BARRICADED THEMSELVES INSIDE THE STORAGE ROOM.
WHAT?
BLOCKED OUR RETREAT? WE KNEW THEY WOULD.
WE NEVER INTENDED TO ESCAPE!
WE'RE TAKING OVER...
...GRACE FIELD FARM!!

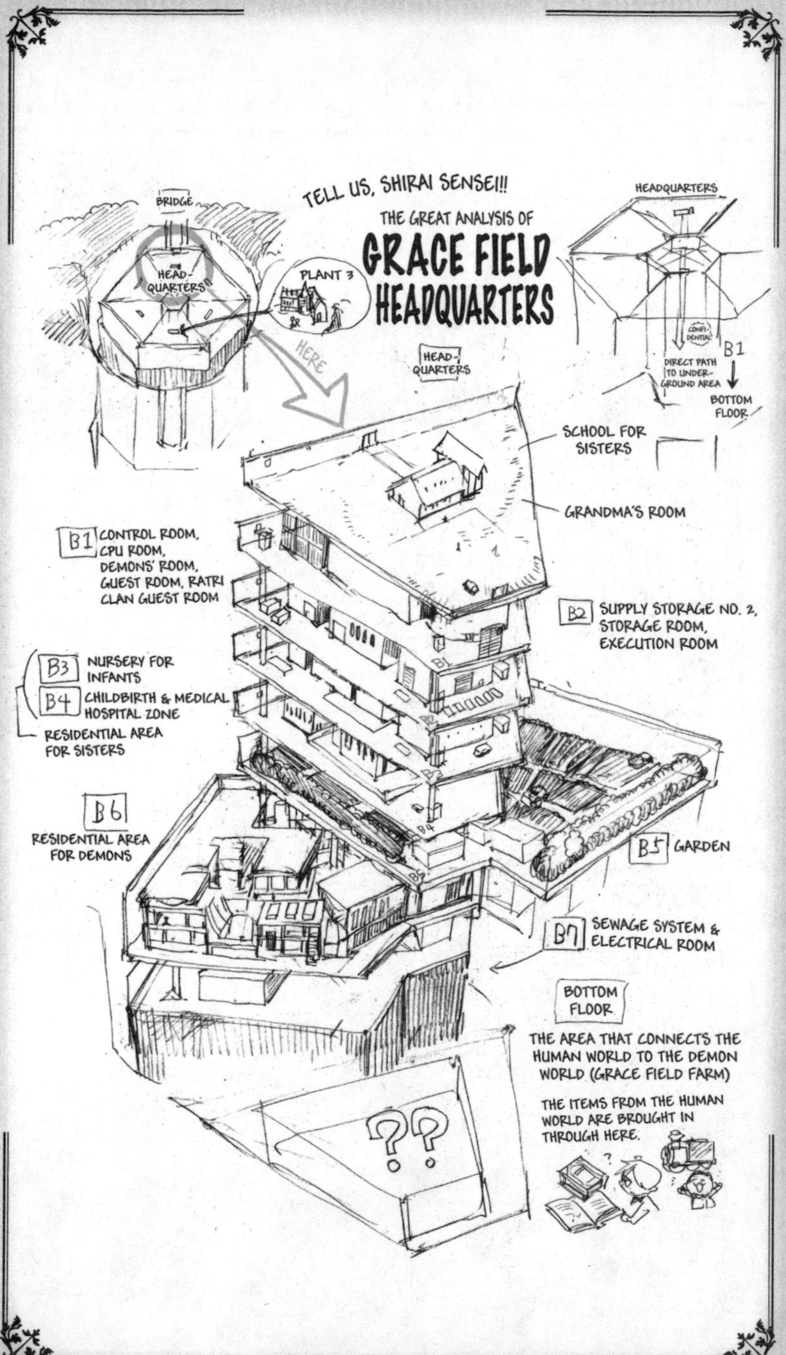
TELL US, SHIRAI SENSEI!!
THE GREAT ANALYSIS OF
GRACE FIELD HEADQUARTERS
BRIDGE
HEAD-QUARTERS
PLANT 3
HERE
HEADQUARTERS
CONFI-DENTIAL
DIRECT PATH TO UNDER-GROUND AREA
B1
BOTTOM FLOOR
HEAD-QUARTERS
SCHOOL FOR SISTERS
GRANDMA'S ROOM
B1 CONTROL ROOM, CPU ROOM, DEMONS' ROOM, GUEST ROOM, RATRI CLAN GUEST ROOM
B2 SUPPLY STORAGE NO. 2, STORAGE ROOM, EXECUTION ROOM
B3 NURSERY FOR INFANTS
B4 CHILDBIRTH & MEDICAL HOSPITAL ZONE
RESIDENTIAL AREA FOR SISTERS
B6
RESIDENTIAL AREA FOR DEMONS
B5 GARDEN
B7 SEWAGE SYSTEM & ELECTRICAL ROOM
BOTTOM FLOOR
THE AREA THAT CONNECTS THE HUMAN WORLD TO THE DEMON WORLD (GRACE FIELD FARM)
THE ITEMS FROM THE HUMAN WORLD ARE BROUGHT IN THROUGH HERE.
??

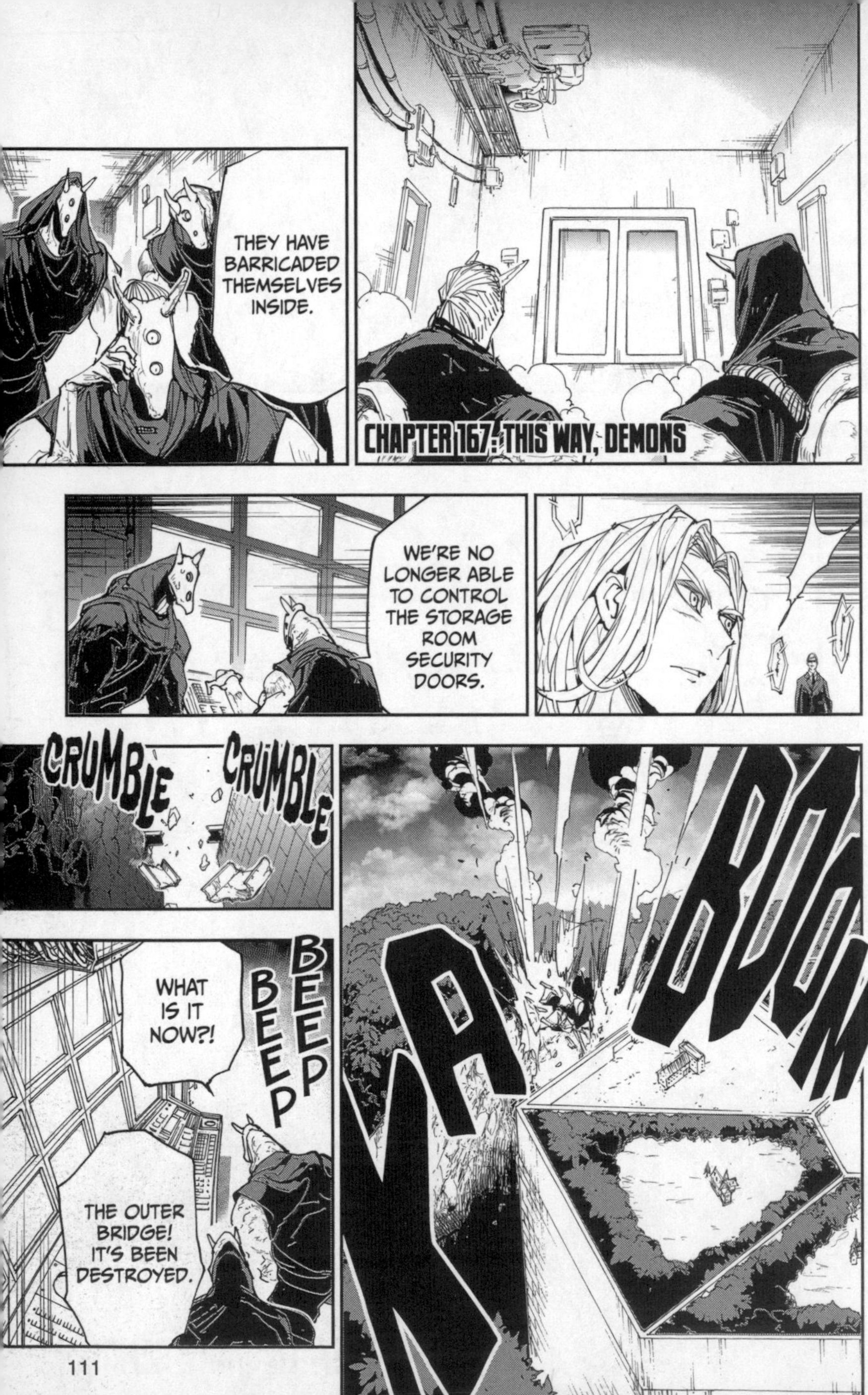
CHAPTER 167: THIS WAY, DEMONS
THEY HAVE BARRICADED THEMSELVES INSIDE.
WE'RE NO LONGER ABLE TO CONTROL THE STORAGE ROOM SECURITY DOORS.
KA BOOM
CRUMBLE
CRUMBLE
BEEP
BEEP
WHAT IS IT NOW?!
THE OUTER BRIDGE! IT'S BEEN DESTROYED.

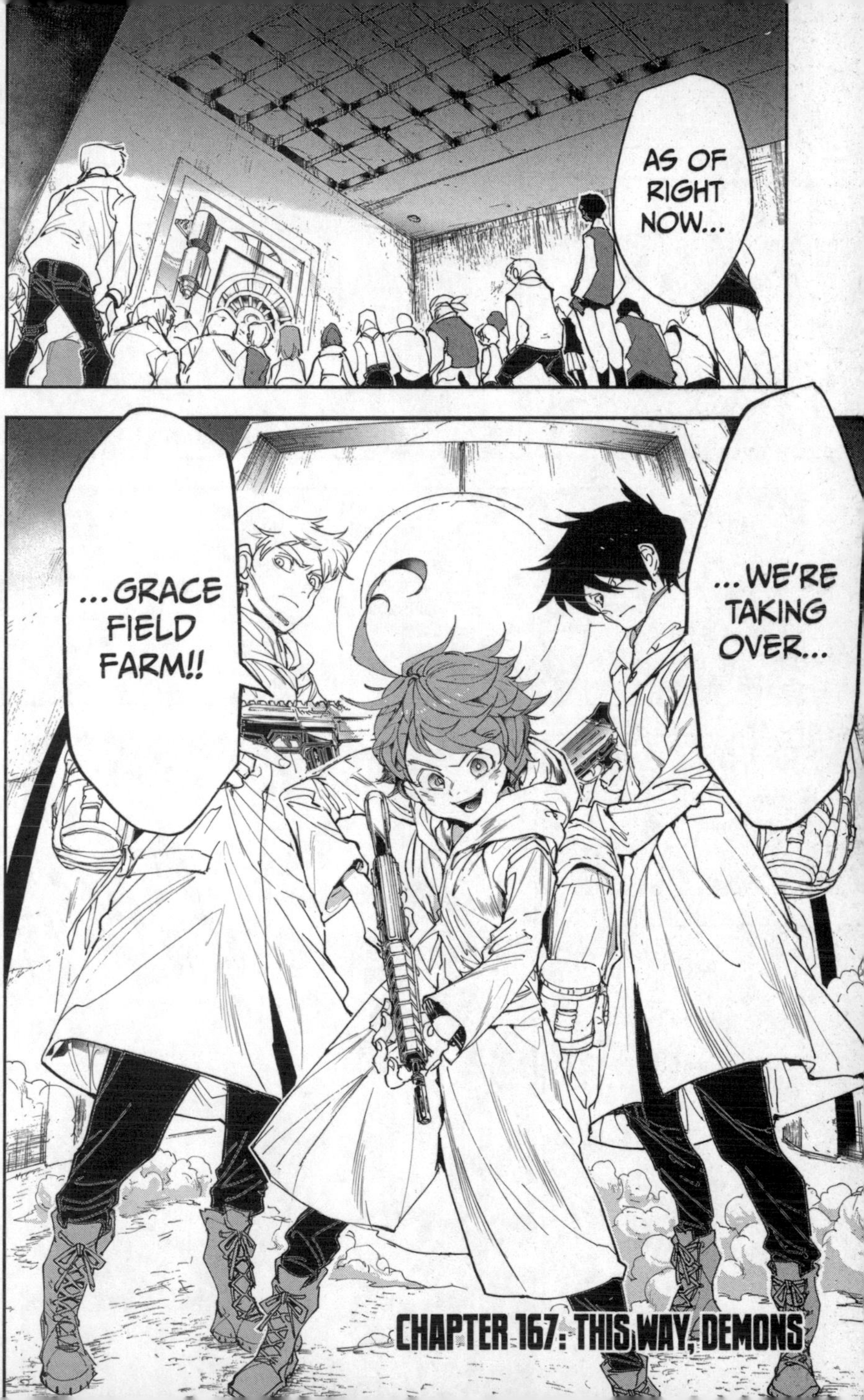
AS OF RIGHT NOW...
...WE'RE TAKING OVER...
...GRACE FIELD FARM!!
CHAPTER 167: THIS WAY, DEMONS

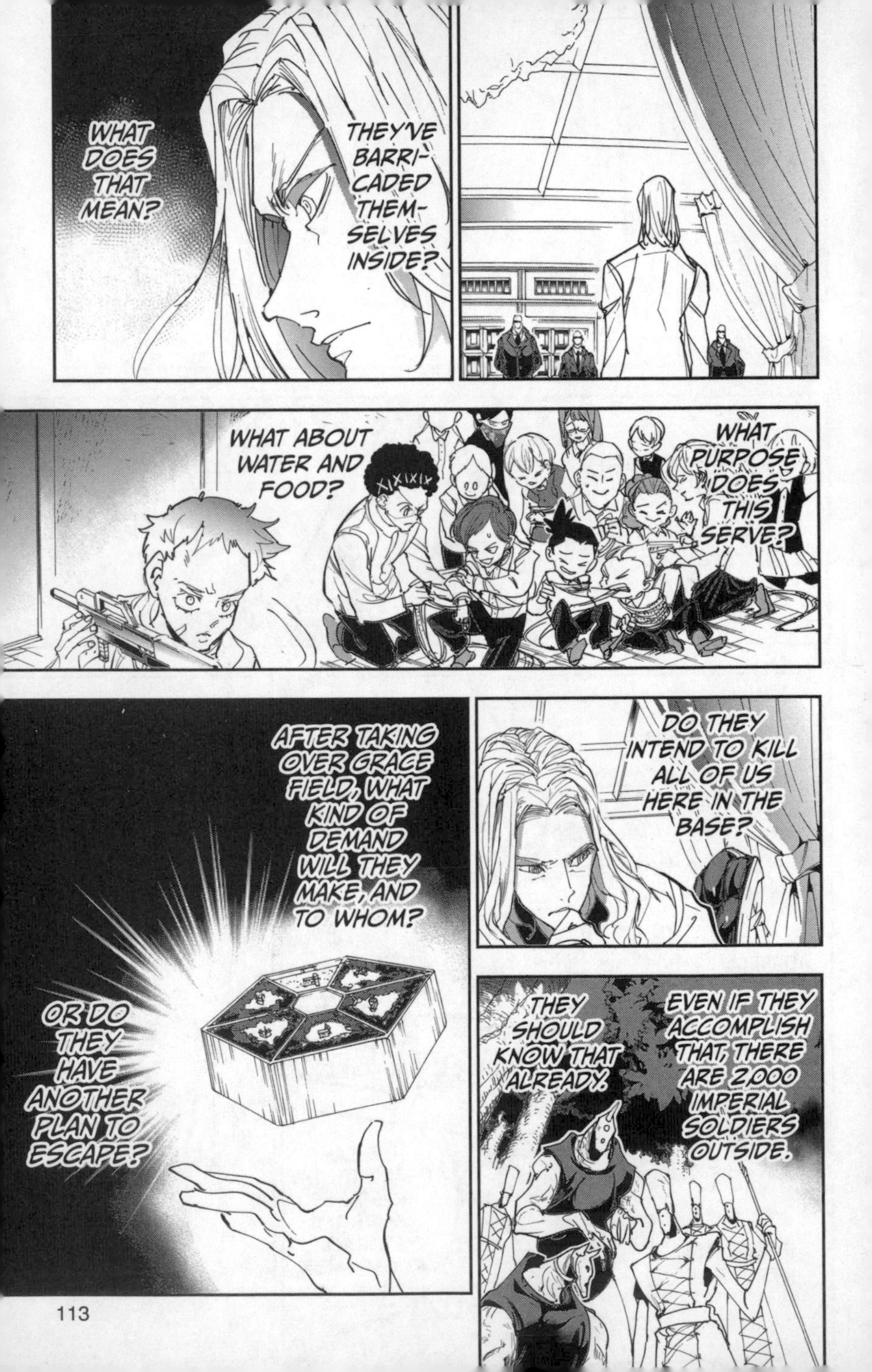
THEY'VE BARRICADED THEMSELVES INSIDE?
WHAT DOES THAT MEAN?
WHAT PURPOSE DOES THIS SERVE?
WHAT ABOUT WATER AND FOOD?
DO THEY INTEND TO KILL ALL OF US HERE IN THE BASE?
EVEN IF THEY ACCOMPLISH THAT, THERE ARE 2,000 IMPERIAL SOLDIERS OUTSIDE.
THEY SHOULD KNOW THAT ALREADY.
AFTER TAKING OVER GRACE FIELD, WHAT KIND OF DEMAND WILL THEY MAKE, AND TO WHOM?
OR DO THEY HAVE ANOTHER PLAN TO ESCAPE?

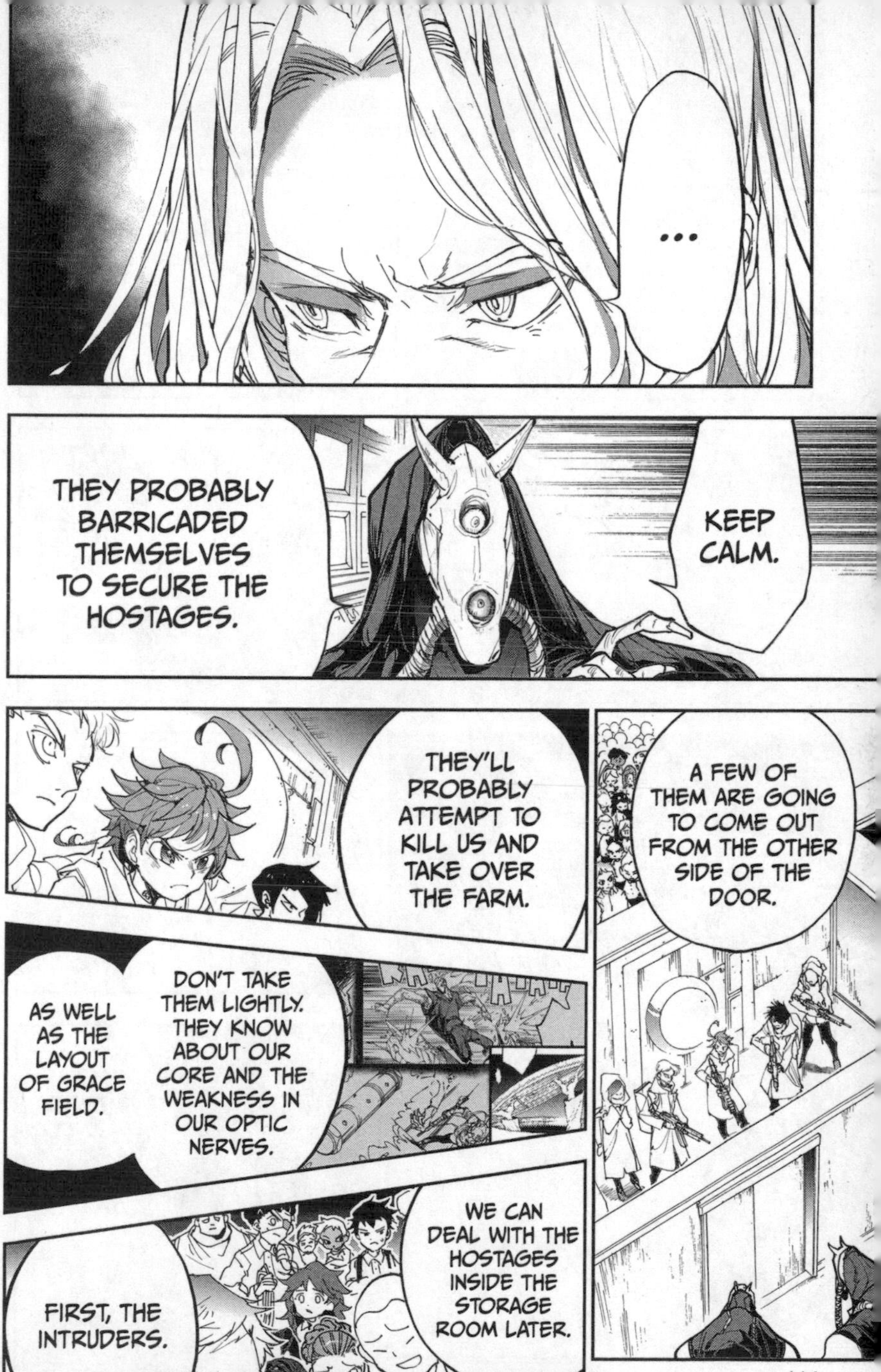
...
KEEP CALM.
THEY PROBABLY BARRICADED THEMSELVES TO SECURE THE HOSTAGES.
A FEW OF THEM ARE GOING TO COME OUT FROM THE OTHER SIDE OF THE DOOR.
THEY'LL PROBABLY ATTEMPT TO KILL US AND TAKE OVER THE FARM.
DON'T TAKE THEM LIGHTLY. THEY KNOW ABOUT OUR CORE AND THE WEAKNESS IN OUR OPTIC NERVES.
AS WELL AS THE LAYOUT OF GRACE FIELD.
WE CAN DEAL WITH THE HOSTAGES INSIDE THE STORAGE ROOM LATER.
FIRST, THE INTRUDERS.

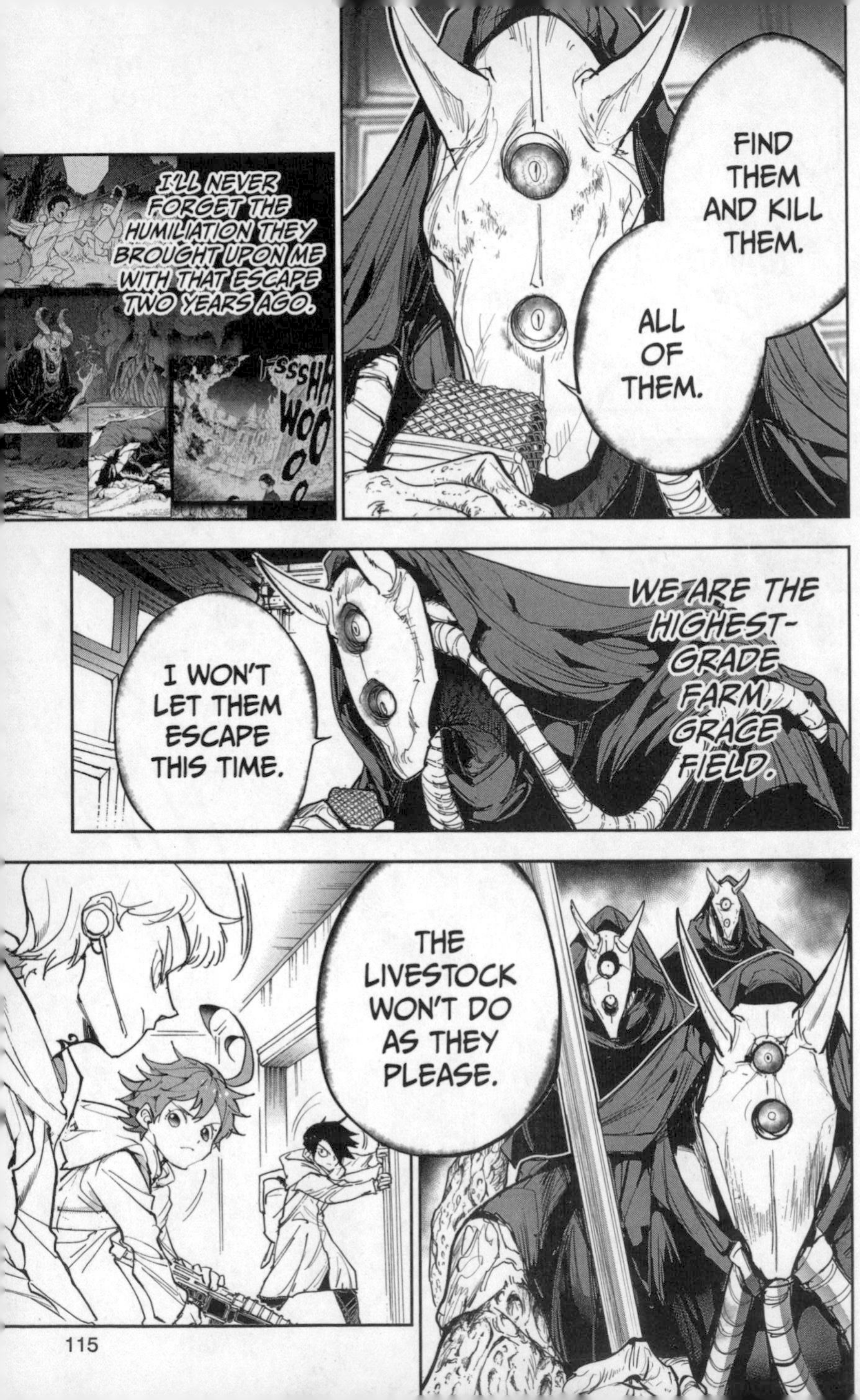
FIND THEM AND KILL THEM.
ALL OF THEM.
I'LL NEVER FORGET THE HUMILIATION THEY BROUGHT UPON ME WITH THAT ESCAPE TWO YEARS AGO.
WOOO
WE ARE THE HIGHEST-GRADE FARM, GRACE FIELD.
I WON'T LET THEM ESCAPE THIS TIME.
THE LIVESTOCK WON'T DO AS THEY PLEASE.

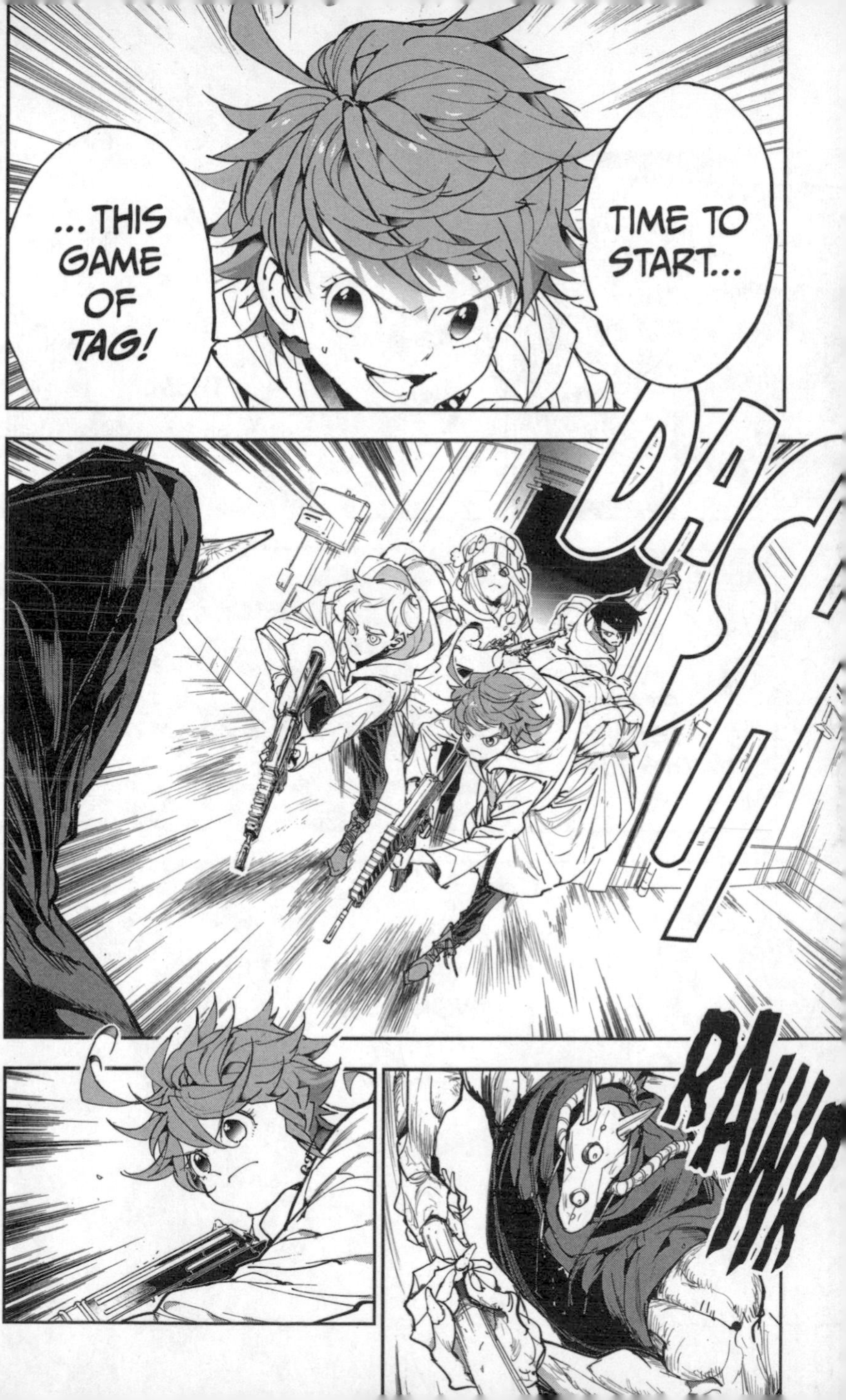
TIME TO START...
...THIS GAME OF TAG!
DASH

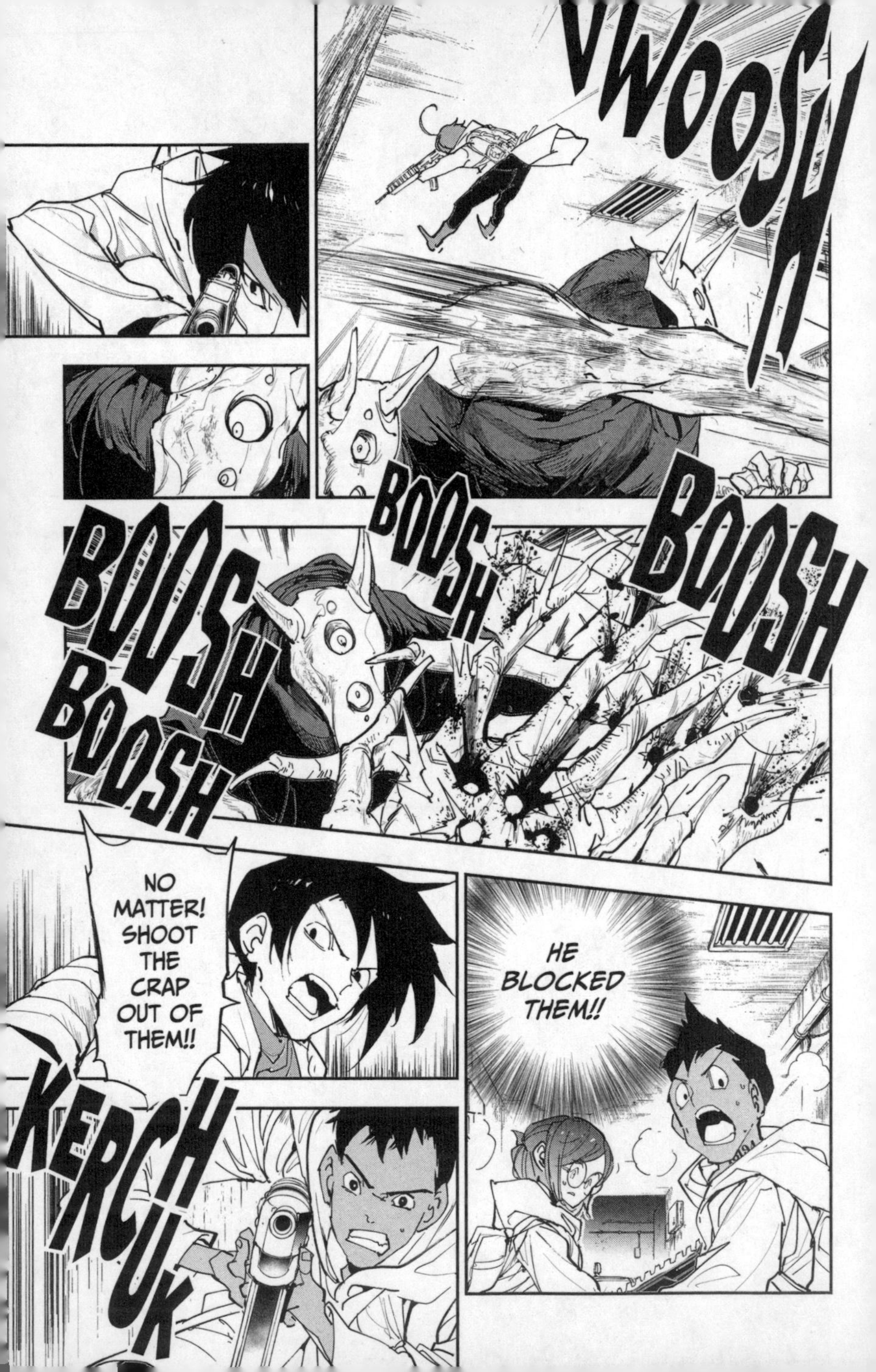
VWOOSH
BOOSH
BOOSH
BOOSH
BOOSH
HE BLOCKED THEM!!
NO MATTER! SHOOT THE CRAP OUT OF THEM!!
KERCHUK

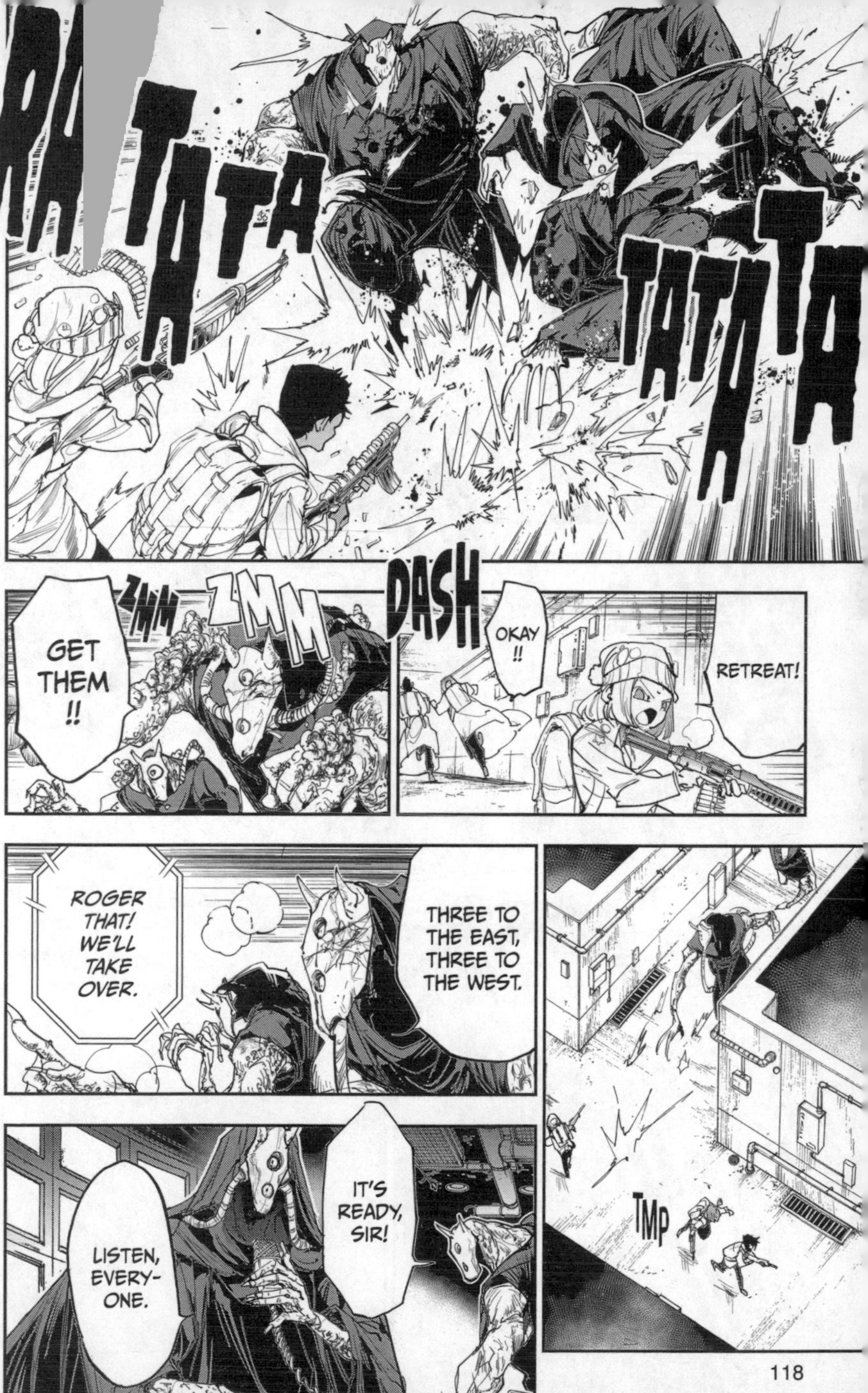
RATATA
TATATA
RETREAT!
OKAY !!
DASH
ZMM
ZMM
GET THEM !!
TMP
THREE TO THE EAST, THREE TO THE WEST.
ROGER THAT! WE'LL TAKE OVER.
IT'S READY, SIR!
LISTEN, EVERYONE.

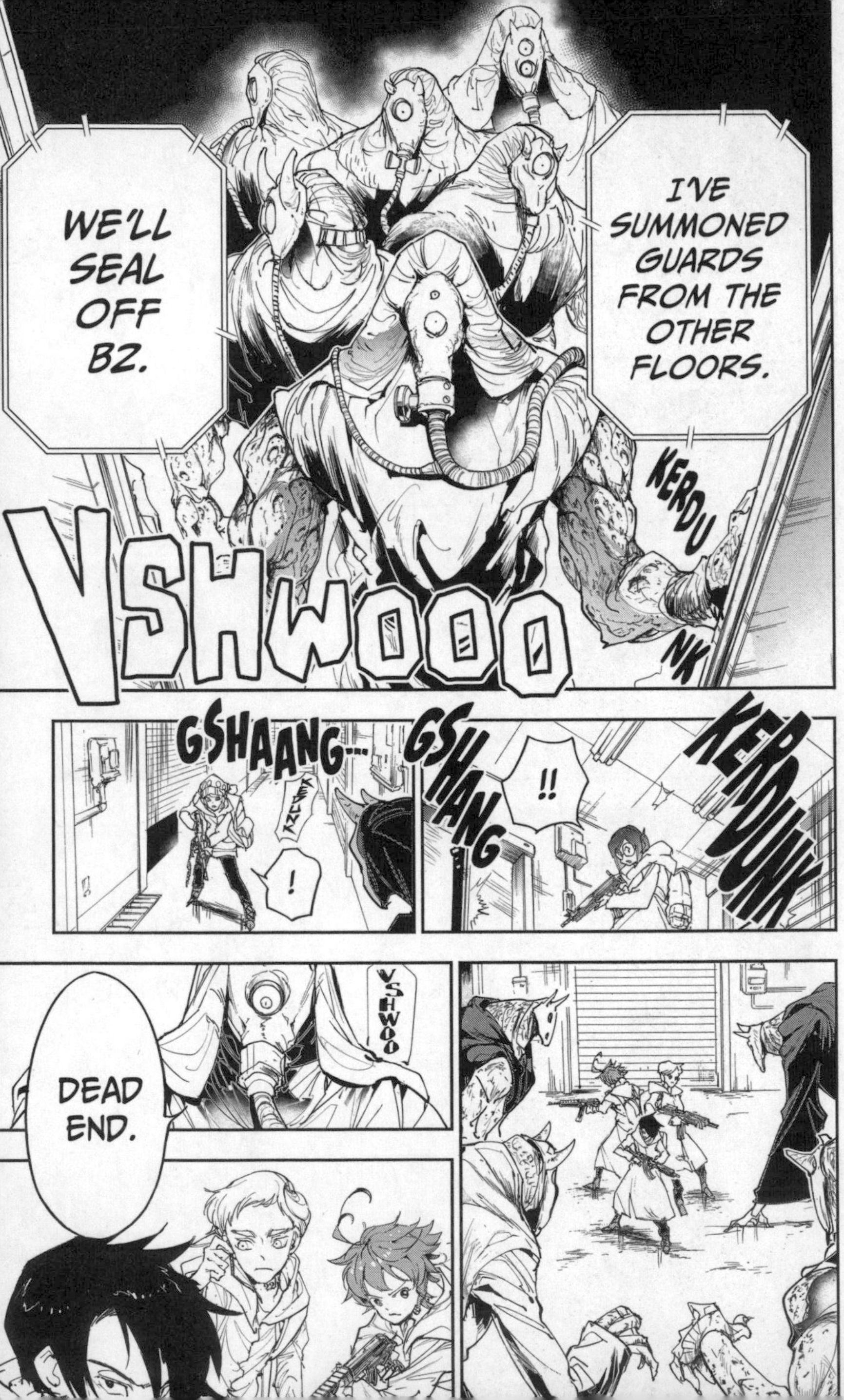
I'VE SUMMONED GUARDS FROM THE OTHER FLOORS.
WE'LL SEAL OFF B2.
KERDUNK
VSHWOOO
KERDUNK
GSHANG
!!
GSHAANG...
KERDUNK
!
VSHWOO
DEAD END.

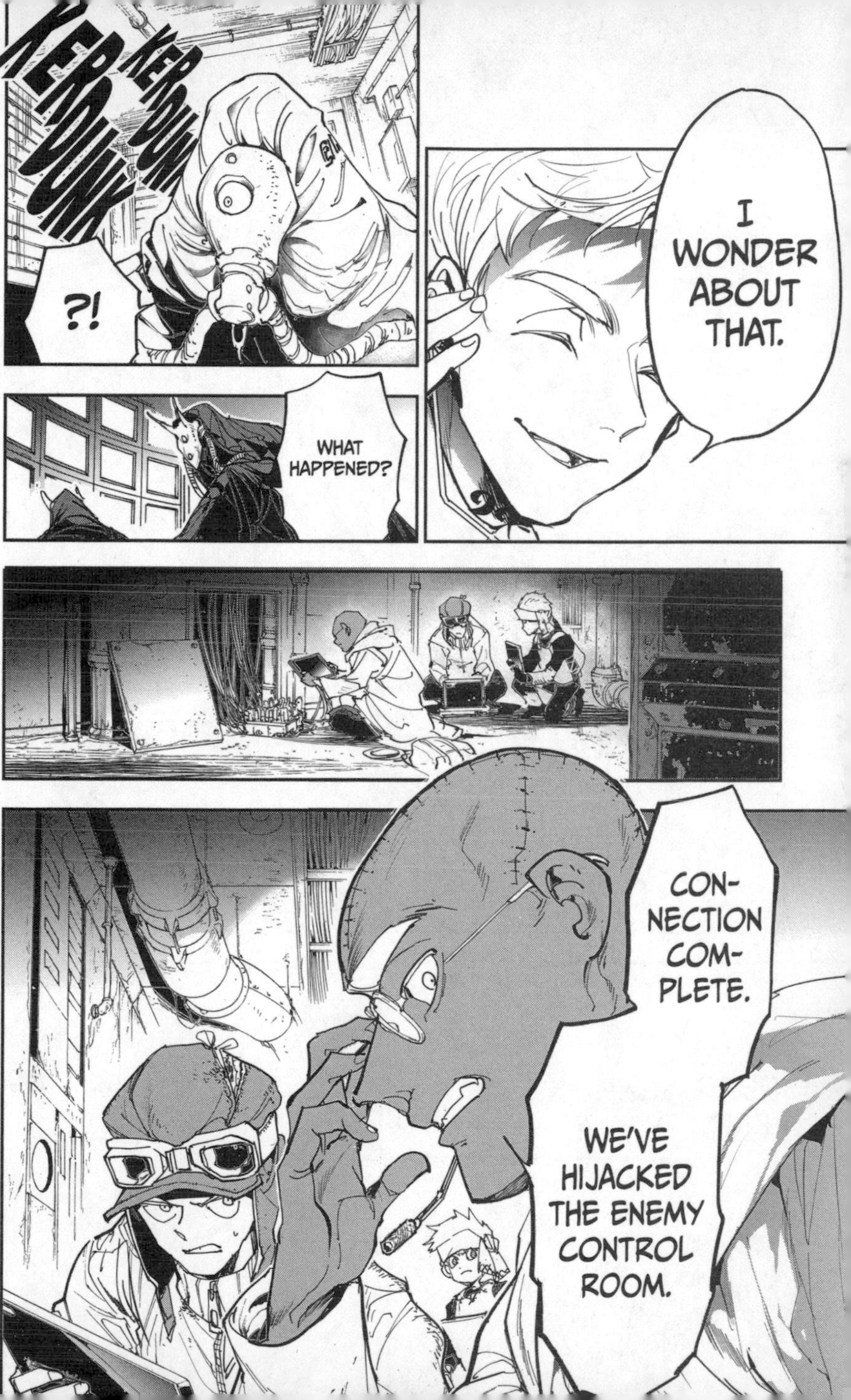
I WONDER ABOUT THAT.
KER DUNK
KER DUNK
?!
WHAT HAPPENED?
CON-NECTION COM-PLETE.
WE'VE HIJACKED THE ENEMY CONTROL ROOM.

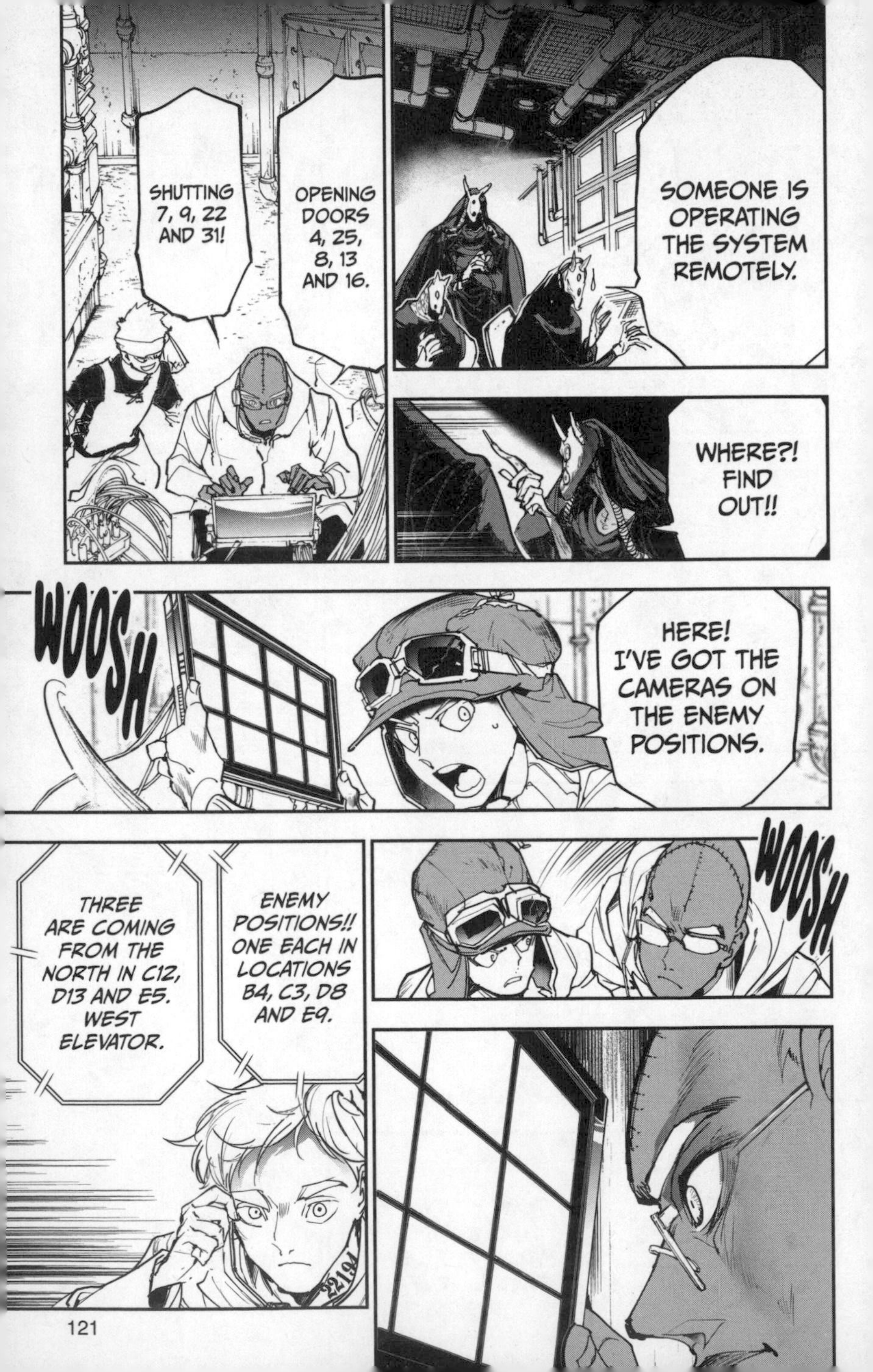

SOMEONE IS OPERATING THE SYSTEM REMOTELY.
WHERE?! FIND OUT!!
OPENING DOORS 4, 25, 8, 13 AND 16.
SHUTTING 7, 9, 22 AND 31!
HERE! I'VE GOT THE CAMERAS ON THE ENEMY POSITIONS.
WOOSH
WOOSH
ENEMY POSITIONS!! ONE EACH IN LOCATIONS B4, C3, D8 AND E9.
THREE ARE COMING FROM THE NORTH IN C12, D13 AND E5. WEST ELEVATOR.
22194

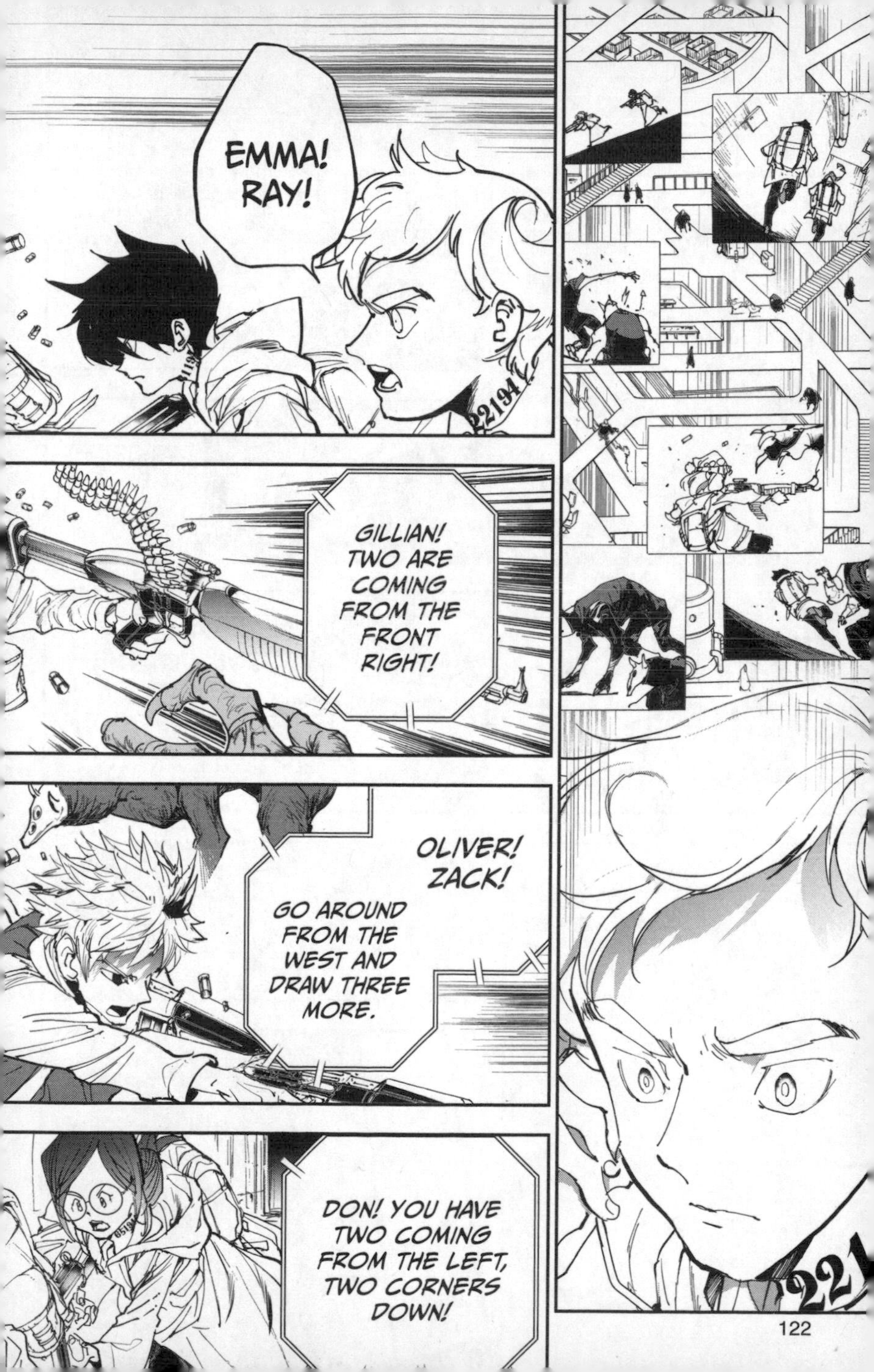
EMMA! RAY!
GILLIAN! TWO ARE COMING FROM THE FRONT RIGHT!
OLIVER! ZACK!
GO AROUND FROM THE WEST AND DRAW THREE MORE.
DON! YOU HAVE TWO COMING FROM THE LEFT, TWO CORNERS DOWN!

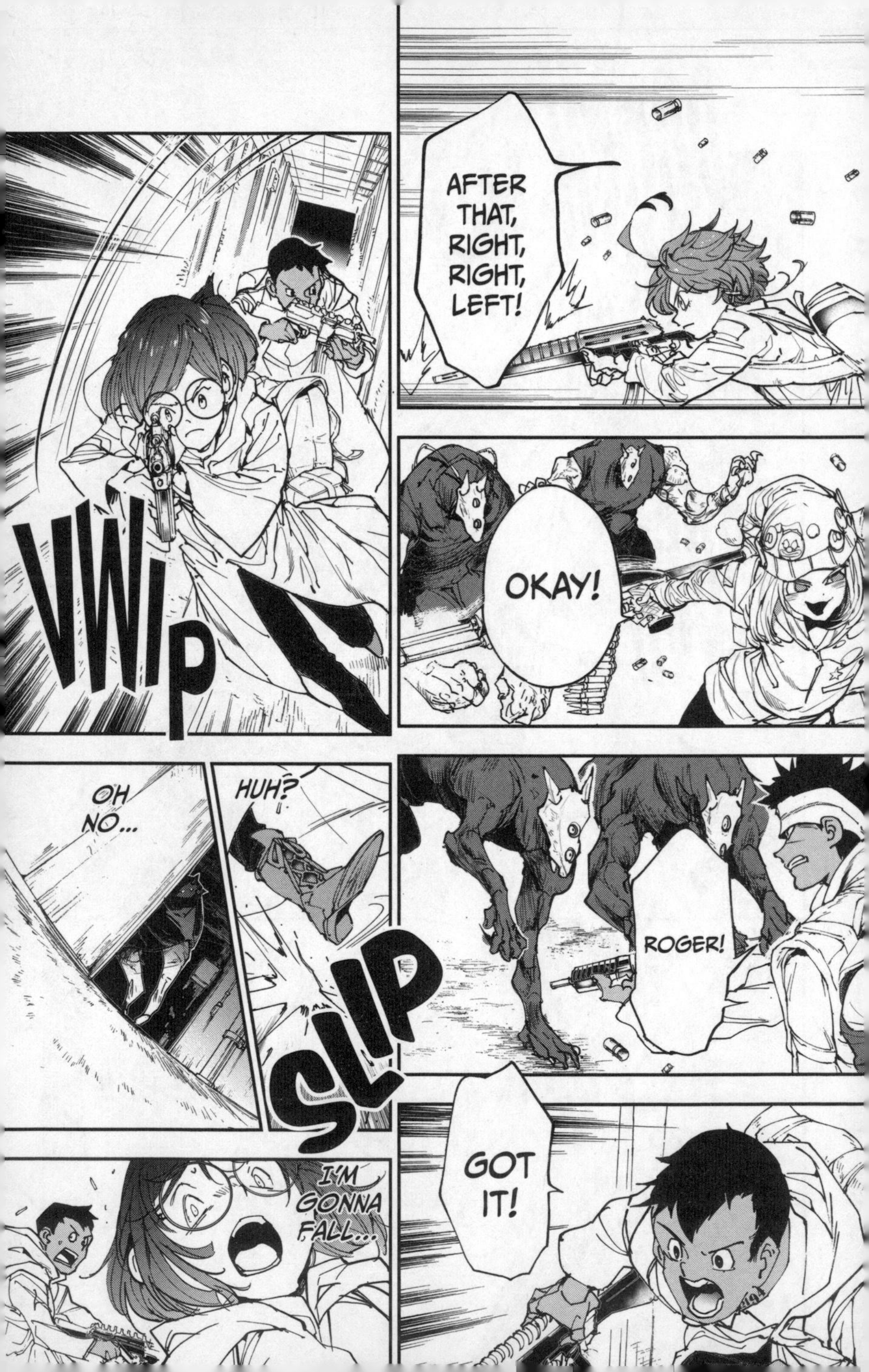

AFTER THAT, RIGHT, RIGHT, LEFT!
OKAY!
VWIP
ROGER!
HUH?
SLIP
OH NO...
GOT IT!
I'M GONNA FALL...

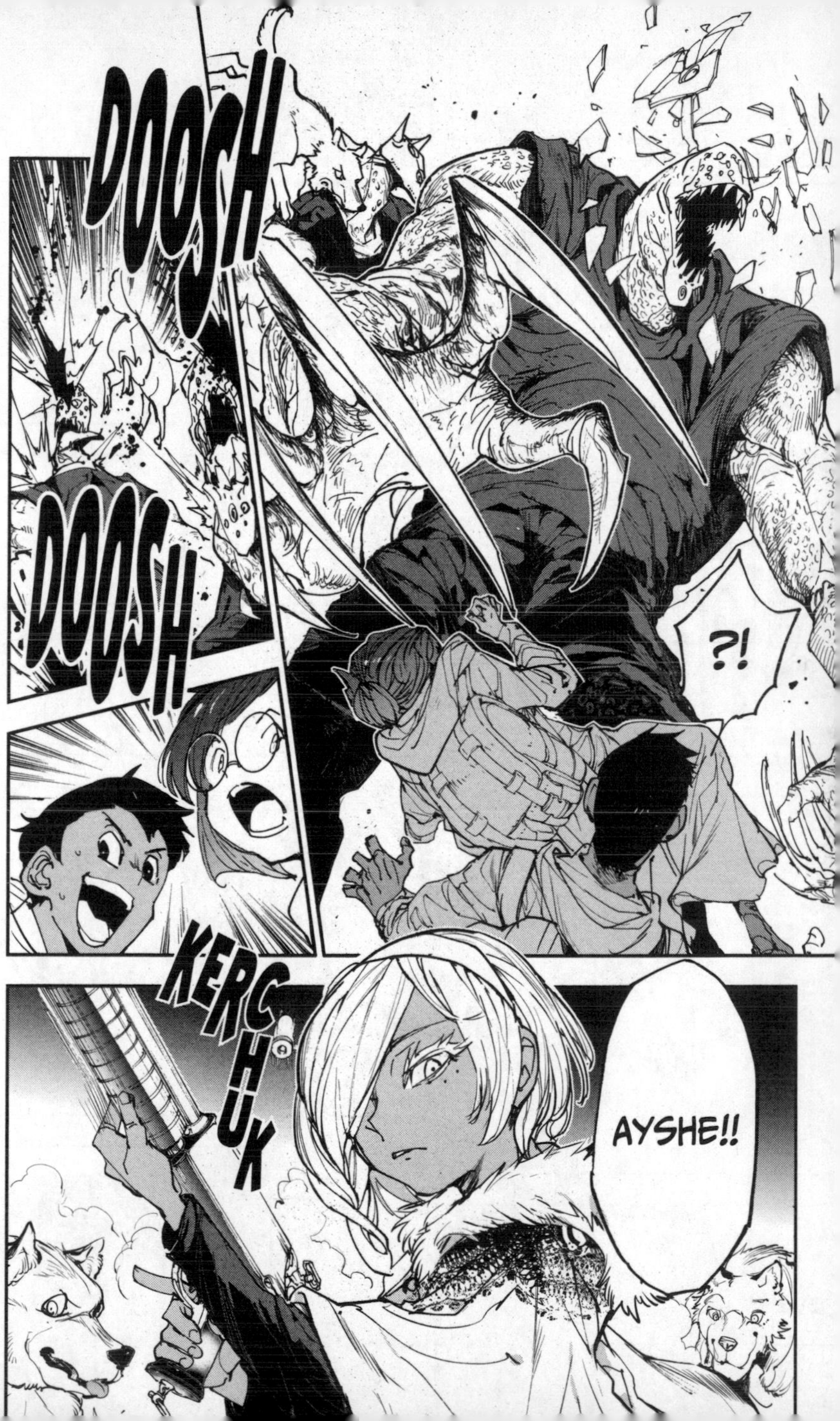
?!
DOOSH
DOOSH
AYSHE!!
KERCHUK

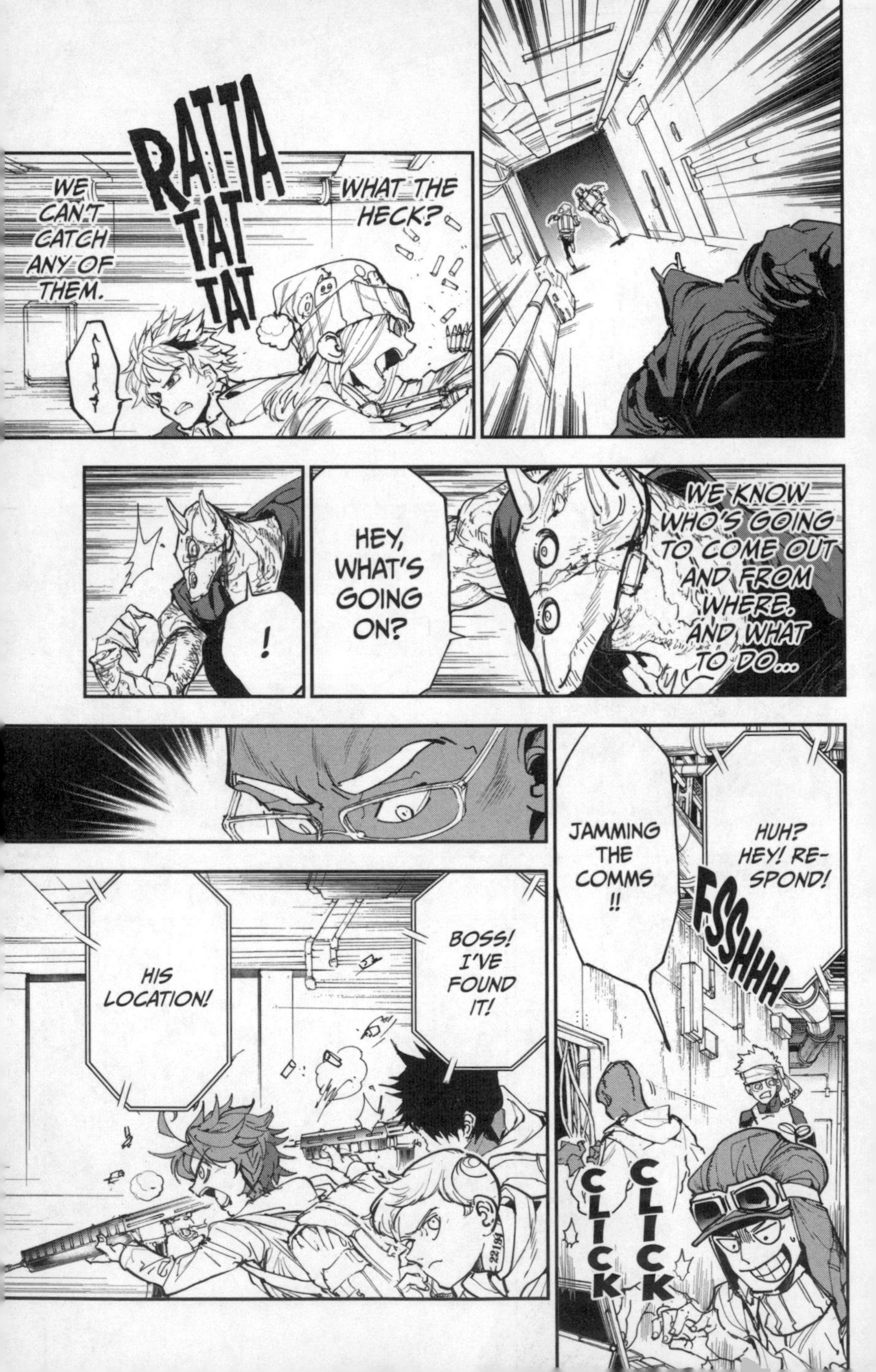
WHAT THE HECK?
RATTA TAT TAT
WE CAN'T CATCH ANY OF THEM.
WE KNOW WHO'S GOING TO COME OUT AND FROM WHERE. AND WHAT TO DO...
HEY, WHAT'S GOING ON?
!
HUH? HEY! RE-SPOND!
FSSHHH
JAMMING THE COMMS !!
CLICK
CLICK
BOSS! I'VE FOUND IT!
HIS LOCATION!

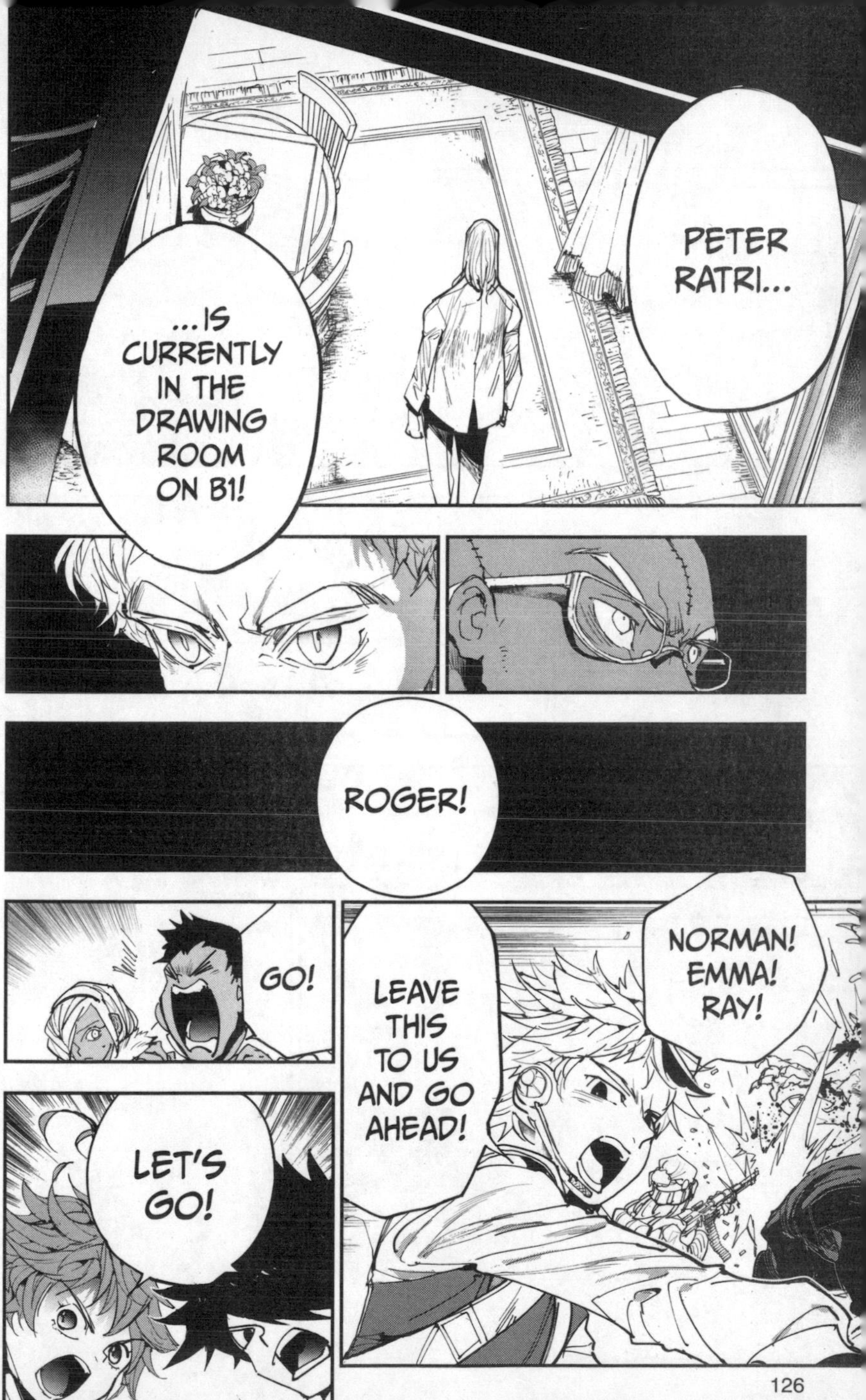
PETER RATRI...
...IS CURRENTLY IN THE DRAWING ROOM ON B1!
ROGER!
NORMAN! EMMA! RAY!
LEAVE THIS TO US AND GO AHEAD!
GO!
LET'S GO!

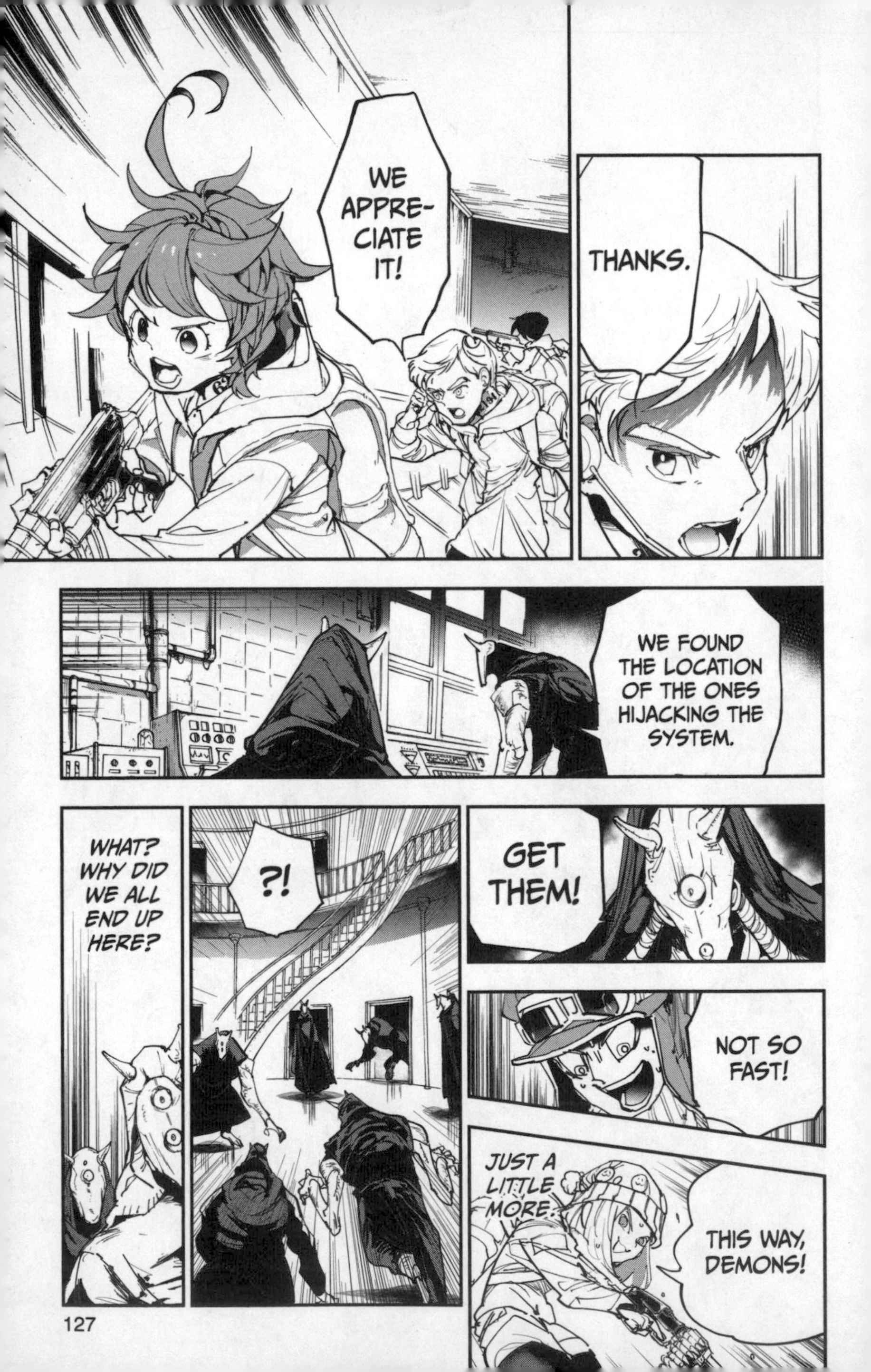
THANKS.
WE APPRECIATE IT!
WE FOUND THE LOCATION OF THE ONES HIJACKING THE SYSTEM.
GET THEM!
NOT SO FAST!
THIS WAY, DEMONS!
JUST A LITTLE MORE.
?!
WHAT? WHY DID WE ALL END UP HERE?

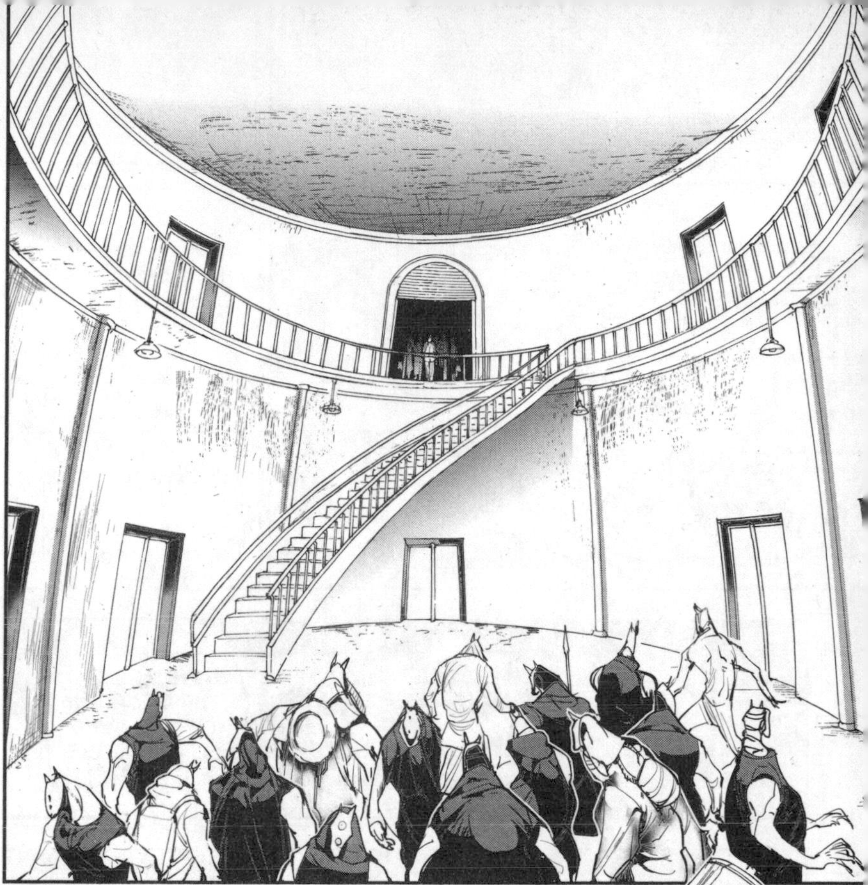
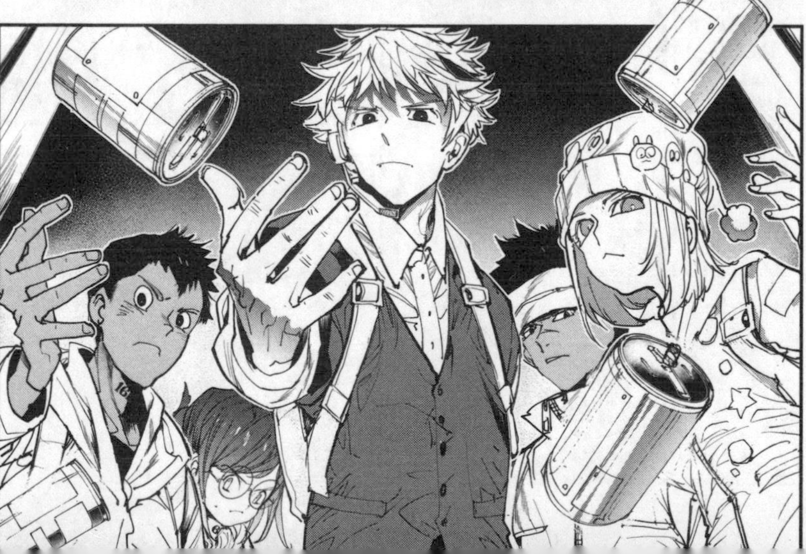

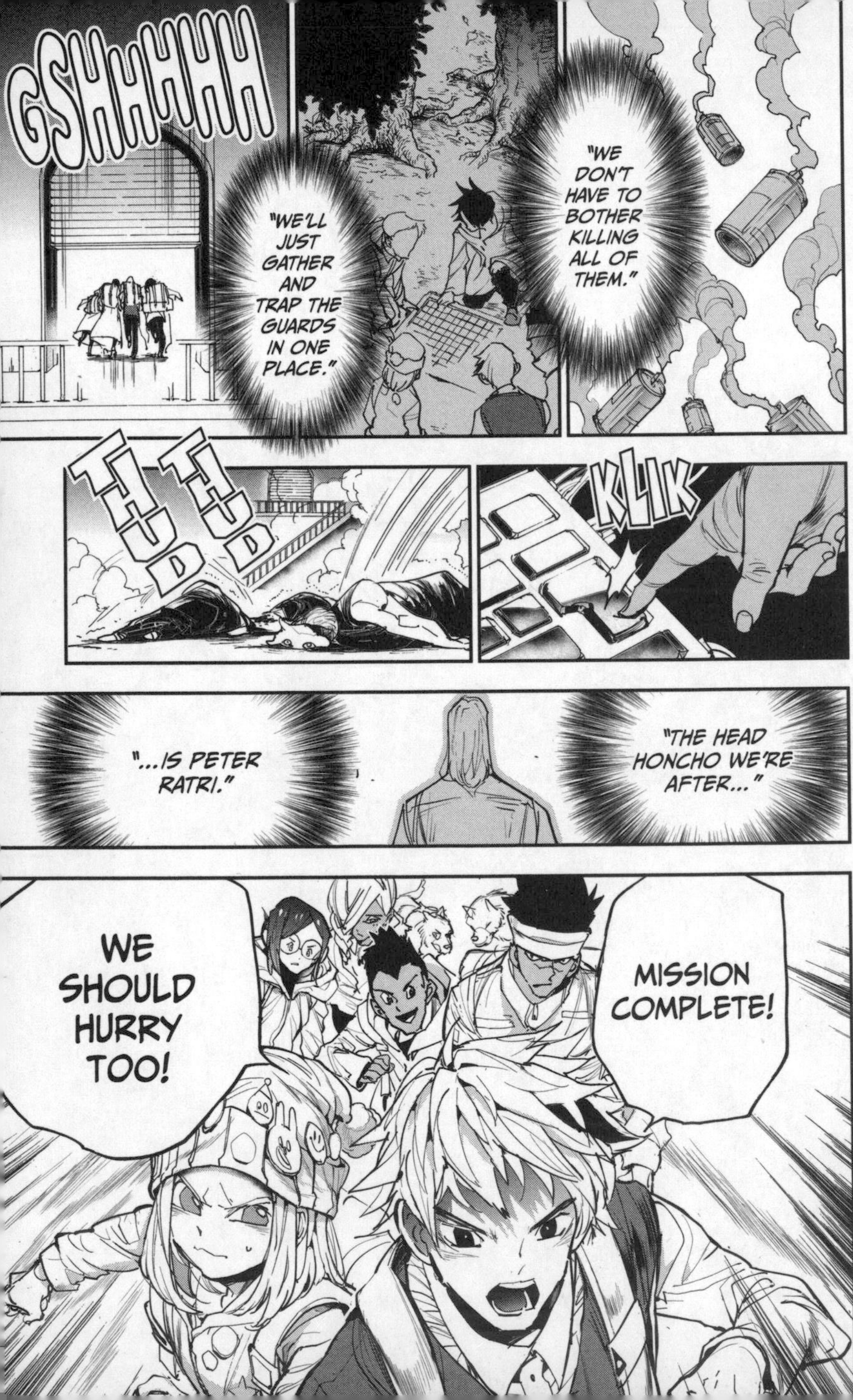
"WE DON'T HAVE TO BOTHER KILLING ALL OF THEM."
"WE'LL JUST GATHER AND TRAP THE GUARDS IN ONE PLACE."
GSHHHHH
KLIK
THUD THUD
"THE HEAD HONCHO WE'RE AFTER..."
"...IS PETER RATRI."
MISSION COMPLETE!
WE SHOULD HURRY TOO!

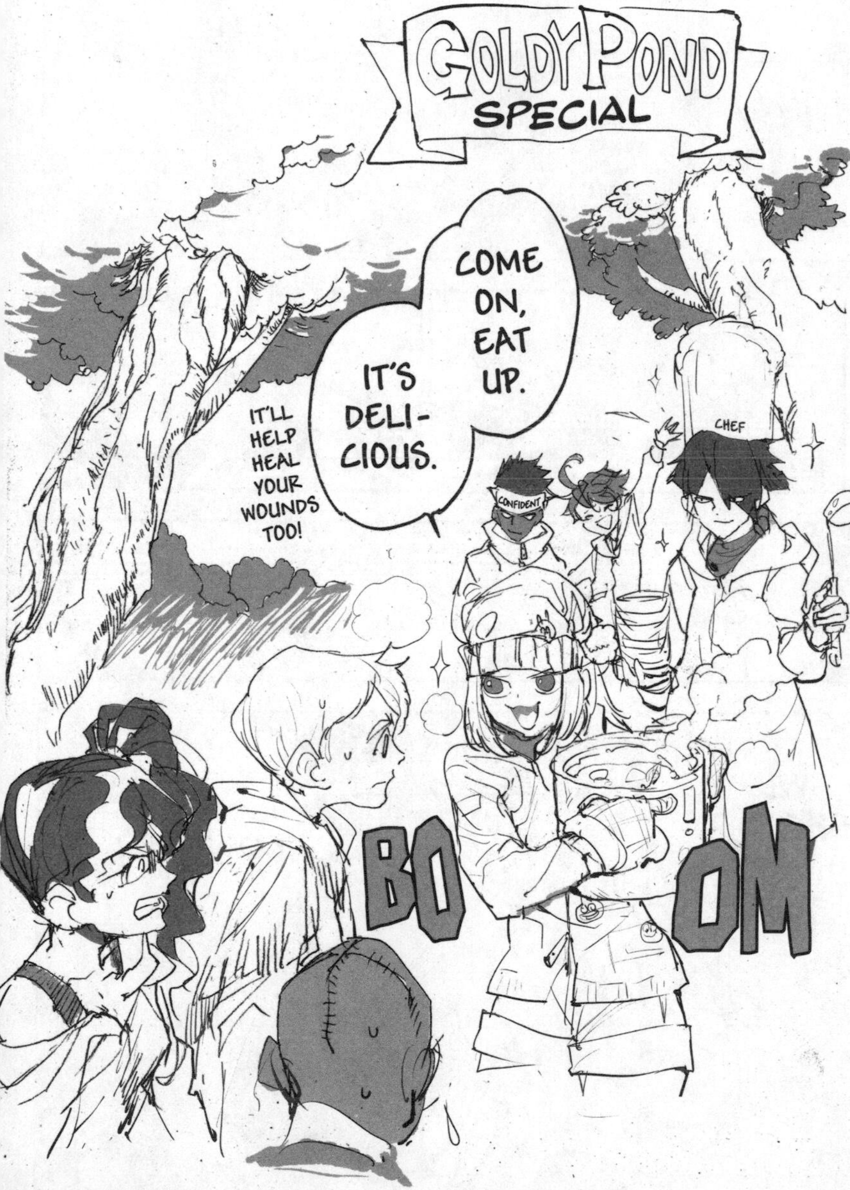
GOLDY POND SPECIAL
CHEF
CONFIDENT
COME ON, EAT UP.
IT'S DELI-CIOUS.
IT'LL HELP HEAL YOUR WOUNDS TOO!
BO OM

CHAPTER 168: DAD

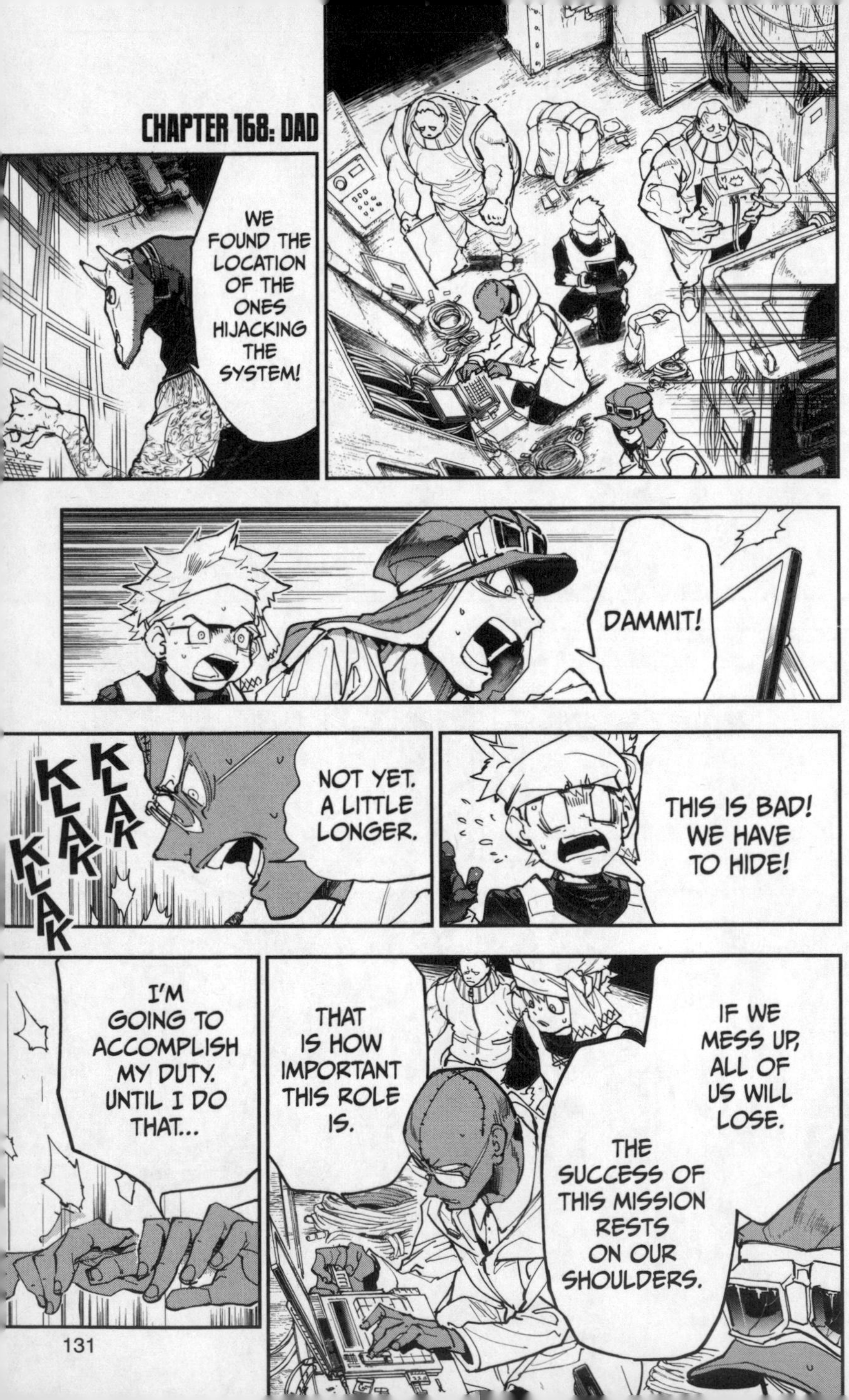
WE FOUND THE LOCATION OF THE ONES HIJACKING THE SYSTEM!
DAMMIT!
THIS IS BAD! WE HAVE TO HIDE!
NOT YET. A LITTLE LONGER.
KLAK KLAK KLAK
IF WE MESS UP, ALL OF US WILL LOSE.
THE SUCCESS OF THIS MISSION RESTS ON OUR SHOULDERS.
THAT IS HOW IMPORTANT THIS ROLE IS.
I'M GOING TO ACCOMPLISH MY DUTY. UNTIL I DO THAT...

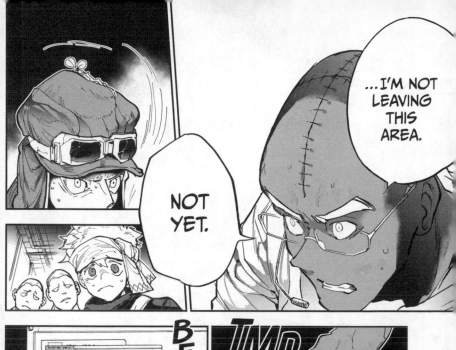

...I'M NOT LEAVING THIS AREA.

NOT YET.

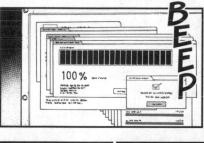

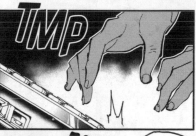

BEEP

TMP

100 %

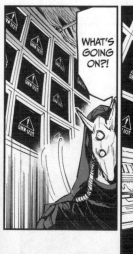

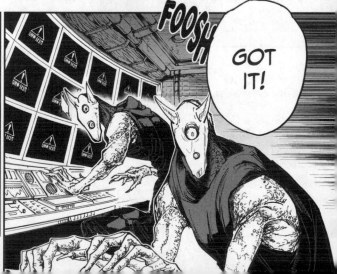

WHAT'S GOING ON?!

FOOSH

GOT IT!

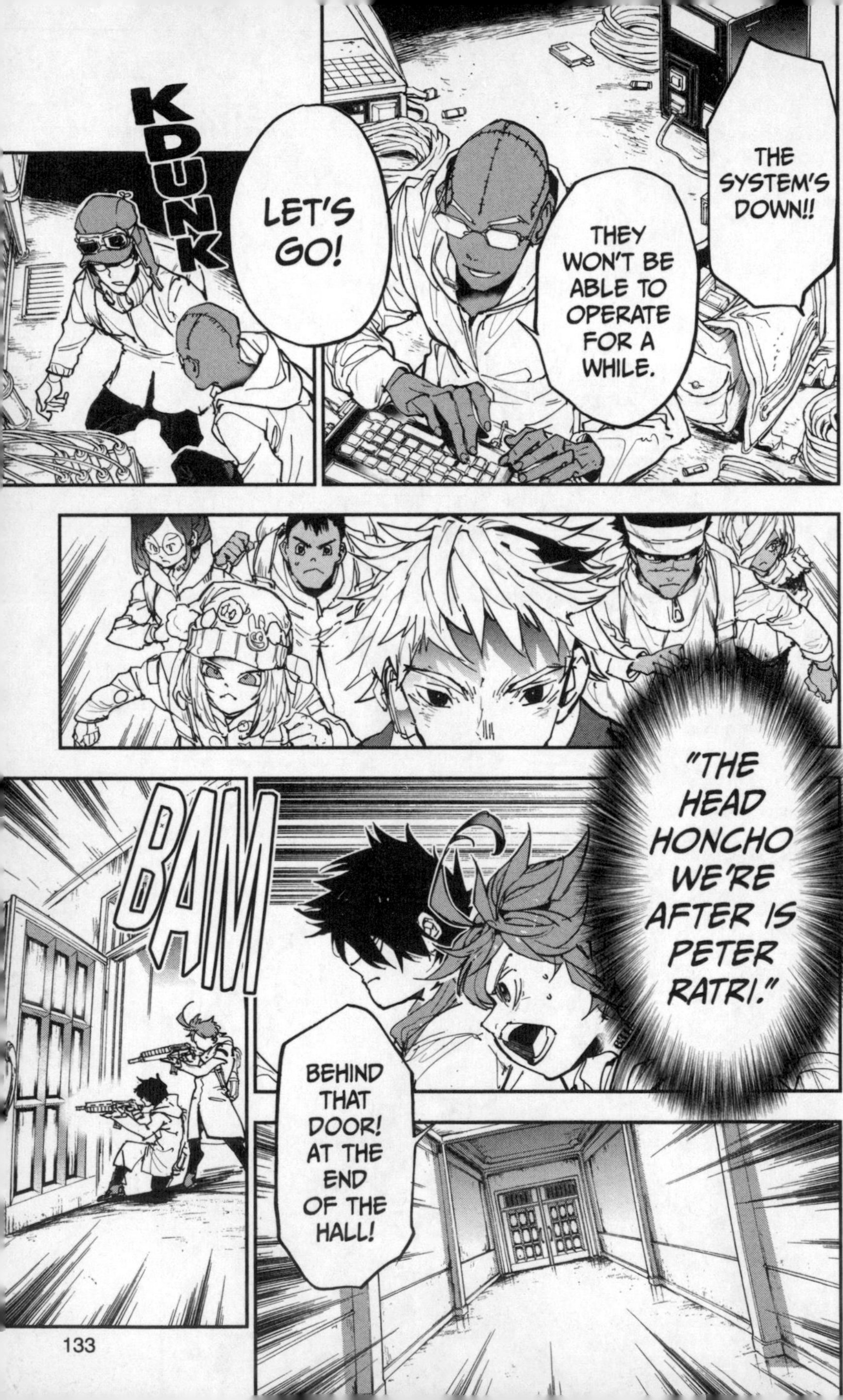
THE SYSTEM'S DOWN!!
THEY WON'T BE ABLE TO OPERATE FOR A WHILE.
LET'S GO!
KDUNK
"THE HEAD HONCHO WE'RE AFTER IS PETER RATRI."
BEHIND THAT DOOR! AT THE END OF THE HALL!
BAM

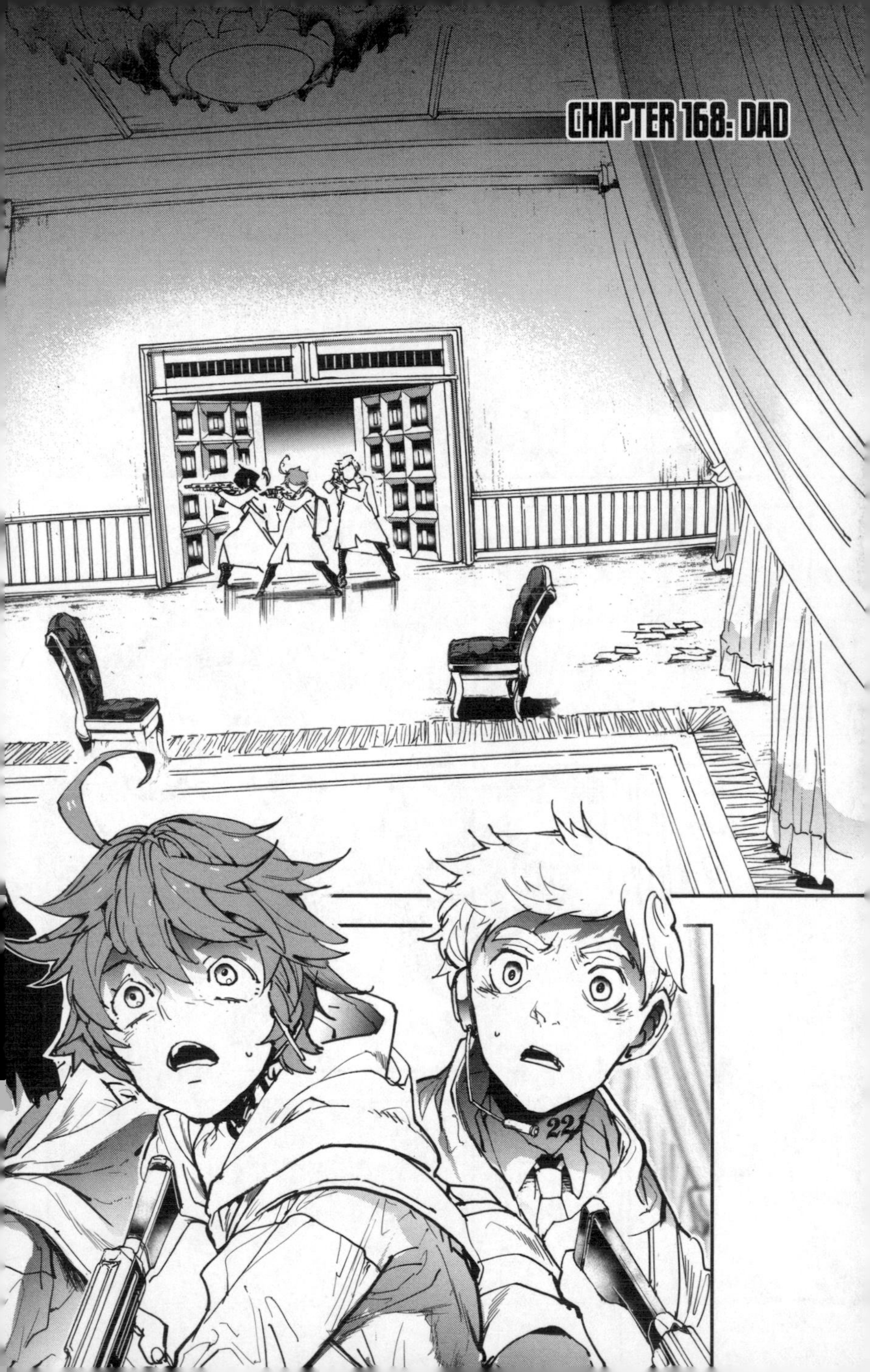
CHAPTER 168: DAD
22

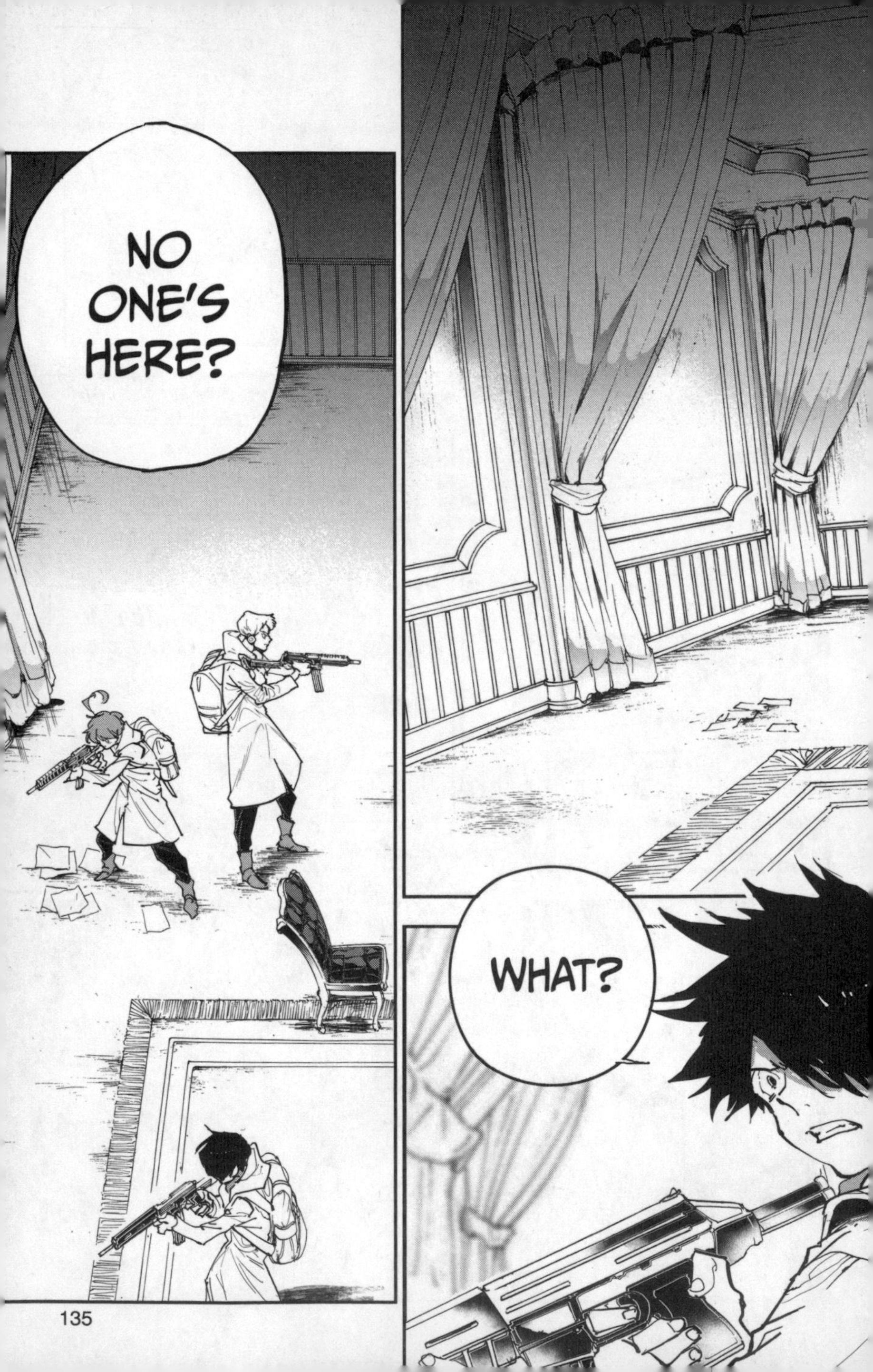
WHAT?
NO ONE'S HERE?

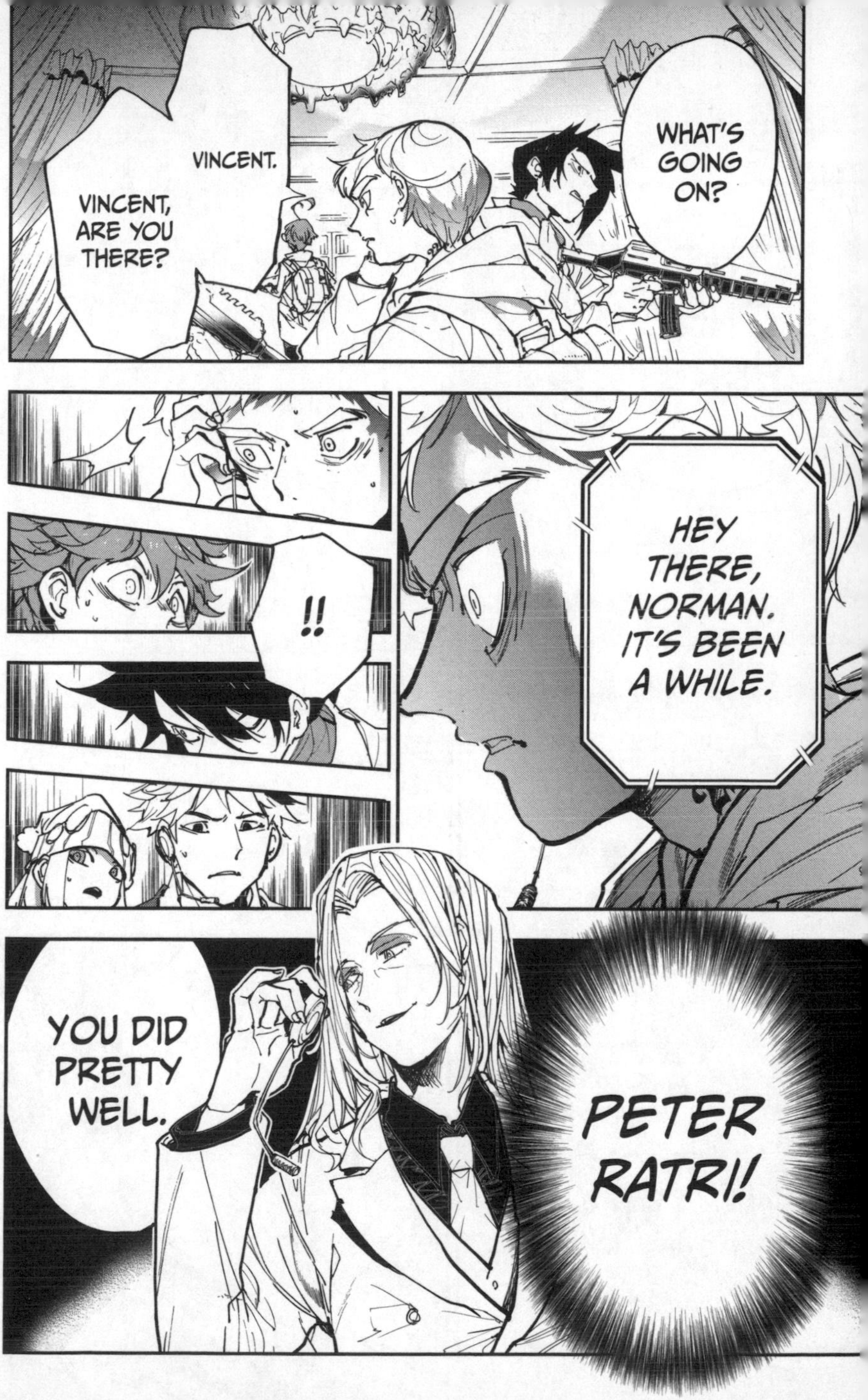
WHAT'S GOING ON?
VINCENT.
VINCENT, ARE YOU THERE?
HEY THERE, NORMAN. IT'S BEEN A WHILE.
!!
PETER RATRI!
YOU DID PRETTY WELL.

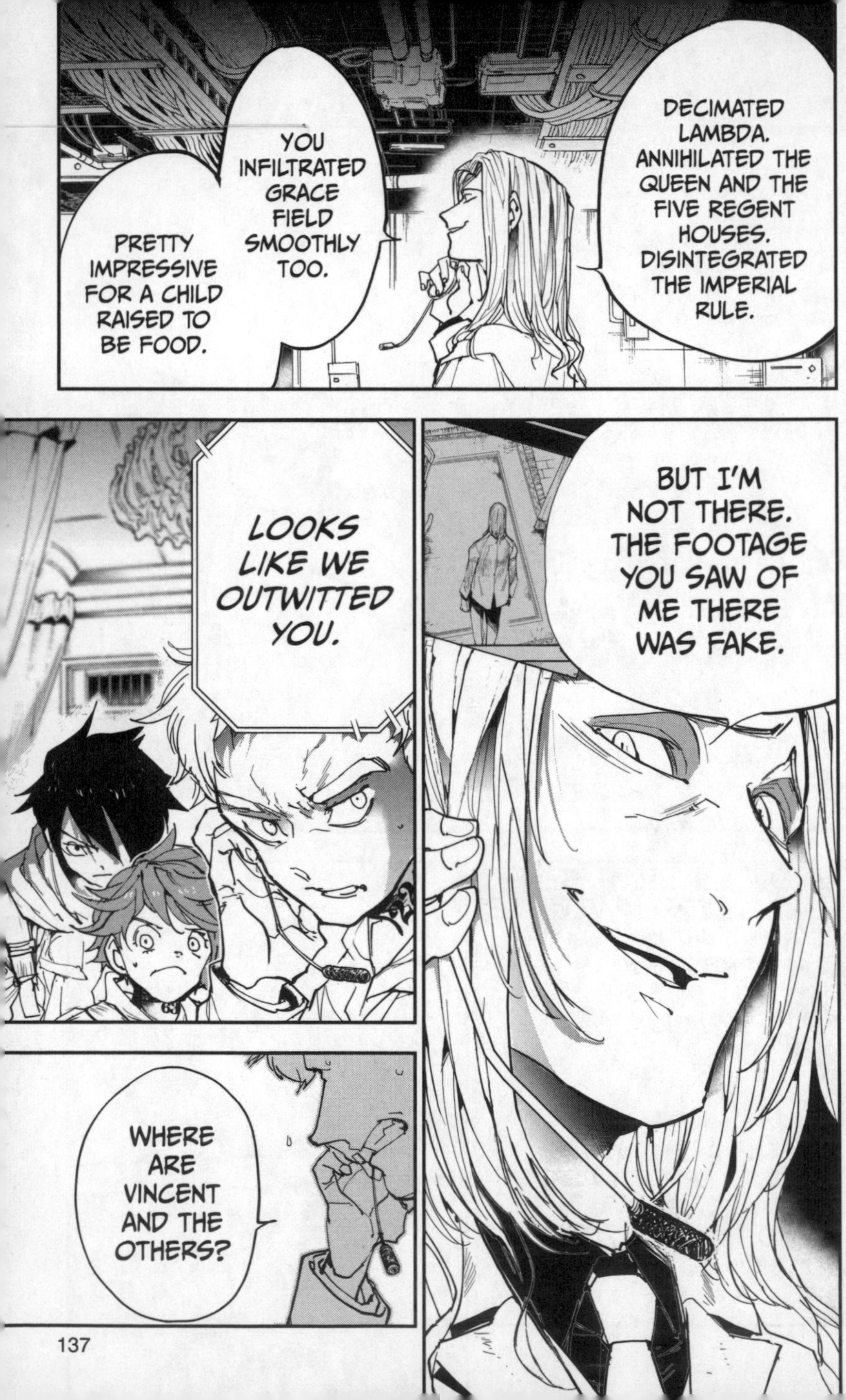
DECIMATED LAMBDA. ANNIHILATED THE QUEEN AND THE FIVE REGENT HOUSES. DISINTEGRATED THE IMPERIAL RULE.
YOU INFILTRATED GRACE FIELD SMOOTHLY TOO.
PRETTY IMPRESSIVE FOR A CHILD RAISED TO BE FOOD.
BUT I'M NOT THERE. THE FOOTAGE YOU SAW OF ME THERE WAS FAKE.
LOOKS LIKE WE OUTWITTED YOU.
WHERE ARE VINCENT AND THE OTHERS?

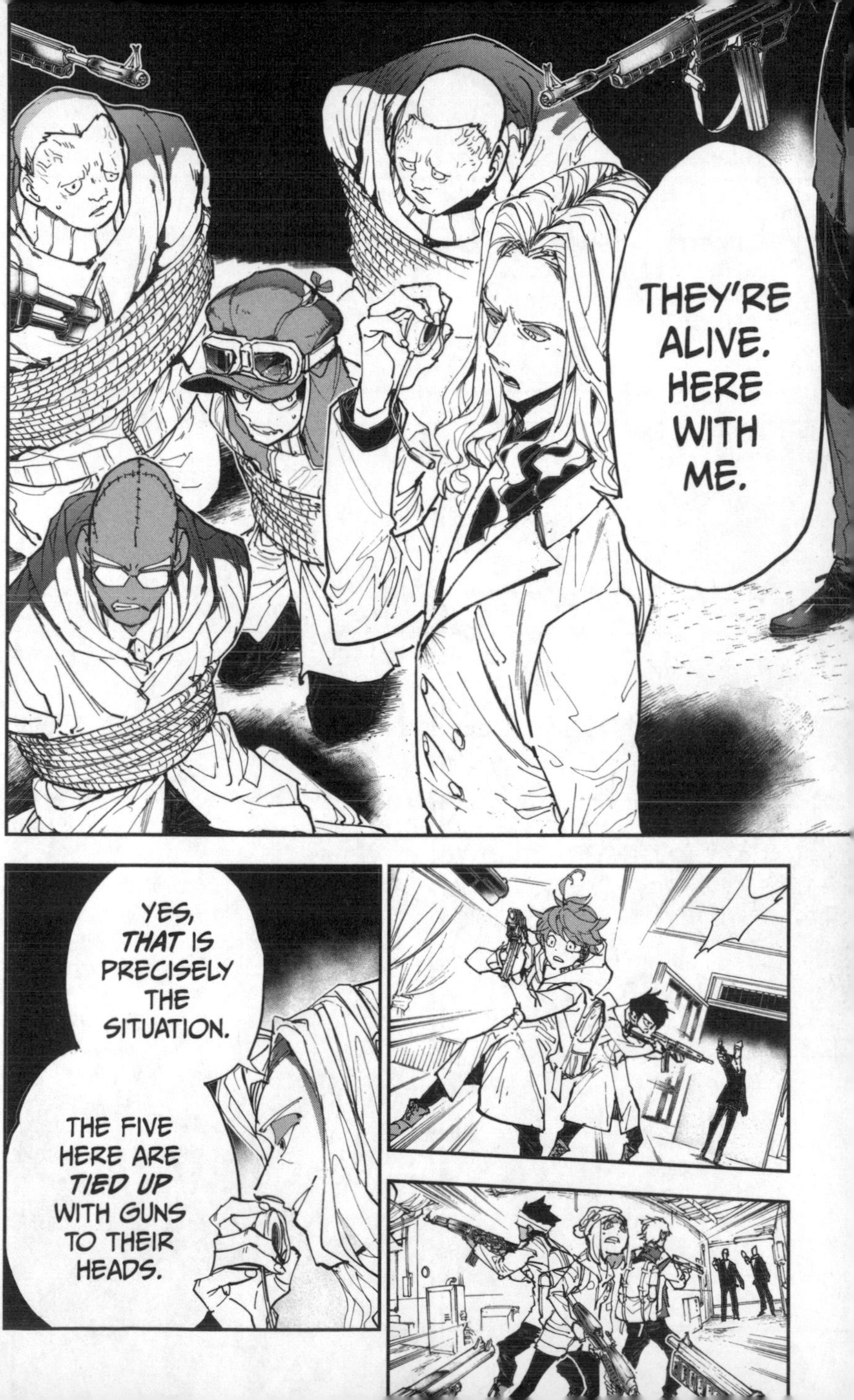
THEY'RE ALIVE. HERE WITH ME.
YES, *THAT* IS PRECISELY THE SITUATION.
THE FIVE HERE ARE *TIED UP* WITH GUNS TO THEIR HEADS.

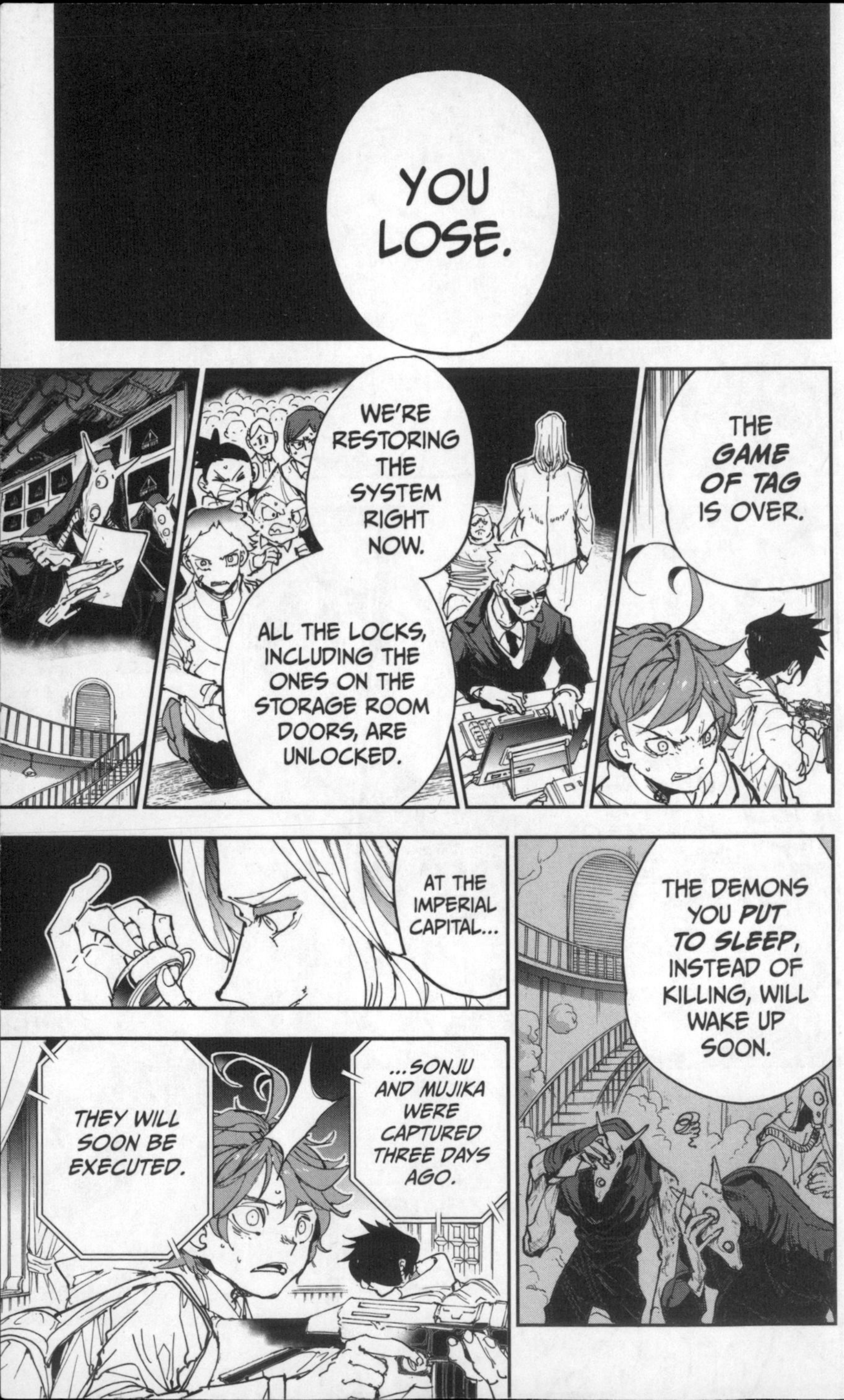
YOU LOSE.
THE *GAME OF TAG* IS OVER.
WE'RE RESTORING THE SYSTEM RIGHT NOW.
ALL THE LOCKS, INCLUDING THE ONES ON THE STORAGE ROOM DOORS, ARE UNLOCKED.
THE DEMONS YOU *PUT TO SLEEP*, INSTEAD OF KILLING, WILL WAKE UP SOON.
AT THE IMPERIAL CAPITAL...
...SONJU AND MUJIKA WERE CAPTURED THREE DAYS AGO.
THEY WILL SOON BE EXECUTED.

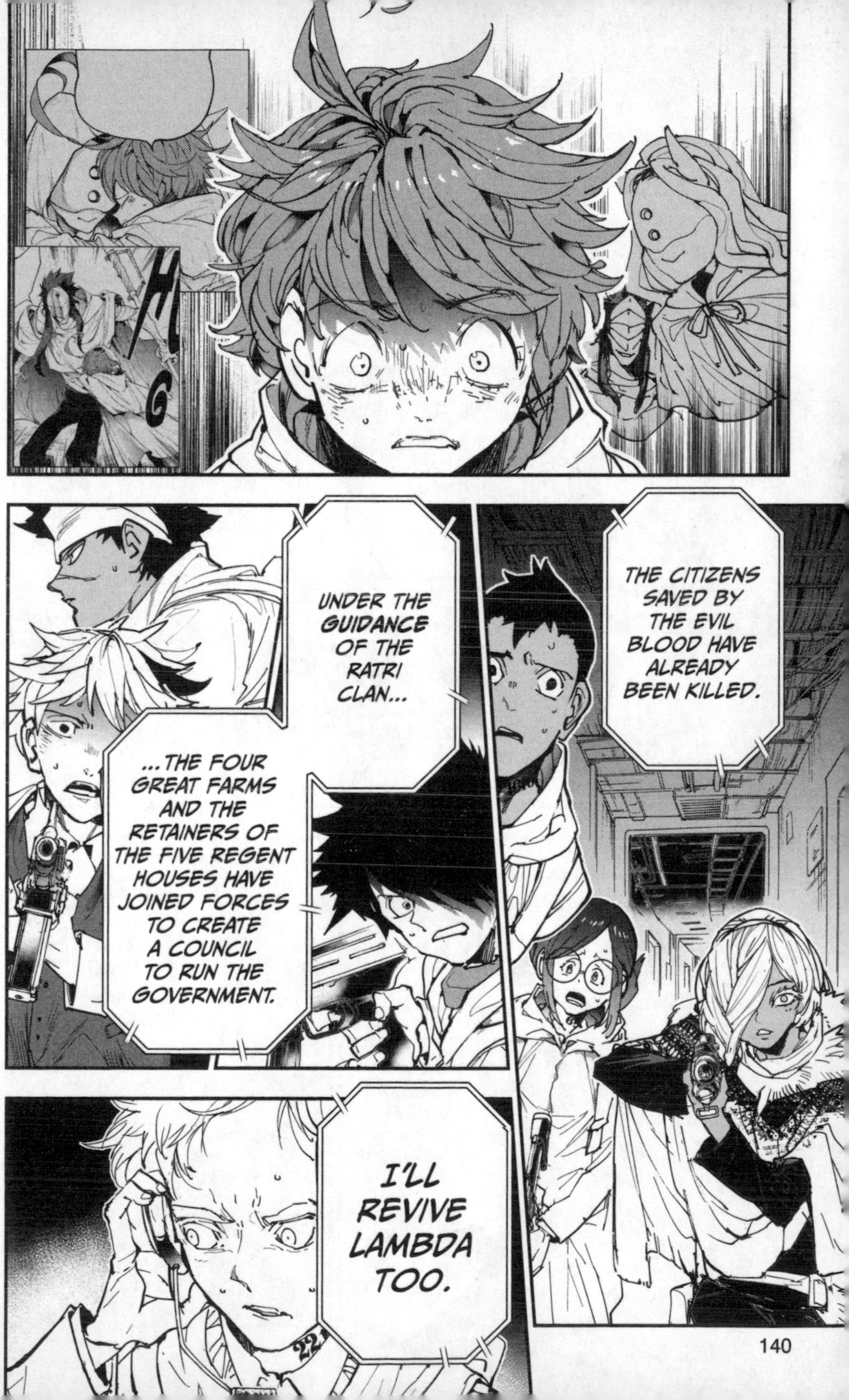
THE CITIZENS SAVED BY THE EVIL BLOOD HAVE ALREADY BEEN KILLED.
UNDER THE GUIDANCE OF THE RATRI CLAN...
...THE FOUR GREAT FARMS AND THE RETAINERS OF THE FIVE REGENT HOUSES HAVE JOINED FORCES TO CREATE A COUNCIL TO RUN THE GOVERNMENT.
I'LL REVIVE LAMBDA TOO.

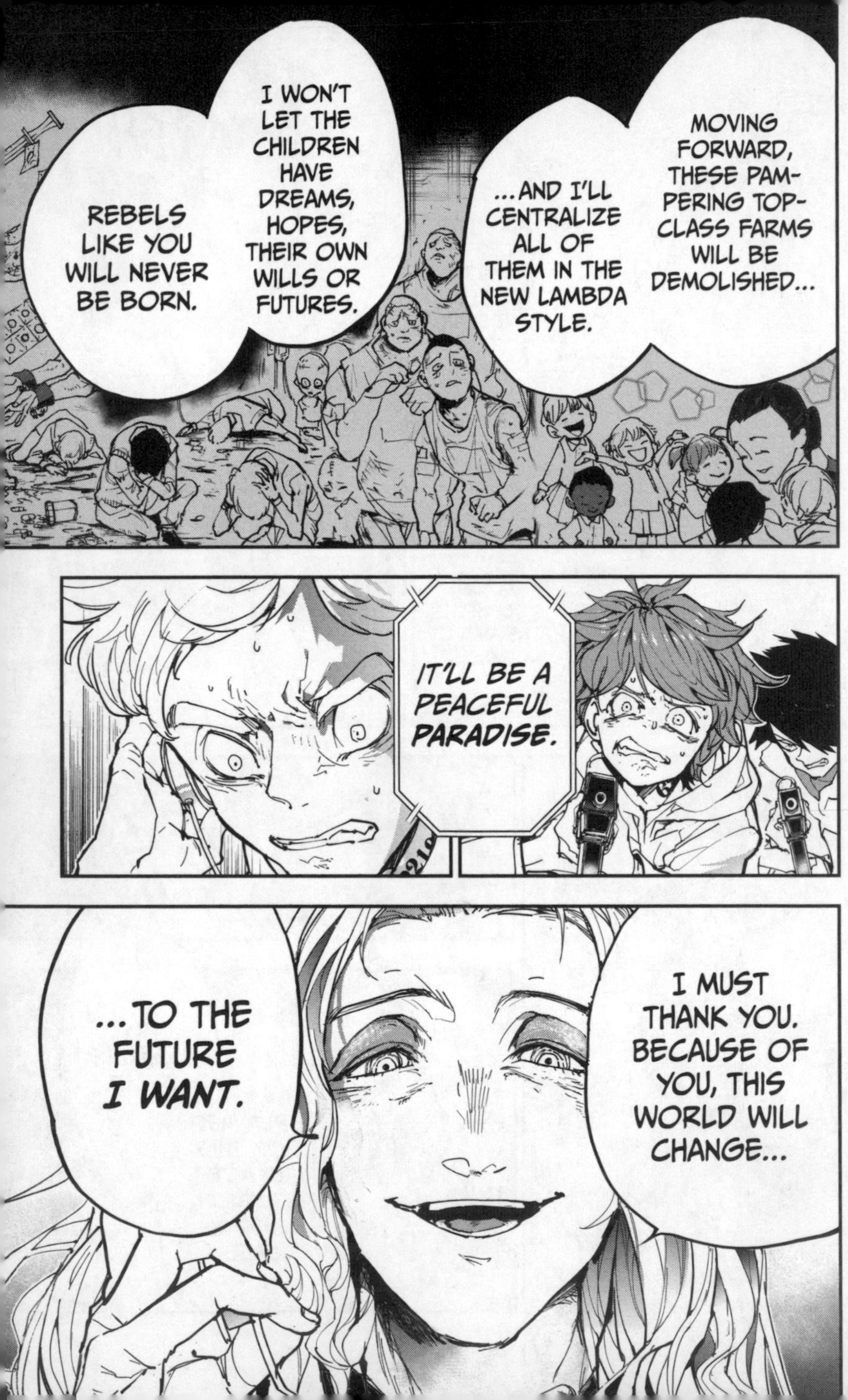
MOVING FORWARD, THESE PAMPERING TOP-CLASS FARMS WILL BE DEMOLISHED...
...AND I'LL CENTRALIZE ALL OF THEM IN THE NEW LAMBDA STYLE.
I WON'T LET THE CHILDREN HAVE DREAMS, HOPES, THEIR OWN WILLS OR FUTURES.
REBELS LIKE YOU WILL NEVER BE BORN.
IT'LL BE A PEACEFUL PARADISE.
I MUST THANK YOU. BECAUSE OF YOU, THIS WORLD WILL CHANGE...
...TO THE FUTURE I WANT.

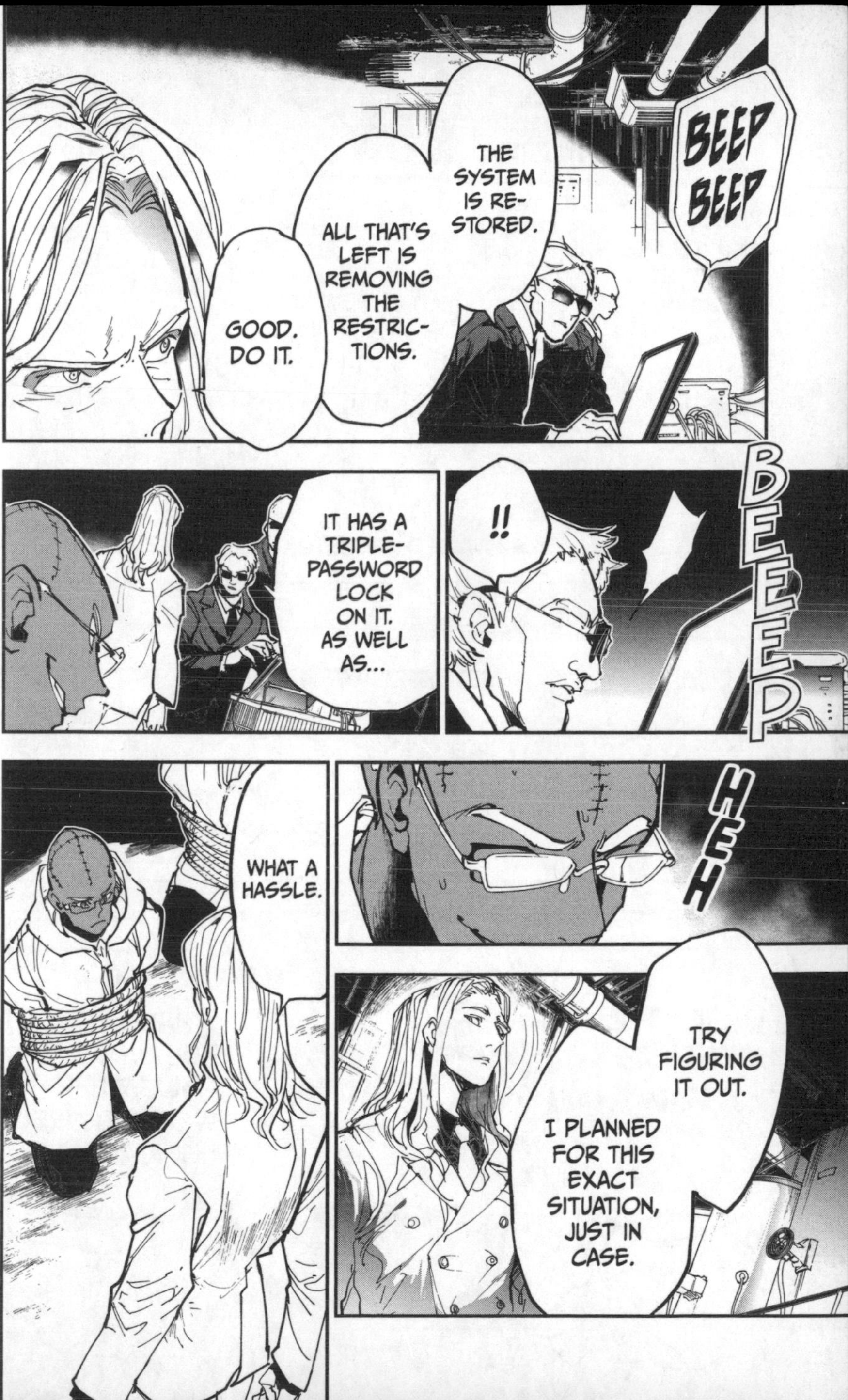
BEEP BEEP
THE SYSTEM IS RE-STORED.
ALL THAT'S LEFT IS REMOVING THE RESTRIC-TIONS.
GOOD. DO IT.
BEEEEP
!!
IT HAS A TRIPLE-PASSWORD LOCK ON IT. AS WELL AS...
HEH
TRY FIGURING IT OUT.
I PLANNED FOR THIS EXACT SITUATION, JUST IN CASE.
WHAT A HASSLE.

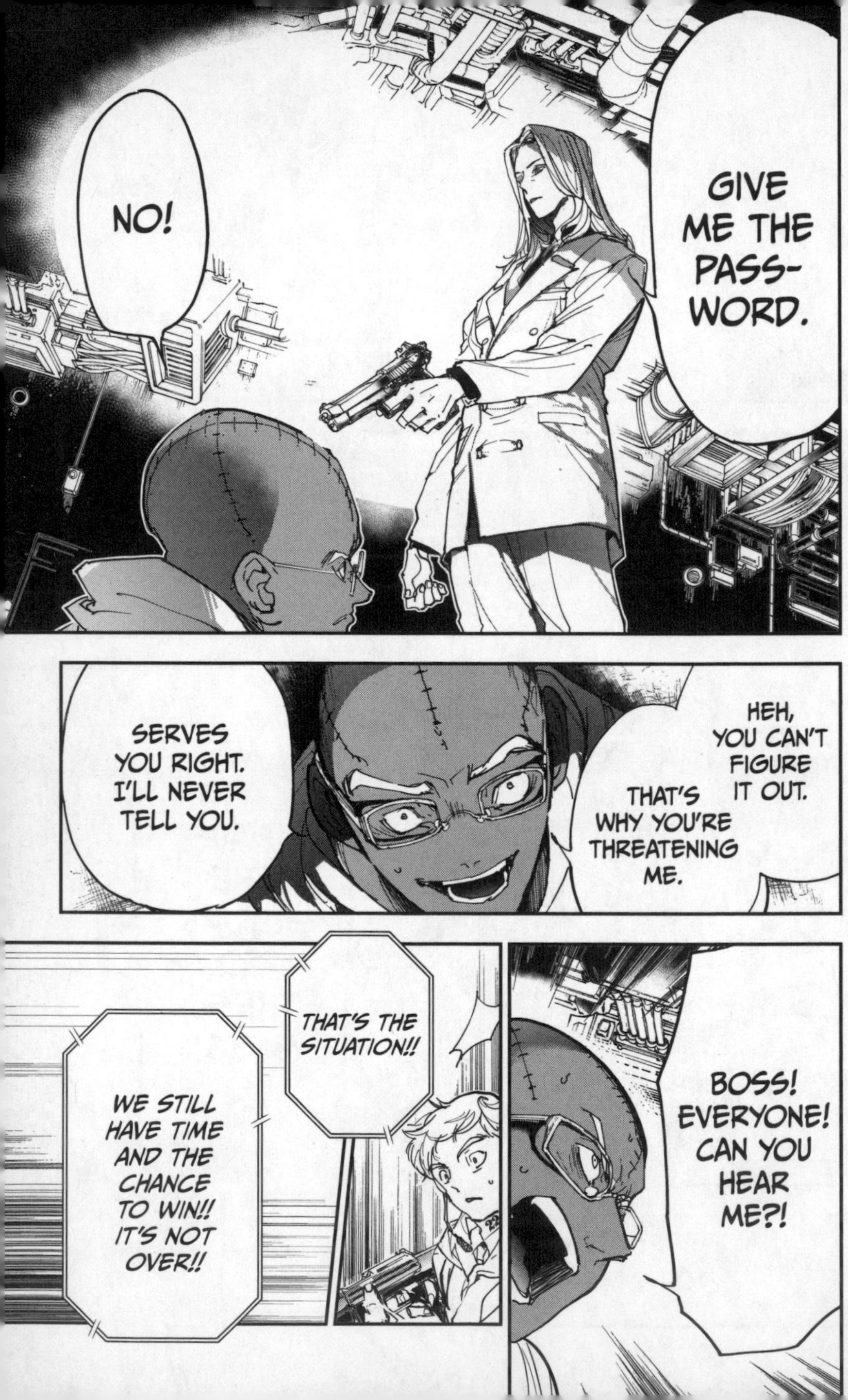
GIVE ME THE PASS-WORD.
NO!
HEH, YOU CAN'T FIGURE IT OUT.
THAT'S WHY YOU'RE THREATENING ME.
SERVES YOU RIGHT. I'LL NEVER TELL YOU.
BOSS! EVERYONE! CAN YOU HEAR ME?!
THAT'S THE SITUATION!!
WE STILL HAVE TIME AND THE CHANCE TO WIN!! IT'S NOT OVER!!

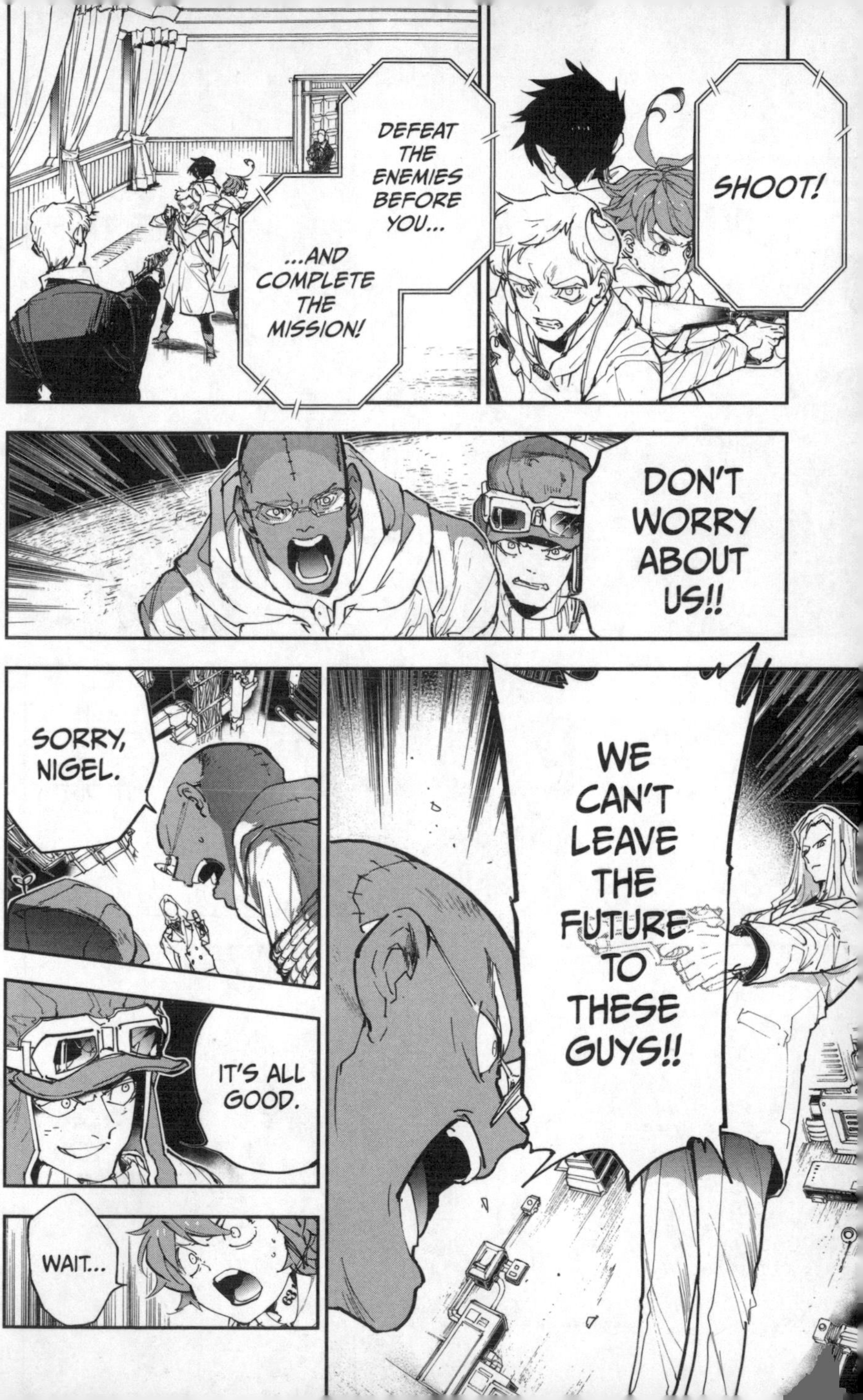
SHOOT!
DEFEAT THE ENEMIES BEFORE YOU...
...AND COMPLETE THE MISSION!
DON'T WORRY ABOUT US!!
WE CAN'T LEAVE THE FUTURE TO THESE GUYS!!
SORRY, NIGEL.
IT'S ALL GOOD.
WAIT...

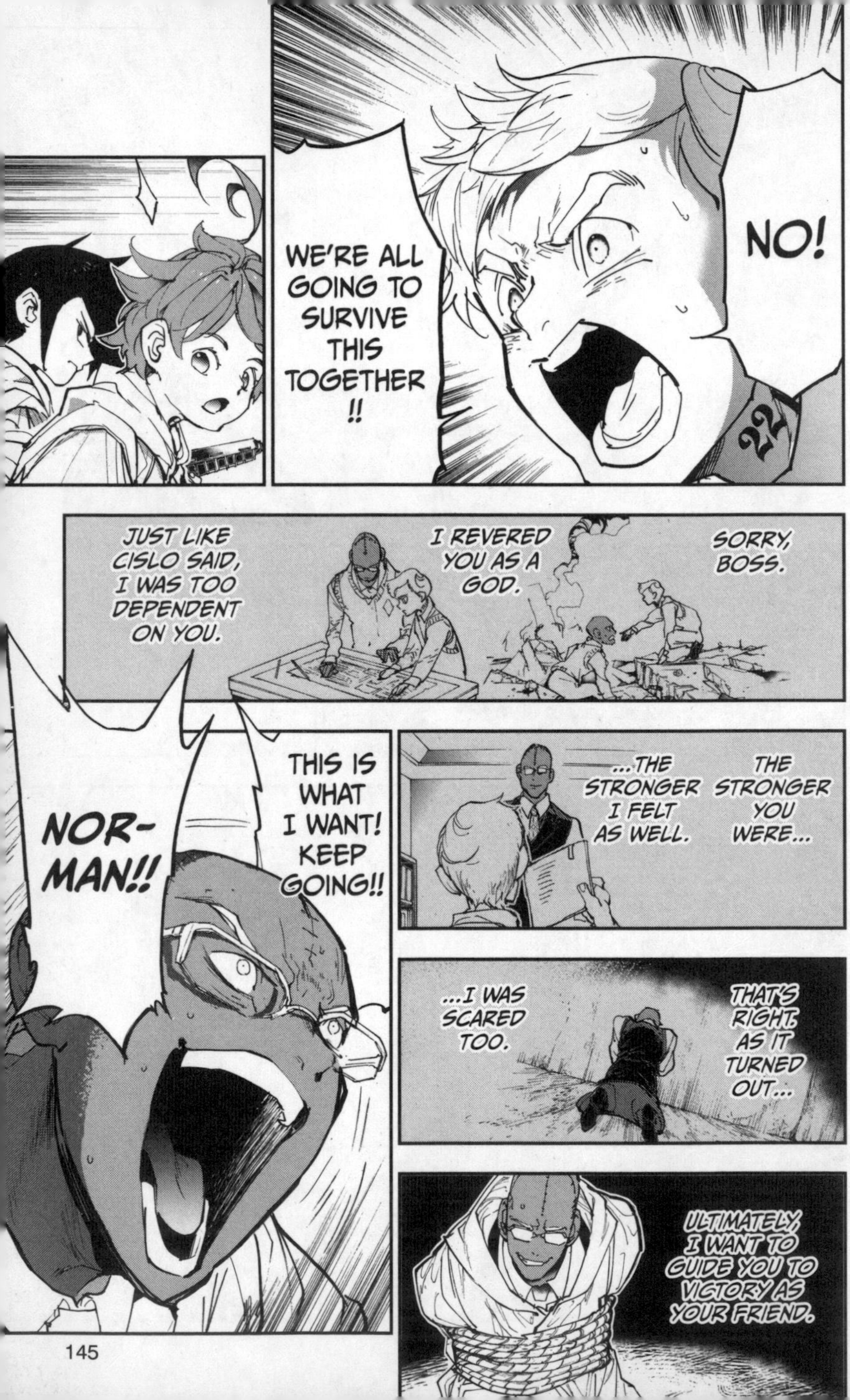
NO!
WE'RE ALL GOING TO SURVIVE THIS TOGETHER !!
SORRY, BOSS.
I REVERED YOU AS A GOD.
JUST LIKE CISLO SAID, I WAS TOO DEPENDENT ON YOU.
THE STRONGER YOU WERE...
...THE STRONGER I FELT AS WELL.
THAT'S RIGHT. AS IT TURNED OUT...
...I WAS SCARED TOO.
ULTIMATELY, I WANT TO GUIDE YOU TO VICTORY AS YOUR FRIEND.
THIS IS WHAT I WANT! KEEP GOING!!
NOR-MAN!!

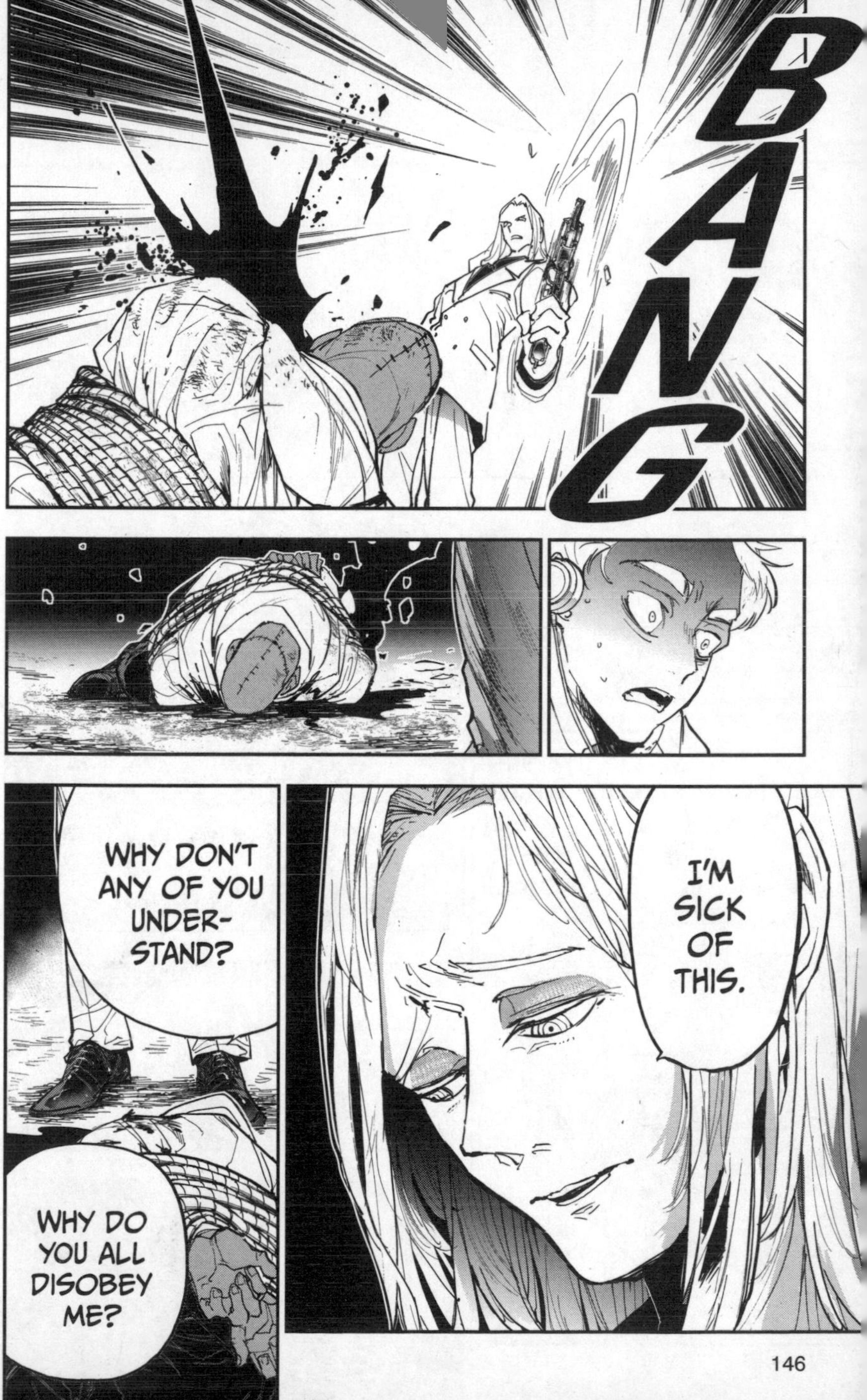
BANG
I'M SICK OF THIS.
WHY DON'T ANY OF YOU UNDER-STAND?
WHY DO YOU ALL DISOBEY ME?

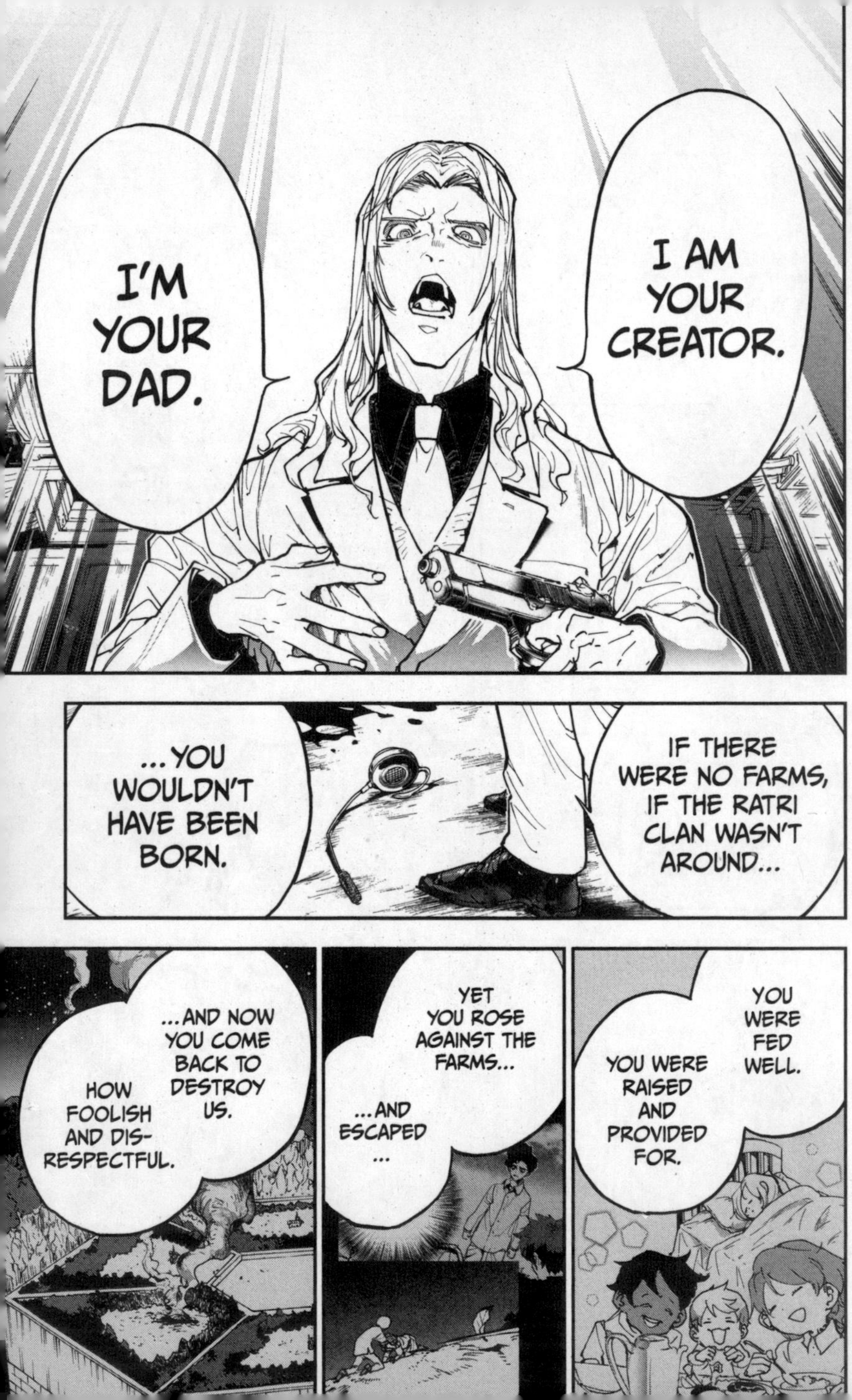
I AM YOUR CREATOR.
I'M YOUR DAD.
IF THERE WERE NO FARMS, IF THE RATRI CLAN WASN'T AROUND...
...YOU WOULDN'T HAVE BEEN BORN.
YOU WERE FED WELL.
YOU WERE RAISED AND PROVIDED FOR.
YET YOU ROSE AGAINST THE FARMS...
...AND ESCAPED...
...AND NOW YOU COME BACK TO DESTROY US.
HOW FOOLISH AND DISRESPECTFUL.

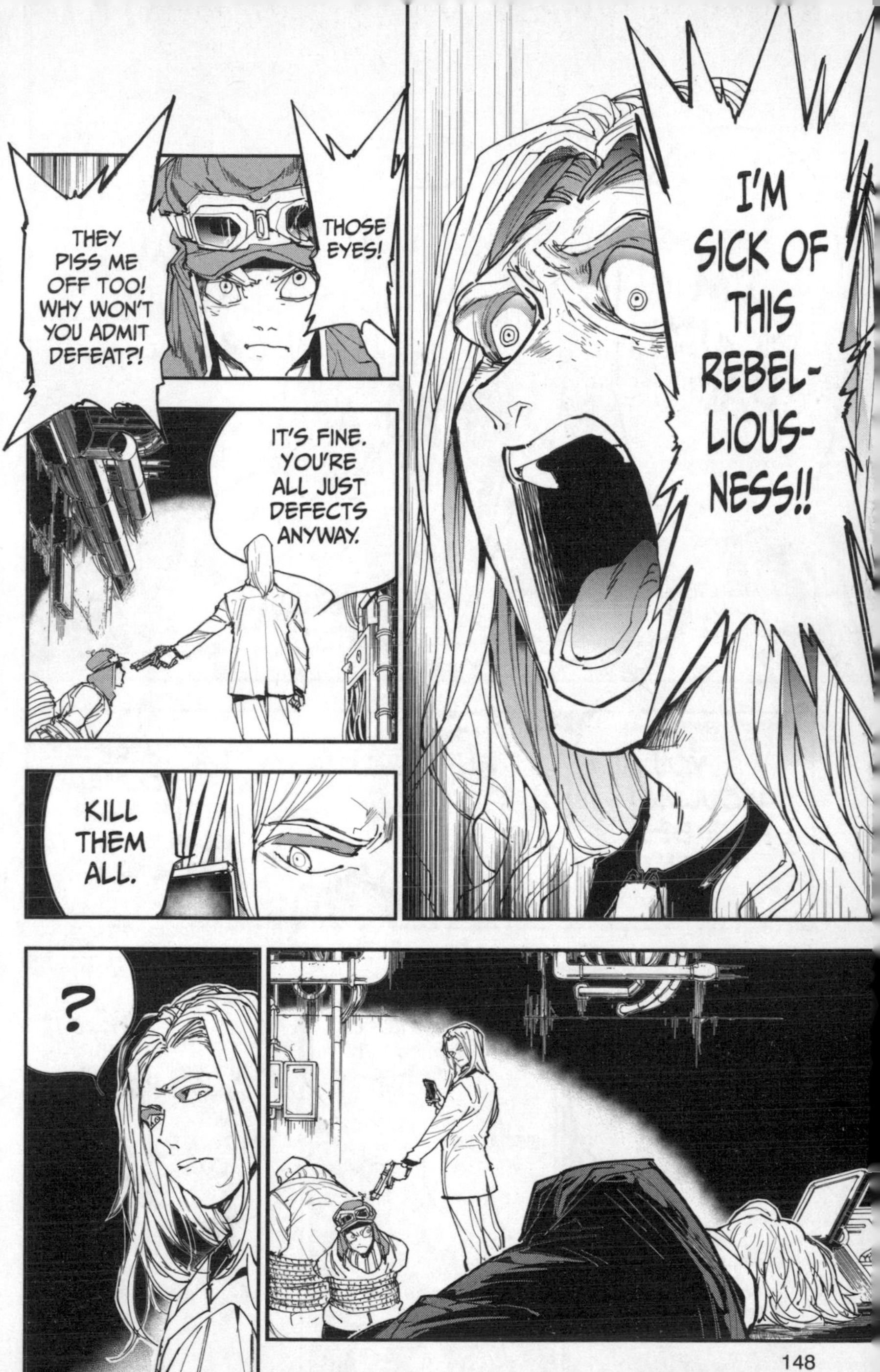
I'M SICK OF THIS REBELLIOUSNESS!!
THOSE EYES!
THEY PISS ME OFF TOO! WHY WON'T YOU ADMIT DEFEAT?!
IT'S FINE. YOU'RE ALL JUST DEFECTS ANYWAY.
KILL THEM ALL.
?

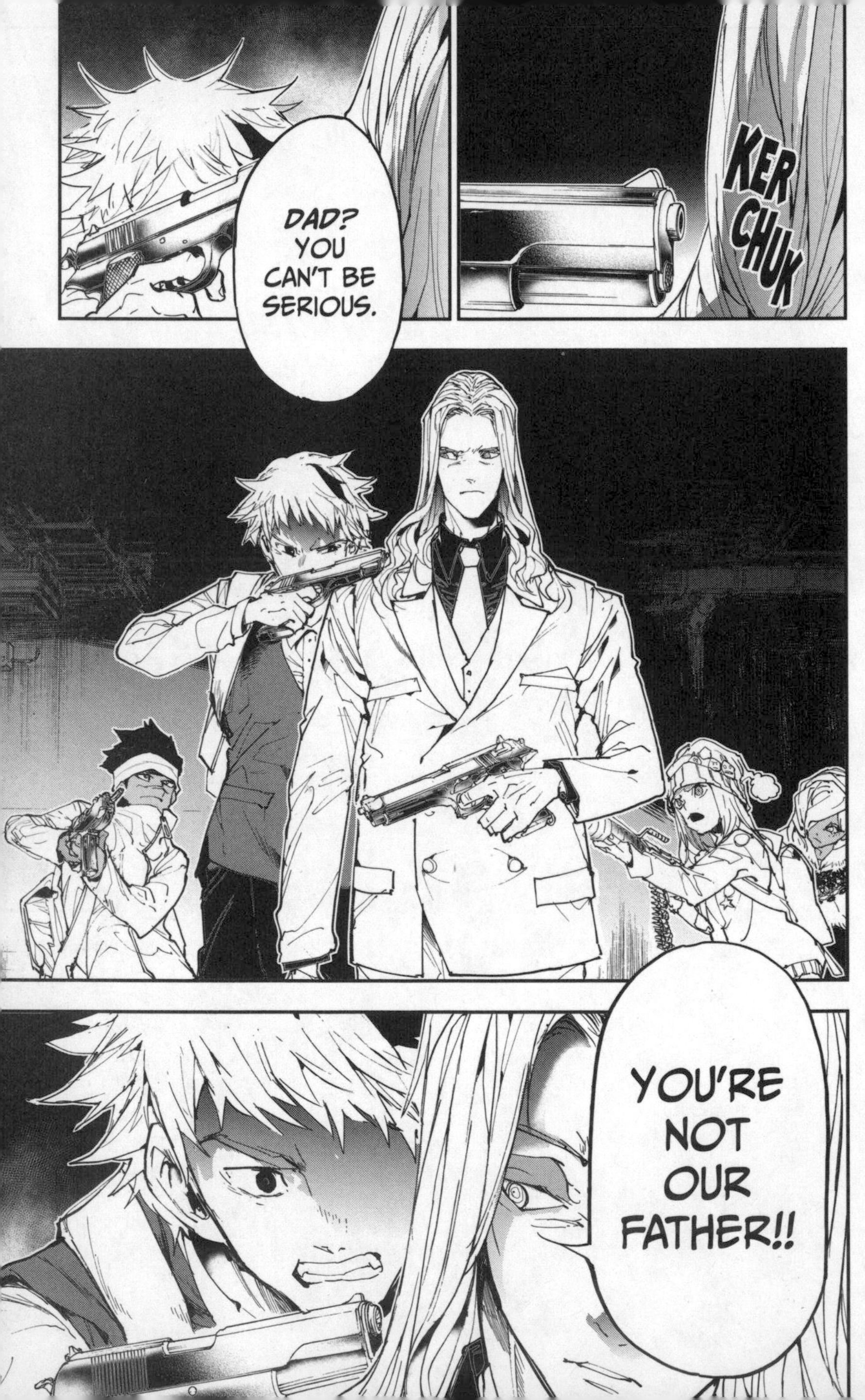
KER CHUK
DAD? YOU CAN'T BE SERIOUS.
YOU'RE NOT OUR FATHER!!

MINION

DEMONS BEHIND THE SCENES

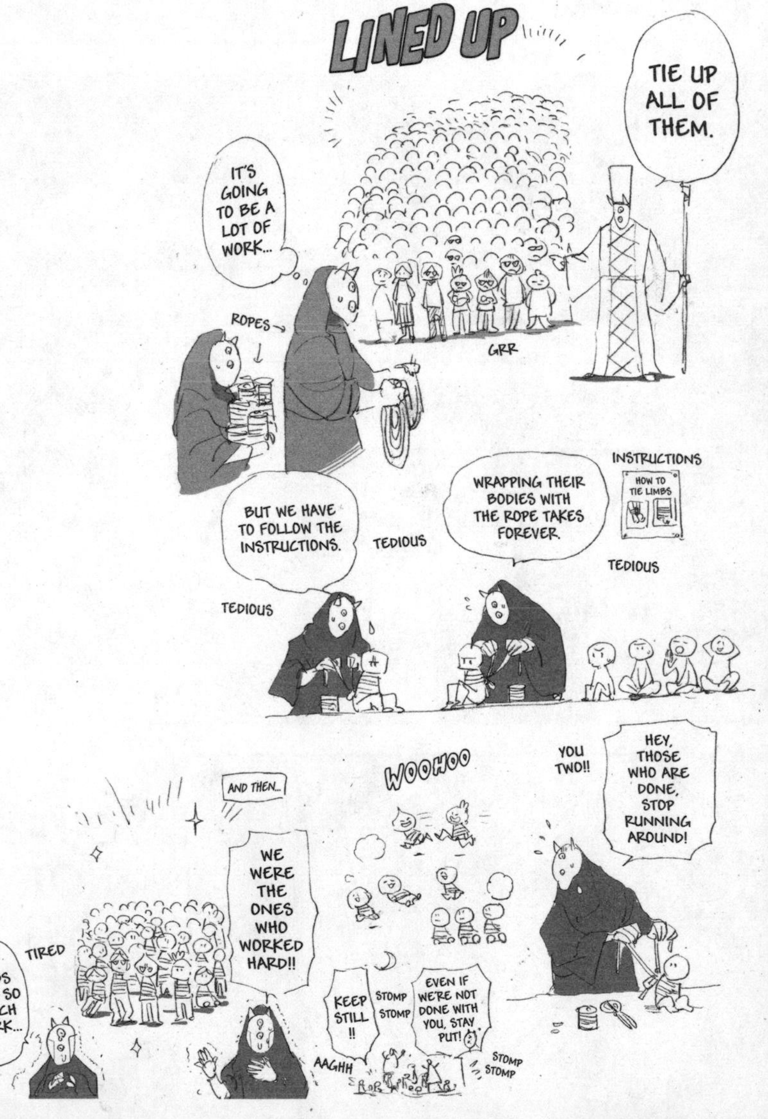
LINED UP
TIE UP ALL OF THEM.
IT'S GOING TO BE A LOT OF WORK...
ROPES
GRR
WRAPPING THEIR BODIES WITH THE ROPE TAKES FOREVER.
INSTRUCTIONS
HOW TO TIE LIMBS
TEDIOUS
TEDIOUS
BUT WE HAVE TO FOLLOW THE INSTRUCTIONS.
TEDIOUS
HEY, THOSE WHO ARE DONE, STOP RUNNING AROUND!
YOU TWO!!
WOOHOO
AND THEN...
EVEN IF WE'RE NOT DONE WITH YOU, STAY PUT!
STOMP STOMP
KEEP STILL!!
STOMP STOMP
AAGHH
WE WERE THE ONES WHO WORKED HARD!!
TIRED
KIDS ARE SO MUCH WORK...

CHAPTER 169: PERFECT SCORES

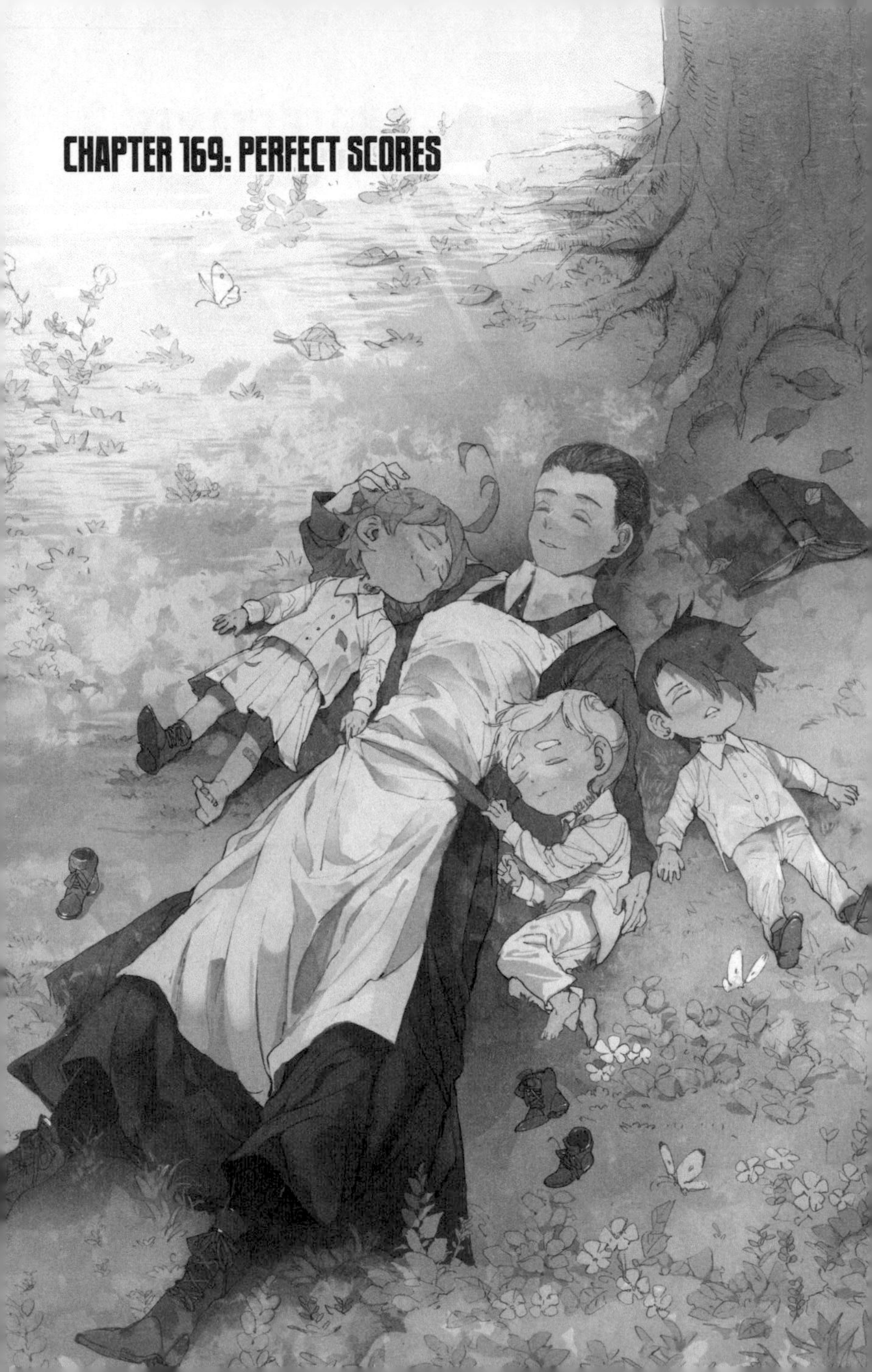

THE PROMISED NEVERLAND DELETED SCENE

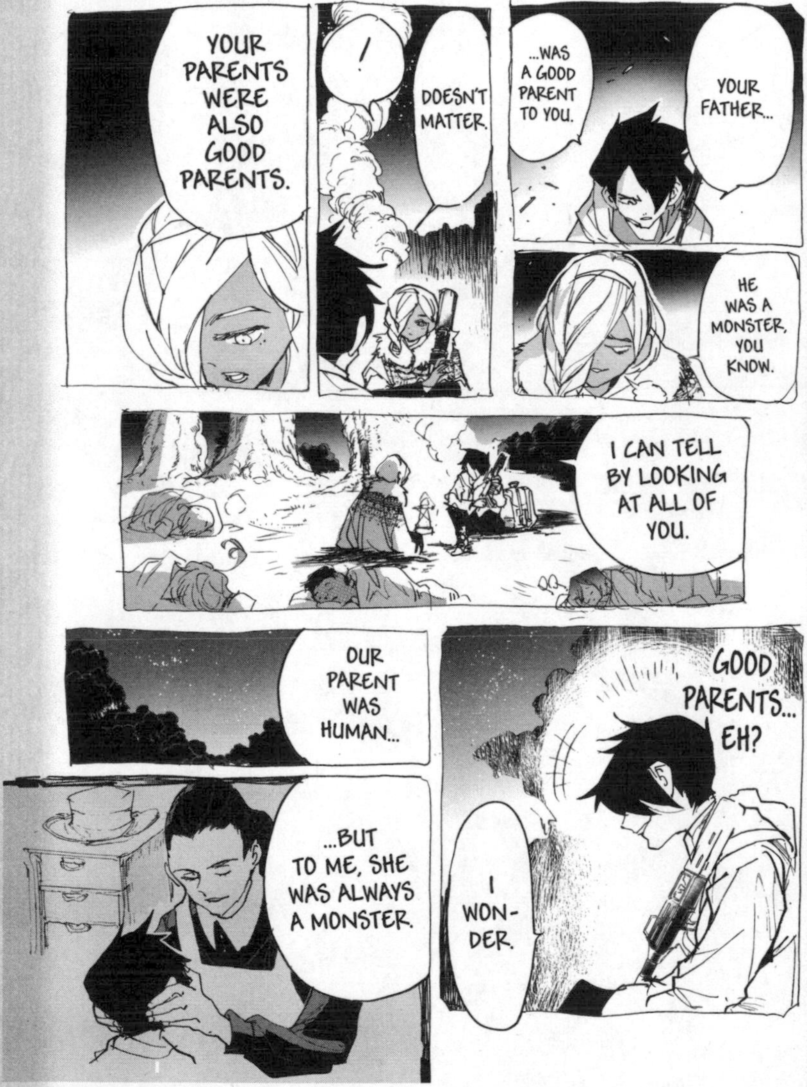
YOUR FATHER...
...WAS A GOOD PARENT TO YOU.
HE WAS A MONSTER, YOU KNOW.
!
DOESN'T MATTER.
YOUR PARENTS WERE ALSO GOOD PARENTS.
I CAN TELL BY LOOKING AT ALL OF YOU.
GOOD PARENTS... EH?
I WON-DER.
OUR PARENT WAS HUMAN...
...BUT TO ME, SHE WAS ALWAYS A MONSTER.

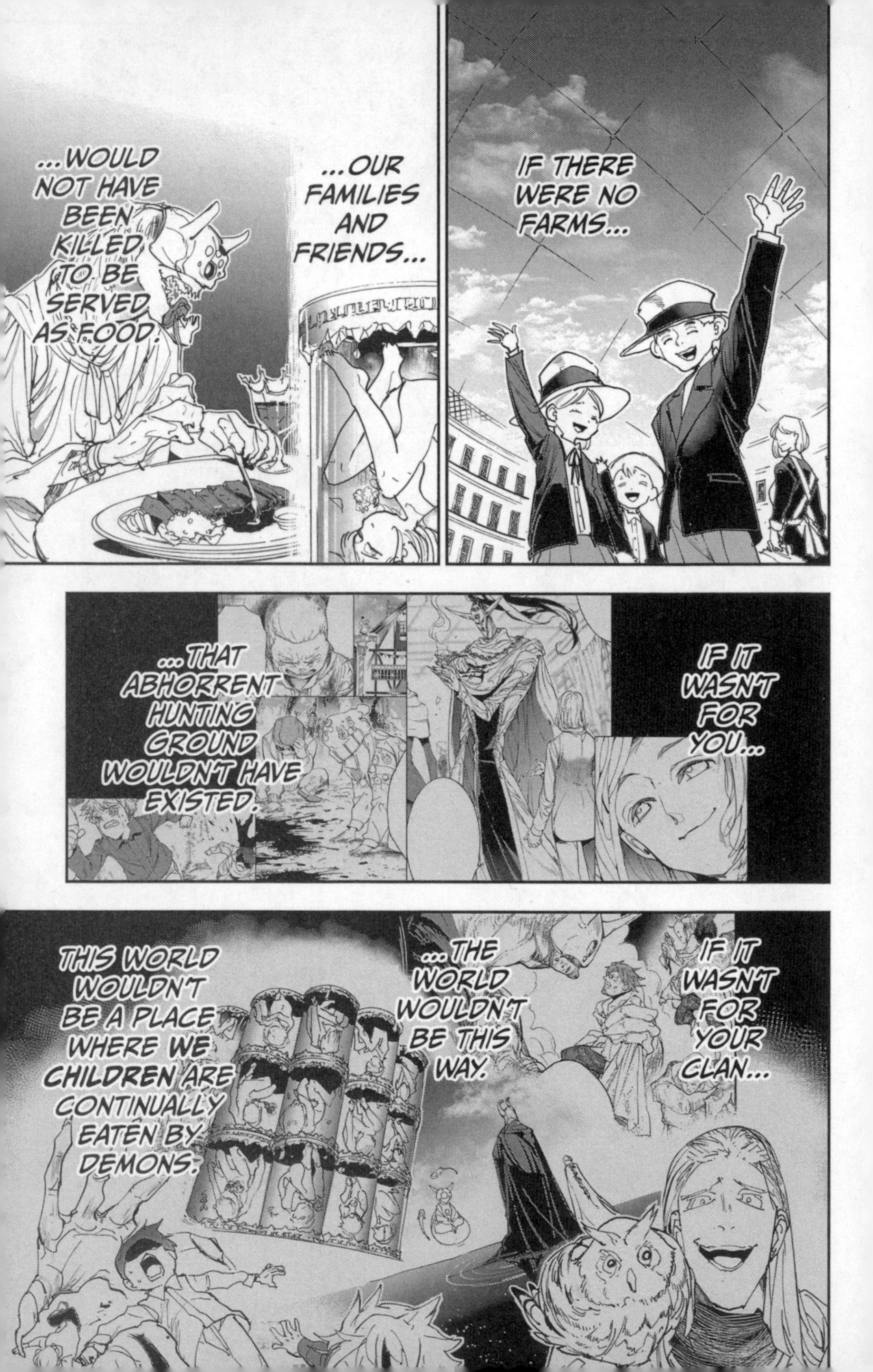
IF THERE WERE NO FARMS...
...OUR FAMILIES AND FRIENDS...
...WOULD NOT HAVE BEEN KILLED TO BE SERVED AS FOOD.
IF IT WASN'T FOR YOU...
...THAT ABHORRENT HUNTING GROUND WOULDN'T HAVE EXISTED.
IF IT WASN'T FOR YOUR CLAN...
...THE WORLD WOULDN'T BE THIS WAY.
THIS WORLD WOULDN'T BE A PLACE WHERE WE CHILDREN ARE CONTINUALLY EATEN BY DEMONS.

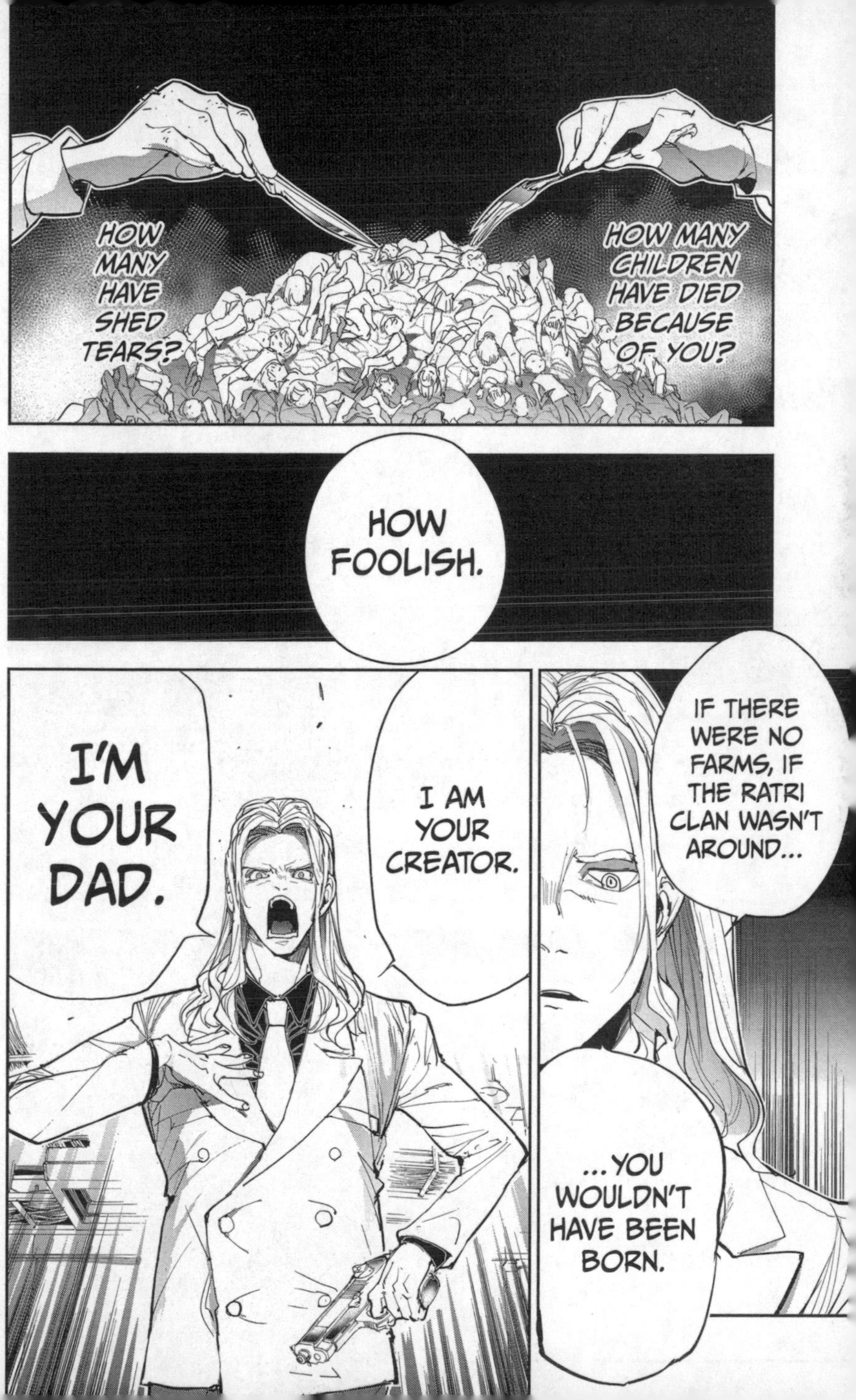
HOW MANY CHILDREN HAVE DIED BECAUSE OF YOU?
HOW MANY HAVE SHED TEARS?
HOW FOOLISH.
IF THERE WERE NO FARMS, IF THE RATRI CLAN WASN'T AROUND...
...YOU WOULDN'T HAVE BEEN BORN.
I AM YOUR CREATOR.
I'M YOUR DAD.

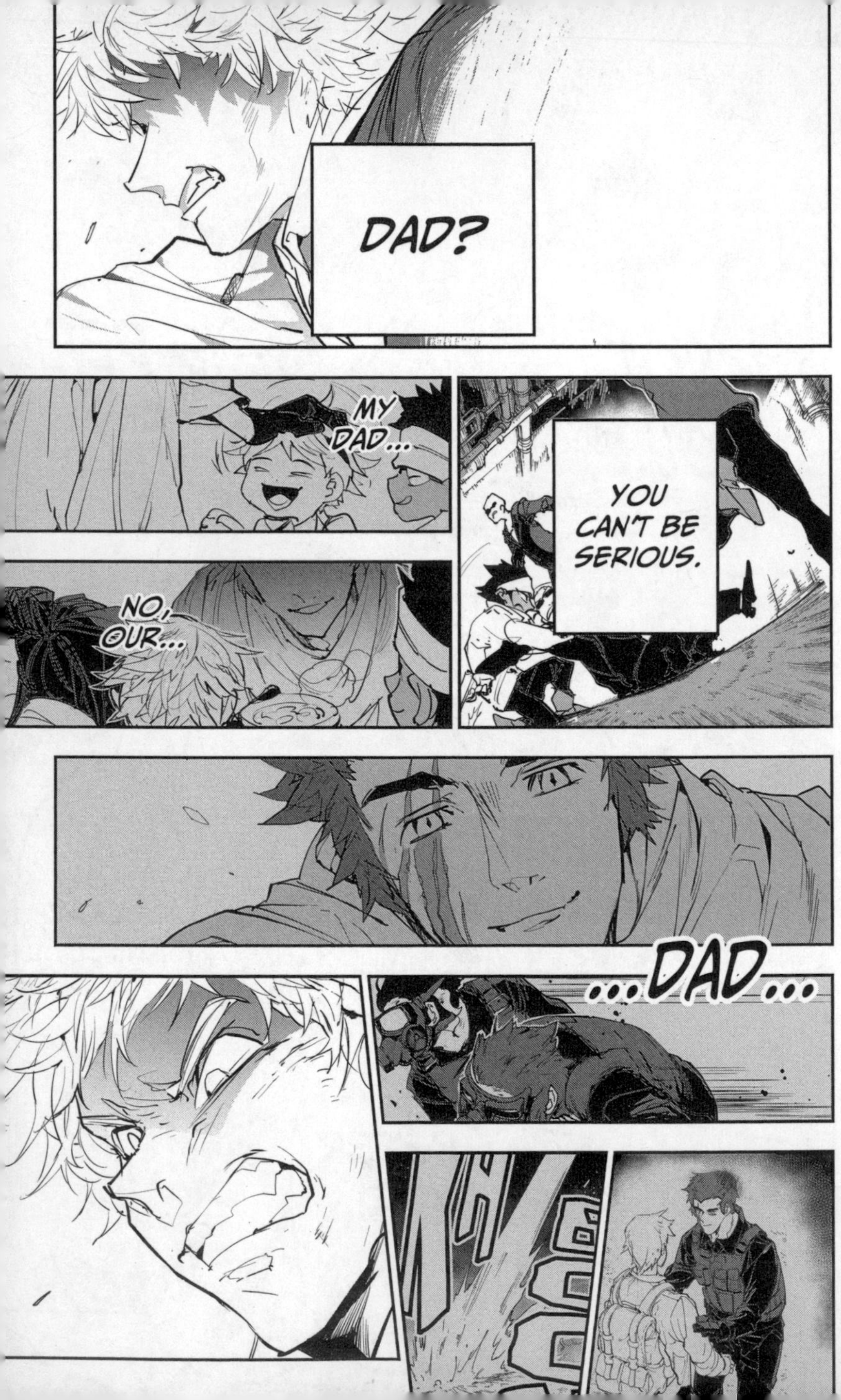
DAD?
YOU CAN'T BE SERIOUS.
MY DAD...
NO, OUR...
...DAD...

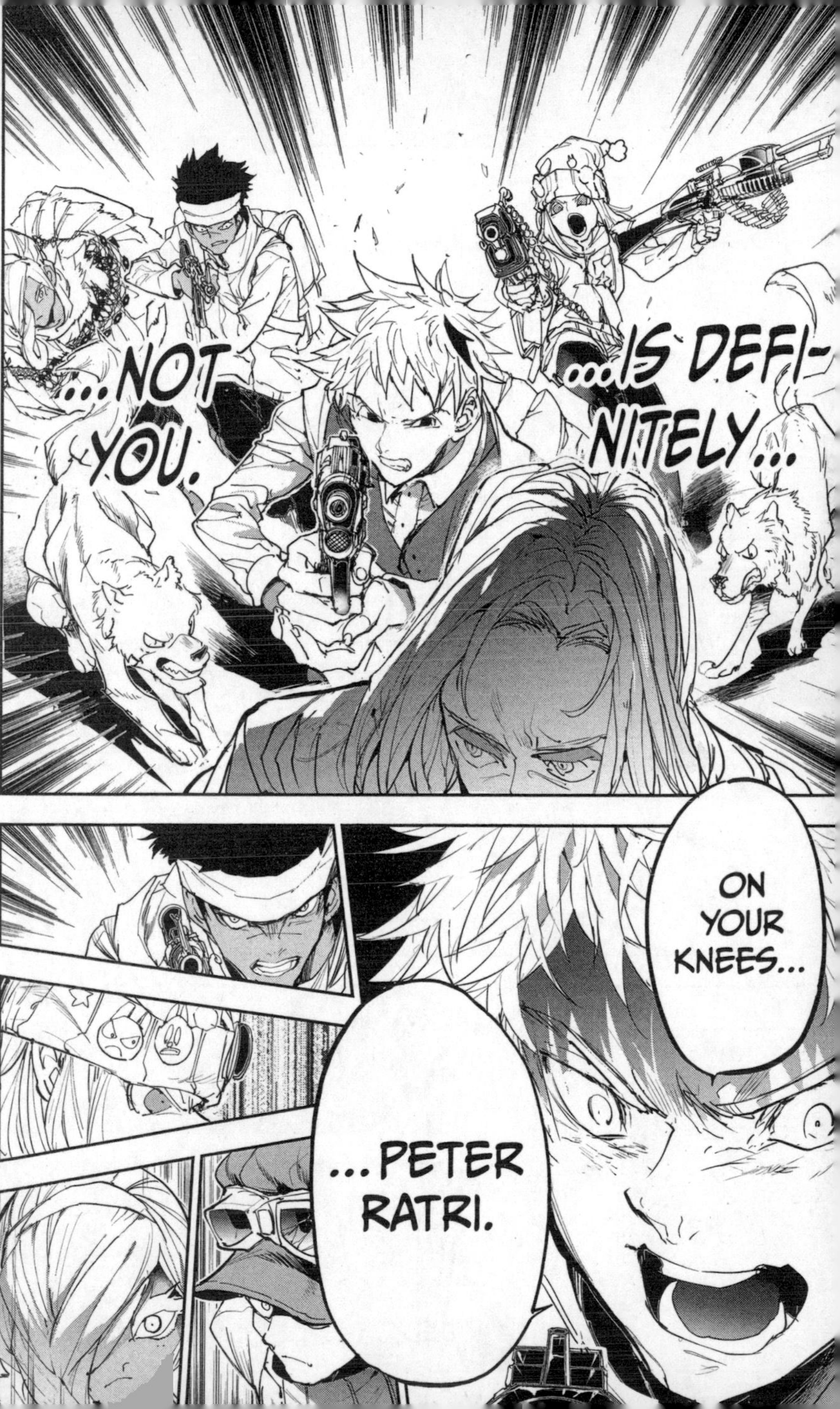
...IS DEFI-NITELY...
...NOT YOU.
ON YOUR KNEES...
...PETER RATRI.

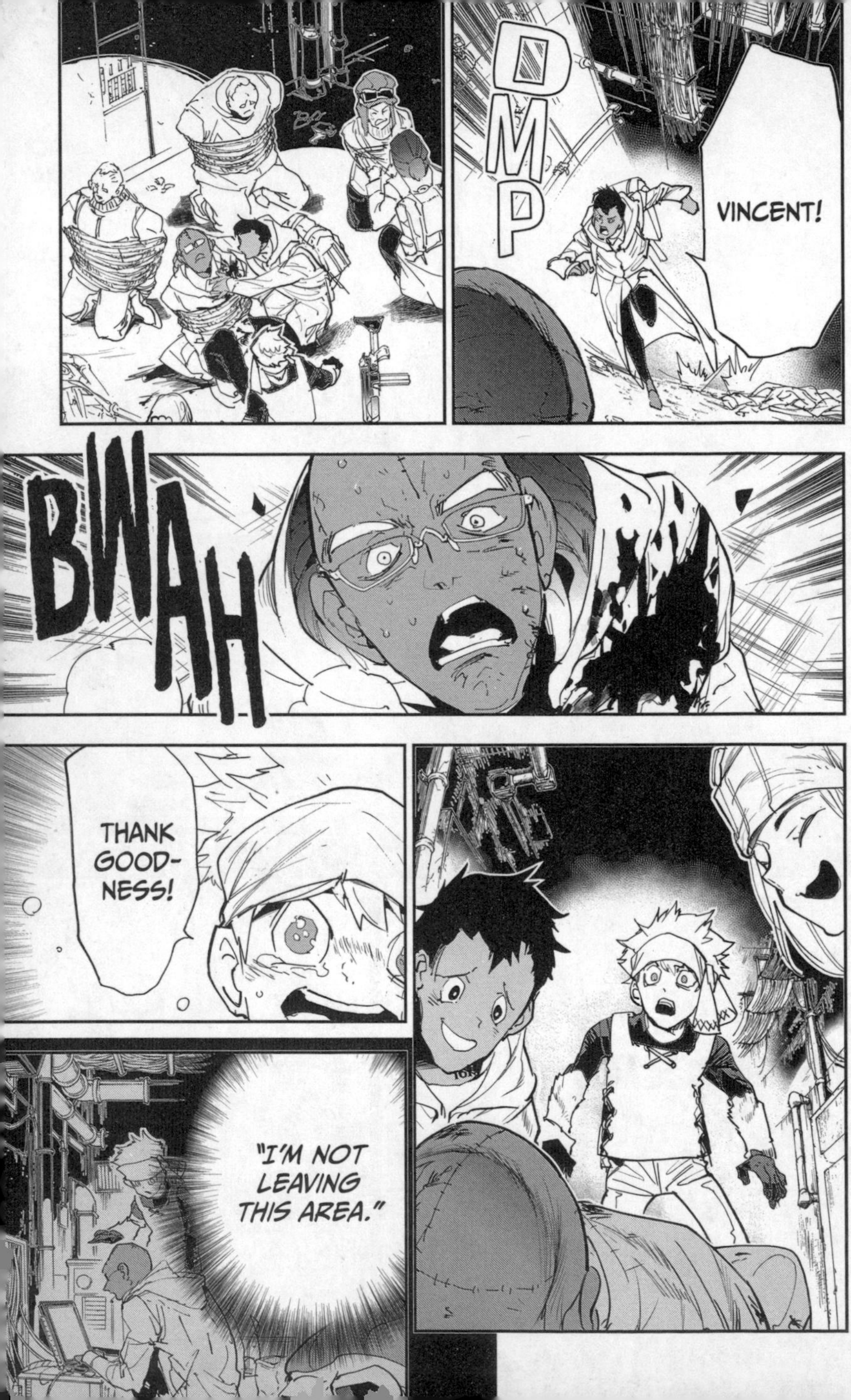
DMP
VINCENT!
BWAH
THANK GOOD-NESS!
"I'M NOT LEAVING THIS AREA."

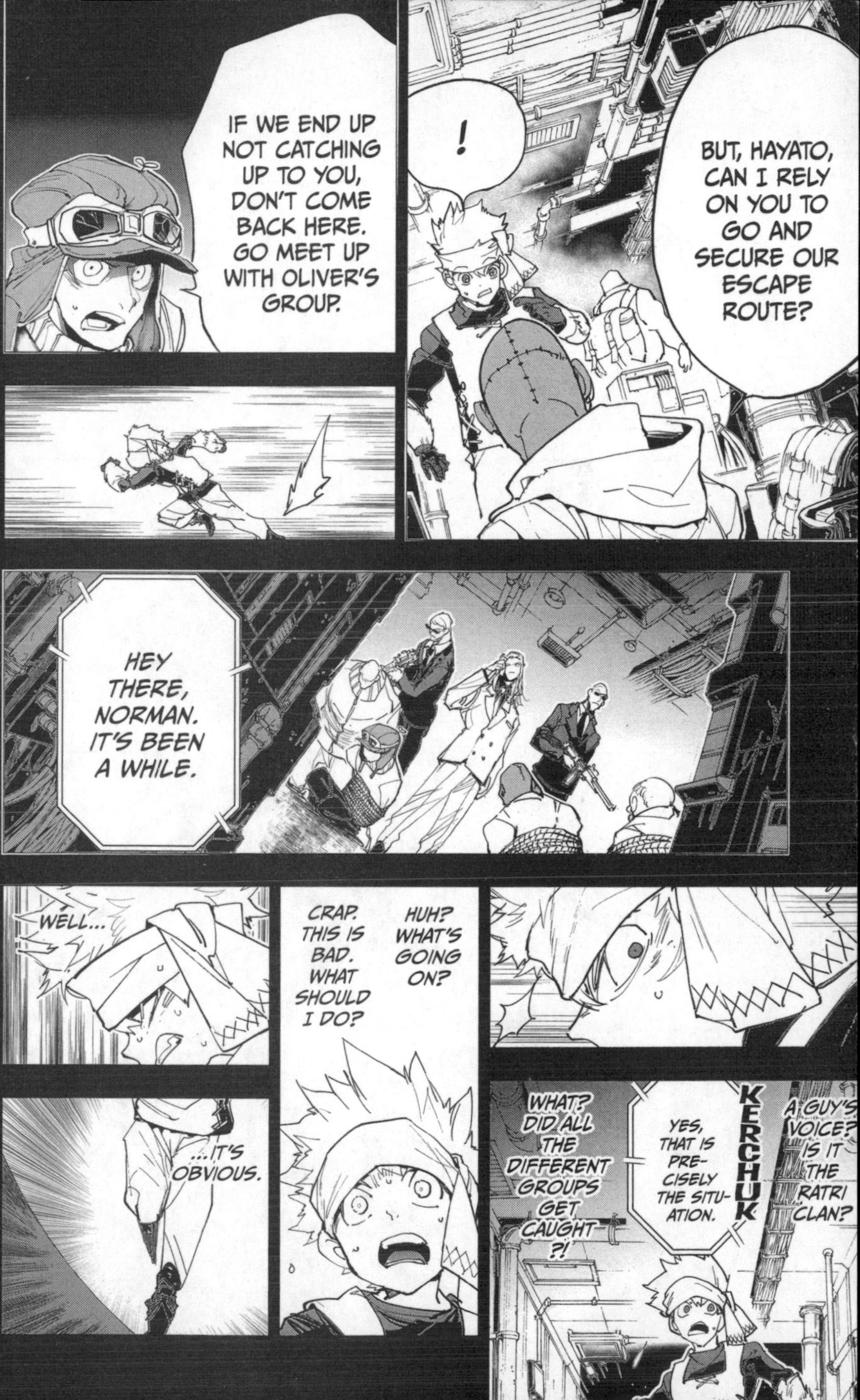
BUT, HAYATO, CAN I RELY ON YOU TO GO AND SECURE OUR ESCAPE ROUTE?
!
IF WE END UP NOT CATCHING UP TO YOU, DON'T COME BACK HERE. GO MEET UP WITH OLIVER'S GROUP.
HEY THERE, NORMAN. IT'S BEEN A WHILE.
A GUY'S VOICE? IS IT THE RATRI CLAN?
KERCHUK
YES, THAT IS PRE-CISELY THE SITU-ATION.
WHAT? DID ALL THE DIFFERENT GROUPS GET CAUGHT?!
HUH? WHAT'S GOING ON?
CRAP. THIS IS BAD. WHAT SHOULD I DO?
WELL...
...IT'S OBVIOUS.

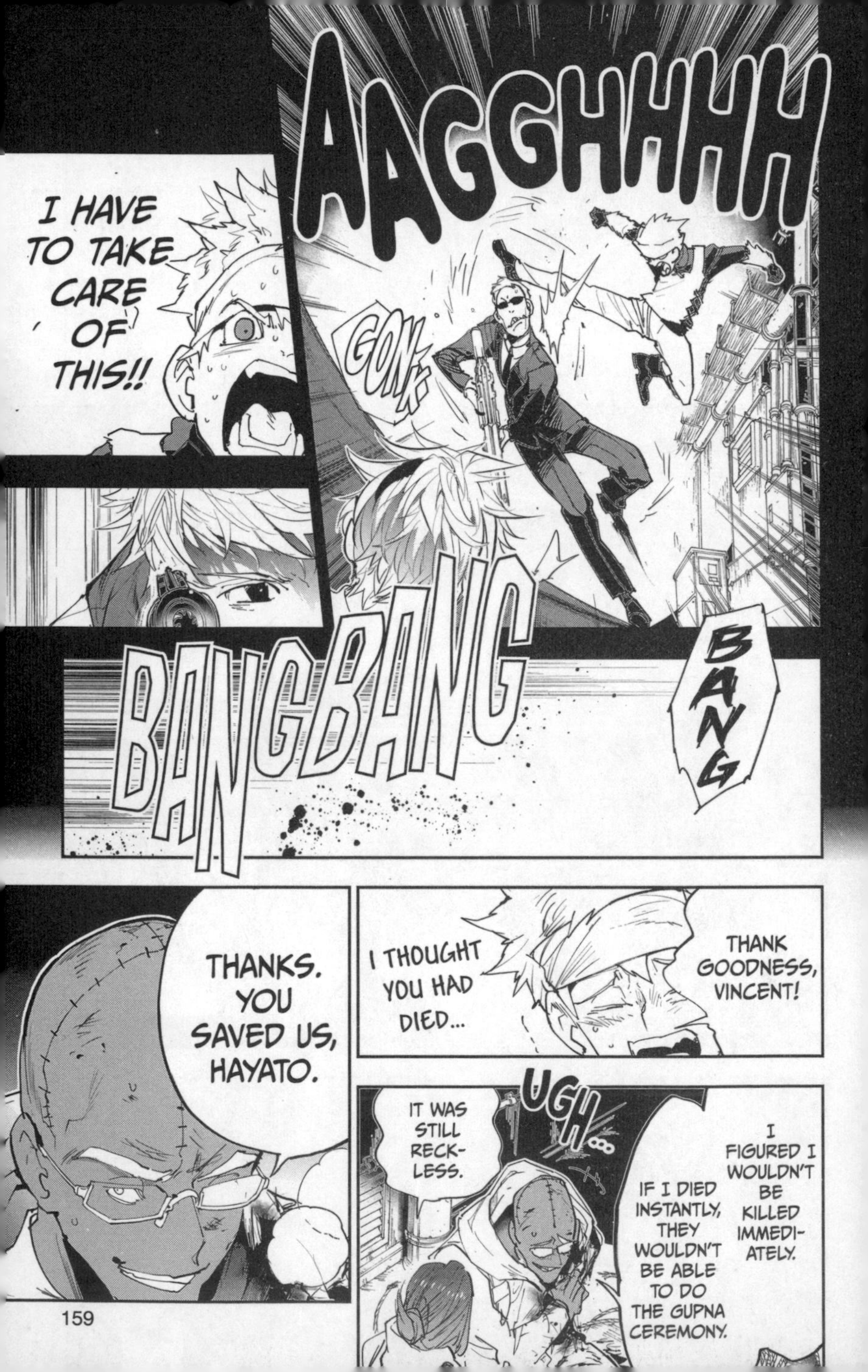
AAGHHHH
GONK
I HAVE TO TAKE CARE OF THIS!!
BANG
BANGBANG
THANK GOODNESS, VINCENT!
I THOUGHT YOU HAD DIED...
UGH...
I FIGURED I WOULDN'T BE KILLED IMMEDIATELY.
IF I DIED INSTANTLY, THEY WOULDN'T BE ABLE TO DO THE GUPNA CEREMONY.
IT WAS STILL RECKLESS.
THANKS. YOU SAVED US, HAYATO.

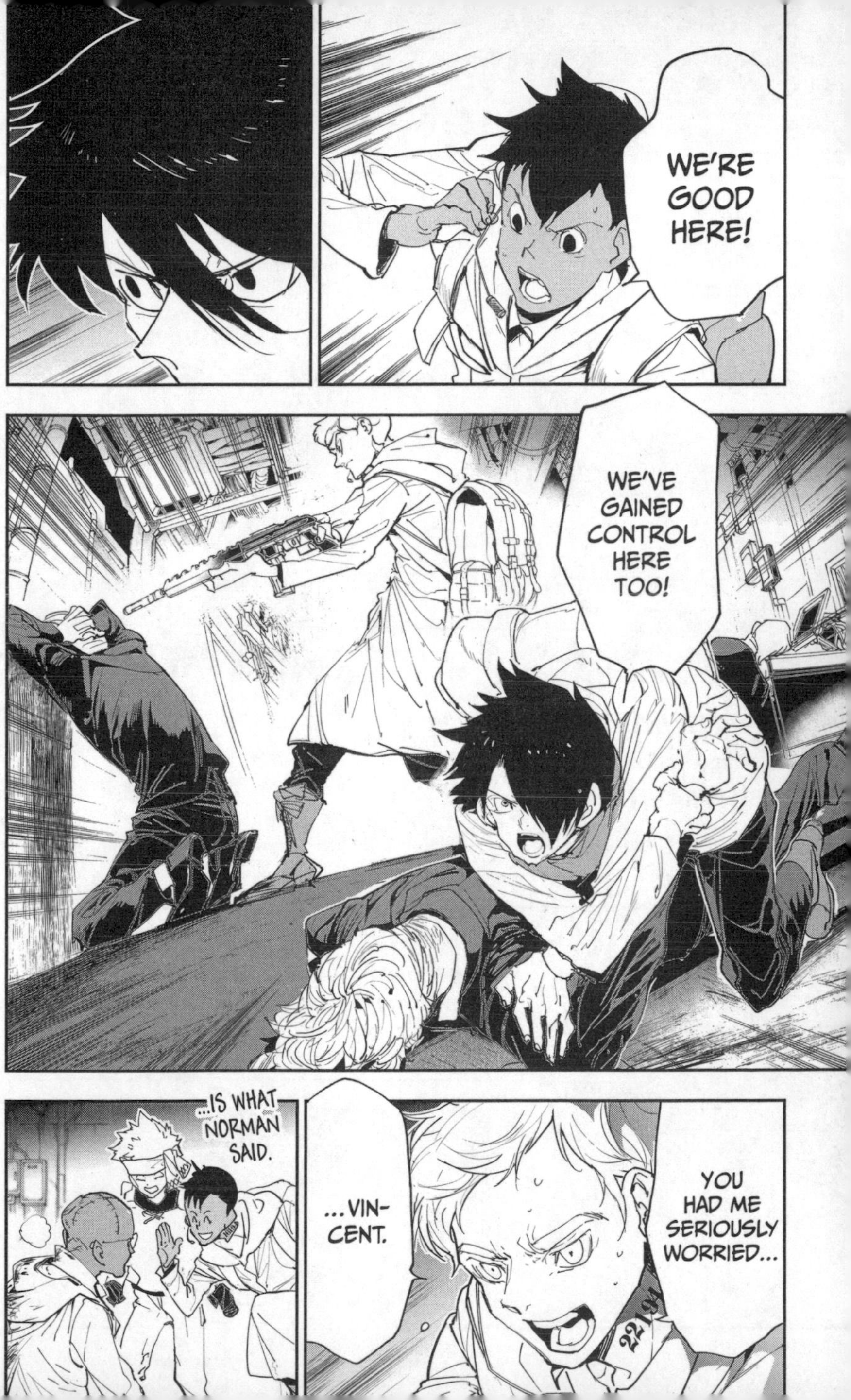
WE'RE GOOD HERE!
WE'VE GAINED CONTROL HERE TOO!
YOU HAD ME SERIOUSLY WORRIED...
...VIN-CENT.
...IS WHAT NORMAN SAID.

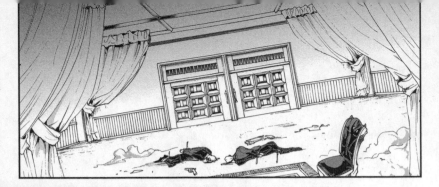

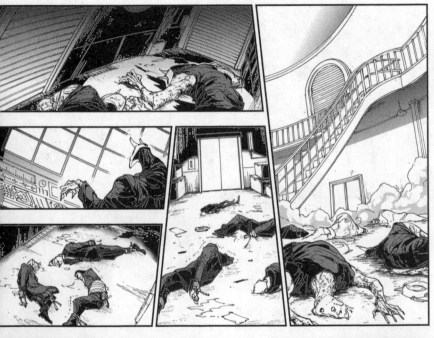

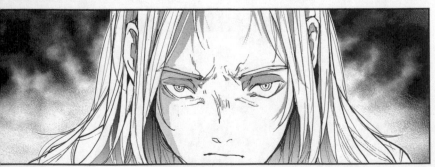

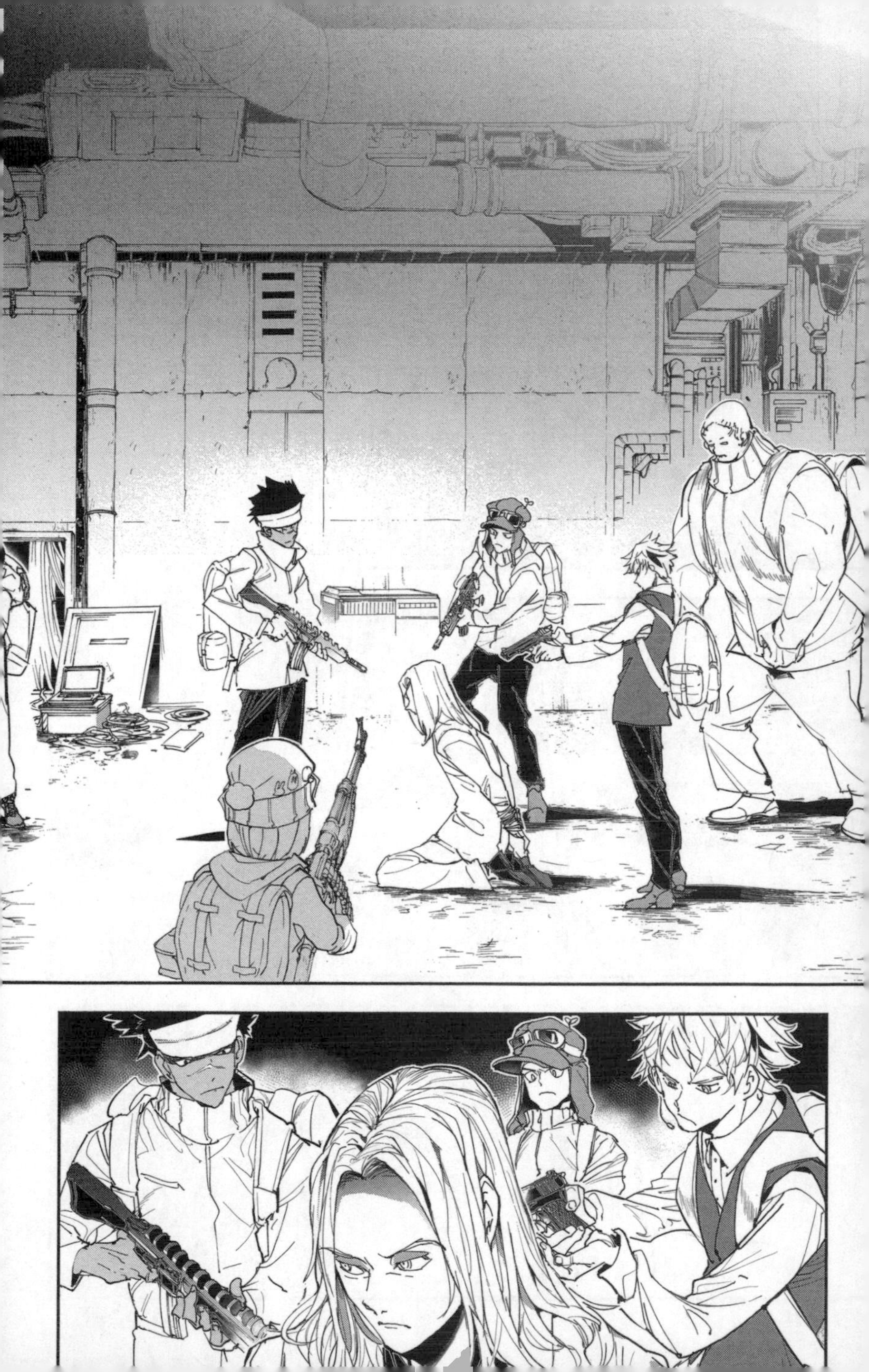

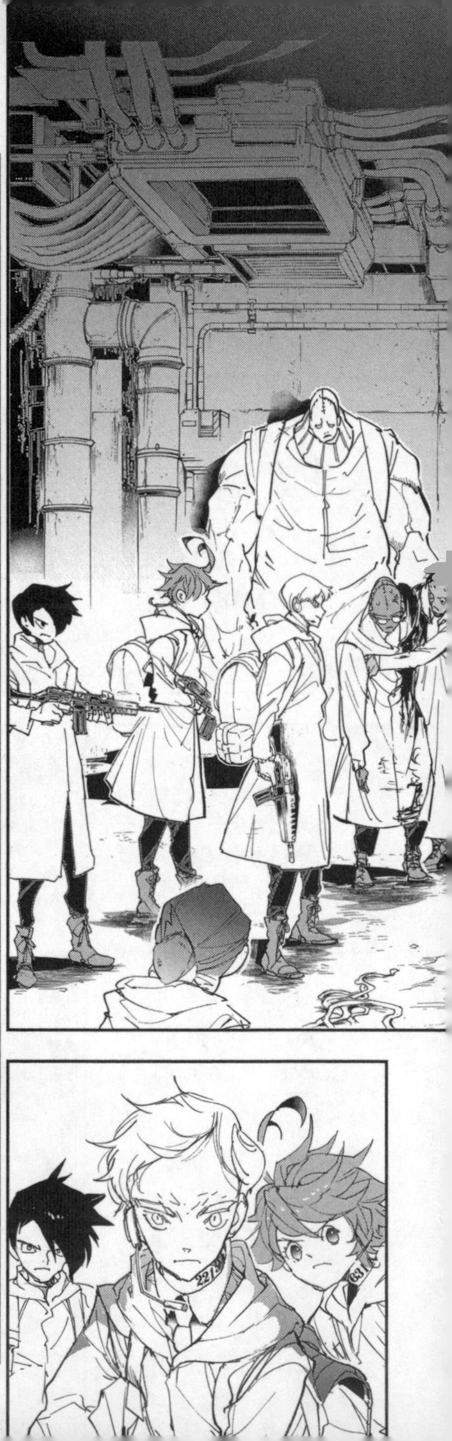

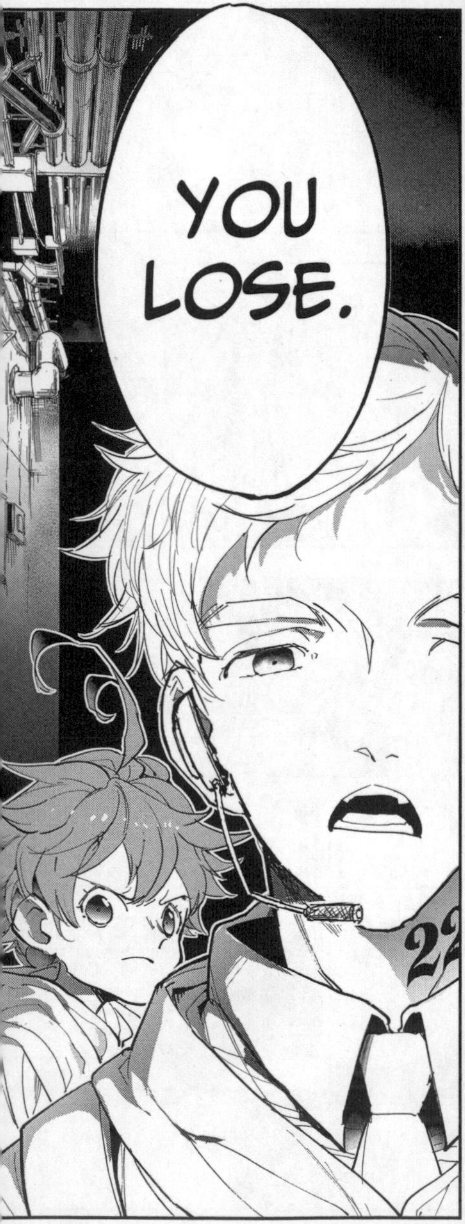
YOU LOSE.

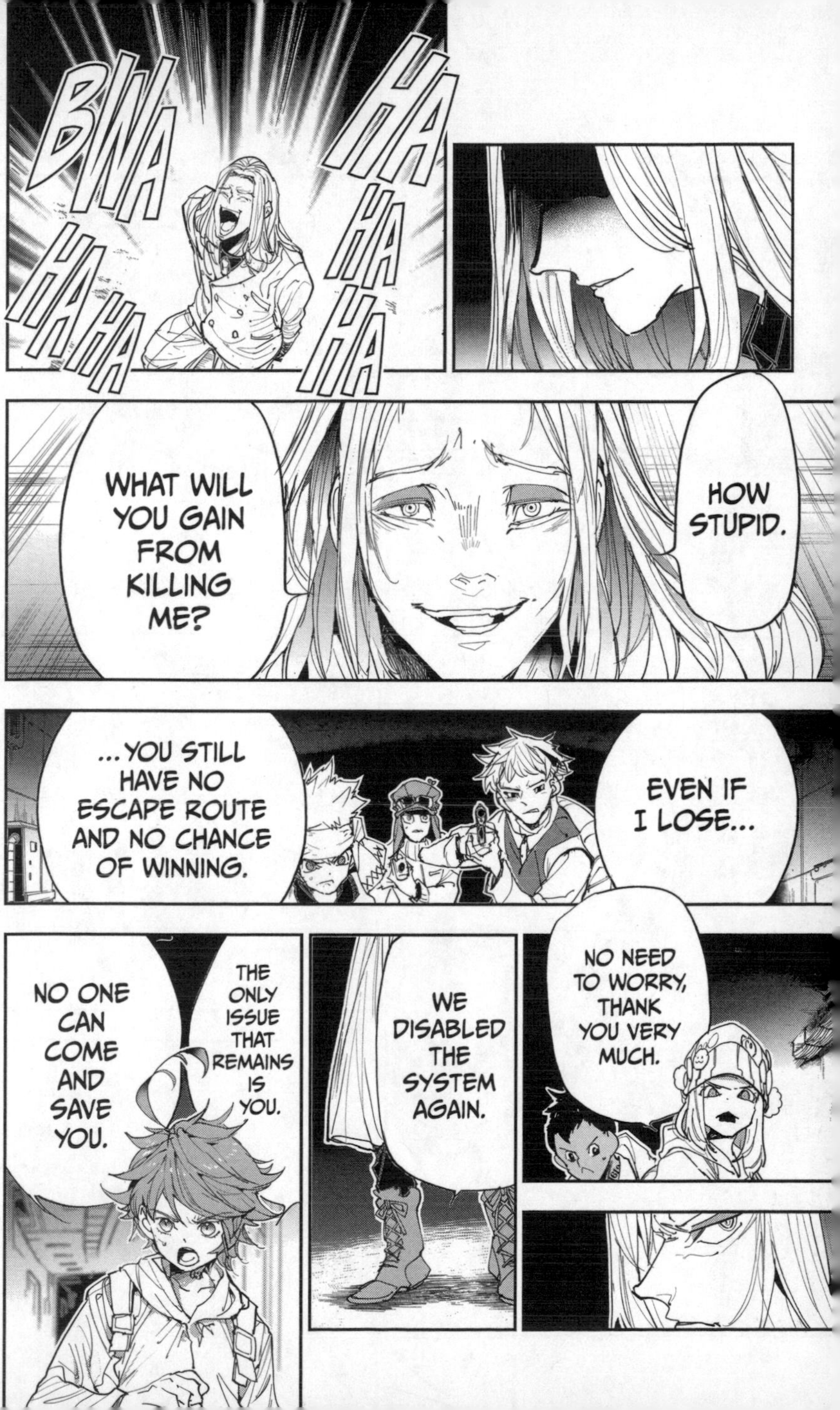
HAHAHAHA
BWAHAHA
HOW STUPID.
WHAT WILL YOU GAIN FROM KILLING ME?
EVEN IF I LOSE...
...YOU STILL HAVE NO ESCAPE ROUTE AND NO CHANCE OF WINNING.
NO NEED TO WORRY, THANK YOU VERY MUCH.
WE DISABLED THE SYSTEM AGAIN.
THE ONLY ISSUE THAT REMAINS IS YOU.
NO ONE CAN COME AND SAVE YOU.

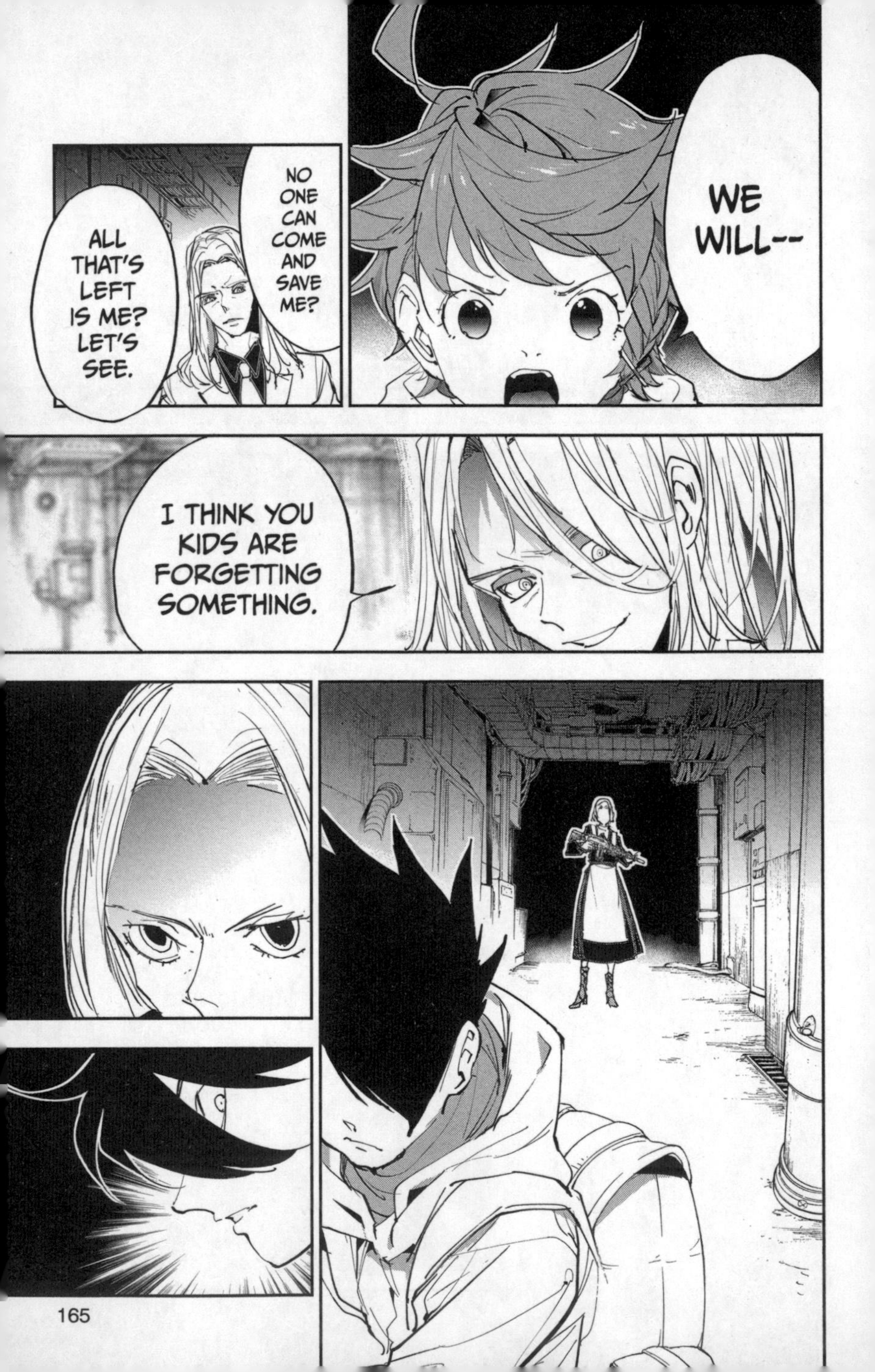
WE WILL--
NO ONE CAN COME AND SAVE ME?
ALL THAT'S LEFT IS ME? LET'S SEE.
I THINK YOU KIDS ARE FORGETTING SOMETHING.

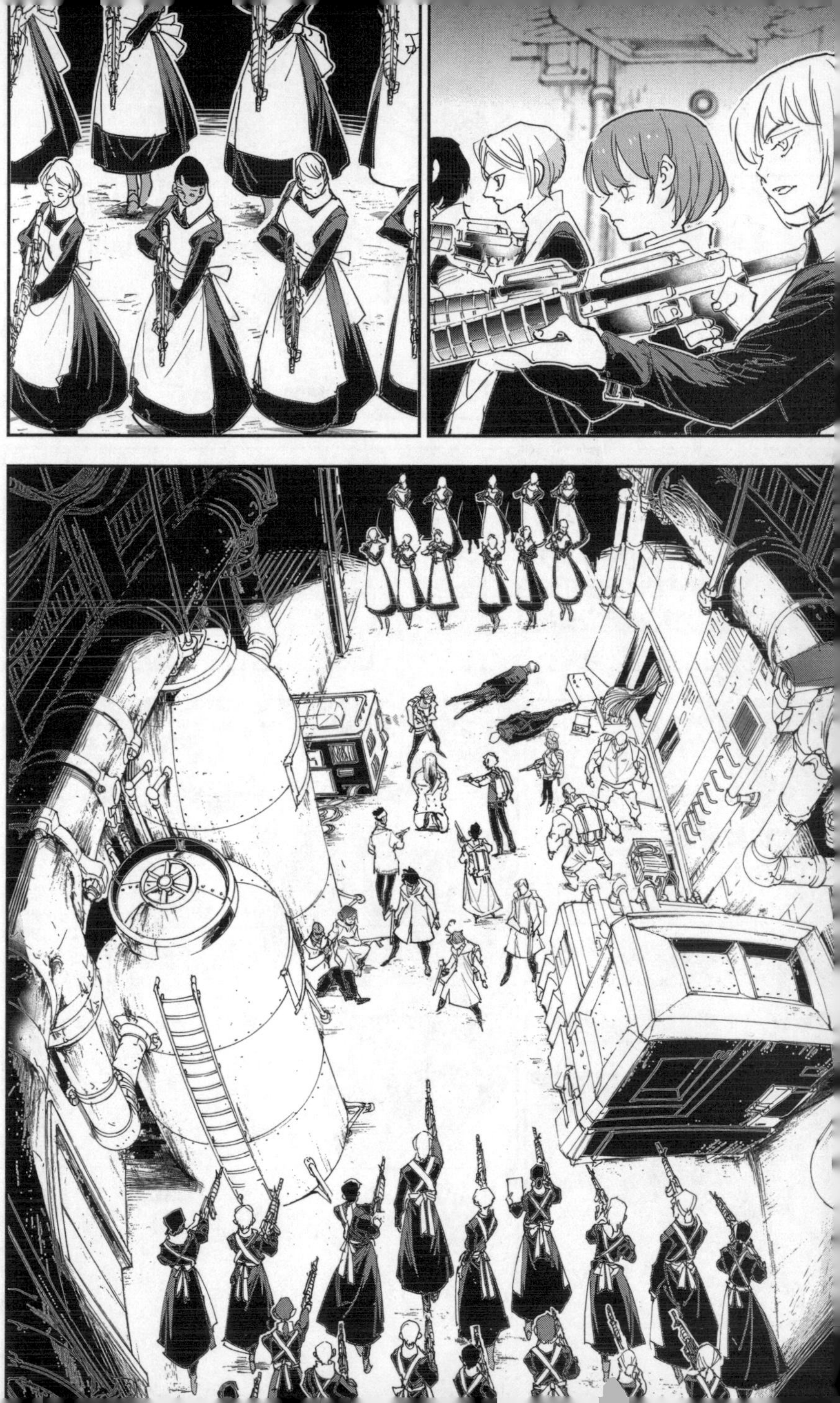

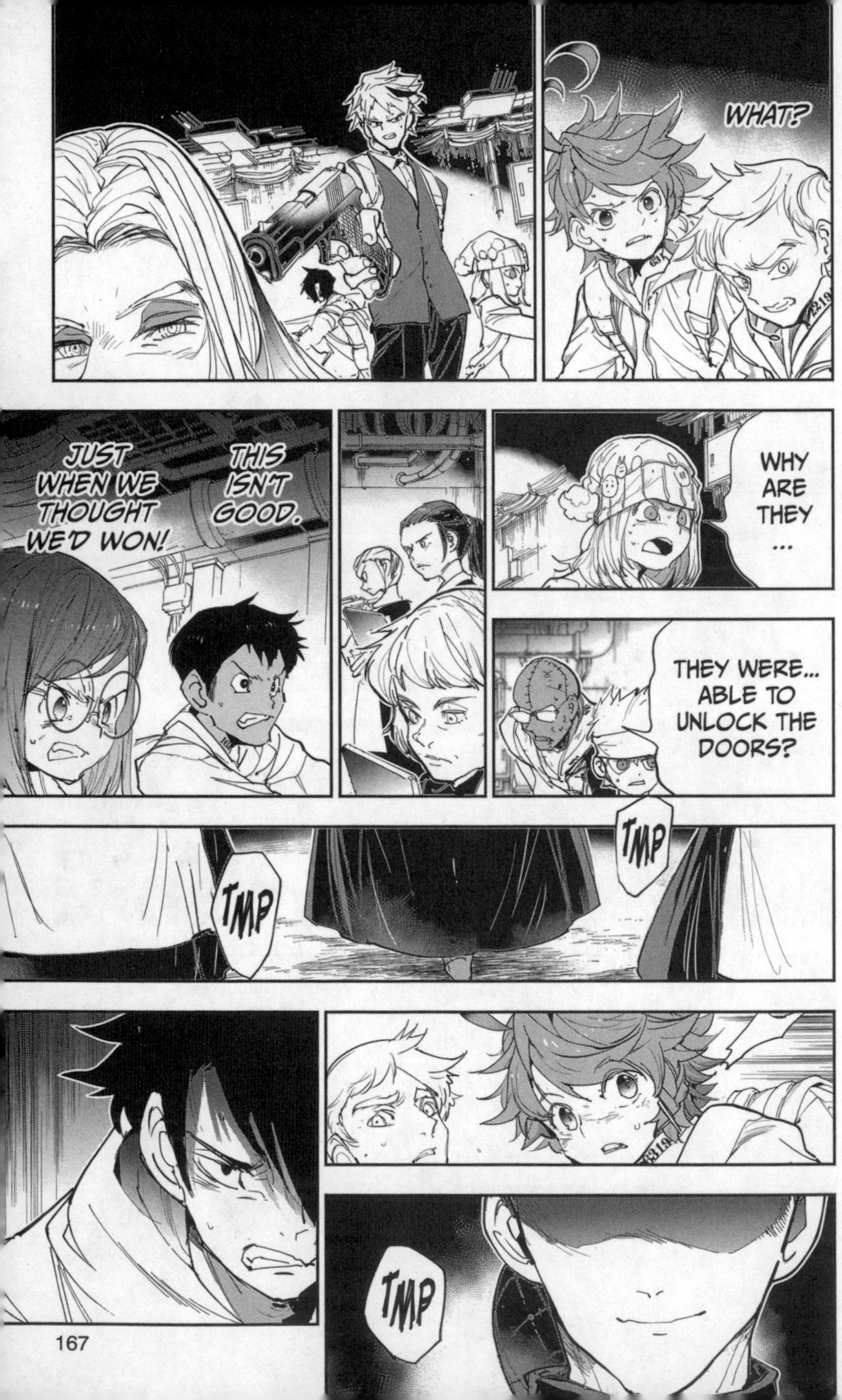

WHAT?
WHY ARE THEY ...
THEY WERE... ABLE TO UNLOCK THE DOORS?
THIS ISN'T GOOD.
JUST WHEN WE THOUGHT WE'D WON!
TMP
TMP
TMP

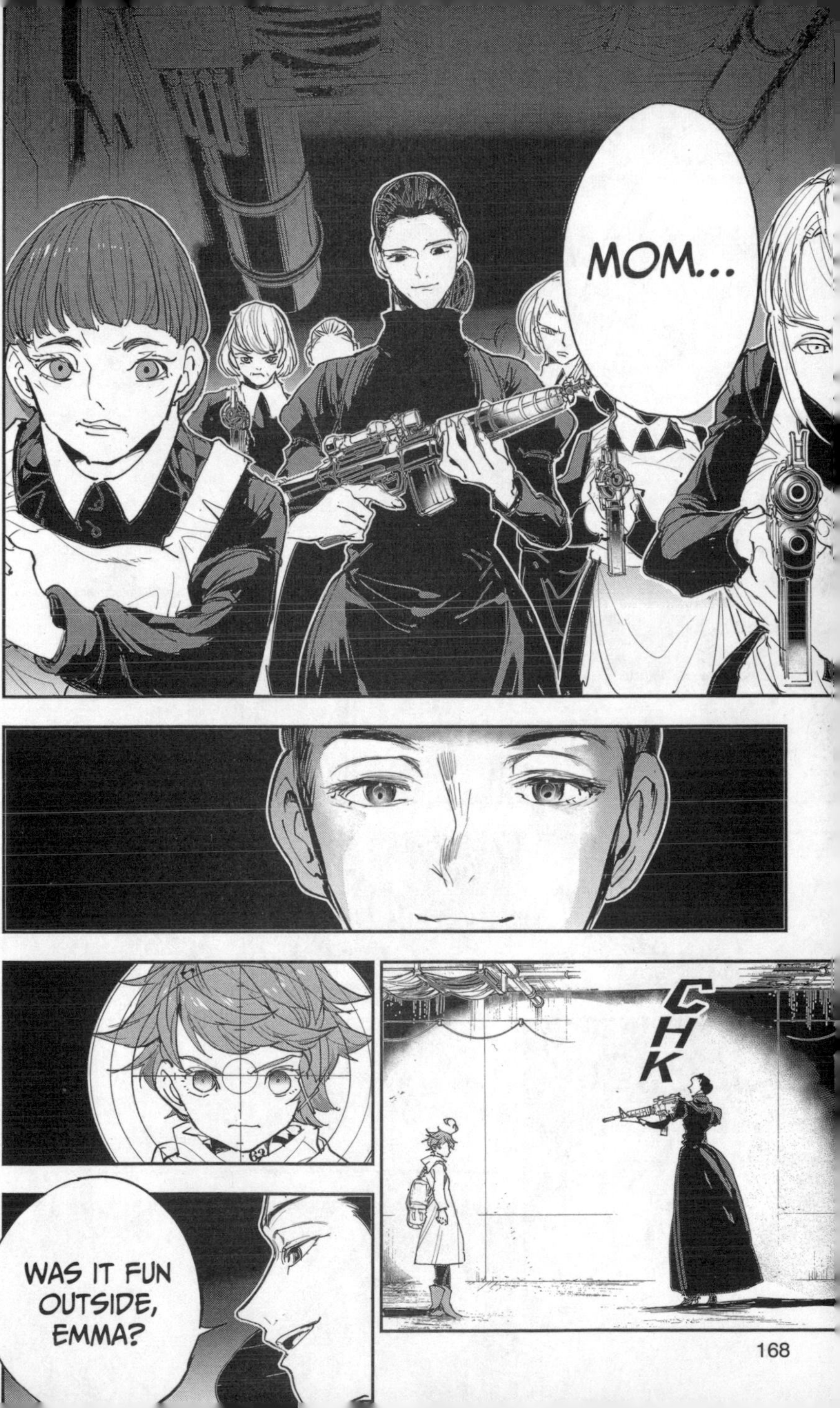
MOM...
CHK
WAS IT FUN OUTSIDE, EMMA?

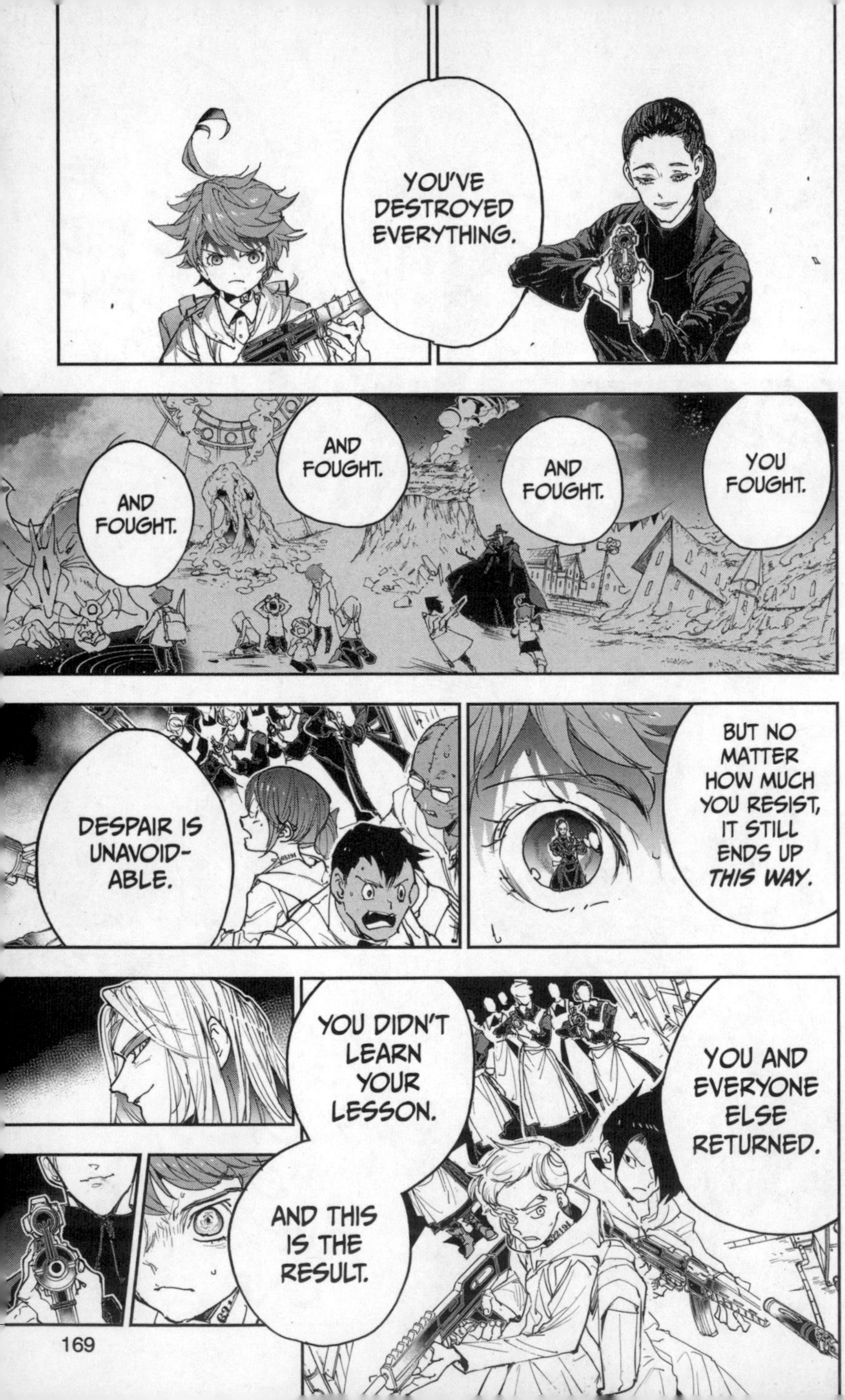
YOU'VE DESTROYED EVERYTHING.
YOU FOUGHT.
AND FOUGHT.
AND FOUGHT.
AND FOUGHT.
BUT NO MATTER HOW MUCH YOU RESIST, IT STILL ENDS UP *THIS WAY.*
DESPAIR IS UNAVOID-ABLE.
YOU AND EVERYONE ELSE RETURNED.
YOU DIDN'T LEARN YOUR LESSON.
AND THIS IS THE RESULT.

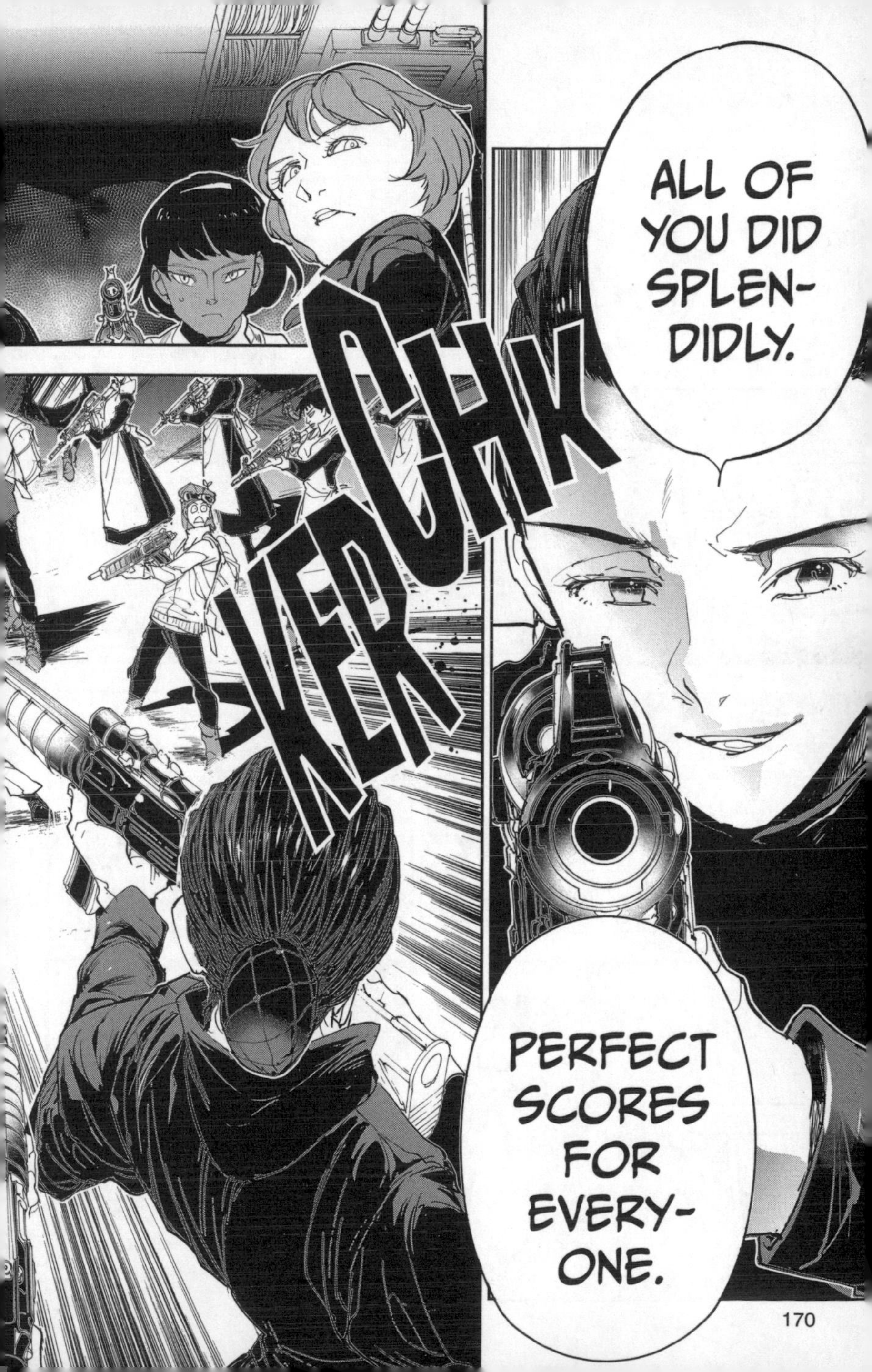
ALL OF YOU DID SPLEN-DIDLY.
PERFECT SCORES FOR EVERY-ONE.
KERCHK

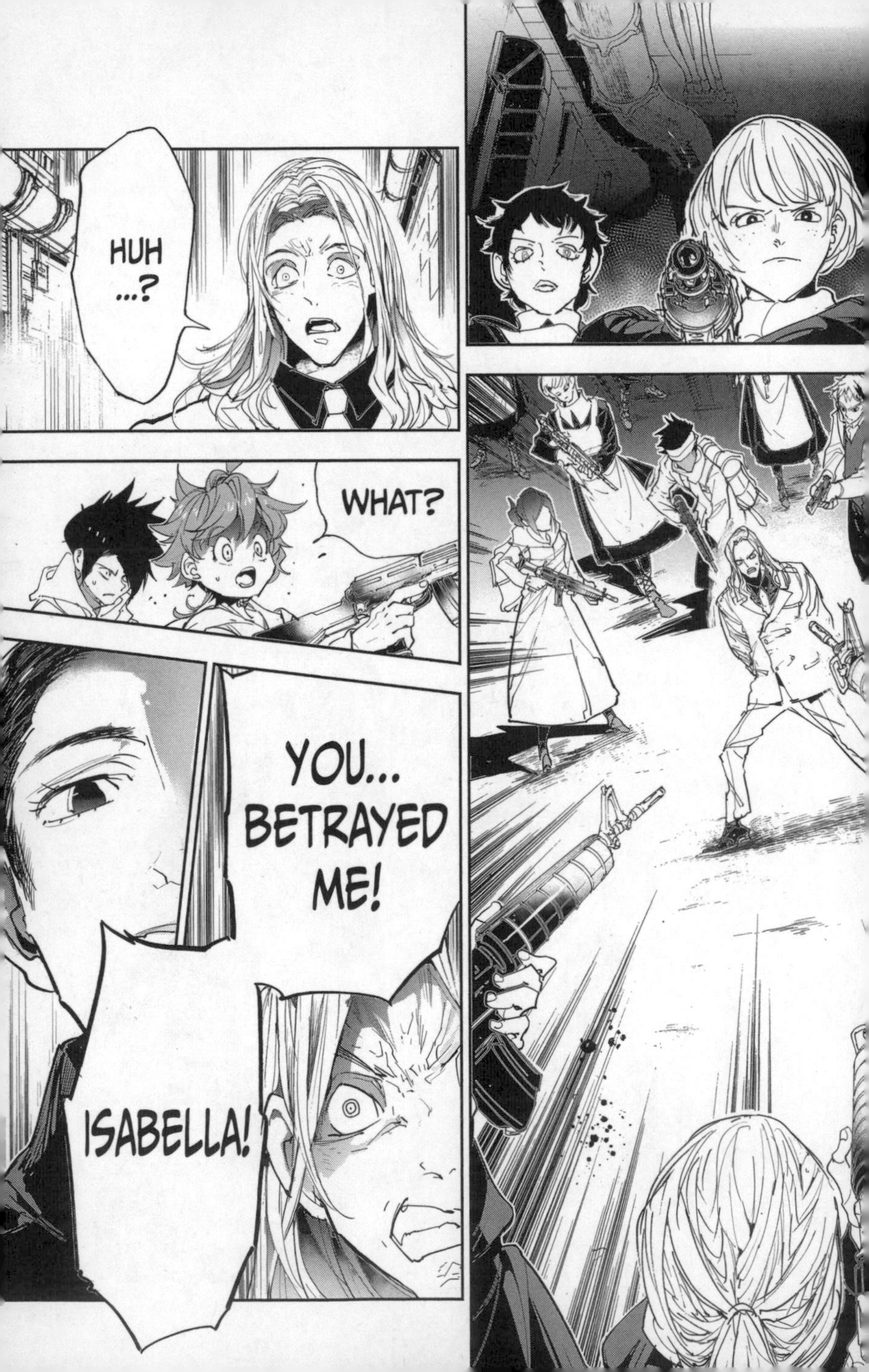
HUH ...?
WHAT?
YOU... BETRAYED ME!
ISABELLA!

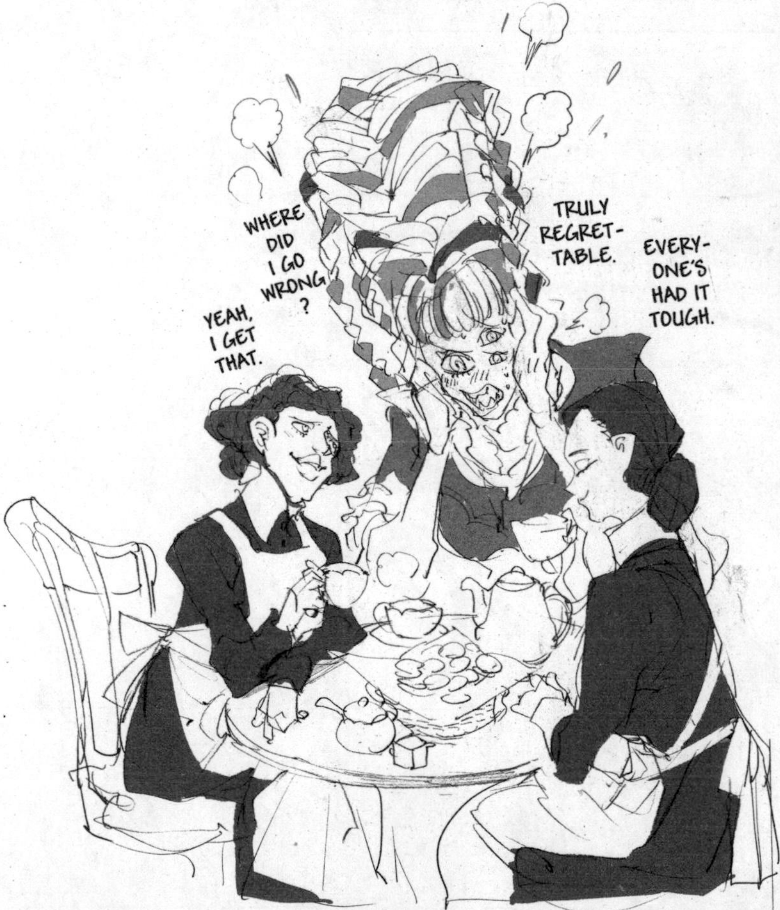
EVERY-ONE'S HAD IT TOUGH.
TRULY REGRET-TABLE.
WHERE DID I GO WRONG?
YEAH, I GET THAT.

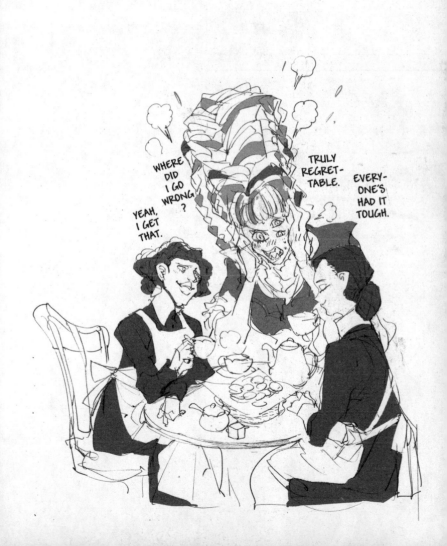

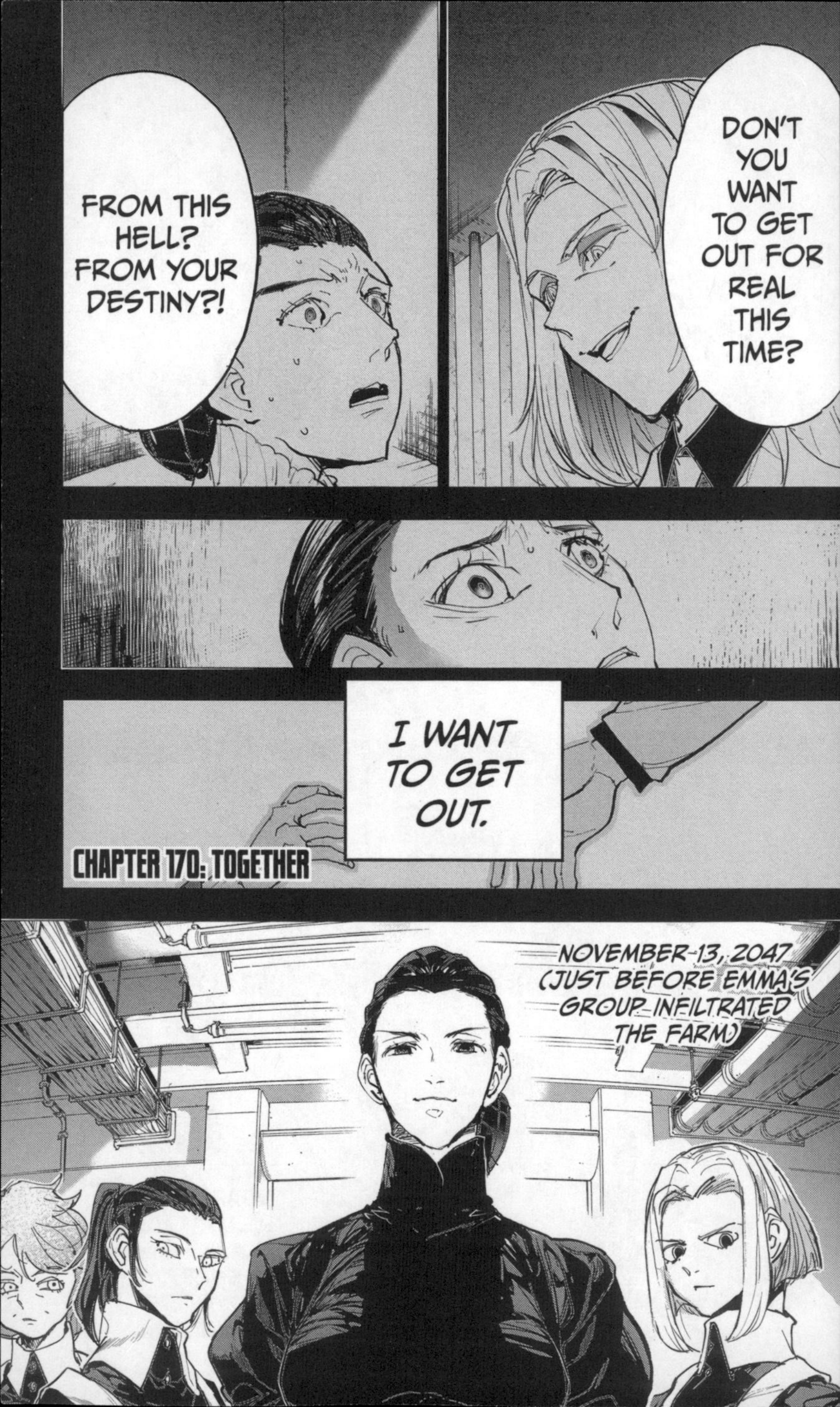
DON'T YOU WANT TO GET OUT FOR REAL THIS TIME?
FROM THIS HELL? FROM YOUR DESTINY?!
I WANT TO GET OUT.
CHAPTER 170: TOGETHER
NOVEMBER 13, 2047 (JUST BEFORE EMMA'S GROUP INFILTRATED THE FARM)

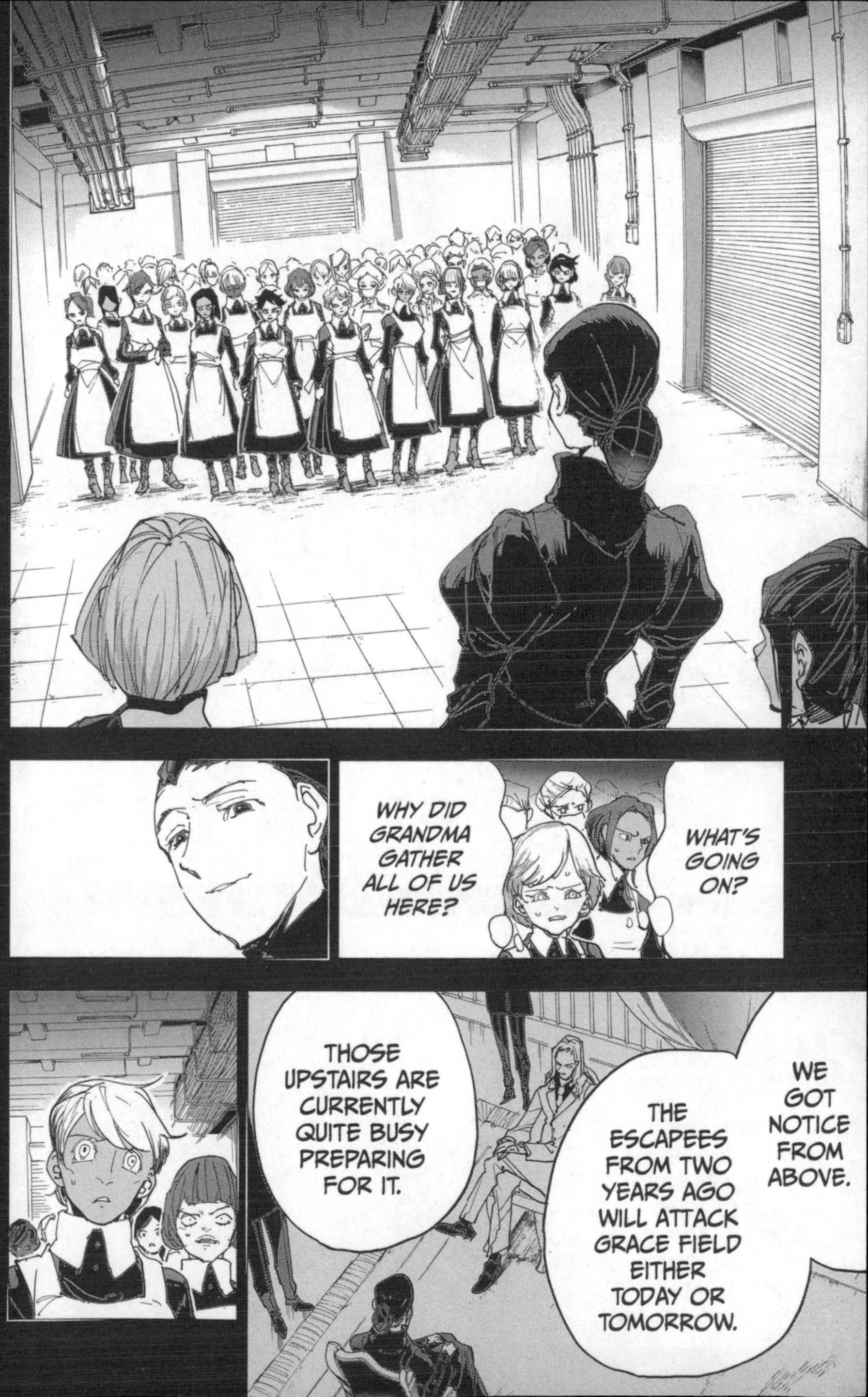
WHAT'S GOING ON?
WHY DID GRANDMA GATHER ALL OF US HERE?
WE GOT NOTICE FROM ABOVE.
THE ESCAPEES FROM TWO YEARS AGO WILL ATTACK GRACE FIELD EITHER TODAY OR TOMORROW.
THOSE UPSTAIRS ARE CURRENTLY QUITE BUSY PREPARING FOR IT.

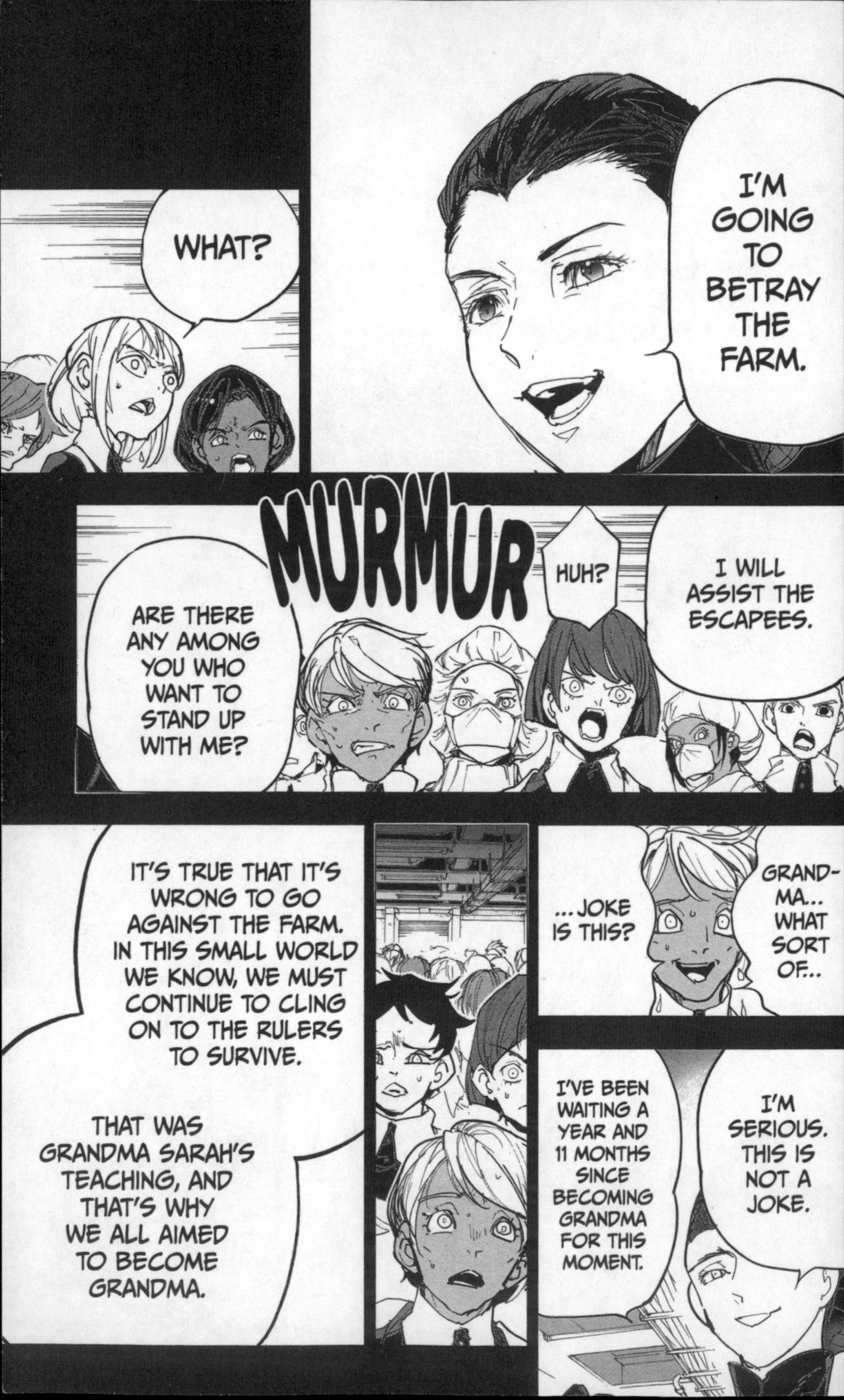
I'M GOING TO BETRAY THE FARM.
WHAT?
I WILL ASSIST THE ESCAPEES.
HUH?
MURMUR
ARE THERE ANY AMONG YOU WHO WANT TO STAND UP WITH ME?
GRAND-MA... WHAT SORT OF...
...JOKE IS THIS?
I'M SERIOUS. THIS IS NOT A JOKE.
I'VE BEEN WAITING A YEAR AND 11 MONTHS SINCE BECOMING GRANDMA FOR THIS MOMENT.
IT'S TRUE THAT IT'S WRONG TO GO AGAINST THE FARM. IN THIS SMALL WORLD WE KNOW, WE MUST CONTINUE TO CLING ON TO THE RULERS TO SURVIVE.
THAT WAS GRANDMA SARAH'S TEACHING, AND THAT'S WHY WE ALL AIMED TO BECOME GRANDMA.

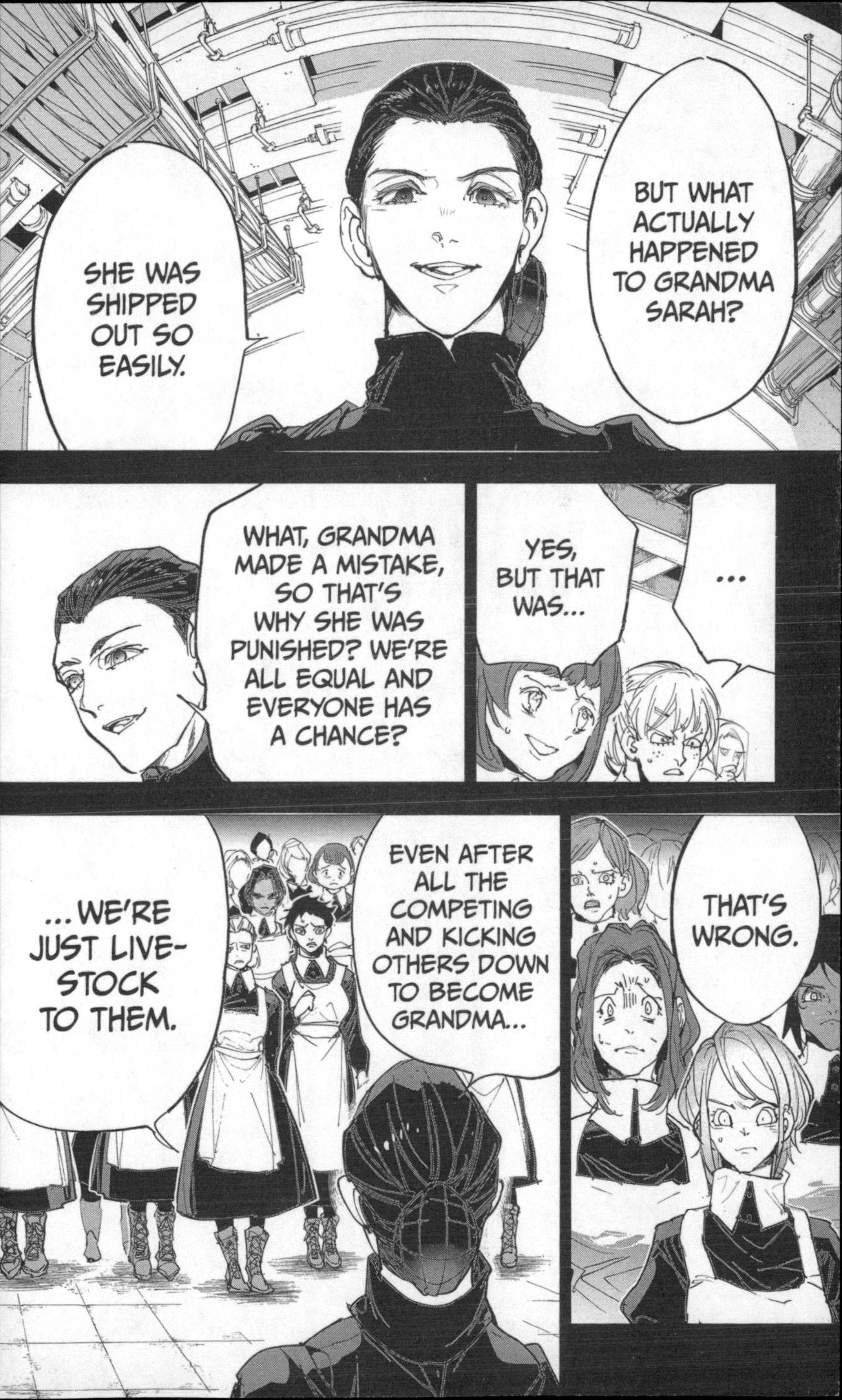

BUT WHAT ACTUALLY HAPPENED TO GRANDMA SARAH?
SHE WAS SHIPPED OUT SO EASILY.
...
YES, BUT THAT WAS...
WHAT, GRANDMA MADE A MISTAKE, SO THAT'S WHY SHE WAS PUNISHED? WE'RE ALL EQUAL AND EVERYONE HAS A CHANCE?
THAT'S WRONG.
EVEN AFTER ALL THE COMPETING AND KICKING OTHERS DOWN TO BECOME GRANDMA...
...WE'RE JUST LIVE-STOCK TO THEM.

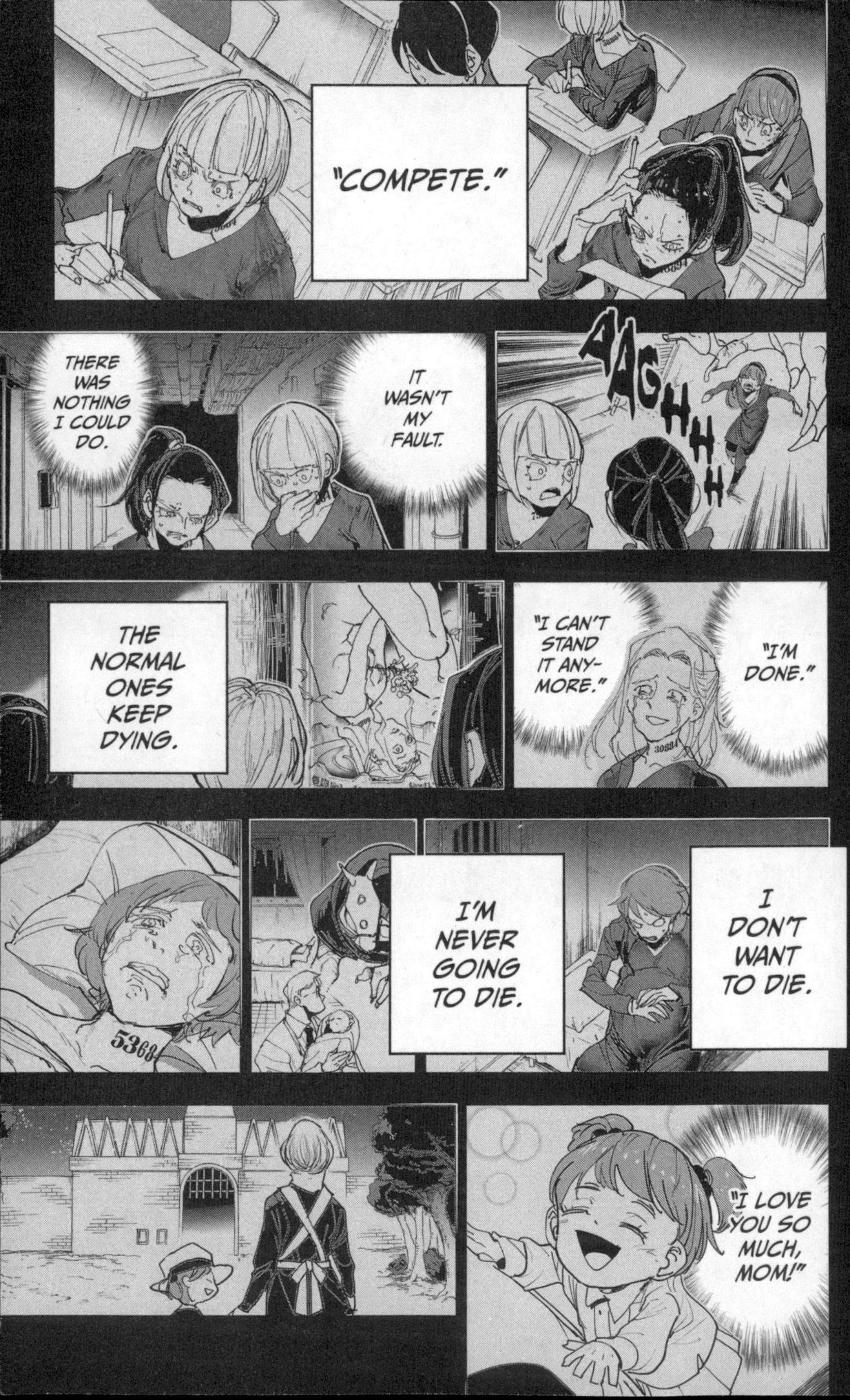
"COMPETE."
AAGHHHH
IT WASN'T MY FAULT.
THERE WAS NOTHING I COULD DO.
"I'M DONE."
"I CAN'T STAND IT ANY-MORE."
THE NORMAL ONES KEEP DYING.
I DON'T WANT TO DIE.
I'M NEVER GOING TO DIE.
"I LOVE YOU SO MUCH, MOM!"

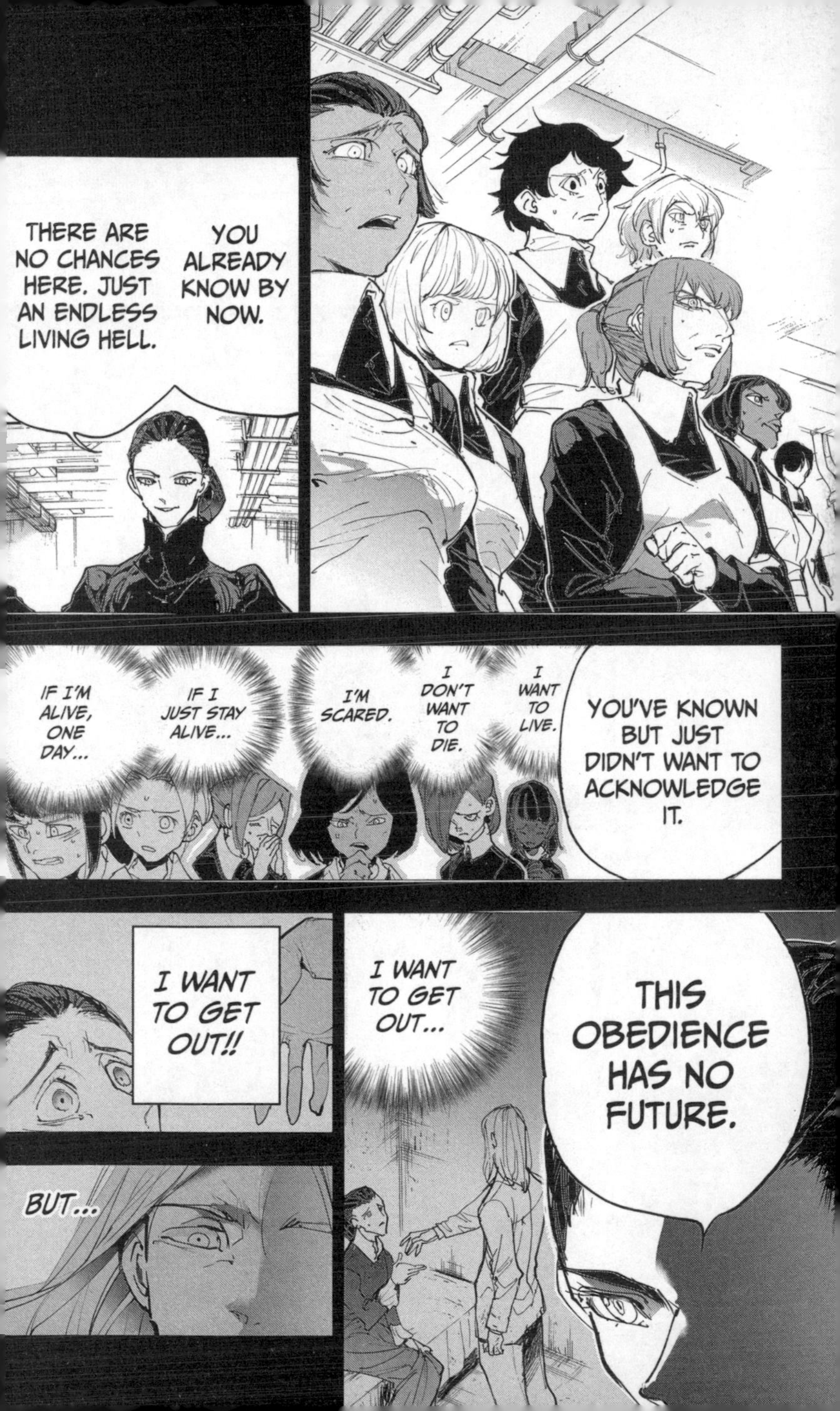
YOU ALREADY KNOW BY NOW.
THERE ARE NO CHANCES HERE. JUST AN ENDLESS LIVING HELL.
YOU'VE KNOWN BUT JUST DIDN'T WANT TO ACKNOWLEDGE IT.
I WANT TO LIVE.
I DON'T WANT TO DIE.
I'M SCARED.
IF I JUST STAY ALIVE...
IF I'M ALIVE, ONE DAY...
THIS OBEDIENCE HAS NO FUTURE.
I WANT TO GET OUT...
I WANT TO GET OUT!!
BUT...

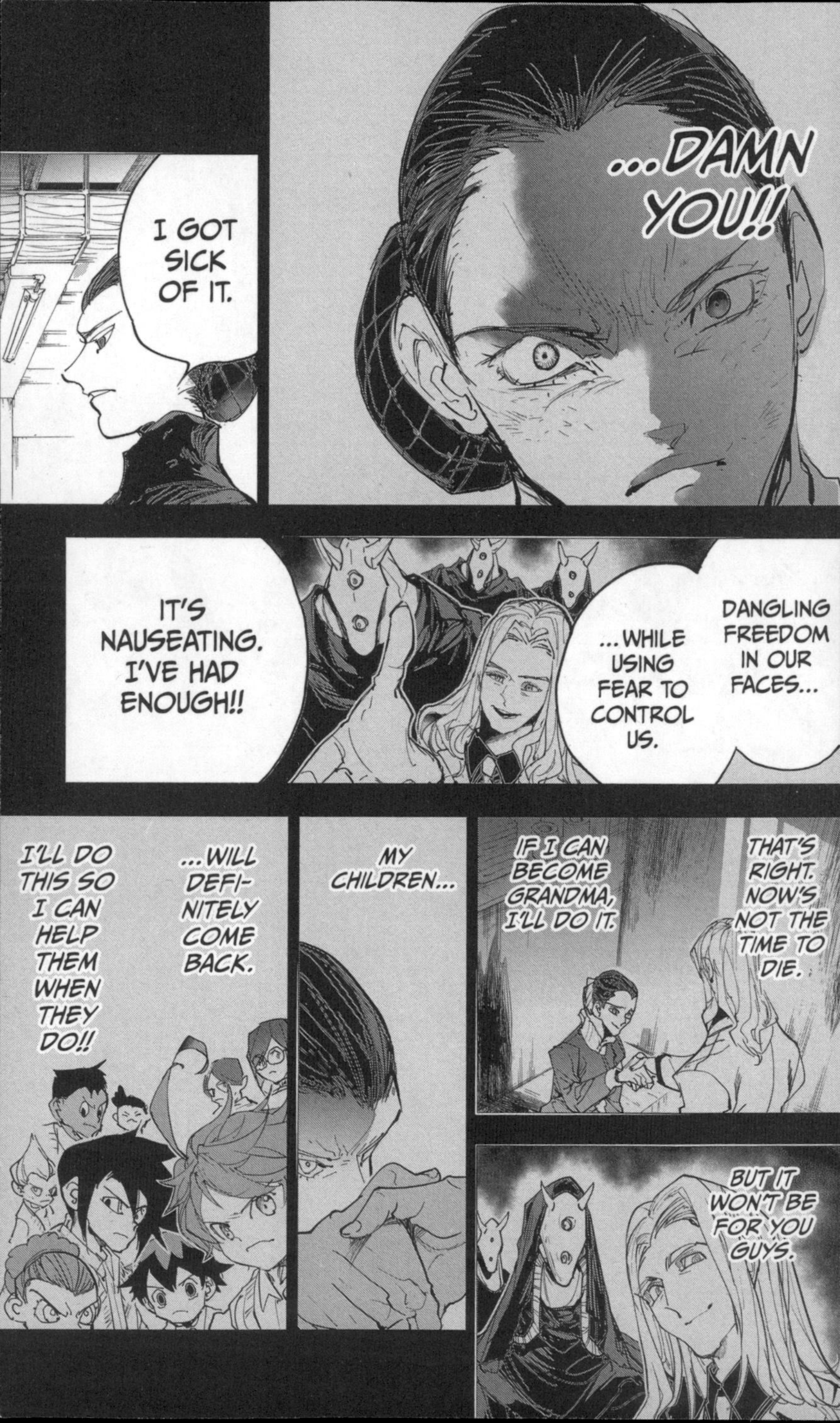
...DAMN YOU!!
I GOT SICK OF IT.
DANGLING FREEDOM IN OUR FACES...
...WHILE USING FEAR TO CONTROL US.
IT'S NAUSEATING. I'VE HAD ENOUGH!!
THAT'S RIGHT. NOW'S NOT THE TIME TO DIE.
IF I CAN BECOME GRANDMA, I'LL DO IT.
BUT IT WON'T BE FOR YOU GUYS.
MY CHILDREN...
...WILL DEFI- NITELY COME BACK.
I'LL DO THIS SO I CAN HELP THEM WHEN THEY DO!!

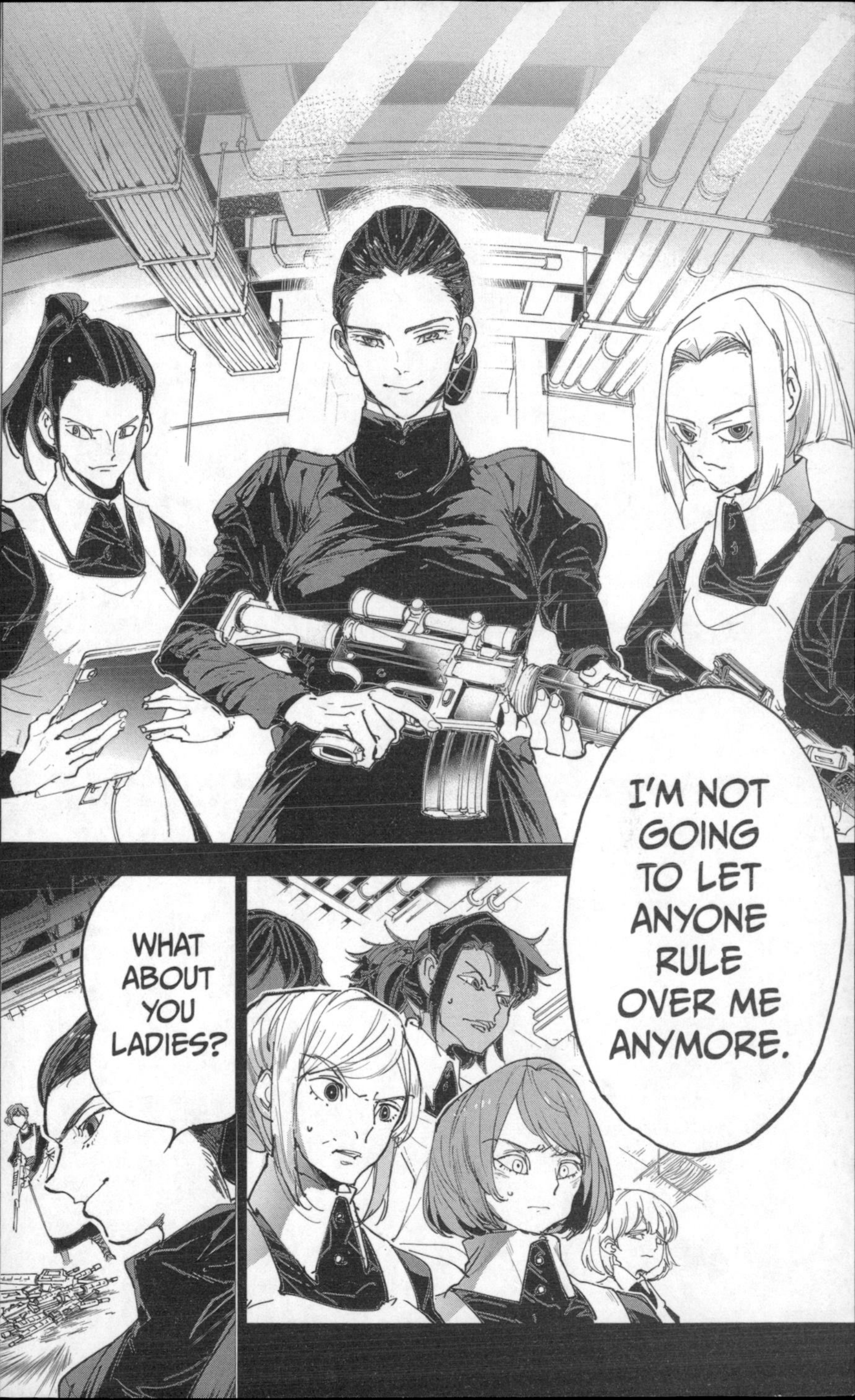
I'M NOT GOING TO LET ANYONE RULE OVER ME ANYMORE.
WHAT ABOUT YOU LADIES?

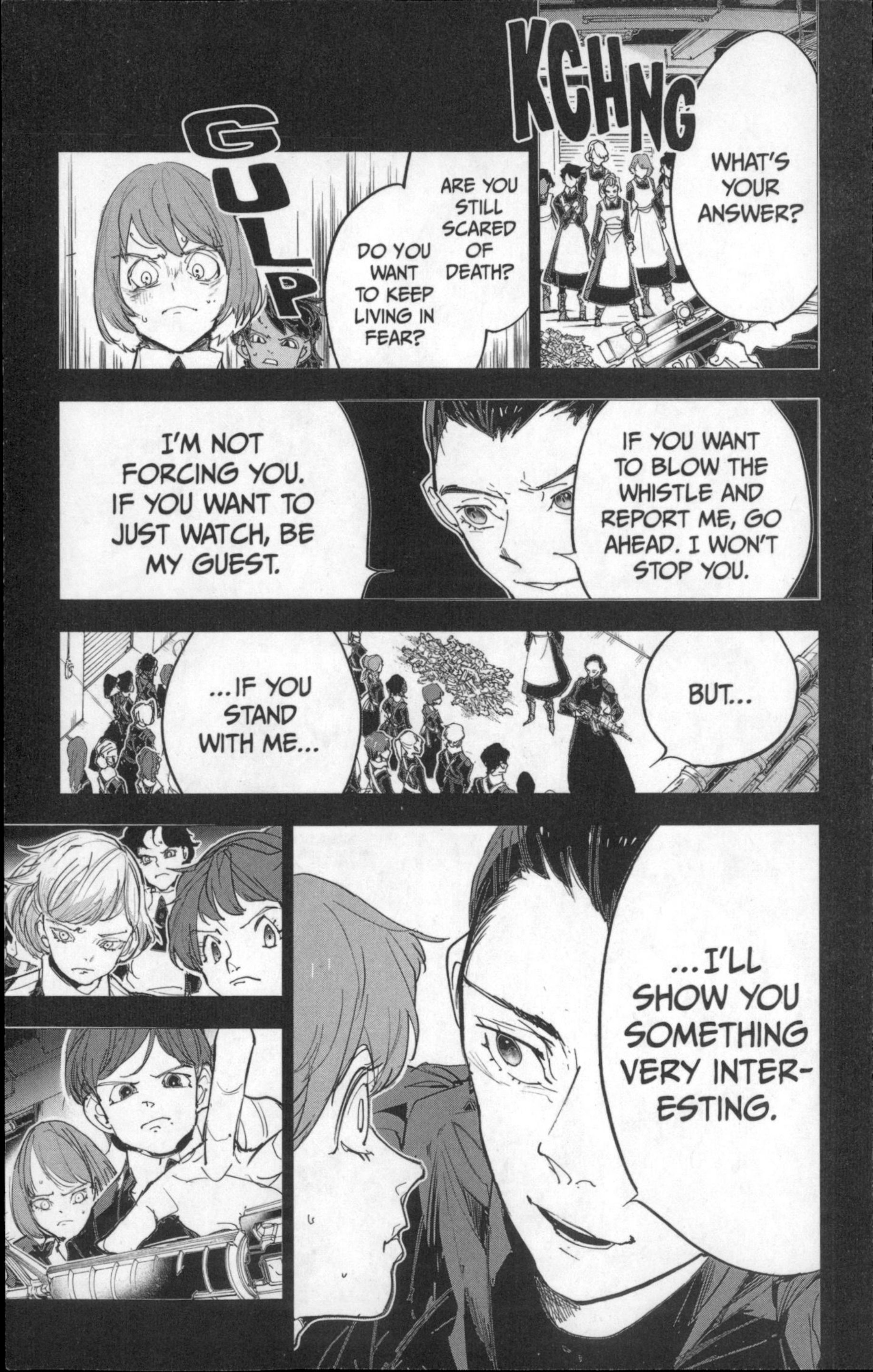
KCHNG
WHAT'S YOUR ANSWER?
ARE YOU STILL SCARED OF DEATH?
DO YOU WANT TO KEEP LIVING IN FEAR?
GULP
IF YOU WANT TO BLOW THE WHISTLE AND REPORT ME, GO AHEAD. I WON'T STOP YOU.
I'M NOT FORCING YOU. IF YOU WANT TO JUST WATCH, BE MY GUEST.
BUT...
...IF YOU STAND WITH ME...
...I'LL SHOW YOU SOMETHING VERY INTER-ESTING.

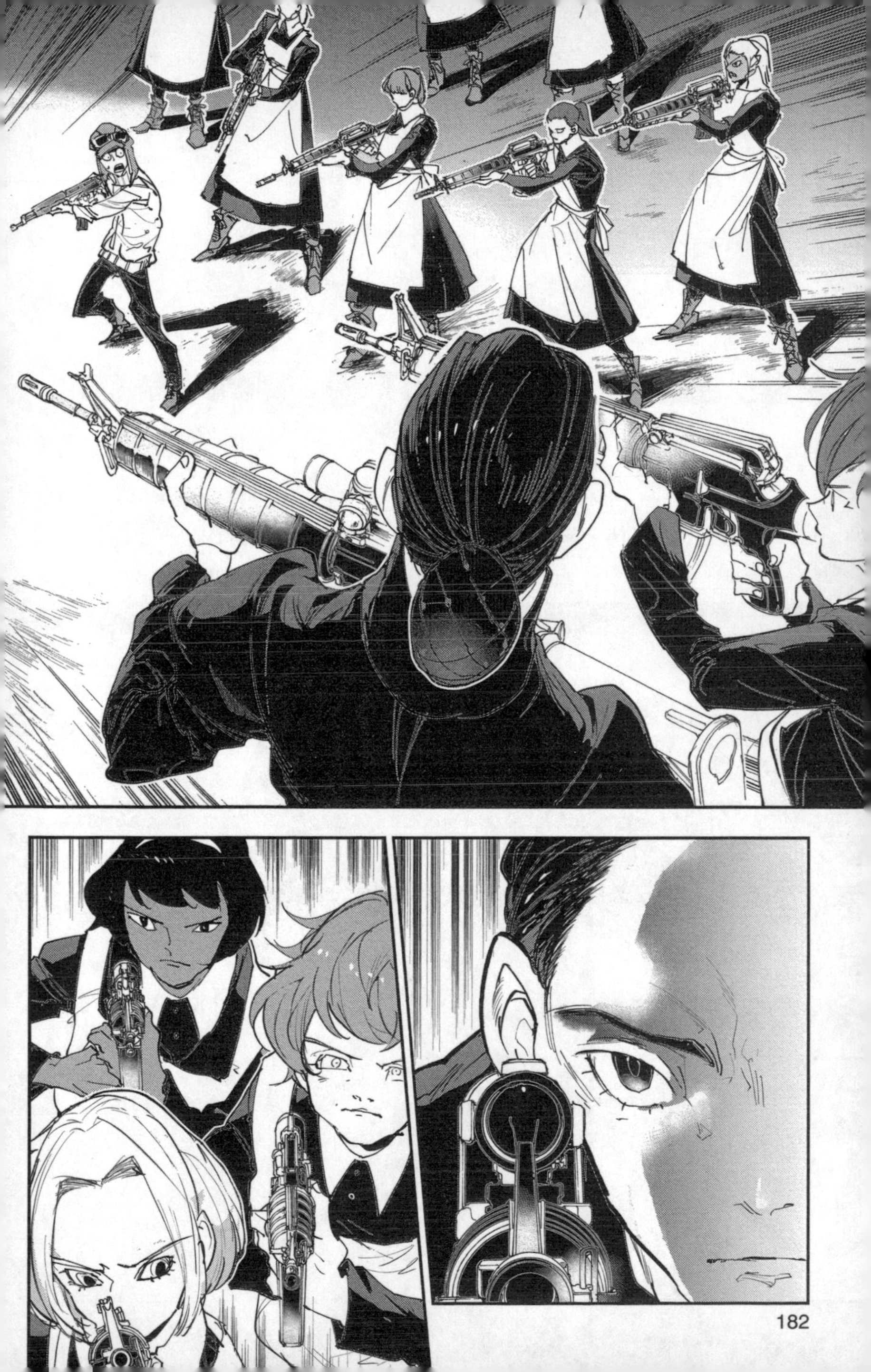

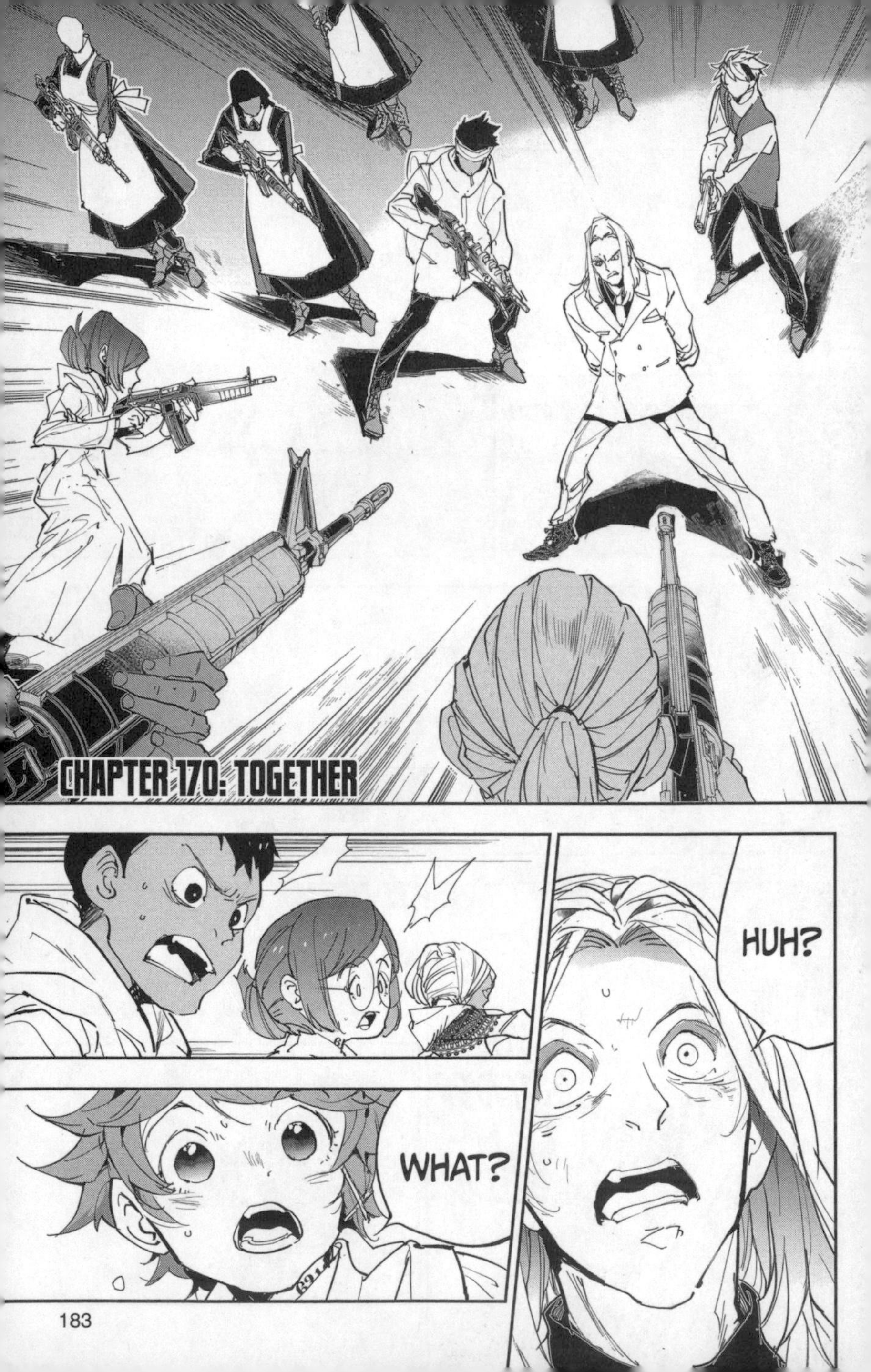
CHAPTER 170: TOGETHER
HUH?
WHAT?

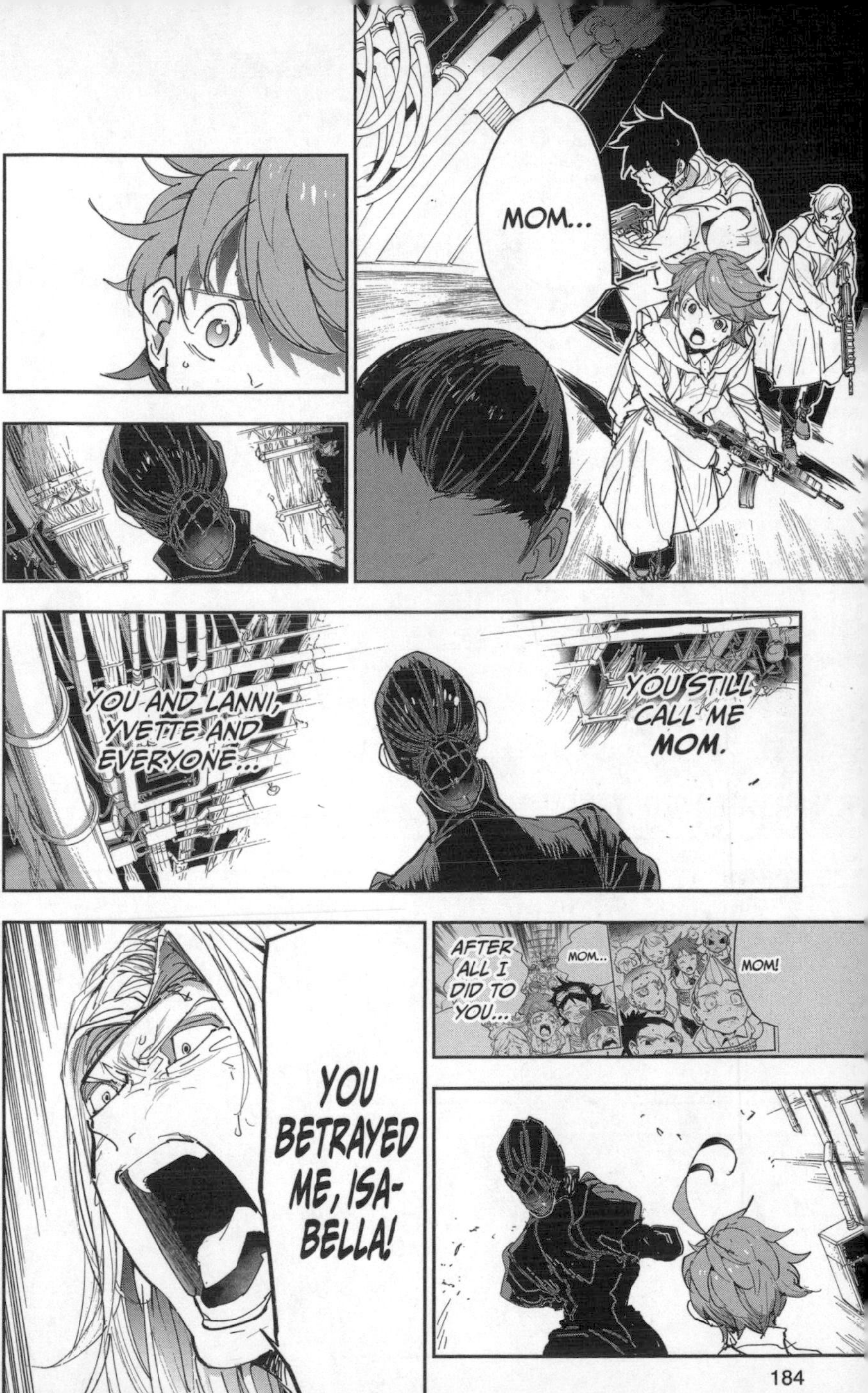
MOM...
YOU STILL CALL ME MOM.
YOU AND LANNI, YVETTE AND EVERYONE...
MOM!
MOM...
AFTER ALL I DID TO YOU...
YOU BETRAYED ME, ISA-BELLA!

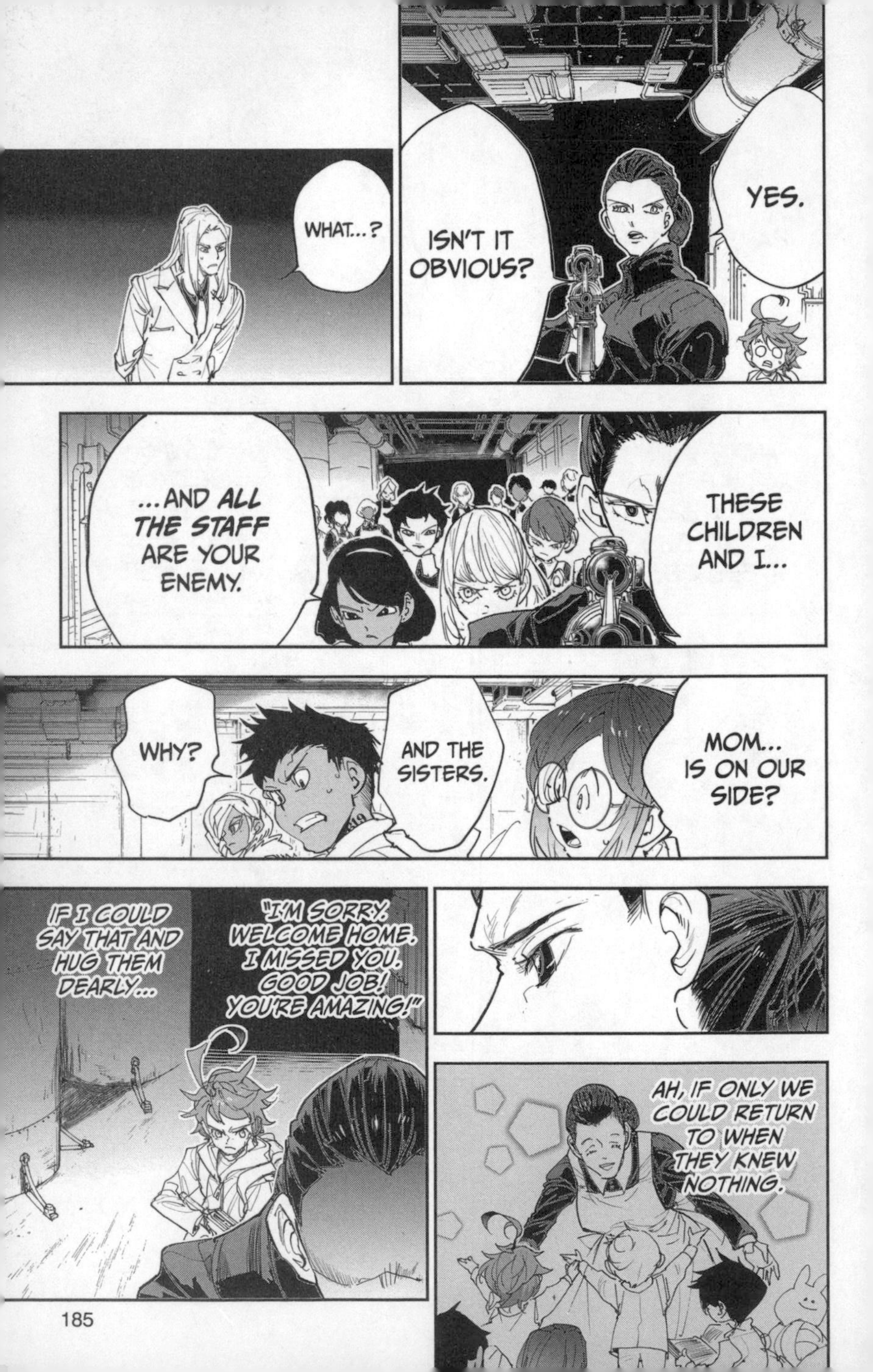
YES.
ISN'T IT OBVIOUS?
WHAT...?
THESE CHILDREN AND I...
...AND ALL THE STAFF ARE YOUR ENEMY.
MOM... IS ON OUR SIDE?
AND THE SISTERS.
WHY?
AH, IF ONLY WE COULD RETURN TO WHEN THEY KNEW NOTHING.
"I'M SORRY. WELCOME HOME. I MISSED YOU. GOOD JOB! YOU'RE AMAZING!"
IF I COULD SAY THAT AND HUG THEM DEARLY...

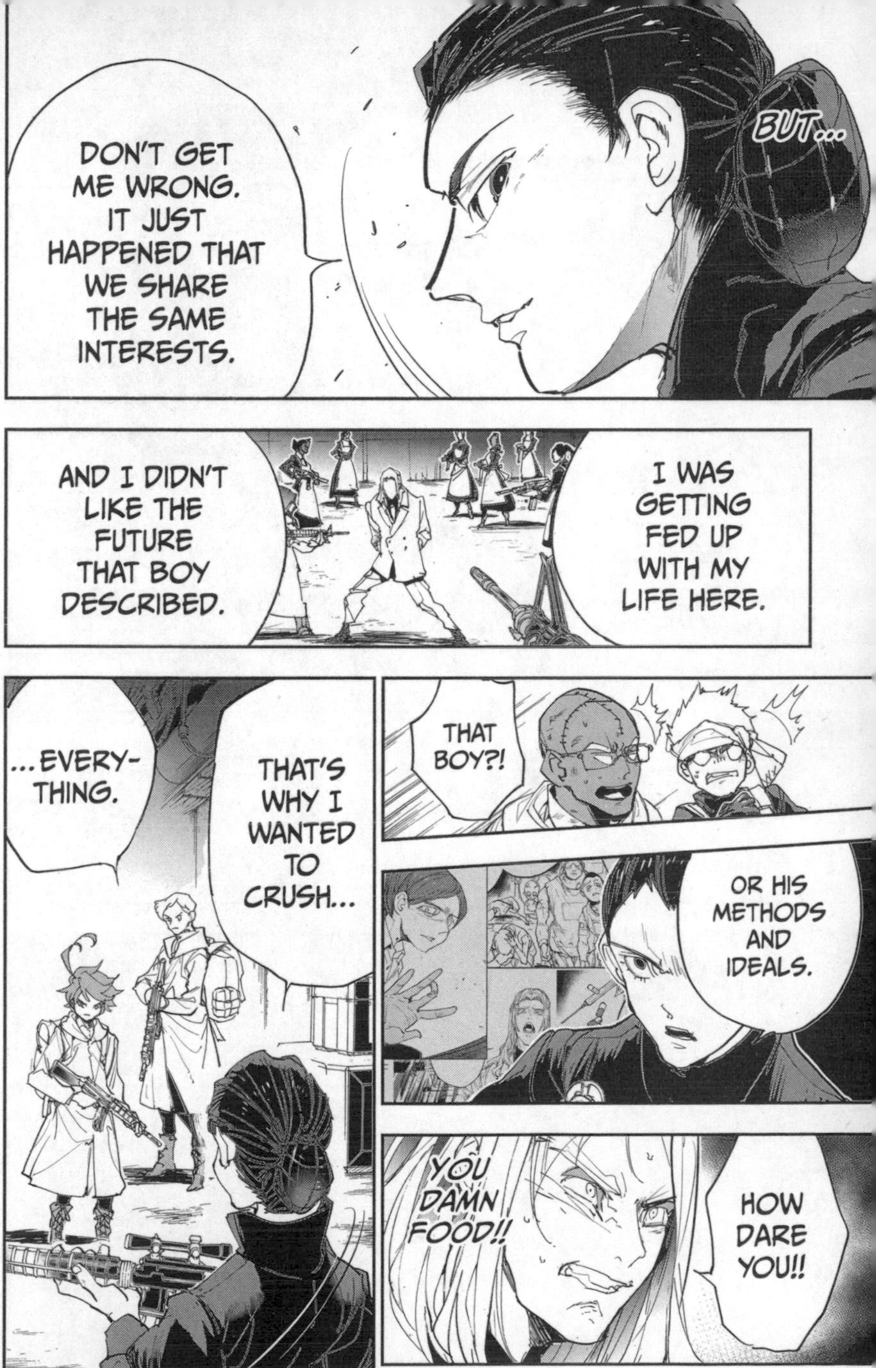
DON'T GET ME WRONG. IT JUST HAPPENED THAT WE SHARE THE SAME INTERESTS.
BUT...
I WAS GETTING FED UP WITH MY LIFE HERE.
AND I DIDN'T LIKE THE FUTURE THAT BOY DESCRIBED.
THAT BOY?!
OR HIS METHODS AND IDEALS.
HOW DARE YOU!!
YOU DAMN FOOD!!
THAT'S WHY I WANTED TO CRUSH...
...EVERY-THING.

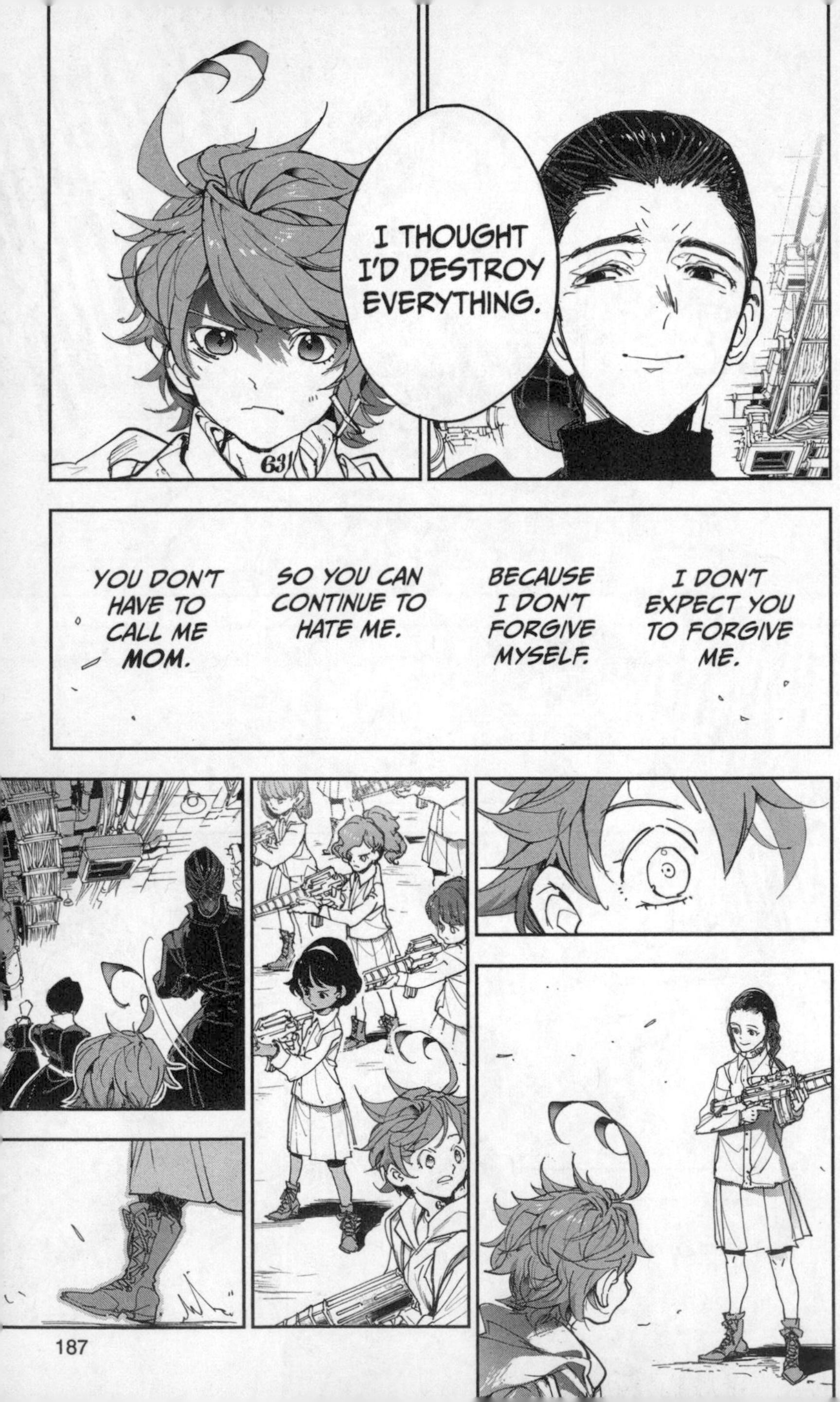
I THOUGHT I'D DESTROY EVERYTHING.
I DON'T EXPECT YOU TO FORGIVE ME.
BECAUSE I DON'T FORGIVE MYSELF.
SO YOU CAN CONTINUE TO HATE ME.
YOU DON'T HAVE TO CALL ME MOM.

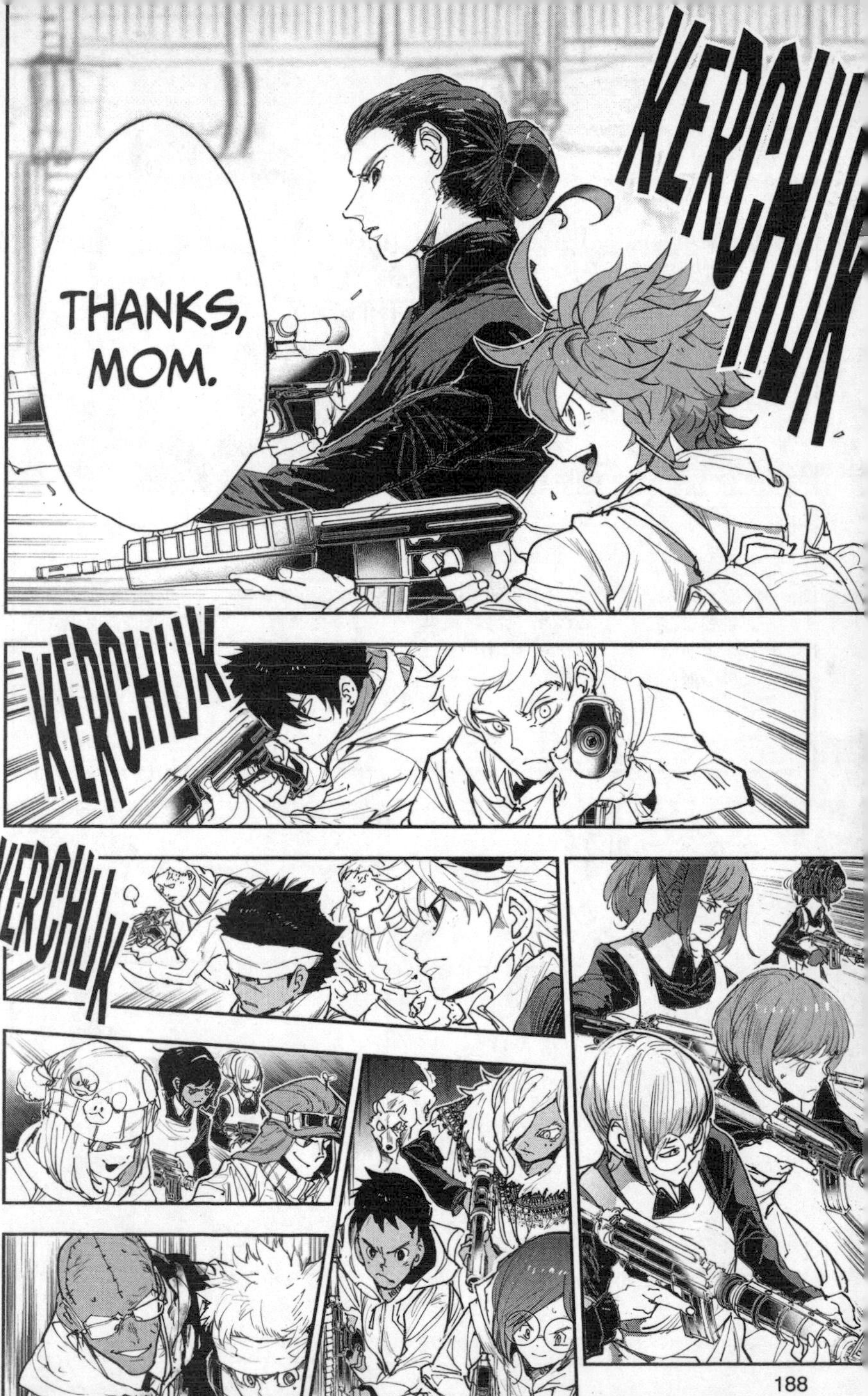
KERCHUK
THANKS, MOM.
KERCHUK
KERCHUK

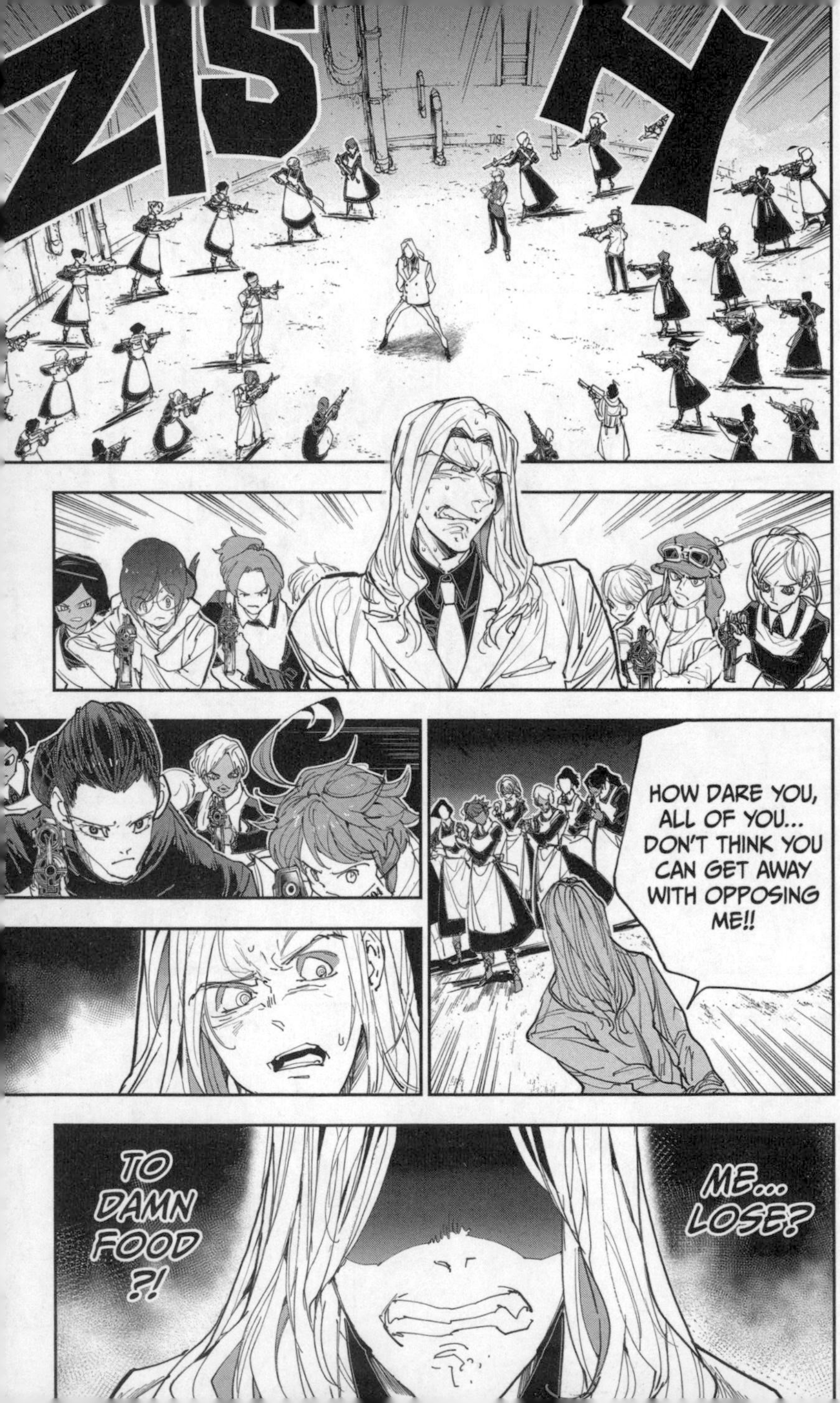
HOW DARE YOU, ALL OF YOU... DON'T THINK YOU CAN GET AWAY WITH OPPOSING ME!!
ME... LOSE?
TO DAMN FOOD ?!

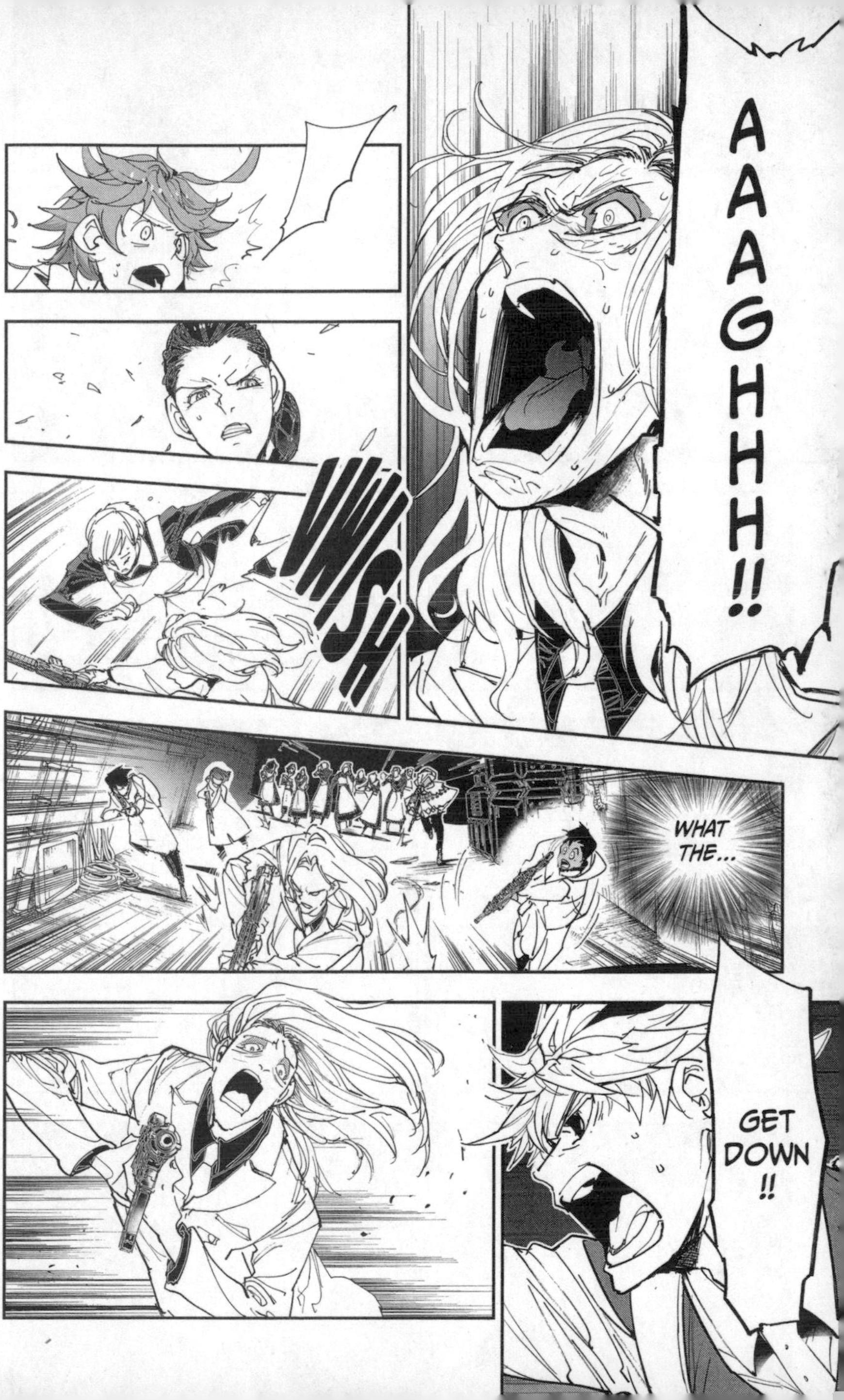
AAAGHHH!!
WWSH
WHAT THE...
GET DOWN!!

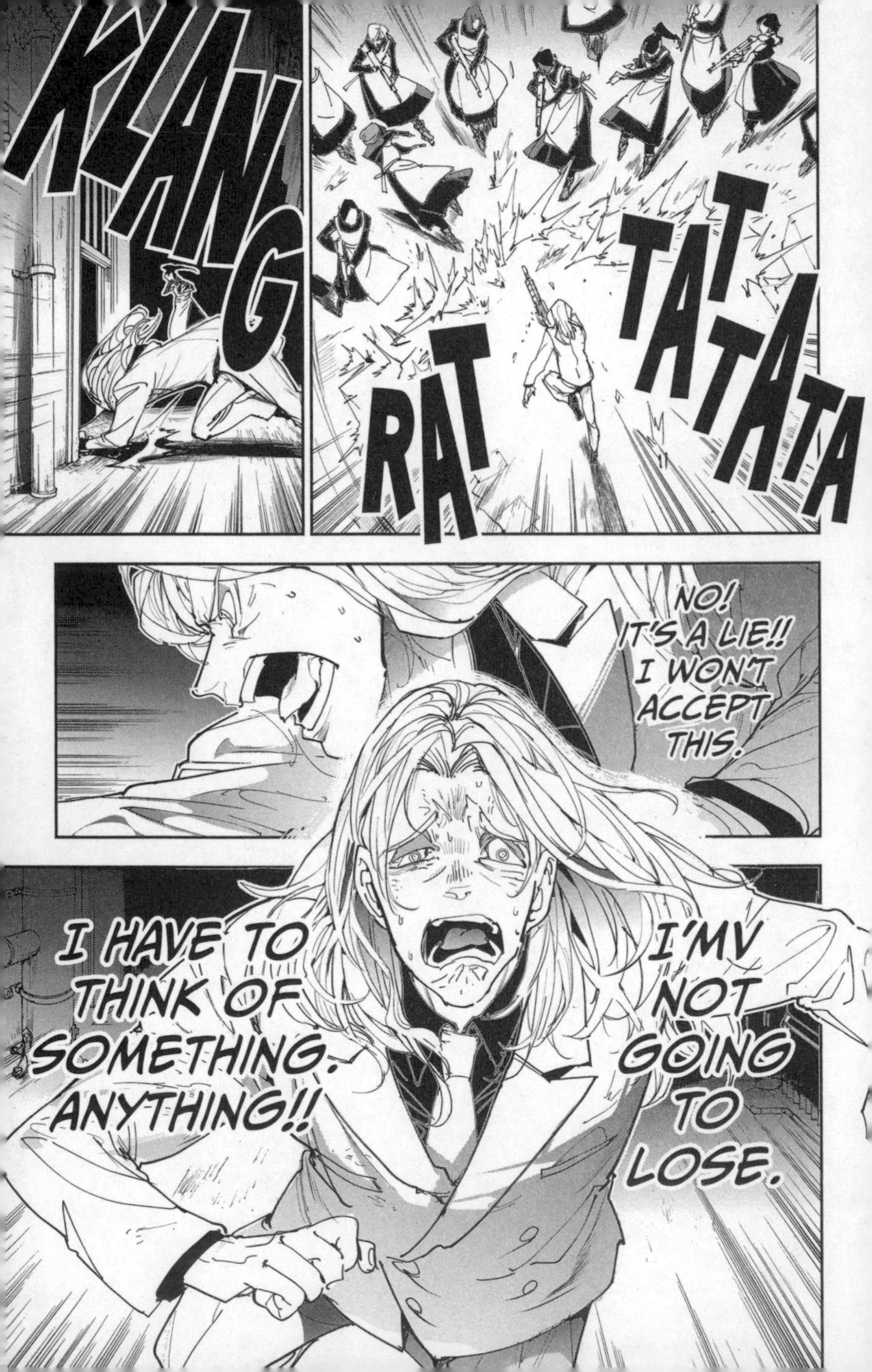
TATATATATA
RAT
KLANG
NO! IT'S A LIE!! I WON'T ACCEPT THIS.
I'M NOT GOING TO LOSE.
I HAVE TO THINK OF SOMETHING. ANYTHING!!

THE SISTERS

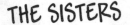

SCARLET WAS AN EXTREMELY KIND GIRL, BUT SHE CHANGED WHEN SHE WAS 12 YEARS OLD. SHE CLOSED OFF HER HEART AND DID ANYTHING TO MOVE UP THE RANKS, EVEN AT THE EXPENSE OF OTHERS.

JESSICA IS CUNNING AND CALCULATING, QUALITIES THAT MADE HER A SISTER EARLY. BUT TO HER, LOVING CHILDREN IS MORE DIFFICULT THAN ANY TEST.

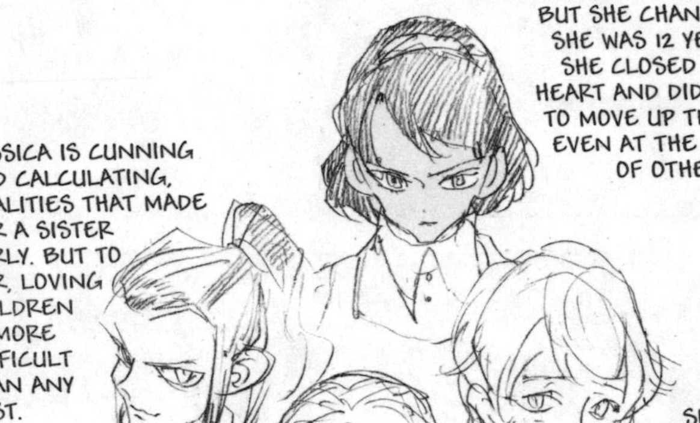

SIENNA'S ONLY DESIRE WAS TO NOT DIE. FOR NOW, THE DEMONS THINK SHE IS VALUABLE BECAUSE SHE IS OBEDIENT AND SUBMISSIVE.

MATILDA CAN BECOME FRIENDS WITH ANYONE, BUT SHE ALSO CRIES THE MOST BEHIND THE SCENES. WHILE PRETENDING TO OBEY SARAH AND ISABELLA, SHE IS AMBITIOUS AND AIMS TO RISE TO THE TOP.

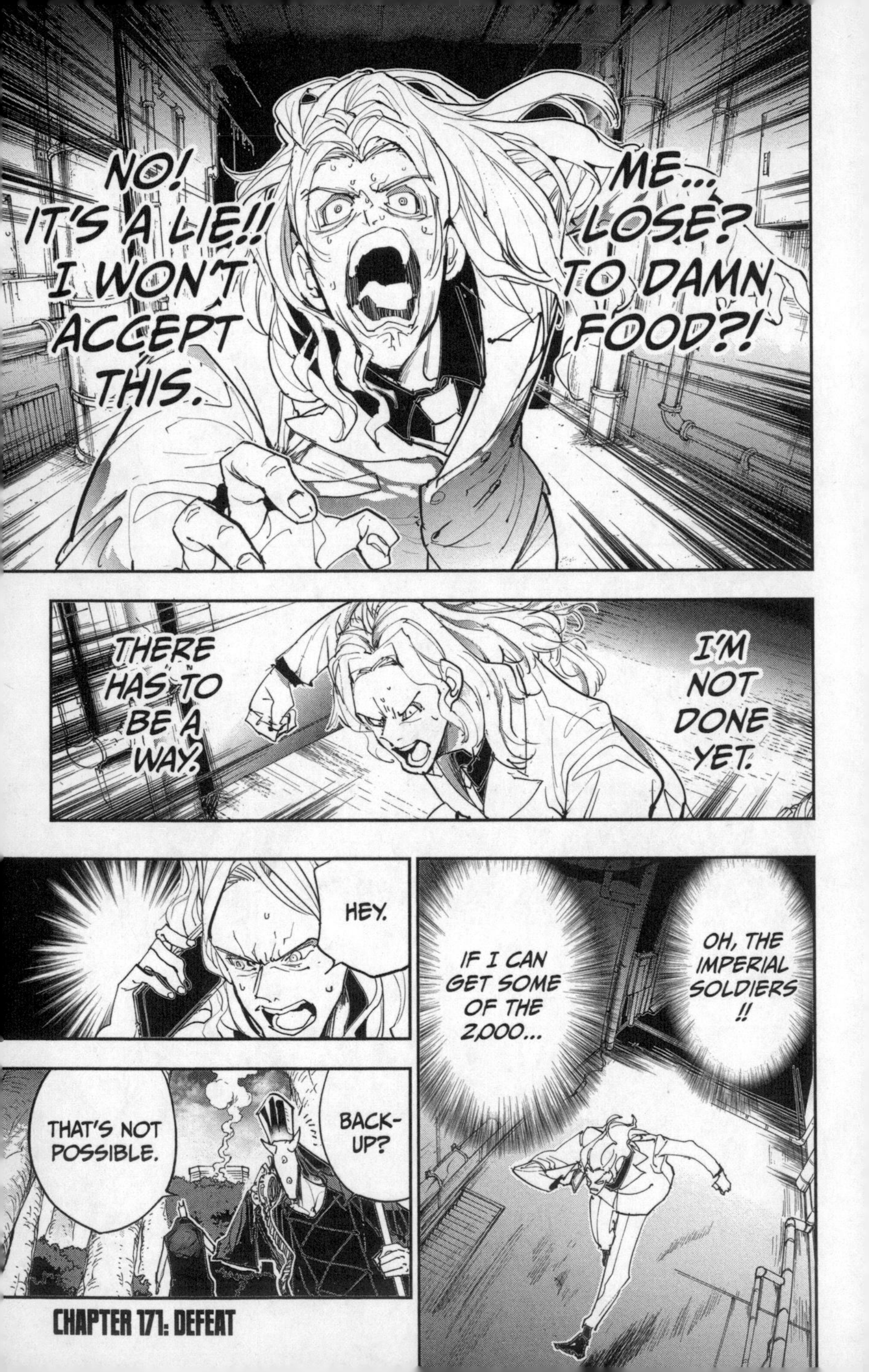
ME... LOSE? TO DAMN FOOD?!
NO! IT'S A LIE!! I WON'T ACCEPT THIS.
I'M NOT DONE YET.
THERE HAS TO BE A WAY.
OH, THE IMPERIAL SOLDIERS!!
IF I CAN GET SOME OF THE 2,000...
HEY.
BACK-UP?
THAT'S NOT POSSIBLE.

CHAPTER 171: DEFEAT

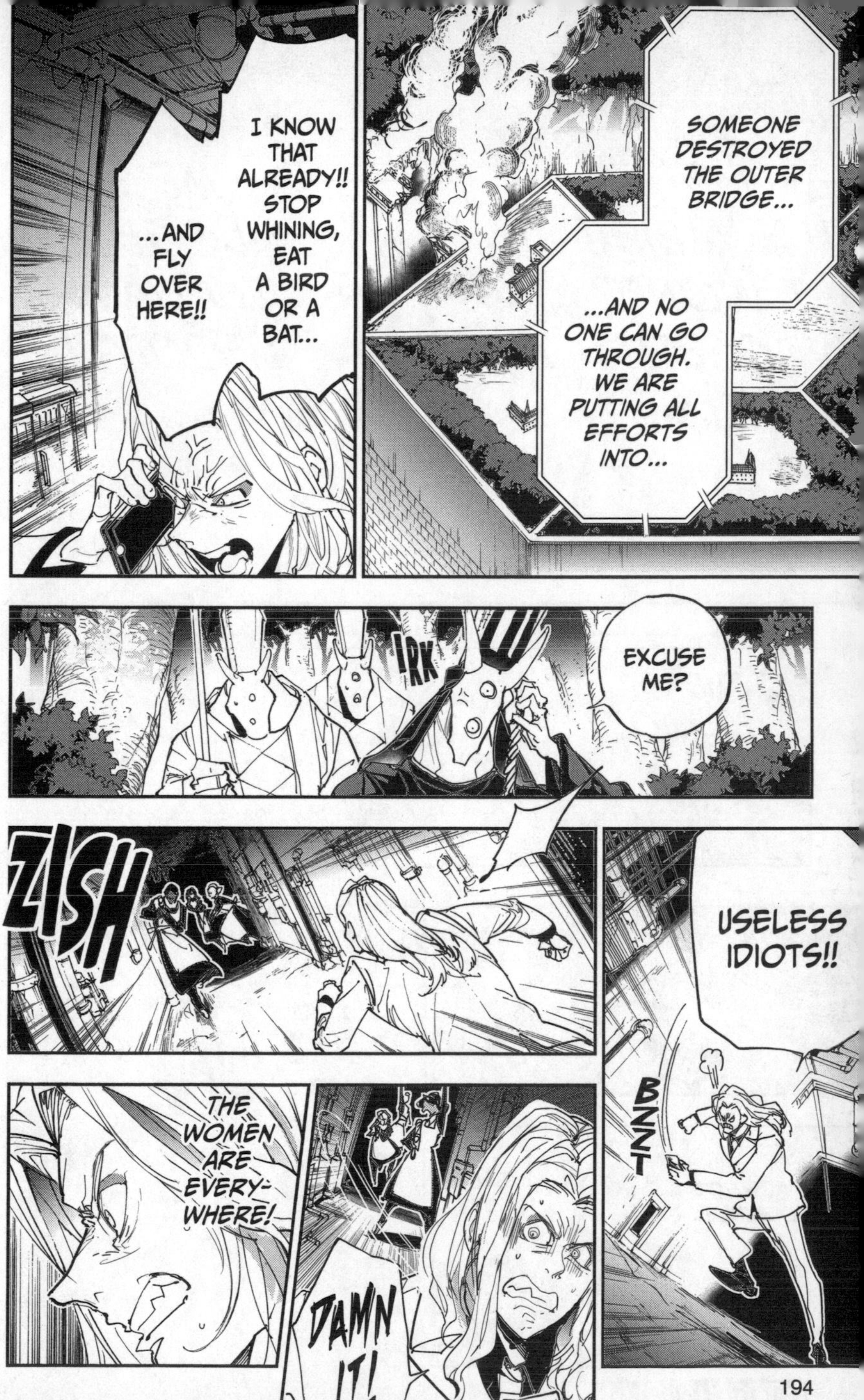
SOMEONE DESTROYED THE OUTER BRIDGE...
...AND NO ONE CAN GO THROUGH. WE ARE PUTTING ALL EFFORTS INTO...
I KNOW THAT ALREADY!! STOP WHINING, EAT A BIRD OR A BAT...
...AND FLY OVER HERE!!
IRK
EXCUSE ME?
USELESS IDIOTS!!
BZZT
ZISH
DAMN IT!
THE WOMEN ARE EVERY-WHERE!

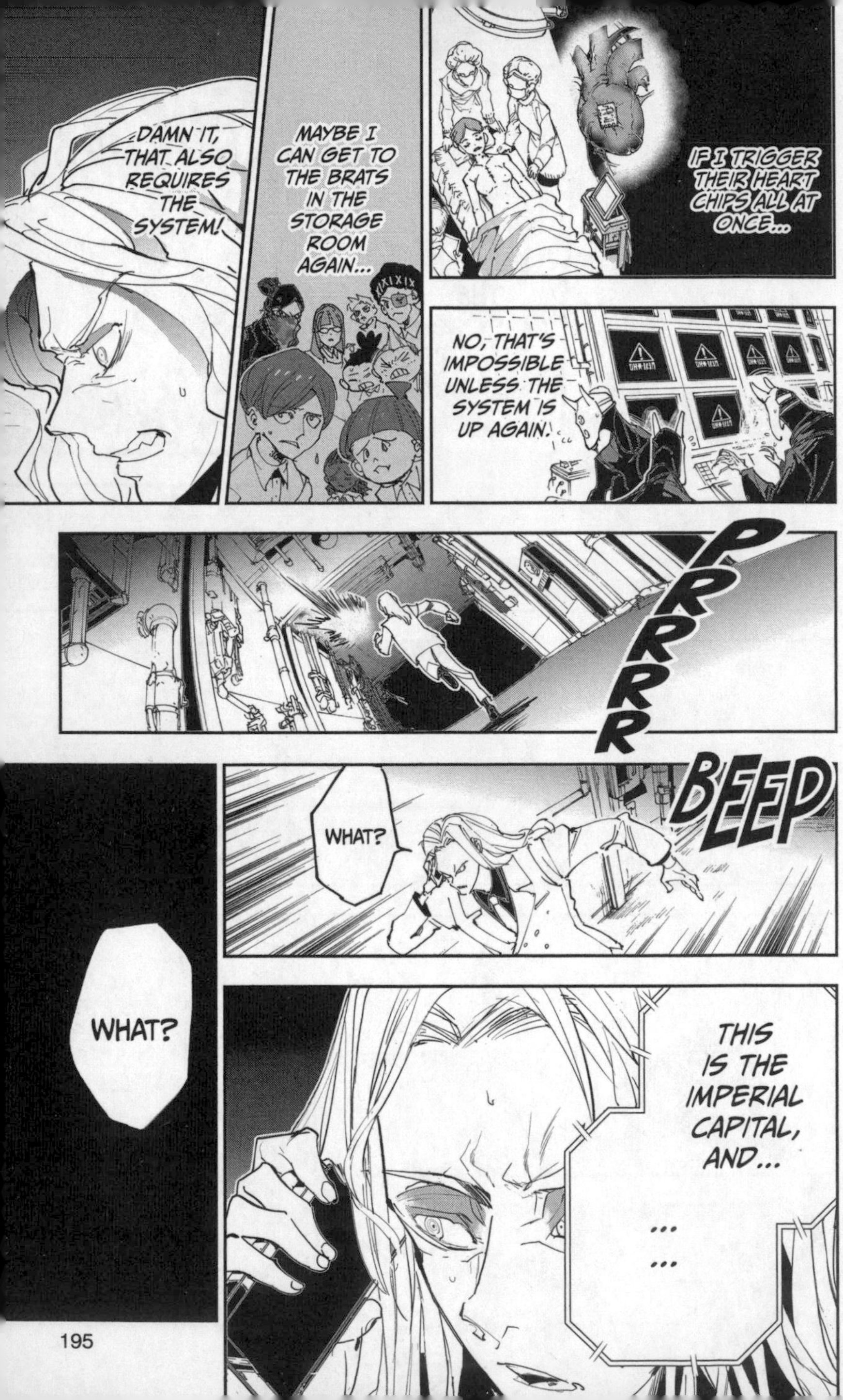
IF I TRIGGER THEIR HEART CHIPS ALL AT ONCE...
NO, THAT'S IMPOSSIBLE UNLESS THE SYSTEM IS UP AGAIN.
MAYBE I CAN GET TO THE BRATS IN THE STORAGE ROOM AGAIN...
DAMN IT, THAT ALSO REQUIRES THE SYSTEM!
PRRRRR
BEEP
WHAT?
THIS IS THE IMPERIAL CAPITAL, AND...
...
...
WHAT?

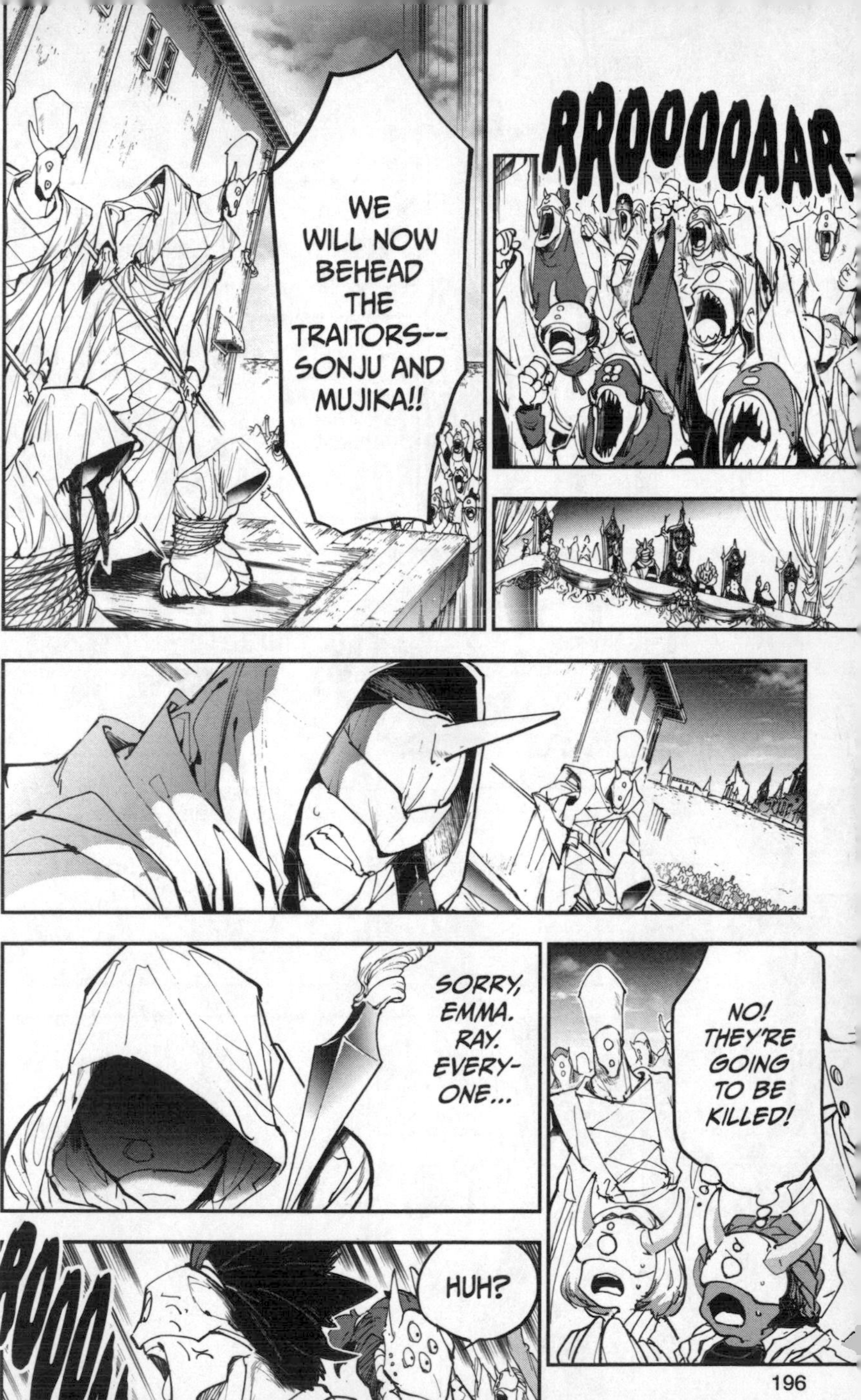
RROOOOAAR
WE WILL NOW BEHEAD THE TRAITORS--SONJU AND MUJIKA!!
NO! THEY'RE GOING TO BE KILLED!
SORRY, EMMA. RAY. EVERY-ONE...
ROOOAA
HUH?

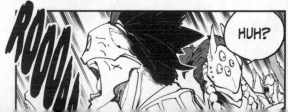

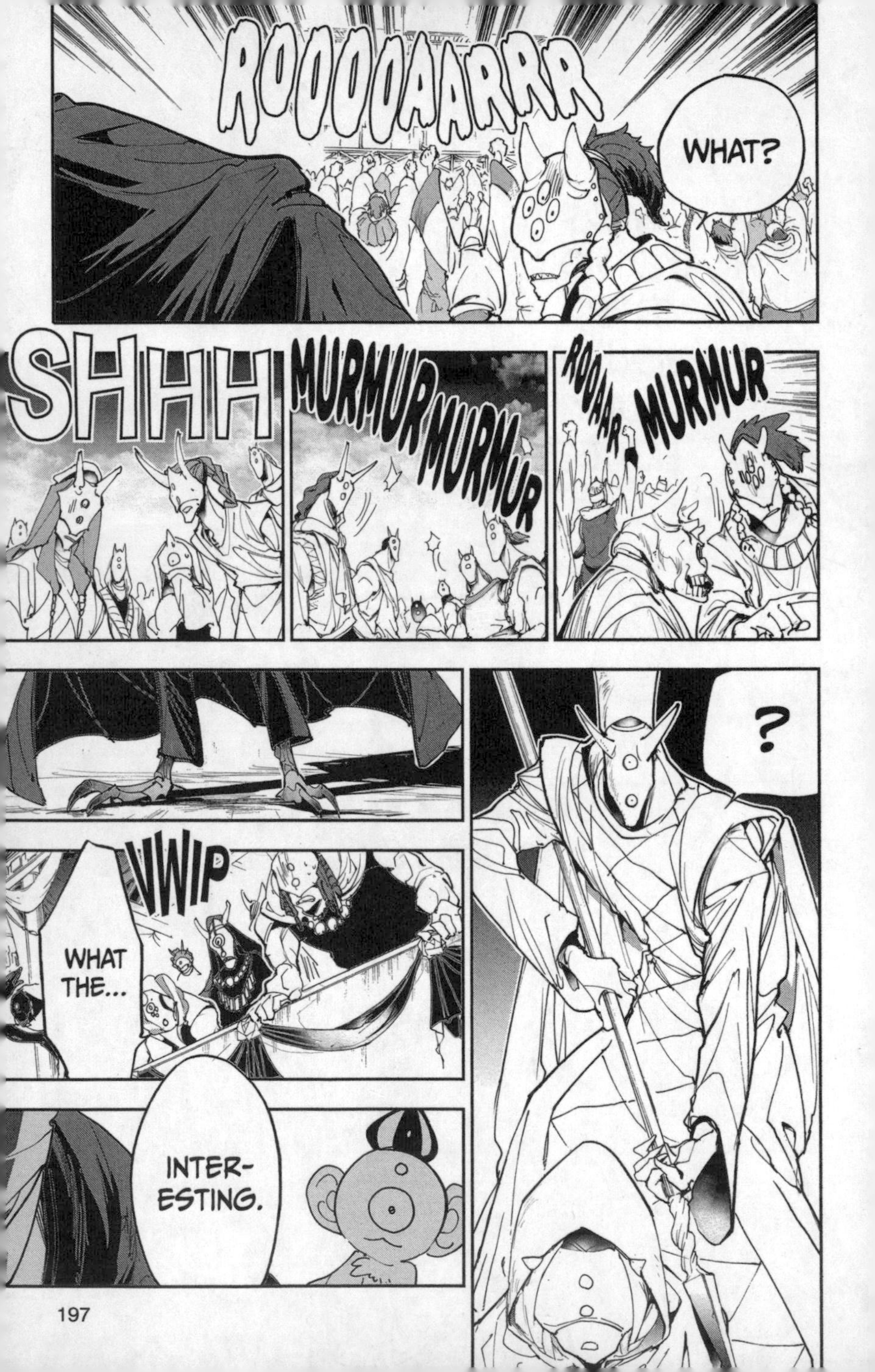
ROOOOAARRR
WHAT?
ROOAARR
MURMUR
MURMUR
MURMUR
MURMUR
SHHH
?
VWIP
WHAT THE...
INTER-ESTING.

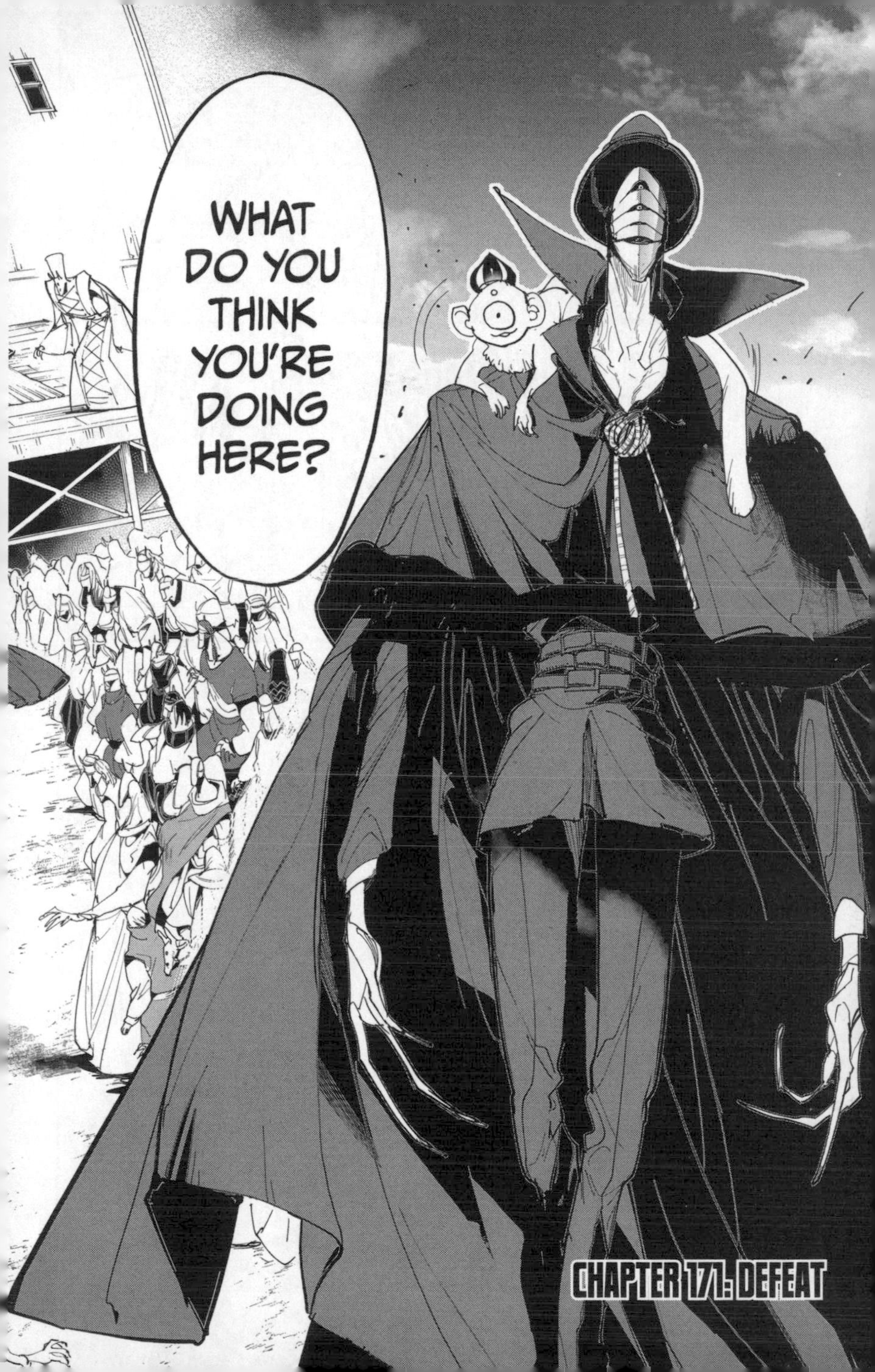
WHAT DO YOU THINK YOU'RE DOING HERE?
CHAPTER 171: DEFEAT

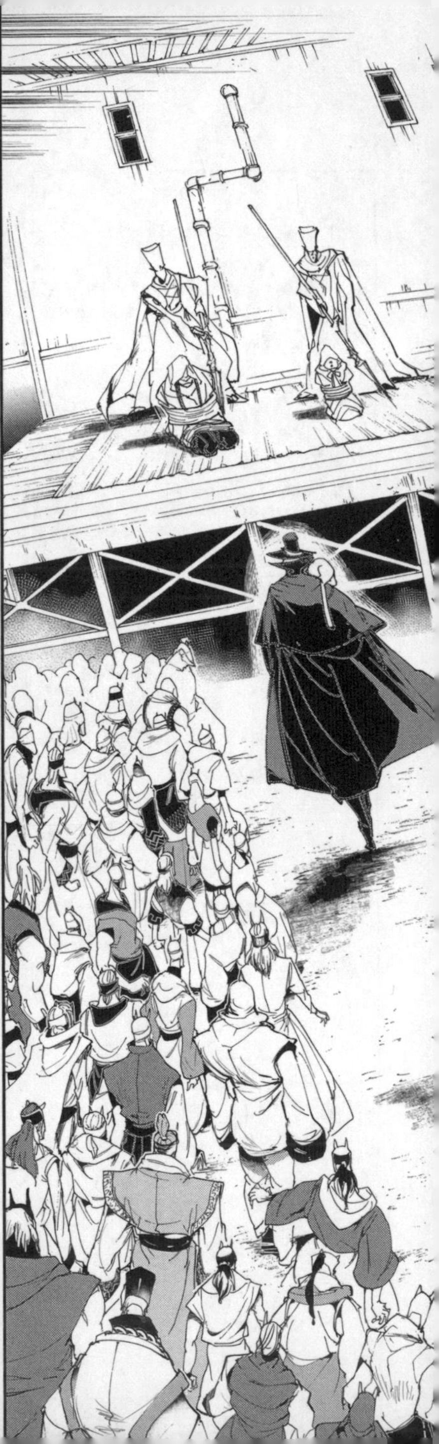

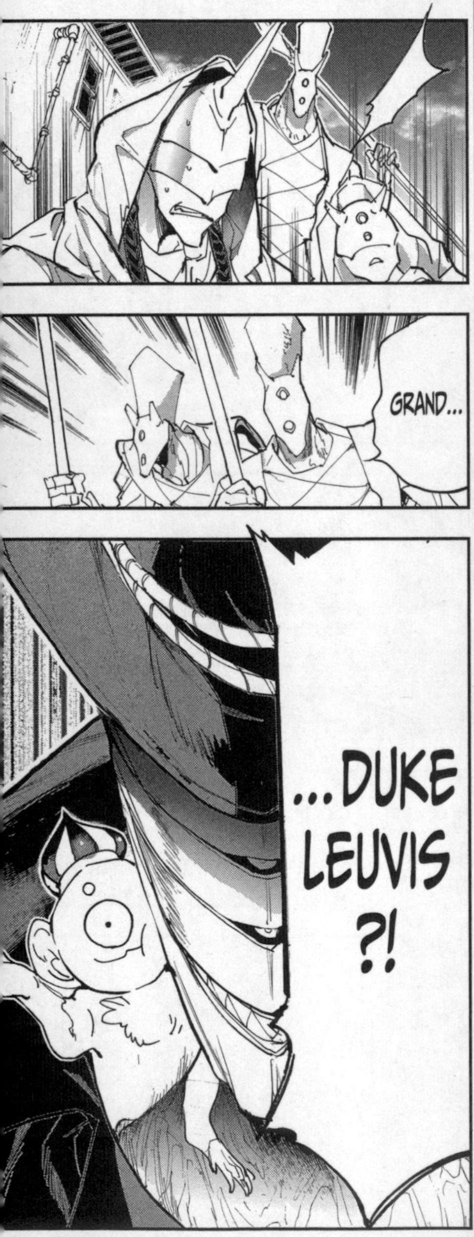
GRAND...
...DUKE LEUVIS ?!

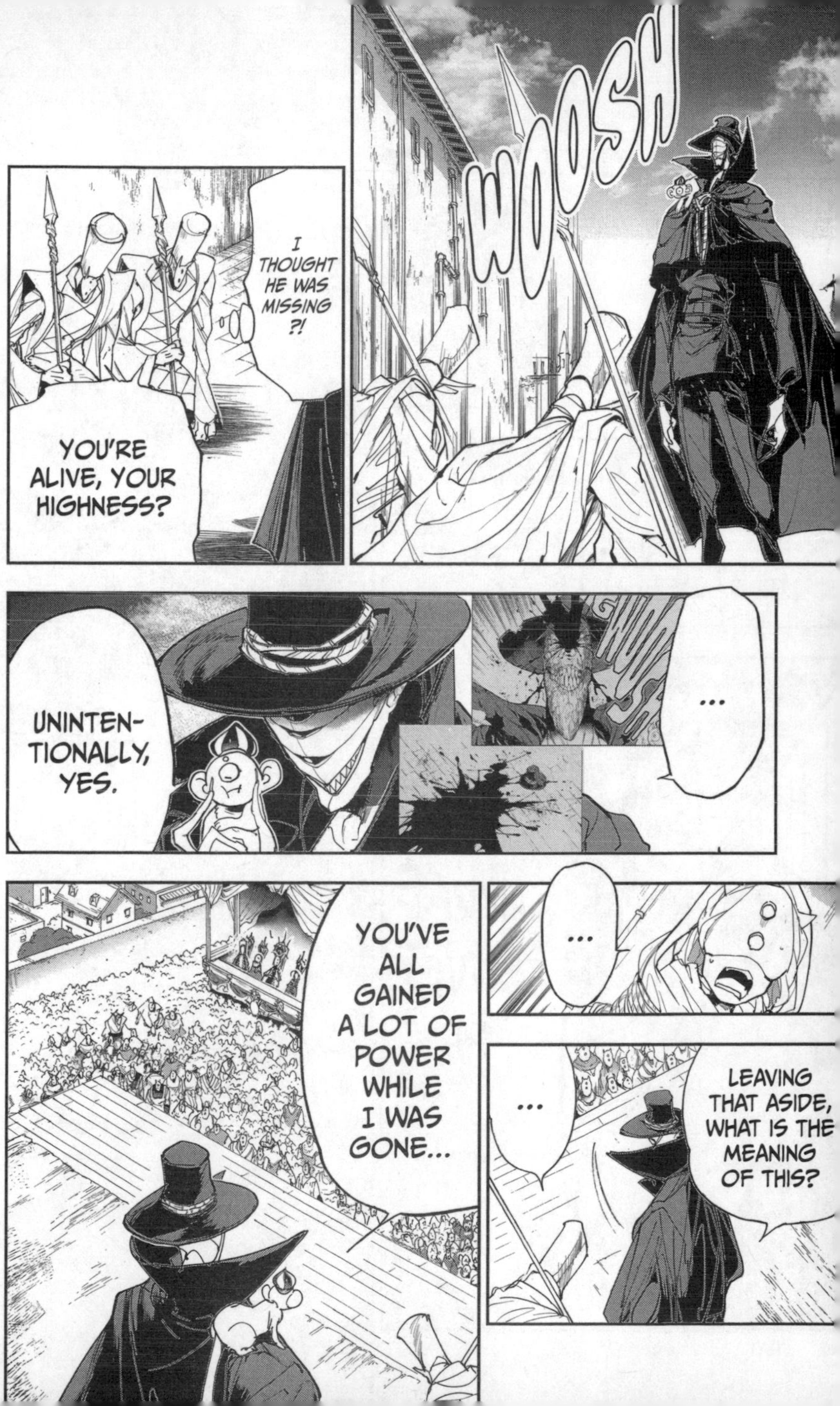
WOOSH
I THOUGHT HE WAS MISSING?!
YOU'RE ALIVE, YOUR HIGHNESS?
...
UNINTEN-TIONALLY, YES.
...
LEAVING THAT ASIDE, WHAT IS THE MEANING OF THIS?
...
YOU'VE ALL GAINED A LOT OF POWER WHILE I WAS GONE...

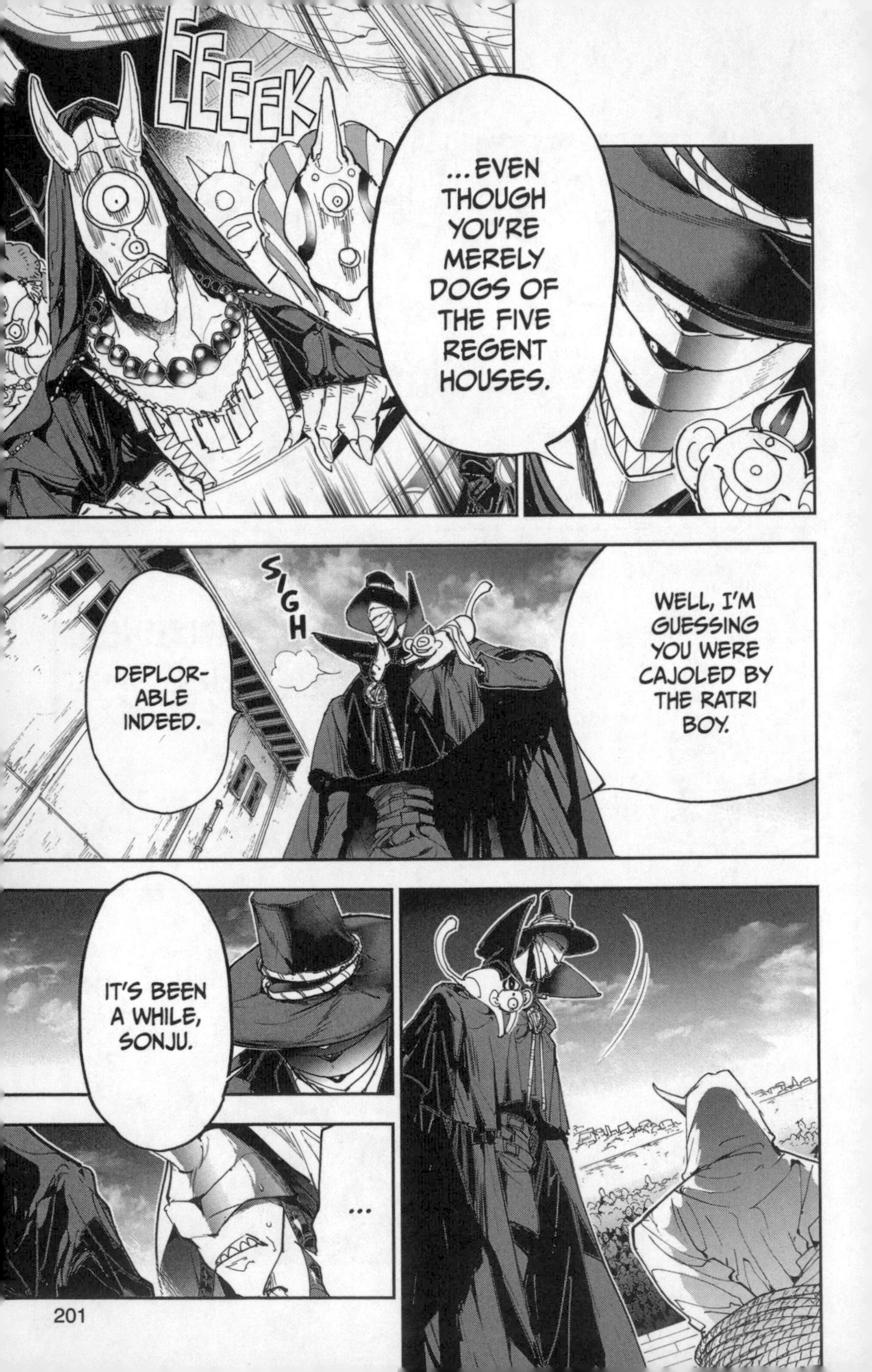
...EVEN THOUGH YOU'RE MERELY DOGS OF THE FIVE REGENT HOUSES.
EEEEK
WELL, I'M GUESSING YOU WERE CAJOLED BY THE RATRI BOY.
SIGH
DEPLORABLE INDEED.
IT'S BEEN A WHILE, SONJU.
...

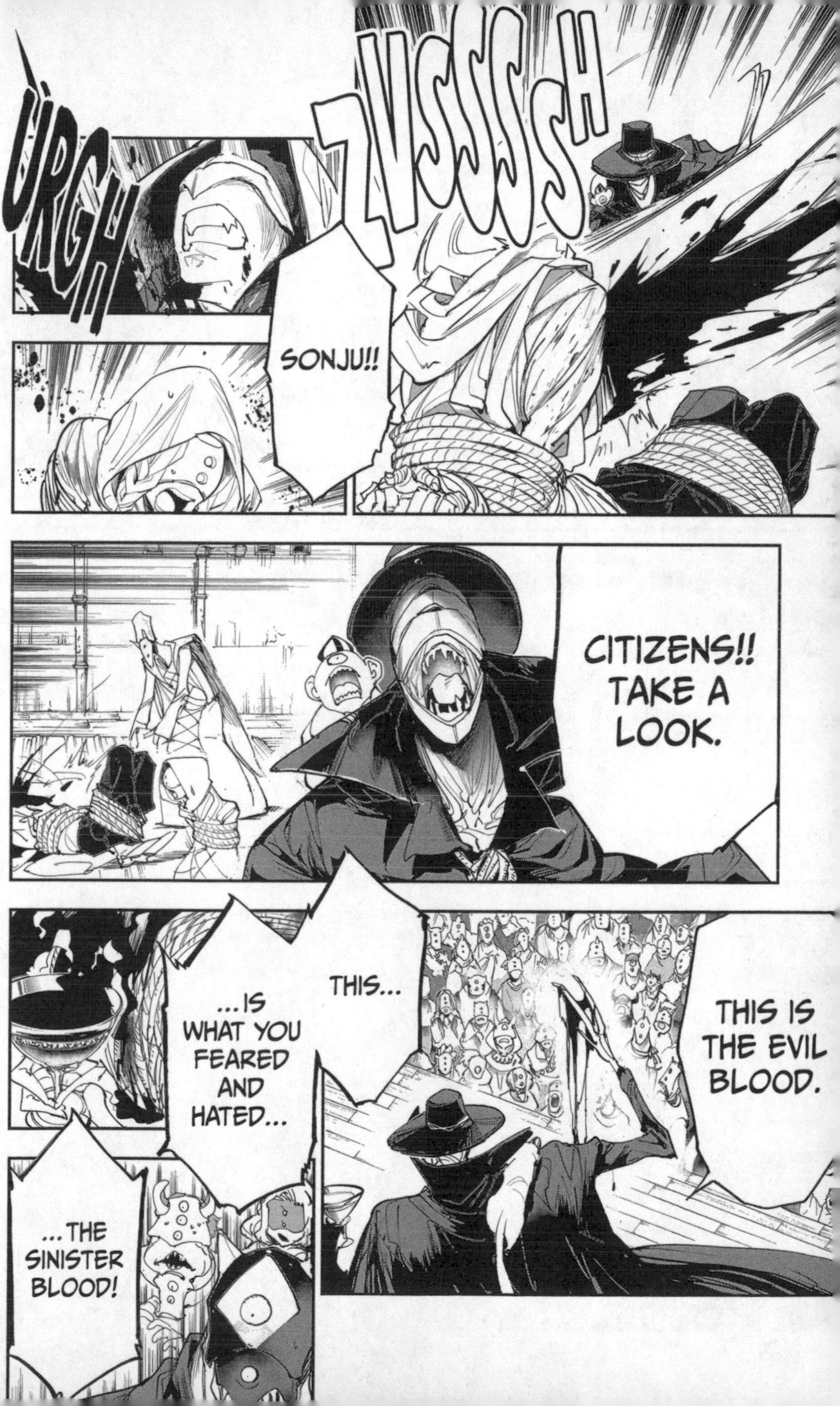
ZVSSSSH
URGH
SONJU!!
CITIZENS!! TAKE A LOOK.
THIS IS THE EVIL BLOOD.
THIS...
...IS WHAT YOU FEARED AND HATED...
...THE SINISTER BLOOD!

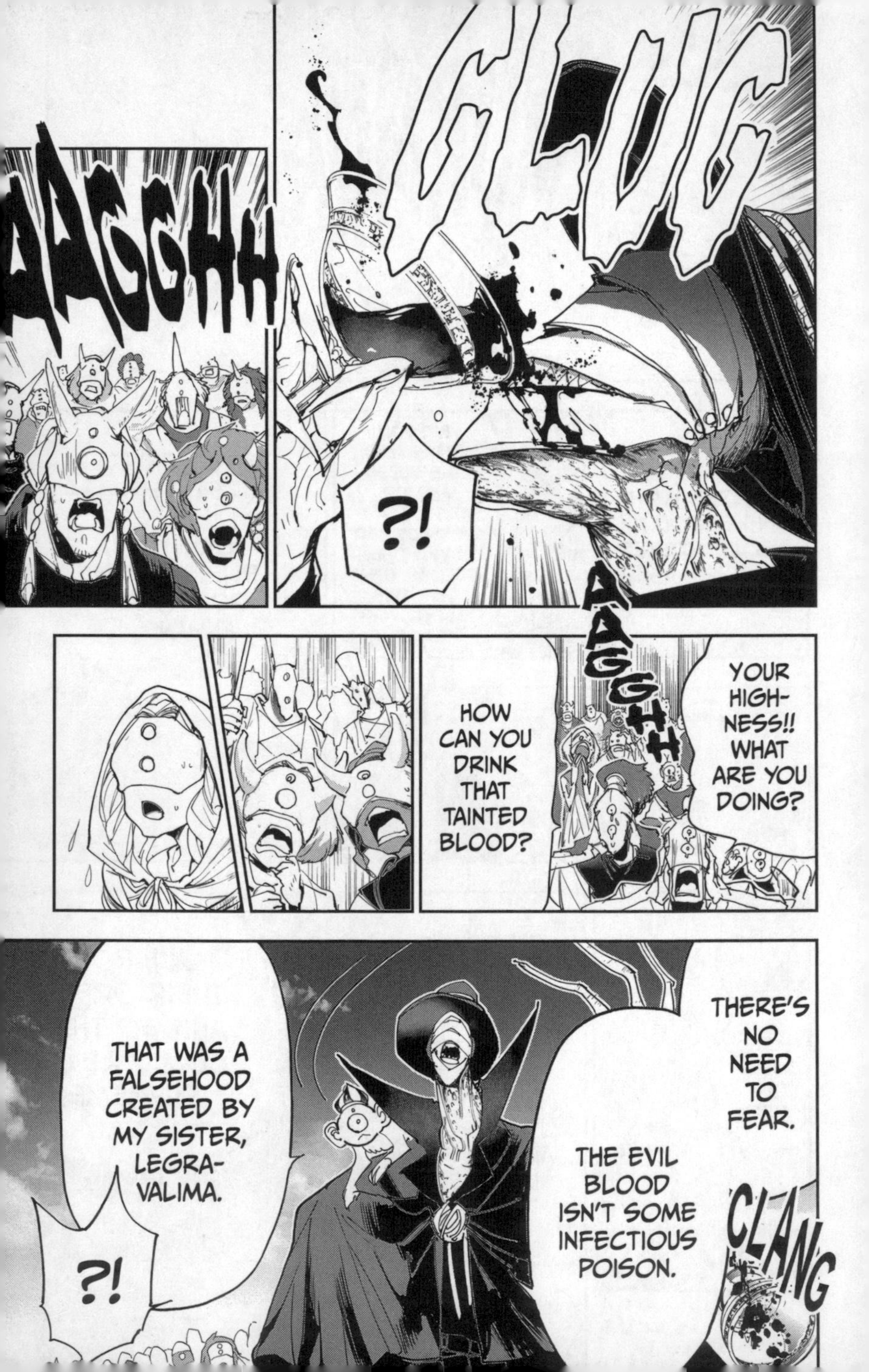
GLUG
?!
AAGGHH
AAGGHH
YOUR HIGH-NESS!! WHAT ARE YOU DOING?
HOW CAN YOU DRINK THAT TAINTED BLOOD?
THERE'S NO NEED TO FEAR.
CLANG
THE EVIL BLOOD ISN'T SOME INFECTIOUS POISON.
THAT WAS A FALSEHOOD CREATED BY MY SISTER, LEGRA-VALIMA.
?!

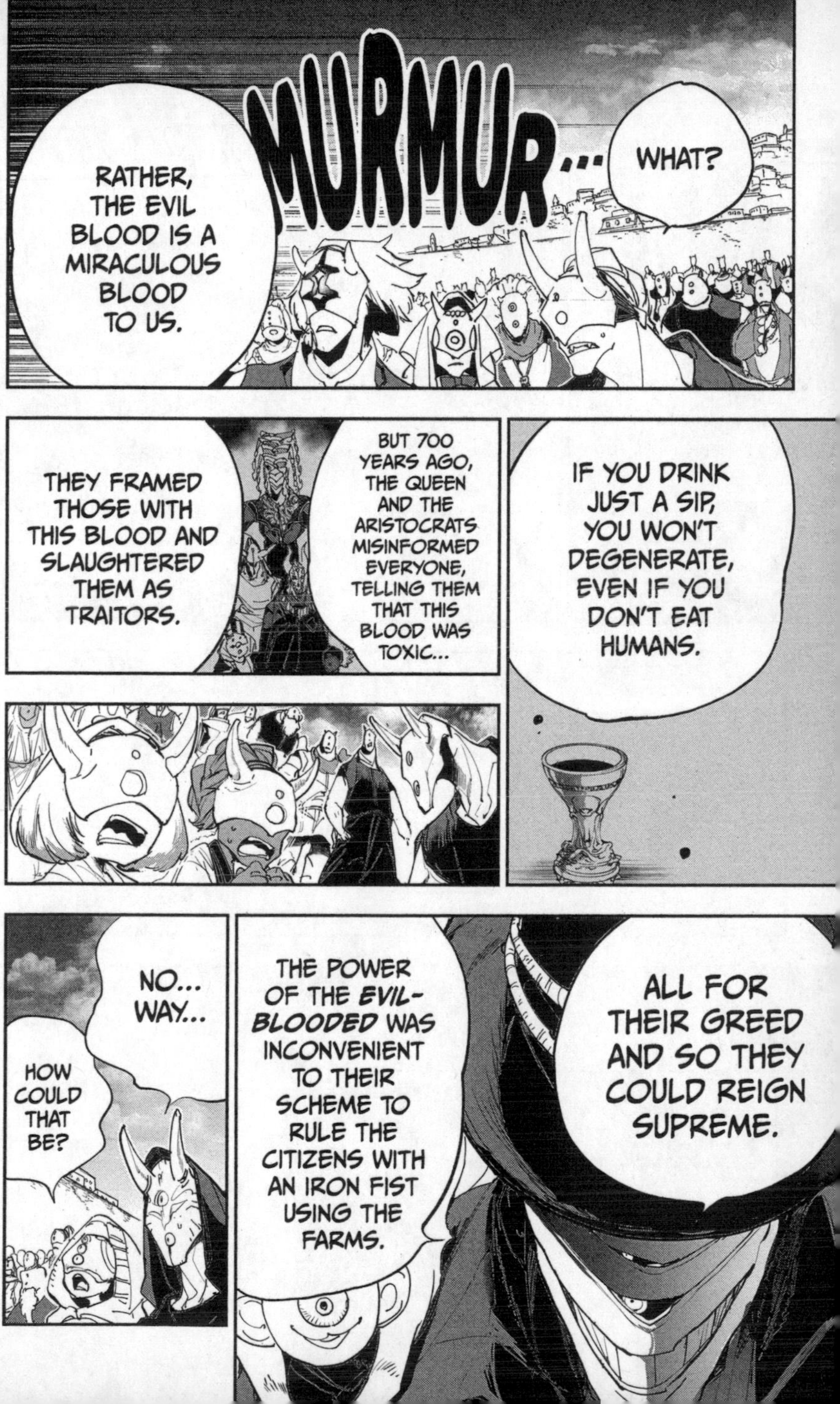
WHAT?
MURMUR...
RATHER, THE EVIL BLOOD IS A MIRACULOUS BLOOD TO US.
IF YOU DRINK JUST A SIP, YOU WON'T DEGENERATE, EVEN IF YOU DON'T EAT HUMANS.
BUT 700 YEARS AGO, THE QUEEN AND THE ARISTOCRATS MISINFORMED EVERYONE, TELLING THEM THAT THIS BLOOD WAS TOXIC...
THEY FRAMED THOSE WITH THIS BLOOD AND SLAUGHTERED THEM AS TRAITORS.
ALL FOR THEIR GREED AND SO THEY COULD REIGN SUPREME.
THE POWER OF THE *EVIL-BLOODED* WAS INCONVENIENT TO THEIR SCHEME TO RULE THE CITIZENS WITH AN IRON FIST USING THE FARMS.
NO... WAY...
HOW COULD THAT BE?

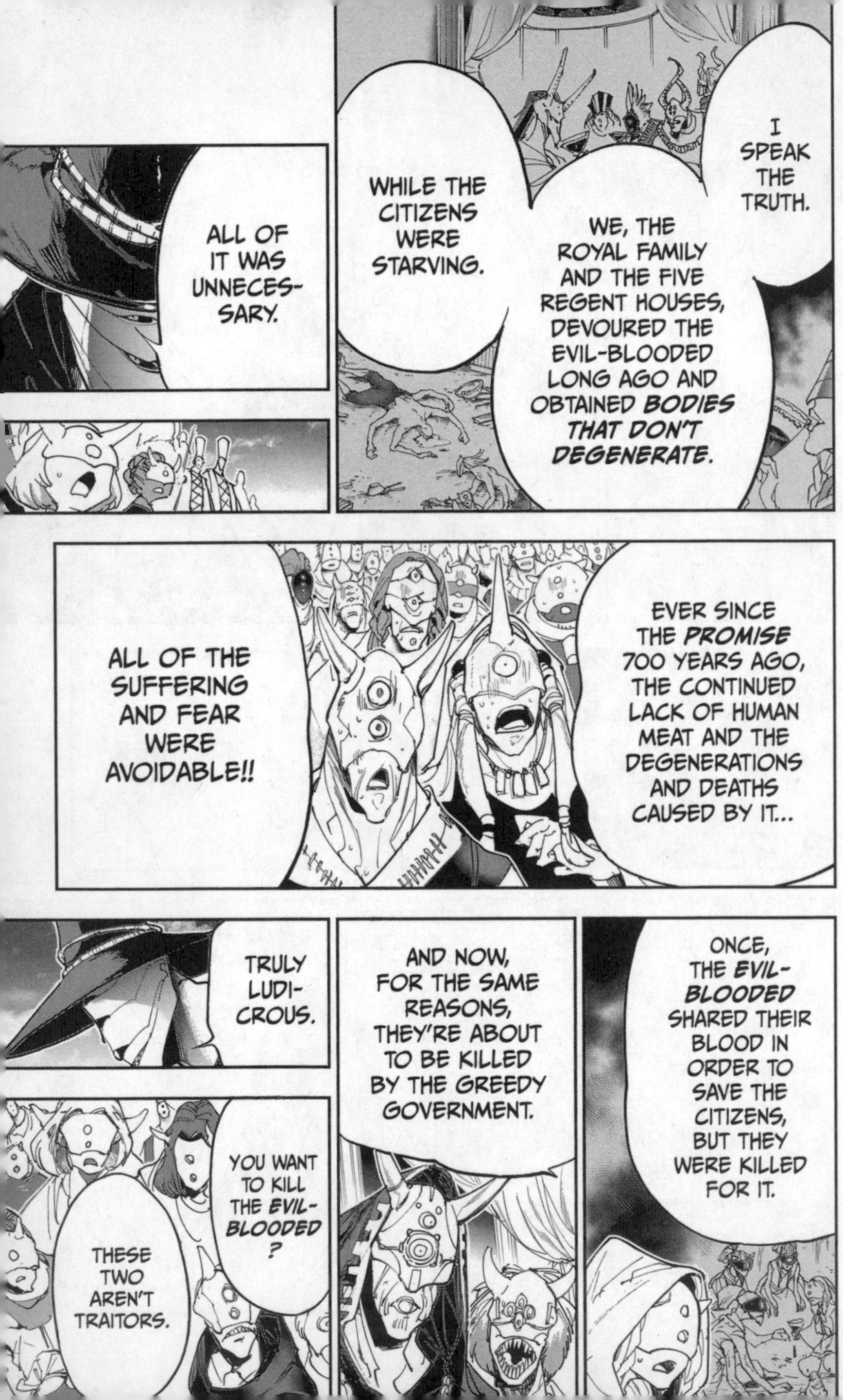
I SPEAK THE TRUTH.
WE, THE ROYAL FAMILY AND THE FIVE REGENT HOUSES, DEVOURED THE EVIL-BLOODED LONG AGO AND OBTAINED *BODIES THAT DON'T DEGENERATE*.
WHILE THE CITIZENS WERE STARVING.
ALL OF IT WAS UNNECES-SARY.
EVER SINCE THE *PROMISE* 700 YEARS AGO, THE CONTINUED LACK OF HUMAN MEAT AND THE DEGENERATIONS AND DEATHS CAUSED BY IT...
ALL OF THE SUFFERING AND FEAR WERE AVOIDABLE!!
ONCE, THE *EVIL-BLOODED* SHARED THEIR BLOOD IN ORDER TO SAVE THE CITIZENS, BUT THEY WERE KILLED FOR IT.
AND NOW, FOR THE SAME REASONS, THEY'RE ABOUT TO BE KILLED BY THE GREEDY GOVERNMENT.
TRULY LUDI-CROUS.
YOU WANT TO KILL THE *EVIL-BLOODED*?
THESE TWO AREN'T TRAITORS.

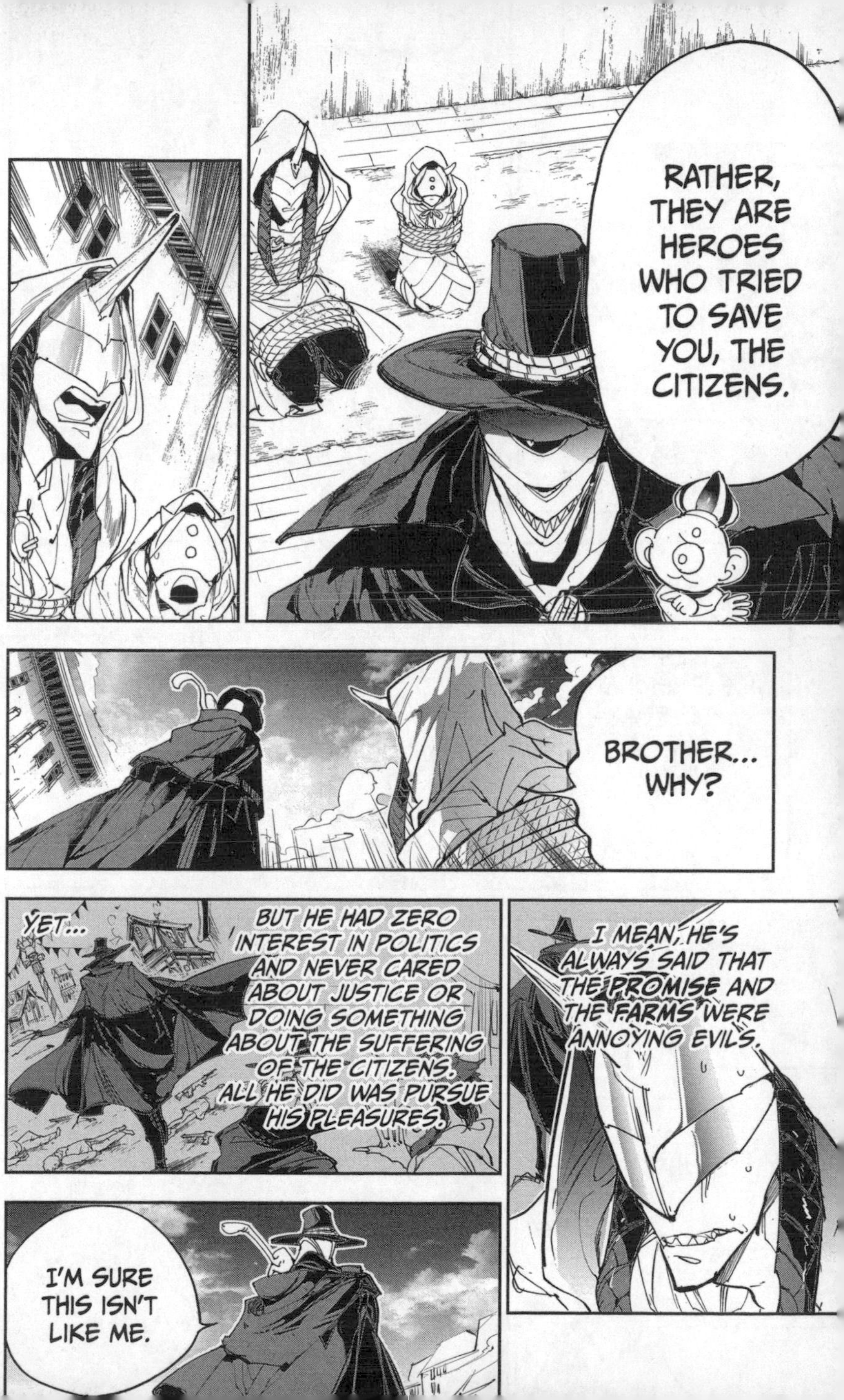
RATHER, THEY ARE HEROES WHO TRIED TO SAVE YOU, THE CITIZENS.
BROTHER... WHY?
I MEAN, HE'S ALWAYS SAID THAT THE PROMISE AND THE FARMS WERE ANNOYING EVILS.
BUT HE HAD ZERO INTEREST IN POLITICS AND NEVER CARED ABOUT JUSTICE OR DOING SOMETHING ABOUT THE SUFFERING OF THE CITIZENS. ALL HE DID WAS PURSUE HIS PLEASURES.
YET...
I'M SURE THIS ISN'T LIKE ME.

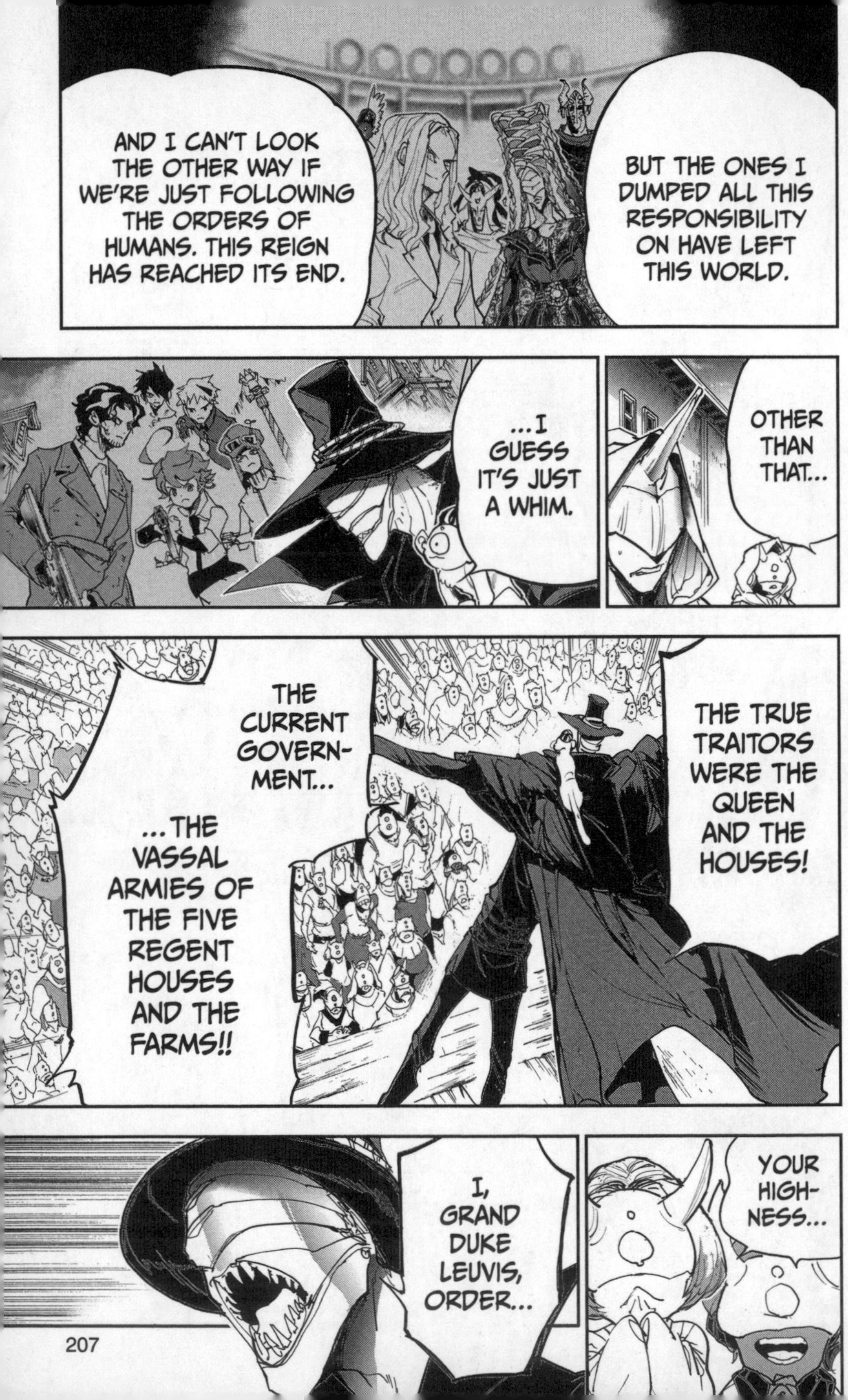
BUT THE ONES I DUMPED ALL THIS RESPONSIBILITY ON HAVE LEFT THIS WORLD.
AND I CAN'T LOOK THE OTHER WAY IF WE'RE JUST FOLLOWING THE ORDERS OF HUMANS. THIS REIGN HAS REACHED ITS END.
OTHER THAN THAT...
...I GUESS IT'S JUST A WHIM.
THE TRUE TRAITORS WERE THE QUEEN AND THE HOUSES!
THE CURRENT GOVERNMENT...
...THE VASSAL ARMIES OF THE FIVE REGENT HOUSES AND THE FARMS!!
YOUR HIGHNESS...
I, GRAND DUKE LEUVIS, ORDER...

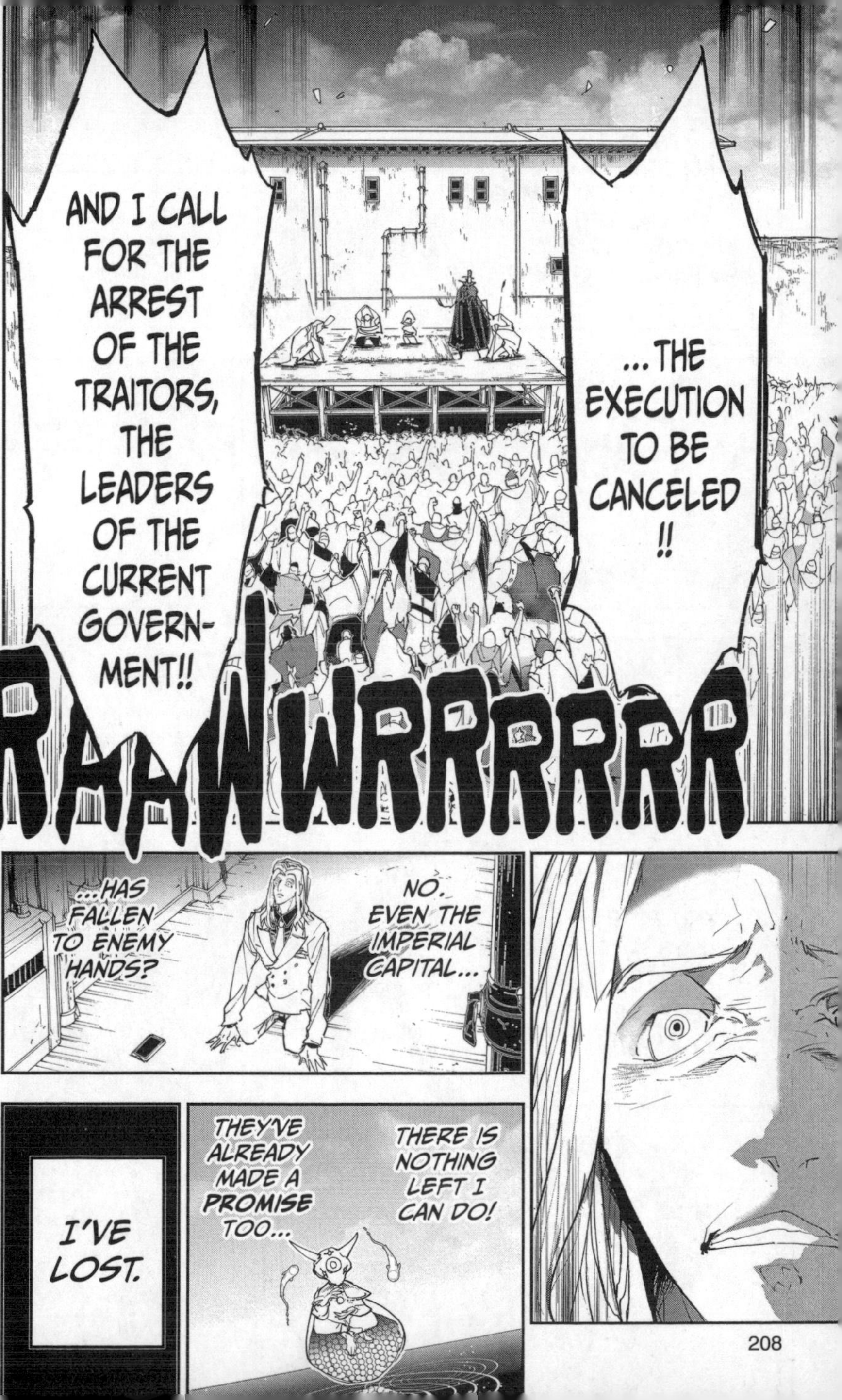
...THE EXECUTION TO BE CANCELED!!
AND I CALL FOR THE ARREST OF THE TRAITORS, THE LEADERS OF THE CURRENT GOVERN-MENT!!
RAAWRRRRRR
NO. EVEN THE IMPERIAL CAPITAL...
...HAS FALLEN TO ENEMY HANDS?
THERE IS NOTHING LEFT I CAN DO!
THEY'VE ALREADY MADE A PROMISE TOO...
I'VE LOST.

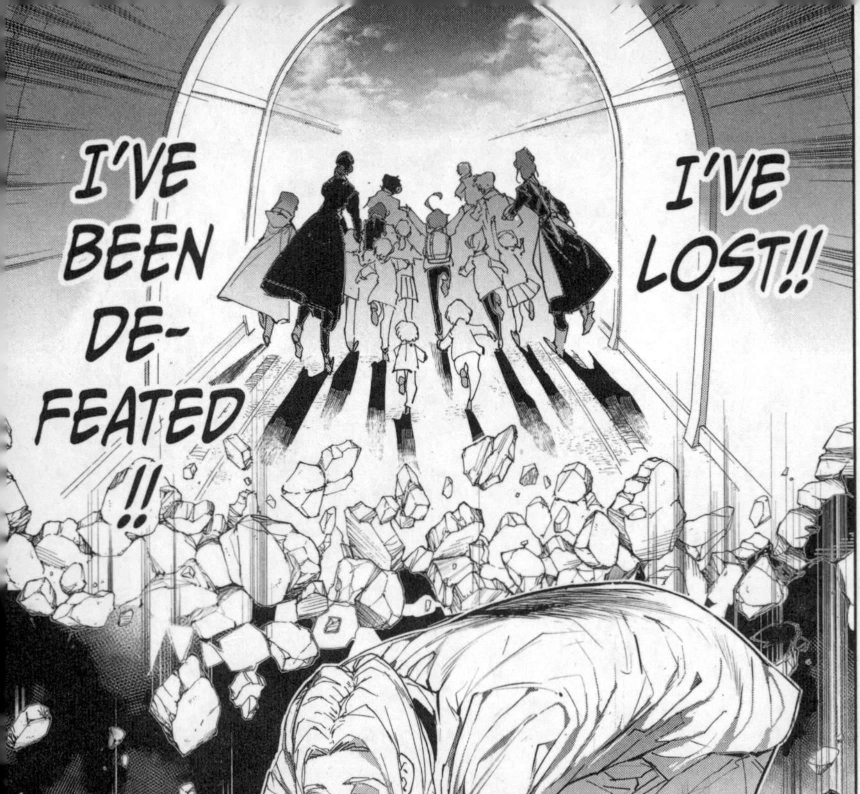
I'VE LOST!!
I'VE BEEN DE-FEATED!!
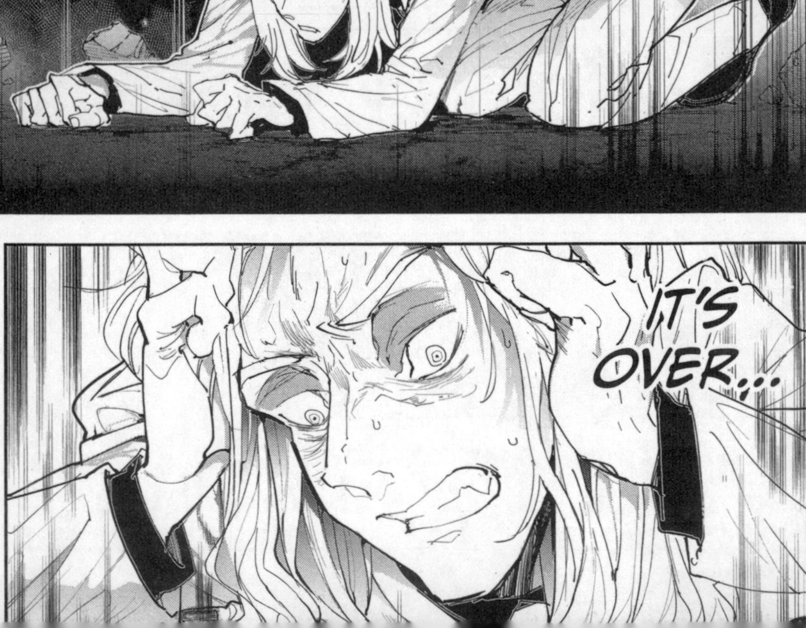
IT'S OVER...

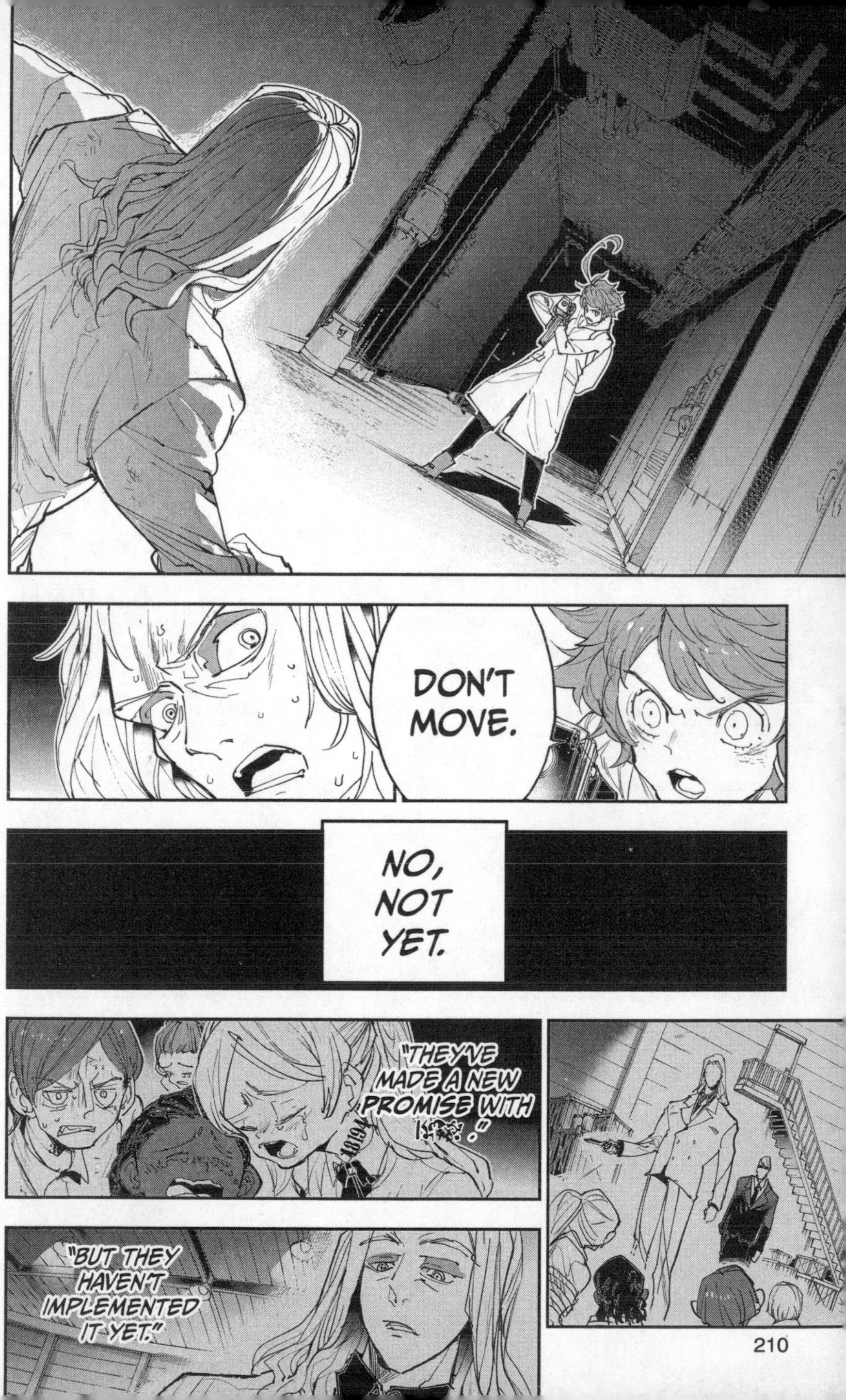
DON'T MOVE.
NO, NOT YET.
"THEY'VE MADE A NEW PROMISE WITH
"BUT THEY HAVEN'T IMPLEMENTED IT YET."

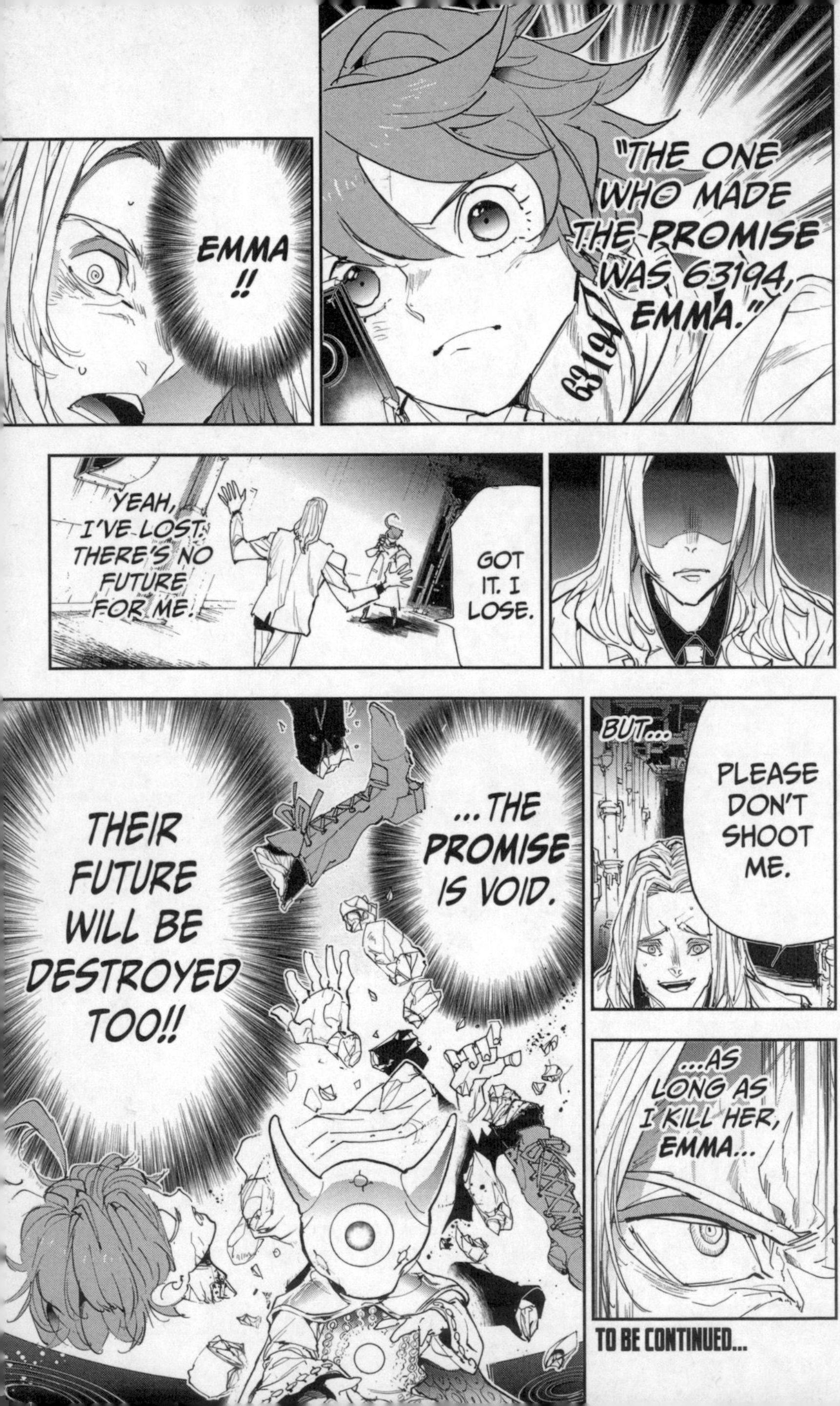
"THE ONE WHO MADE THE PROMISE WAS 63194, EMMA."
63194
EMMA!!
GOT IT. I LOSE.
YEAH, I'VE LOST. THERE'S NO FUTURE FOR ME.
BUT...
PLEASE DON'T SHOOT ME.
...AS LONG AS I KILL HER, EMMA...
...THE PROMISE IS VOID.
THEIR FUTURE WILL BE DESTROYED TOO!!

TO BE CONTINUED...

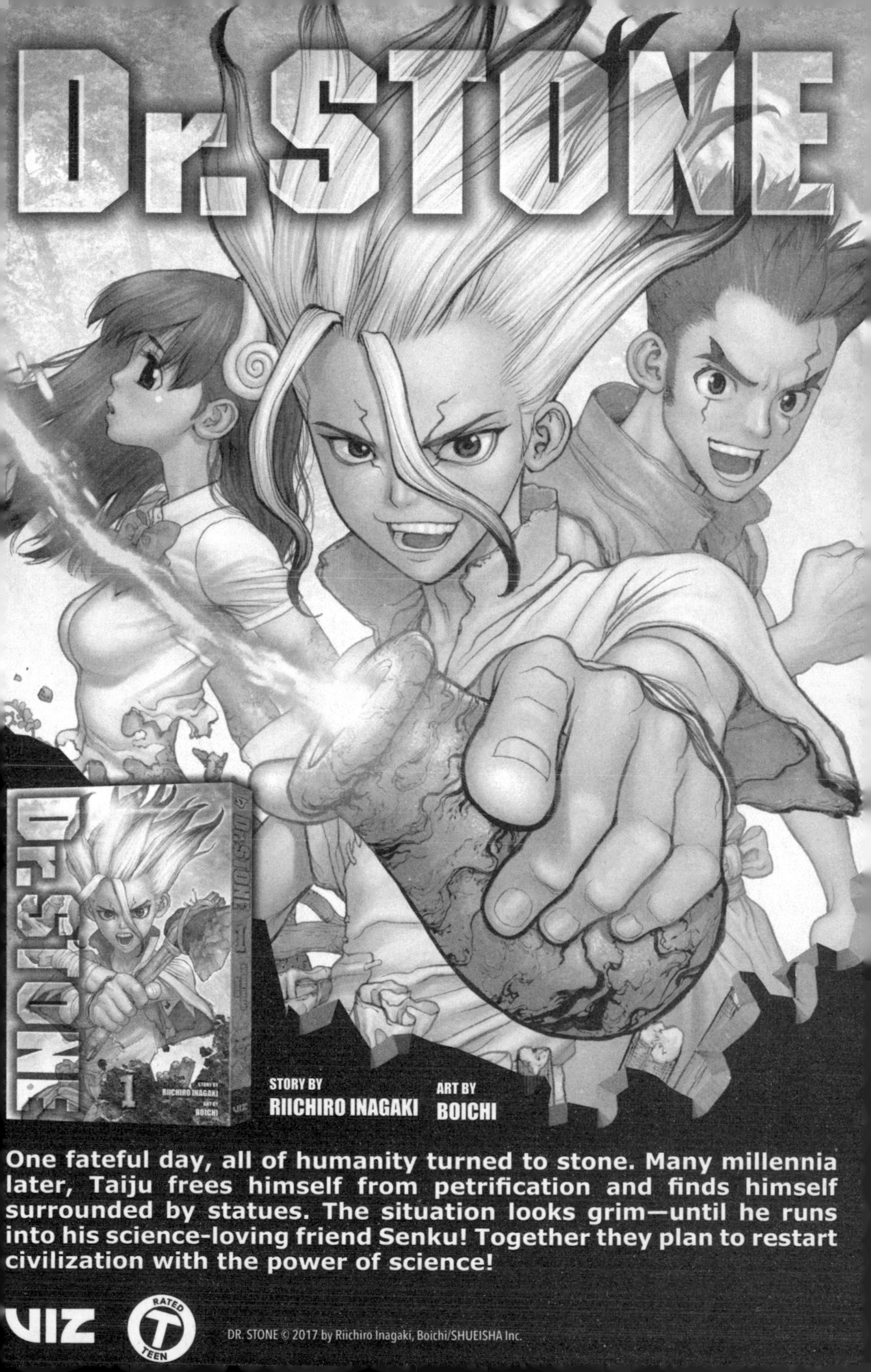
Dr. STONE
Dr. STONE 1
STORY BY RIICHIRO INAGAKI
ART BY BOICHI
VIZ
STORY BY
RIICHIRO INAGAKI
ART BY
BOICHI

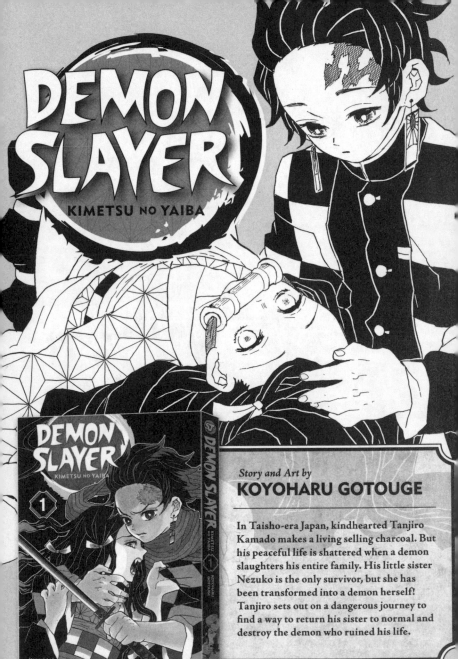

DEMON SLAYER
KIMETSU NO YAIBA

Story and Art by
KOYOHARU GOTOUGE

In Taisho-era Japan, kindhearted Tanjiro Kamado makes a living selling charcoal. But his peaceful life is shattered when a demon slaughters his entire family. His little sister Nezuko is the only survivor, but she has been transformed into a demon herself! Tanjiro sets out on a dangerous journey to find a way to return his sister to normal and destroy the demon who ruined his life.

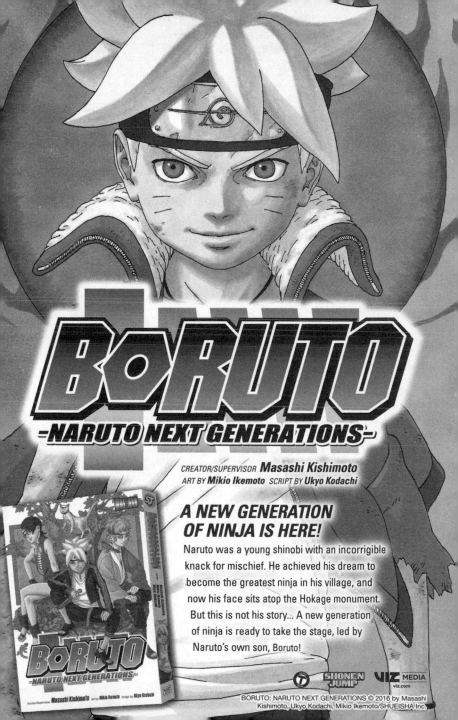

YOU'RE READING THE **WRONG WAY!**

The Promised *Neverland* reads from right to left, starting in the upper-right corner. Japanese is read from right to left, meaning that action, sound effects and word-balloon order are completely reversed from English order.

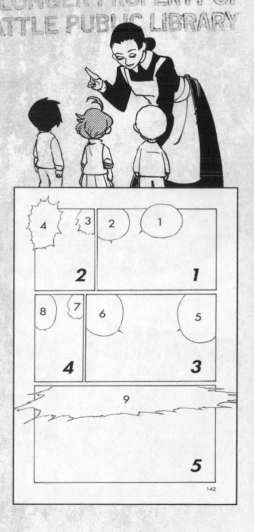